EVOLUTION AND
CHRISTIAN FAITH

EVOLUTION AND CHRISTIAN FAITH

by

Bolton Davidheiser

THE PRESBYTERIAN AND REFORMED PUBLISHING COMPANY
1969

Library of Congress Catalog Card Number: 70-76782

First printing, August 1969
Second printing, March 1970
Third printing, January 1971
Fourth printing, December 1971
Fifth printing, March 1973
Sixth printing, January 1975

Copyright, 1969, by

Presbyterian and Reformed Publishing Company

FOREWORD

One of the few things that Christianity and evolution have in common is that it may be said of both that they "have turned the world upside down." The amazing take-over of evolution from what originally was merely a theory in one particular science to an accepted fact affecting a dozen or more areas of learning is one of the most amazing phenomena of our time. The effect of this theory on theology, the church, and the individual Christian has largely gone unnoticed, probably because it has happened so gradually.

But effect it has had, and this fact must be met. Some have simply accepted the teachings of evolution; others have attempted a compromise of one sort or another which usually has resulted in adjusting, if not contradicting, the teachings of the Bible. A few have rejected evolution — usually without knowing much about it.

Dr. Davidheiser's book is not the first which has tried to expose the deficiencies and contradictions in the evolutionary theory, but it is an exceedingly important and distinctive one. In the first place, the author is eminently qualified to write on this subject. His doctorate from the Johns Hopkins University is in Zoology with a specialty in Genetics. His conversion to Christ was out of a theologically liberal background and did not occur until some time after he had earned his Ph.D. In other words, the author does not write from a sense of need to defend his childhood faith by superficial investigations into fields in which he is not competent. Rather he writes as a trained and once-convinced evolutionist whose doubts of that theory grew out of painstaking research into its teachings. What he has produced is no small effort, for the scope of evolution demands that one writing on the subject acquaint himself with many technical fields of knowledge. This Dr. Davidheiser has done in a remarkable way.

As the author himself points out, if, on the basis of the Bible, a creationist says that some aspect of evolution is not true he will not be heard. But if an evolutionist says the same thing on the basis of the inconclusiveness of his scientific investigations, people will listen. Because this has been the approach of Dr. Davidheiser — that is, he has collected evidence from evolutionists' writings as to the fallacies in the theory — people will be obliged to pay attention to this book. In it they will hear evolutionists who are recognized experts in their various fields expressing serious doubts as to the reliability of the basic tenets of their theory. All who accept any form of evolution, including the many varieties of theistic evolution, will find this book required reading.

CHARLES C. RYRIE

INTRODUCTION

The purpose of this book is threefold. It is hoped that it will be of value to mature Christians, who do not have a background in science, to use in counselling young people concerning the relationship of evolution and science to Christian faith. It is hoped it will be of value to those who are still seeking with an open mind for answers to problems in this area. Finally, it is hoped that it will serve as a warning to Christians who have grown complacent or who have been deceived into thinking that evolution is not a real issue.

It is of the utmost importance for Christians to realize that a very real struggle is going on and that the theory of evolution is a very important factor in the accelerating trend toward apostasy.

This book has not been written to convince evolutionists that they are wrong. The Bible has not done this; it would be presumptuous of any author to expect to do it. There is Christian faith and there is evolutionary faith. Each has its evidences. Everyone who considers them both must make his choice.

Evolutionists may be roughly grouped into three classes. There are those who use evolution as a weapon against Christian faith, and even against that which in general is good and decent. There are those who are convinced that evolution is true, and therefore they can take no other position. Finally, there is a multitude who know very little about it but who follow along because they have been told that everyone who is not narrow-minded and bigoted accepts evolution as a fact.

A book like this will do nothing for the first type. It is very unlikely that it will do much for the second type. It may help those of the third type who are open-minded. Moreover, it is hoped that it will be a significant aid to Bible-believing Christians who are faced with problems in this area.

A PERSONAL TESTIMONY

I am Pennsylvania Dutch. One of my ancestors, William Ritten-house, came to this country in 1688 and built the first paper mill in America. It is said that he was the first Mennonite preacher in America. His great-grandson, David Rittenhouse, became famous as a self-made mathematician and astronomer. Also he was the first Treasurer of the state of Pennsylvania.

I cannot remember starting to go to Sunday school, for it seems I always went. Because of lack of transportation I went to the only church within walking distance. It was so liberal that for a time commercial moving pictures were shown Saturday nights for an admission price, there being no theater in town. Later in another small town I went to a church of the same denomination, again it being the only one within walking distance.

The first book I read besides my first grade reader was the Bible. I remember the occasion well. We were visiting relatives and my father handed me a Bible and asked me to read. I did not think I could do it and was surprised to find that I could.

When I went to high school I lived in a town which had seven churches. Although a rather wide choice was offered, I joined the denomination in which I had grown up. I remember that one time I asked my Sunday school teacher what it meant that "Christ died for us." I had heard this and did not understand what it meant. The teacher did not know either, so I did not find out at that time.

About this time and for quite a few years my religion amounted to a strong respect for Christian ethics, a real interest in Biblical history, and a great aversion for ritual and ceremony. At no time did I have any tendency toward atheism or agnosticism.

Later I understood what it means that Christ died for us. Being God incarnate in human flesh, He alone was sinless and therefore able to pay the penalty for sin. This atonement was necessary since we all have a sin nature through an act of disobedience in defiance of God's declaration that disobedience would bring death. When I understood this I could not accept it because it is incompatible with belief in the evolution of man and I was convinced that evolution is a fact.

If man evolved, the process was gradual and there never was a first pair of human beings distinct from the animal kingdom. If man evolved and there never was a first pair of human beings, then the Biblical account of the fall of man is not true but is a myth or an allegory. If man evolved, we are getting better and what is called sin is just a remnant of selfish animal nature. If man evolved, Christ was just a reformer and not the Redeemer; He was a martyr and not the Savior. Then the Christian religion becomes a code of ethics and not the way of eternal life through a risen Lord. As Paul said, "If in this life only we have hope in Christ, we are of all men most miserable" (I Cor. 15:19).

More years went by and my religious associates were people more liberal than those of my earlier years. I became dissatisfied but did not know why. One time I walked out in the middle of a church service. People probably thought I was ill — I hoped so — but the reason I left was because I could not endure what was being said.

One day a religious leader whom I admired said that those he represented did not believe in sending missionaries to the heathen because they had their own religions and it was better to let them alone. This was the first time I found myself in disagreement with a specific statement, though I had nothing to say since I did not at that time accept the gospel of salvation by grace. Then one evening a young man gave a testimony, prefacing it with the explanation that his convictions were not really religious. The fact is that they were not, and I knew it. But when he finished, one of the prominent persons present commented, "Why, that's lousy with religion!" That was too much for me. I knew something was wrong but I did not know where to turn. My impression of fundamentalists and anti-evolutionists was that they were dull, ignorant, and uninteresting people.

The Second World War approached. Being idealistic, naive, and desirous to do something about it, I spent much time doing such things as collecting clothes for Europe and attending "peace meetings." Long before the war came I took a stand as a conscientious objector, basing my decision entirely upon the New Testament. Looking back with the advantage of a wider perspective, I can see what influences motivated my activities and what could have brought a change in my life at that time. I remember particularly one "peace meeting" where I was applauding the speaker so vigorously that he seemed to turn his attention toward me in particular. But as his talk progressed I sensed duplicity in his motives and stopped applauding altogether. I walked out of that meeting feeling very depressed.

If some understanding person who knew the Lord had spoken to me during this time, I believe my life would have been changed and the following wasted years would have been spent profitably. But no one did and I continued on in this way. I got into difficulty just once, when I stayed in a room where a light was on and prayed during a practice blackout. My motives were religious and sincere, and I did what seemed right to me during those years. Out of context, this may sound good, but it is not. In the days of the Judges "every man did that which was right in his own eyes" (Judges 17:6), and this was not good. Without the restraining control of the Holy Spirit, this can lead to civil disobedience and anarchy.

One evening in the spring of 1944 in North Dakota I attended a church service. The pastor was not gifted, and everything he said I had heard many times before. He preached a simple gospel message of salvation by grace, and that evening I found myself saying, "I believe that," to everything he said. This surprised me for I had said many times that I could not believe unless someone would first disprove evolution to me. But there I was, agreeing with everything he said and telling myself I believed it. There was no request for anyone to respond publicly. I was the only one who knew that something had happened to me. All my life I had considered myself a Christian, but I was not really a believer. It was not just a mental assent — the acceptance of a point of view I had previously rejected — it was a transforming experience. The Bible calls it a second birth. Speaking to the eminent Nicodemus, the Lord Jesus Christ told him, "You must be born again" (John, chapter 3). The second birth is a spiritual birth. Those who accept the Lord Jesus Christ as Saviour and Lord are born again, into the family of God.

Later I was employed in cancer research in Baltimore and had access to a good library. In my spare time I looked up articles on evolution in *Biological Abstracts,* and then read them in the scientific journals. I was surprised to find that things which I had taken as assured were not so sure after all. The more I read the more amazed I became. As evolution had been the great stumblingblock in my life, I felt a desire to aid others who might have the same problem.

Evolution is commonly presented to the public as proved beyond any real doubt. It is good to know something of the "other side" of the evolution problem, and I have tried to present that in my writing and speaking. But this is not enough. It is the preaching of the gospel that leads to salvation.

CONTENTS

CHAPTER I

EVOLUTION AND CHRISTIAN FAITH

It might seem that there is no need to define what is meant by the terms *evolution* and *Christian faith*. This is not the case, however, for at the present time people have widely divergent views as to what is meant by each of these terms.

There are many who believe that the theory of evolution can be reconciled with Christian faith rather easily, and therefore that no problem exists. Then there are those who say that they believe in the Bible in its entirety, but who take a position in which they admit a great deal of evolution. At the same time many of these deny that they are evolutionists. Finally there is the position that evolution and Christian faith cannot be reconciled.

Therefore, in discussing evolution and Christian faith it is necessary to define terms and clarify what is meant by words which are used.

WHAT IS EVOLUTION?

As taught in all college textbooks of General Biology, General Botany, and General Zoology, evolution means that all life on earth developed from one or a few simple forms of life. It is now generally held that these alleged simple ancestors also developed in a natural way from non-living matter.

This being so, there should be no problem about what evolution is. But there is a problem. At the famous Scopes trail in Tennessee in 1925, Professor H. H. Newman of the University of Chicago defined evolution as the philosophy of change, and said that everyone who admits a changing world admits the essence of evolution. Some authors who write for college students and for the general public have stressed the idea that evolution is change, and that to admit change is to admit evolution. Thus everyone who is aware of changes in the world is an evolutionist in spite of himself.

It is not uncommon for evolutionists to distinguish between *macro-*

evolution and *micro-evolution. Macro-evolution* is real evolution. The term *micro-evolution* is used for small hereditary changes which do occur and can be observed in animals and plants. As previously mentioned, there are those who say that because change does occur, everyone is an evolutionist in spite of himself. It is purely an assumption however that there is any connection between these observable changes and real evolution.

Evolutionists are trying to break down resistance to the word *evolution,* and so every anti-evolutionist who says, "We believe in micro-evolution," is aiding the evolutionary cause. *Micro-evolution* is a misnomer and use of the term should be avoided by everyone who does not accept evolution.

To say that evolution is merely change, or even to say that it is a hereditary change and that therefore everyone must be an evolutionist, is comparable to the situation in which the gambler says that gambling is merely taking a chance, and therefore everyone is a gambler in spite of himself because it is not possible to live without taking some chances. But gambling is trying to get something for less than its value through risking the loss of a smaller amount. Risking an accident by driving on the highway to the place of one's employment involves taking a chance, but it is not gambling. Some people will be able to see this and not be deceived, but others will be brainwashed by repeated assertions that since they cannot avoid taking some chances they are gamblers, and presently they will find real gambling much less objectionable than they had supposed. Thus it is with evolution.

Recently a number of Christian men of science have adopted this technique. They are telling Christian audiences that now it is all right to accept at least a certain amount of evolution, and indeed that it is impossible to do otherwise.

For example, Wilbur L. Bullock, Associate Professor of Zoology at the University of New Hampshire, says in an article published in *Eternity* magazine, reprinted from the *Gordon Review,* that "we can say that evolution is an orderly change in living organisms, and that, regardless of the label placed on any particular viewpoint, some degree of evolution is accepted by all — even those who refuse to admit it by that name."[1] He continues that "while all biologists 'accept evolution' as a principle, we have yet to explain the mechanisms whereby it has taken place above the species and genus level." Concerning the reluctance to be dogmatic about the way evolution has come about he says, "This reluctance does not mean that we are anti-evolutionary — although it is often so interpreted. . . ."

Another point of view taken by some Christian men of science is that since the Biblical word *kind* as used in the Genesis account of creation cannot be defined in terms of any man-made category of classification, they can define it according to their own decisions and thereby remain strictly Biblical. According to their own words, they most frequently consider the taxonomic group known as an *order* to represent a *kind*.[2] If any two creatures of the Order Carnivora belong to the same kind, then according to these men, anyone who believes the Bible in its entirety may believe that a weasel and a walrus and a skunk and a polar bear descended from the same ancestry.[3]

It is true that the term *kind* used in the Biblical account of creation cannot be defined in terms of any of the man-made taxonomic categories, but equating the kind to an order as the general rule to be followed in most or many cases gives license for a great deal of real evolution and opens the way for evolution to become acceptable and to be considered compatible with Scripture.

Strangely, men of these apparently opposite views have much in common, and in many cases it seems that individuals accept and teach both of these views at the same time: 1. trivial changes which really do occur may properly be called examples of evolution, and therefore everyone is an evolutionist in spite of himself; 2. really large changes are not necessarily evolutionary, for the Biblical term *kind* may include animals which are quite diverse. Thus these men can say in effect: "Although *I* believe that a giraffe and a hippopotamus have the same ancestry, *I* am a creationist and not an evolutionist, because a giraffe and a hippopotamus both belong to the same kind;[4] but if *you* admit that some strains of flies have become resistent to DDT, then *you* are an evolutionist."

Some anti-evolutionists are being caught in the trap and are saying that *if* evolution can be defined to mean observable changes, *then* this sort of evolution must be accepted. Changes of this sort are a fact, but agreeing that it is proper to define them as evolution is playing into the hands of those who wish to see opposition to the concept of evolution broken down. These matters will be considered in more detail in a later chapter.

NOTES

1. Bullock, Wilbur L., "Evolution and/or Creation," *Eternity*, 11:7:10, July, 1960, p. 10 *et seq*. Reprinted from the *Gordon Review*.

2. For example, see *Evolution and Christian Thought Today*, Russell L. Mixter, editor (Wm. B. Eerdmans Pub. Co., 1959). One of the authors, Professor James O. Buswell III, proposes that "since in a percentage of *orders*, major gaps appear between them, perhaps the *order* is as near to being what Genesis 1 means by the term 'kind' as any single taxonomic category can be. This proposal implies simply that God created the orders, and natural selection took it from there," (page 183). In a footnote on the same page he says that Dr. Mixter arrived at the same conclusion.

3. Since the categories of classification are man-made they may be changed from time to time. At present a weasel and a walrus are in the same order, although it is possible that at some time in the future the order will be divided into two. It may be that at some future time the aquatic carnivores will be classified in a different order from the terrestrial carnivores.

4. The giraffe and the hippopotamus are both even-toed ungulates and belong to the same order, Artiodactyla.

WHAT IS CHRISTIAN FAITH?

Among those who consider themselves Christians there is no agreement as to what is meant by Christian faith. Apostasy has already gone so far that some who do not even believe in God desire to retain for themselves the name Christian, as is illustrated in the "God-Is-Dead" movement. This is a long way from the beliefs of the martyrs of the early church, who preferred suffering horrible deaths rather than to deny their faith in a risen Lord. It is necessary to define the term *Christian* as it will be used in this discussion.

Christian faith is not "another way to God," comparable with non-Christian faiths. The Lord Jesus Christ said, "I am the way, the truth, and the life. No one comes to the Father except through Me"[1] (John 14:6). The apostle Paul said, "No one can lay any other foundation than the one which is laid, which is Jesus Christ" (I Cor. 3:11). Peter the disciple spoke boldly to the rulers of Israel and said concerning Christ, "There is no salvation in anyone else, for there is no other name under heaven that has been given among men by which we are able to be saved" (Acts 4:12). Some people do not like this. They say it is too narrow. But it is Scripture. These are the words of Peter and of Paul and of the Lord Jesus Christ.

Christian faith is not a way of life. It is not the acceptance of a code of ethics based upon "the teachings of Jesus." The apostle Paul said, "If our hope in Christ is for this life only, we are of all men most miserable" (I Cor. 15:19). Many other verses of the Bible could also be quoted to show that Christian faith is not for this life only. The best known reference is John 3:16, where the Lord said to Nicodemus, "For God so loved the world that He gave His only begotten Son, that whosoever believes in him should not perish, but have everlasting life."[1] In the last verse of the same chapter we read, "He who believes in the Son has eternal life, and he who does not believe the Son shall not see life, but the wrath of God abides on him."

Since Christian faith includes faith in Christ beyond this life, and indeed for eternity, it follows that the Christian has faith in Christ in a way in which he cannot have faith in any human being. The Christian looks to Christ with faith in Him not only as Lord of his life but also as his Savior. He is our Savior because He died upon the cross as our substitute, taking the penalty of our sins upon Himself. He alone could do this because He was with God in the beginning and at the same time He was God, and He made all things. He alone as God and as the only sinless one could become a man and pay the penalty for our sins.

Speaking to Nicodemus, the Lord compared His coming crucifixion to a historical event which was well known to this ruler of the Jews. He said, "As Moses lifted up the serpent in the wilderness, even so must the Son of Man be lifted up, that whosoever believes in Him should not perish but have eternal life" (John 3:14, 15). Because of the sinning of the Israelites while on their journey to the Promised Land, God sent serpents among them, and the bite of the serpents caused death. The people repented and asked for deliverance. Following God's instructions, Moses made a replica of a serpent in brass and raised it upon a pole. Those who looked upon it with faith lived (Num. 21:5-9). We are told in the Bible that all of us are guilty of sin and are worthy of condemnation, but if we look with faith to Christ raised upon the cross as the One who took away the penalty for our sins by His atoning sacrifice, we are made free.

At the time of the crucifixion Christ took upon Himself the sins of the world. Because the penalty for sin is separation from God, He was at this time separated from God the Father, and in fulfillment of prophecy He cried from the cross, "My God, my God, why hast Thou forsaken me?" These are the opening words of the twenty-second

Psalm, which describes the crucifixion in considerable detail though written about a thousand years before the event.[2] Since Christ paid the penalty for sin, those who will confess their need of salvation and will accept His sacrifice as being for them will never be forsaken by God and will have eternal life.

As proof of the reality of salvation, the Lord Jesus Christ arose from the grave on the third day, as He said He would. He was seen by many people during a period of forty days, at one time by more than five hundred persons. Then He ascended into heaven in the sight of His disciples, until a cloud obscured Him from their vision (The Acts of the Apostles, chapter 1, and I Cor. 15:3-8).

The Bible says that without the shedding of blood there is no remission of sins (Heb. 9:22). Before the Lord Jesus Christ shed His blood upon the cross for the redemption of sinners, the blood of animals was shed in sacrifice in the Temple at Jerusalem. However the blood of animals cannot take away sin, and those who offered these sacrifices were thereby expressing their faith in the providence of God, that these sacrifices would be accepted as a type of the blood of Christ, which was to be shed at a time that was then still in the future (Hebrews, chapter 10). When Christ died upon the cross, the penalty for sin was paid, and there was no longer any need for the symbolic shedding of animal blood. As Christ died on the cross, the veil of the Temple was torn from the top to the bottom (Matt. 27:50, 51). This curtain closed the most holy place, where the high priest took sacrificial animal blood and sprinkled it upon the mercy seat for the atonement of the sins of the people. As the veil was torn, the most holy place was no longer closed, and the mercy seat was no longer inaccessible. Through the sacrifice of Christ all may now come boldly into the presence of God without any other intermediary. But this access was made possible only through the shed blood of Christ, and it is only through Christ that anyone can come. He said, "I am the way, the truth, and the life. No one comes to the Father except through Me" (John 14:6). Some try to by-pass the cross in coming to God, but this cannot be done. "There is one God, and one mediator between God and man, the man Christ Jesus, who gave Himself a ransom for all. . ." (I Tim. 2:5, 6).

In order for Christ to be able to do what He did, it follows that He was not a man as other men. He was equal with God, and He was God. He became incarnate in human flesh in order to perform His redemptive work. This is told both in the New Testament and in the

Old Testament. "In the beginning was the Word, and the Word was with God, and the Word was God. All things were made by Him and without Him was not anything made that was made. . . . . And the Word became flesh and dwelt among us, and we beheld His glory, the glory of the Only Begotten from the Father, full of grace and truth" (John 1:1-3, 14). "For unto us a child is born, unto us a Son is given, and the government shall be upon His shoulder. His name shall be called Wonderful, Counsellor, the mighty God, the everlasting Father, the Prince of Peace" (Isa. 9:6).

Christian faith is the faith which the sinner exercises when he professes that he is unable to save himself through any merits of his own or by anything he can do other than accepting the death of Christ upon the cross as being a sacrifice in his place, assuring him of eternal life. The Christian believes that since he has taken Christ as his Saviour, the penalty for his sins has already been paid at Calvary, and he has eternal life through the merits of Jesus Christ his Lord.

Christian faith is faith in a living, risen Saviour. Christian faith is faith in what He has done for us, and not faith in what we can do for ourselves. The best and most that we can do is altogether inadequate. What He did is altogether adequate. Thus He is our Redeemer and Saviour. Because we belong to Him and wish to show our appreciation and love for Him, we also accept Him as our Lord and strive, with His help, to do His will.

NOTES

1. This is an age of many translations. The quotations presented here are a modernizing of the wording of the King James and are not from any published translation.
2. In the Douay-Rhiems version this is the 21st Psalm.

THE ISSUE

The basis of the Christian faith is the sacrificial death of Christ on the cross as a vicarious atonement for sin, followed by His resurrection. The occasion which made this redemption necessary was the disobedience of the first pair of human beings. Because of this disobedience all people have a sin nature and are sinners. To be acceptable in the sight of God it is necessary for the sinner to be redeemed. He must acknowledge that Christ's sacrifice on the cross was the payment of the ransom price by the sinless One for the sinner, and accept this as the atonement for his own sins.

According to the theory of evolution there never were two human beings who were progenitors of the human race, for man emerged gradually from an animal ancestry. According to the theory of evolution, that which the Bible calls sin is merely a remnant of a bestial nature, which will be overcome in time as man continues to improve. These two views contradict at every point.

It is common for authors of college textbooks in biological science to say, as Darwin did, that there is nothing about the theory of evolution which should cause any religious difficulty. It is said that the apparent conflict between the theory of evolution and Christian faith is due to a misunderstanding of terms, and it is assumed that the misunderstanding is on the part of those who are looking at it from the religious side. But those who say there is no real conflict between evolution and Christian faith are ignorant of the most basic Christian doctrines, or else they repudiate them. Some will say that to ascribe such importance to these doctrines is to be narrow and bigoted. But these things are according to Scripture. They are not man-made doctrines or private views. If the Bible is true, those who put their confidence in erroneous religious doctrines will one day find that this is of all conditions the most tragic.

Many authors write about an evolutionary process in religion. Casting aside the fulfillment of the law and the prophets in Christ, they say that He taught a way which is superior to previous teachings, a way of love in which all men are brothers and God is Father of all. ("The fatherhood of God and brotherhood of man.") This sounds good, but it is not the way Christ taught. To the hypocritical religious leaders of that day He said, "You are of your father the devil" (John 8:44). God was not their father, nor is He the Father of unregenerate men today. He said that a time is coming when because of wickedness men will desire that the mountains fall on them and cover them (Luke 23:28-30). It is recorded five times in the gospel of Matthew that He said, "There shall be weeping [or wailing] and gnashing of teeth." There is another side to the picture besides love. Everyone who is aware of the world situation today knows that there is in the world much hatred for the Lord Jesus Christ. Bibles and Christian literature cannot be taken openly into large areas of the earth's surface. Yet He loves the sinner and died to redeem all who will turn to Him from their evil ways and accept Him as Saviour.

Evolutionists generally believe that unless man destroys himself or overpopulates the earth, he will improve until wars cease and prosperity is the rule. The Bible presents the opposite picture. Wickedness and lawlessness will increase. Apostasy will also increase until there is a large, ecumenical, corrupt, nominally Christian church (II Tim. 3; Rev. 17 and 18). Because of man's sinful nature and his rebellion against God and Christ, he can never achieve peace. Peace will come only when the Lord returns to rule in righteousness. The Bible indicates that even during that time man's sinful nature will be manifest, and some men will rebel even against the righteous rule of the Lord Jesus Christ.

Evolutionists cannot accept the first human family as real, historical persons, but rather as symbolic types. But the Lord Jesus Christ and the writers of the Bible considered them as real. The apostle Paul says that Adam was made before Eve, and that she was deceived and that he was not (I Tim. 2:13 and II Cor. 11:3). Paul also declares that because of the disobedience of Adam, all are sinners; but because of the obedience of Christ in submitting to the role of sacrifice, many are made righteous (Rom. 5:14-19). Death came through Adam, but life came through Jesus Christ (I Cor. 15:22).

John the beloved disciple, writing about Christian love, mentions the case of Cain and Abel, sons of Adam (I John 3:12). Cain, the first son of Adam, slew his brother Abel. Thus in the Biblical record of the human race, the very first human born on earth became a murderer. The writer of the book of Hebrews (generally assumed to have been Paul) mentions that Abel offered to God a better sacrifice than Cain did (Heb. 11:4). It will be remembered that Abel offered animals from the flock while Cain offered fruits of the field. Abel's sacrifice was acceptable because atonement can be made only with the shedding of blood (Heb. 9:22), looking forward in faith to the time when Christ would shed His blood in atonement on the cross. After the crucifixion there was no need of further blood sacrifices (see also Heb. 9:11-14 in context).

The Lord Jesus Christ referred to Abel as a real person when He denounced the hypocritical Pharisees (Matt. 23:35) and when He denounced the unjust lawyers (Luke 11:51).

Some evolutionists say that they believe the Bible when it says that Adam was made from the dust of the ground. "Of course," they say, "Adam was not a man made directly from the dust of the ground but a type of mankind made from the dust by way of a long animal ancestry." This is not the way the Bible presents it, and this evolutionary interpretation is completely invalidated by the fact that the Bible says that Eve, the mate of the first man, was made from a portion of his side, generally considered to be a rib. There was no mate for Adam until the Lord provided the first woman in this way. If this is true, mankind could not have evolved from an animal ancestry. The creation of Eve, the first woman, cannot be reconciled with any theory of evolution. The honorable thing for religious evolutionists to do about the creation of Adam and Eve is to say outright, "I don't believe it," rather than to say that reconciliation with the theory of evolution is possible.

In summary, the issue is twofold. In the first place, the theory of evolution cannot be reconciled with the historical account of creation as presented in the Bible. In the second place, the theory of evolution cannot be reconciled with the basic Christian doctrine of salvation by grace, because this is based upon the historical account of the fall of man. If there never was a historical fall of man through disobedience to God, then there is no need of a redeemer, and Christ therefore was a martyr instead of the Savior. Acceptance of a theory of evolution leads logically to a religious position which, if called Christian, is Christian in name only.

DO EVOLUTIONISTS BELIEVE WE CAME FROM MONKEYS OR APES?

It is natural that people are more interested in the evolution of man than in the evolution of other creatures. If all life evolved from simple beginnings, as evolutionists affirm, it follows that we evolved from quite a number of different things, including protozoa, fish, and reptiles. An important question is this: According to evolutionary theory, what were the creatures like which preceded our earliest human ancestors? Monkeys and apes immediately come to mind, but people are often reluctant to say that according to the theory of evolution we descended from monkeys or apes, because we have been told so often that scientists do not believe this and that it is merely a misconception of the uninformed. If a person who is told this presses for more details, he is told that we did not evolve from monkeys or apes, but that we and monkeys and apes all evolved from a common ancestor. This is supposed to make an important difference. But the fact is that evolutionists in general and Charles Darwin in particular have made it a matter of record in print that they *do* believe we evolved from monkeys or apes or both.

Let us first look at some quotations from people who say that the evolutionists do not say we came from such an ancestry.

Dr. E. Adamson Hoebel, Professor of Anthropology at the University of Utah, says, "Man is not, as the common misconception has it, 'descended from the monkeys.' Such a popular idea is a vulgar corruption of the evolutionary concept of the descent of man; it was never advocated by Darwin nor by any of his scientific followers in biology or anthropology . . . man is not descended from the apes."[1]

Russell L. Mixter of Wheaton College said concerning Charles Darwin, "He did not, as popularly believed, hold that man descended from monkeys. A more accurate way of expressing Darwin's idea is to say that man and the apes descended from a common ancestor through a process termed 'natural selection.' "[2]

Professor James O. Buswell III, formerly of Wheaton College, says, "One of the biggest false notions of many creationists concerns what evolutionists believe. Evolutionists no longer believe that the older the fossil remains are, the more ape-like they become, while finally man merges into ape."[3]

Professor J. Frank Cassel of the University of North Dakota says, "One thing that evolution does not mean is that man descended from apes."[4]

Even the outstanding geneticist, Professor Theodosius Dobzhansky of Columbia University, says this, and he charges that it was the *anti-evolutionists* who started the idea. He says that their motive was to make the theory of evolution appear as shocking as possible. He says that "to make Darwin's theory as shocking as possible the proposition 'man and apes have descended from common ancestors' was garbled into 'man has descended from the apes.' This, of course, is obvious nonsense, since man's remote ancestors could not have descended from animals which are our contemporaries."[5] It is naive of Professor Dobzhansky to assert that the theory of evolution prohibits the existence of apes in the past which were not our contemporaries.

Professor William Howells of Harvard says, "Darwin is supposed, by those who have not read him, to be the man who thought of evolution and who said that men were descended from monkeys. Neither notion is even half true."[6]

It seems that it is Professor Howells and the others quoted here who have not read Darwin, for Darwin did say very plainly that men descended from monkeys.

Stanley Edgar Hyman of Bennington College makes a statement which may be a classic example of quoting out of context. He says, "Every fool has greeted Darwin's theory, as earlier fools have greeted earlier evolutionary theories, with the statement that it would make a man a descendant of a baboon or chimpanzee. He [Darwin] writes: 'But we must not fall into the error of supposing that the early progenator of the whole Simian stock, including man, was identical with, or even closely resembled, any existing monkey or ape.' "[7]

What Darwin said at this particular place in his book *The Descent of Man* was, "But a naturalist would undoubtedly have ranked as an ape or monkey an ancient form which possessed many characters common to the Catarrhine and Platyrrhine monkeys, other characters in an intermediate condition, and some few, perhaps, distinct from those now found in either group. And as man from a genealogical point of view belongs to the Catarrhine or Old World stock, we must conclude, however much the conclusion may revolt our pride, that our early progenitors would have been thus designated." *Then* Darwin makes the statement which Professor Hyman quotes: "But we must not fall into the error of supposing that the early progenitor of the whole Simian stock, including man, was identical with, or even closely resembled, any *existing* ape or monkey." (Emphasis added.) This is from the sixth chapter of Darwin's *The Descent of Man.*

In the same chapter Darwin says, "The Simiadae then branched off into two great stems, the New World [western hemisphere] and Old World [eastern hemisphere] monkeys; and from the latter, at a remote period, Man, the wonder and glory of the Universe proceeded."

Darwin could hardly have said more plainly that he believed we evolved from monkeys. To bring this up-to-date, we may quote a statement by the famous anthropologist M. F. Ashley Montagu, made in 1964, in which he says the same thing. "It was from the Old World monkey stock that the early anthropoids arose, and from these, in turn, that the line which led to man came into being."[8]

Darwin's *Descent of Man* was published twelve years after his *Origin of Species.* In the earlier work he avoided a discussion of human origins. Meanwhile various of his followers had taken the position that we evolved from monkeys or from some sort of ape.

This has been the evolutionary point of view ever since. Why then do some authors try to persuade the public that it is not so? The reason seems to be in order to make evolution more acceptable to those who have a distaste for a simian ancestry.

George Gaylord Simpson is one of the most outstanding evolutionists in our country today. Concerning this matter he says, "On this subject, by the way, there has been too much pussyfooting. Apologists emphasize that man cannot be a descendant of any living ape — a statement that is obvious to the verge of imbicility — and go on to state or imply that man is not really descended from an ape or monkey at all, but from an earlier common ancestor. In fact, that earlier ancestor would certainly be called an ape or monkey in popular speech by anyone who saw it. Since the terms *ape* and *monkey* are defined by popular usage, man's ancestors *were* apes or monkeys (or successively both). It is pusillanimous if not dishonest for an informed investigator to say otherwise."[9]

Professor Simpson says further that before Darwin published *The Descent of Man,* when *The Origin of Species* was his only published work on evolution, it was not only his opponents but also his followers who recognized his belief in a simian ancestry for man. Dr. Simpson says, "In *The Origin of Species* Darwin deliberately avoided the issue, saying only in closing, 'Light will be thrown on the origin of man and his history.' Yet his adherents made no secret of the matter and at once embroiled Darwin, with themselves, in arguments about man's origin from monkeys. Twelve years later (in 1871) Darwin published *The Descent of Man,* which makes it clear that he was indeed of that opinion."[10]

H. J. Muller, the Nobel Prize-winning geneticist of Indiana University, says: "It is fashionable in some circles to refer slurringly to the inference that apes were ancestral to men, and to insinuate that Darwin's theory to this effect has been discredited and that it is more proper to say that men and apes, perhaps even men, apes, and monkeys, diverged long ago from a stem form that was more primitive than any of these. This is mere wishful thinking on the part of those who resent too vivid a visualization of their lowly origin and their present-day poor relations."[11]

William L. Straus Jr., the famous anthropologist of the Johns Hopkins University, also explodes the myth that the scientists do not believe that we evolved from apes. Writing in 1949 he said that "perhaps the majority of anthropologists and comparative anatomists . . . believe that man has evolved from a true anthropoid ape at a relatively late geological date."[12]

Thomas Henry Huxley was Darwin's staunchest defender, and we are told that when he gave a series of lectures in Edinburgh he was greeted with applause when he made an "unequivical declaration that man has descended from a simian ancestry."[13] Professor Straus says that Huxley was "the godfather, if not the father, of the anthropoid-ape theory of man's origin." (That is, as opposed to belief in man's origin from a kind of ape which could not be described as anthropoid.) He continues, "Indeed his concept of man's relationship to the other primates today remains the orthodox one, differing only in details imposed by the advance of knowledge. . . . In its present orthodox form, this theory assumes that man evolved from an animal that would be classified as an anthropoid ape. In fact, in one form or another, this anthropoid ape theory has been so often and so continuously expostulated and propagandized that it has become almost a fundamental tenet of biological and more particularly anthropological belief, a sort of canon or article of faith."[14]

Although he was not the first to do so, a biologist named Klaatch, about 1910, derived the Negroes from the gorilla, the Mongolians from the orangutan, and the Caucasians from the chimpanzee.[15] Another biologist, named Crookshank, seems to have had a similar idea when he declared that Negroes sit on the ground the way a gorilla does and that Mongolians sit down like orangutans. The philosopher Immanuel Kant said, "It is possible for a chimpanzee or orangutan, by perfecting its organs, to change at some future date into a human being."[16] Thus it is not correct to say that even the idea that man evolved from a *living* kind of ape was a misconception of some anti-evolutionists.

There was a time when some living apes were thought to *be* men, and some men were thought to be apes. When Europeans first saw the Australian aborigenes some thought they might be some sort of ape, although they used fire and were skillful with the boomerang.

Anyone can go to a public library and find statements in books on biological science which show that the authors believe we evolved from apes. Following are a few illustrations of this.

G. Elliot Smith, the famous anatomist of the University of London, wrote: "The earliest members of the Human family must have been merely apes with an overgrown brain. . . . The vast continents of

Africa and Asia represented the laboratory in which, for untold ages, nature was making her greatest experiments to achieve the transformation of the base substance of some brutal Ape into the divine form of Man."[17]

Raymond Dart, discoverer of the Australopithecines, agrees with Professor Smith and says: "As Elliot Smith put it: 'The acquisition of speech was, in fact, an essential part of the process of transforming an ape into a human being.' "[18]

Arthur Keith, the great British anthropologist, wrote: "All the evidence now at our disposal supports the conclusion that man has arisen, as Lamarck and Darwin suspected, from an anthropoid ape not higher in the zoological scale than a chimpanzee."[19]

Professor Keith also says, "No matter what line of evidence we select to follow — evidence gathered by anatomists, by embryologists, by physiologists, or by psychologists — we reach the conviction that man's brain has been evolved from that of an anthropoid ape. . . ."[20] A little further on he continues, "Was Darwin right when he said that man, under the action of biological forces which can be observed and measured, has been raised from a place amongst anthropoid apes to that which he now occupies? The answer is yes! And in returning this verdict I speak but as foreman of the jury — a jury which has been empanneled from men who have devoted a lifetime to weighing the evidence."[21]

Harry L. Shapiro, anthropologist of the American Museum of Natural History, says: "About a million years ago . . . the curtain rose on man . . . a creature with a small skull, a massive mandible, and trailing in many parts of his anatomy evidences of his recent emergence from the world of apes."[22]

Ernest Albert Hooton, the famous anthropologist of Harvard, said concerning man: "He made himself from an ape and created human culture."[23]

William Howells, the well-known Harvard anthropologist, wrote of man: "In body and brain he is simply a made-over ape, with no fundamental distinctions at all."[24]

Sherwood L. Washburn, anthropologist of the University of California, said, "Man began when populations of apes . . . started the bipedal, tool-using way of life that gave rise to the man-apes of the genus *Australopithecus*."[25]

F. H. T. Rhodes of University College, Swansea, wrote: ". . . a great variety of anthropoid apes lived in Europe, Asia, and Africa during Miocene times, and it is amongst these that our remote ancestors will probably be found."[26]

William Lee Stokes of the University of Utah says of man: "Either he diverged from the apes at a relatively late time and is a 'made over ape' or he split off from the primates much earlier at the evolutionary stage represented by the tarsiers or lower monkeys."[27]

Thomas S. Hall et al., of Washington University, wrote in their textbook: "Beyond the farthest reach of archaeology is the vast stretch of time in which apes became ape-men and then men."[28]

John S. Hensill of San Francisco State College said, "From some such early ancestor as Dryopithecus, the primitive ape, appeared the earliest man. . . ."[29]

Charles L. Camp of the University of California's Museum of Paleontology wrote: "Man's structure declares his ancestral life in a tree, but the fossil record does not tell from which particular group of tree-dwelling ape creatures man arose."[30]

Frank B. Livingstone of the University of Michigan wrote, "This paper will attempt to reconstruct this transition from ape to man. . ."[31]

Loren Eiseley of the University of Pennsylvania put it this way: "The ape whose cultural remains at the beginning of the first glaciation can scarcely be distinguished from chance bits of stone has, by the end of the fourth ice age, become artist and world rover, penetrator of the five continents, and master of all."[32] He also said concerning man, "Once he was thought a fallen angel; then we found him to be an ascended ape."[33]

Weston La Barre of Duke University said, ". . . it is much more likely that he [man] is an ape fallen from arboreal grace than that he is a fallen angel."[34]

Roy Chapman Andrews of the American Museum of Natural History said, "The evolution of our ancestral Forest Apes took place in widely separated areas. . . ."[35]

Wilfred Le Gros Clark of the University of Oxford said: "That man has been derived from a form which — without any strain on commonly recognized definitions — can be properly called 'an anthropoid ape' is a statement which no longer admits doubt."[36]

Conway Zirkle of the University of Pennsylvania said that our prehuman ancestors lived in the trees and "before the change our ancestors were tree-living apes. . . ."[37]

This may seem like an unduly large sample of quotations to illustrate a point, but since so much pressure has been put upon the public to have people believe that the evolutionists do not derive human beings from monkeys or apes, and since this is not true, it seems desirable to present a wide selection of quotations to document the fact that evolutionists *do* believe we came from apes or monkeys or both.

Since it is commonly believed by evolutionists that we evolved from apes more recently than from monkeys, it is natural that more is said about our ape ancestry than about our monkey ancestry. Some deny that monkeys are in our ancestral line. In 1957 William Scheele, Director of the Cleveland Museum of Natural History, said that around the 1920's "scientists realized that it would have been impossible for men to have been derived from monkeys, simply because man's body is too unspecialized to enable him to act and live like a monkey."[38] He said this in spite of the fact that Dr. William L. Straus Jr. of the Johns Hopkins University, an outstanding anthropologist and authority on the primates, had published a paper in 1949 in which he gave his reasons for believing not only that we *did* evolve from monkeys, but that we evolved directly from monkeys and not by way of the apes. Professor Straus agrees with Charles Darwin that we evolved from the catarrhine monkeys, and he lists fifteen respects in which we are more like monkeys than we are like anthropoid apes.[39] Professor Straus also refers to a French scientist named Boule who "accuses the anthropologists of being biased and having assumed *a priori* that man is closest to apes disregarded the possibility of being closer to monkeys."

Here are a few sample statements by scientists who refer to our monkey ancestry.

Ralph Linton, anthropologist of the University of Pennsylvania, says, "From everything we know, it seems that our remote ancestors were monkeys."[40]

Carleton Coon, Harvard anthropologist, says, "Some of the descendants of the monkeys that had learned to walk upright went back to the forest, there they became the ancestors of the apes. Only those upright ones that stayed out in the open grew to be men."[41]

M. F. Ashley Montagu, the eminent anthropologist recently of Rutgers and the University of California at Santa Barbara, says, "Some authorities interpret the facts to indicate that man . . . originated either from a tarsioid or generalized catarrhine monkey. . . ."[42] As previously mentioned, he agrees with Darwin that "it was from the Old World monkey stock that the early anthropoids arose, and from these, in turn, that the line which led to man came into being."[43]

Professor George A. Dorsey of the University of Chicago says, "If mankind has received no more from his monkey ancestor, he might as well have had an opossum for an ancestor."[44]

Marston Bates of the University of Michigan says, "After all, no part of the zoo is more popular than the monkey house, and whatever our ancestors might have been like, there is a lot of monkey still left in us."[45]

Professor Julian Huxley, grandson of the famous Thomas Henry Huxley ("Darwin's bulldog"), lecturer at the University of London, says, "Man, it seems could only have evolved from a tree-living mammal which came down from the trees. Tree life as a monkey gave him grasping hands able to manipulate objects, and binocular vision."[46]

It seems that no matter what an evolutionist may say, a search of the biological literature will reveal that some other evolutionist has said just the opposite. In some cases it may even seem like satire, while in fact it is serious science. In 1947 C. J. van der Horst published a paper in which he proposed that monkeys evolved from man instead of man from monkeys. The evidence for this was an abnormal embryo of a tree shrew which he had found.[47]

Somewhat along this same line W. E. Le Gros Clark says that "Professor Wood Jones has pointed out that there are some anatomical features that make it easier to believe that the apes are descended from man rather than man from an extinct ape."[48]

Professor F. Wood Jones is well known for his theory that we evolved from a tarsius-like creature, bypassing both the monkeys and the apes. (There is only one living species of tarsier. It is about the size of a squirrel, has large ears and enormous eyes, eats insects and lizards, moves by jumping, and is active at night.) Strangely enough, his views were first published by an organization called The Society for Promoting Christian Knowledge! Some contemporary anti-evolutionists seem to have been pleased with this theory of Professor Wood Jones, apparently because it contradicted the generally accepted theories of evolution. This was indeed a short-sighted and unintelligent stand to take.

Tracing our supposed ancestry back to the beginning of the primate line, one comes to the tree shrews or tupaiids. These little animals were formerly classed as insectivores, but are now rather generally accepted as primates. Loren Eiseley of the University of Pennsylvania says, "Before the coming of the flowering plants our ancestral stock, the warm-blooded mammals, consisted of a few mousy little creatures hidden in trees and underbrush."[49]

Professor William Howells of Harvard has said, "A visitor from another world, happening along seventy million years ago, would probably have laughed at the idea the Paleocene primates could ever produce a man. But they did."[50] As a native of this planet at the present time, Professor Howells has a distinct advantage over such a hypothetical visitor from elsewhere. He says that "a tree shrew remains a pretty unpromising object for a grandfather. Luckily it is all over now, and we can use hindsight."[51]

The accusation is frequently made that religious people who reject the theory of evolution do so because it hurts their pride to think that they had an animal ancestry. The implications seem to be that they should overcome a false pride, and that in so doing they will achieve a greater measure of maturity. Of all people, Christians should have the least false pride, for they acknowledge that their eternal destiny depends upon nothing they have done or can do, except their acceptance of the atonement of the Lord Jesus Christ and His merits as the means of their eternal security. But there is something about monkeys that seems to make them particularly distasteful as relatives to many people. Missionaries from widely separated areas have reported that when they asked natives why they file or cut off the front teeth of their young people, the answer was that they do not wish to look like monkeys.

The Bible says that man was made in the image of God (Gen. 1:26, 27; 5:1; 9:6). We know that God the Father is a Spirit, but God the Son, Christ, had a body when He walked the earth. There are good reasons for believing that physical manifestations of God in the Old Testament were God the Son. Man was made in the Image of God. This is not said of any other creature.

As to the matter of pride interfering with the acceptance of evolution, it is interesting to note the case of an outstanding scientist who was a personal friend of Charles Darwin, but who refused to accept the theory of evolution for a long time, to Darwin's dismay and distress, because he did not like the thought of being related to monkeys. This was Charles Lyell, whose *Principles of Geology* was responsible for starting Darwin in his evolutionary thinking. Lyell popularized the uniformitarian view of geology and made it acceptable to the scientist. This uniformitarian view leads logically to the evolutionary theory of life. Yet Lyell dreaded the logical conclusion of what he himself was largely responsible for having started.

Concerning the concept that man evolved from apes, Henshaw Ward, one of Darwin's biographers, says, "Lyell confessed in private that he shuddered at the thought of the idea."[52] He further says, "For thirty years Lyell had loathed the thought of being descended from apes: to accept the *Origin* [*of Species*] was to lose faith in his gentlemanly superiority to the beasts."[53] According to Ward it was also the deliberate judgment of Thomas Henry Huxley that "Lyell would have adopted Darwinism much sooner if he had not dreaded all the consequences that must follow — the simian ancestry."[54]

Except that monkeys are in some ways distasteful creatures, it may seem strange that so much has been done to cover up the evolutionists' belief in our simian ancestry. If it hurts our pride to think of having a monkey or ape ancestry, should it not hurt our pride as much or more to think we came from fish and worms?

Professor Garrett Hardin of the University of California at Santa Barbara says that the phrase "amoeba to man" may have become popular because it does not sound so offensive as does a reference to our ape or monkey ancestry. He says, "Perhaps to *descend* from — well, why not say from an innocuous amoeba, without mentioning any closer cousins? 'From amoeba to man' became a catchword after Darwin."[55] But, alas, the amoeba has had to give up this place of honor in our ancestry to a flagellate of the *Euglena* type. Besides, there are different kinds of amoebas. People who have had amoebic dysentery may not look upon the amoeba as innocuous.

Some evolutionists may not like to think about their ancestry, but Professor Loren Eiseley does not mind. In fact he seems to prefer it. He says, "I lift up my hands under the light. There is no fur, black upon them, any longer. For a moment I wish there were — for a moment of desperate terror I wish to hurtle backward like a scuttling crab into my evolutionary shell, to be a swinging ape or leaping tupaiid [tree shrew]; yes, or sleeping reptile on a stream bank — anything but the thing I have become."[56]

NOTES

1. Hoebel, E. Adamson, *Man In the Primitive World* (McGraw-Hill, 1949), p. 21.

2. Mixter, Russell L., "Man In Creation," *Christian Life*, 23:6:24. October, 1961, p. 25.

3. Buswell, James O. III, "The Story of Creation. IV. The Creation of Man," *Christian Life*, 18:1:14, May, 1956, p. 17.

4. Cassel, J. Frank, "Comments on the Origin of Species," *Journal of the American Scientific Affiliation*, 13:2:42, June, 1961. p. 44.

5. Dobzhansky, Theodosius, *Mankind Evolving* (Yale University Press, 1962), p. 5.

6. Howells, William, *Mankind So Far* (Doubleday and Co., 1945), p. 6.

7. Hyman, Stanley Edgar, *Darwin for Today* (The Viking Press, 1963), p. 9.

8. Ashley Montagu, M. F., *The Science of Man* (Odessy Press, 1964), p. 14.

9. Simpson, George Gaylord, "The Word into which Darwin Led us." (Part of his book: *This View of Life*), *Science*, 131:3405:966, April 1, 1960, p. 969.

10. *Ibid.*, p. 969.

11. Muller, H. J., "Man's Place in Living Nature," *Scientific Monthly*, 84:5:245, May, 1957, p. 250.

12. Straus, William L. Jr., "The Riddle of Man's Ancestry," *Quarterly Review of Biology*, 24:3:200, September, 1949, p. 203.

13. *Ibid.*, p. 202.

14. *Ibid.*, p. 202.

15. This is mentioned by a number of authors. See Franz Weidenreich, *Apes, Giants, and Man* (University of Chicago Press, 1946), p. 24. Also William Howells, *Scientific American*, 203:3:113, September, 1960, p. 113.

16. Wendt, Herbert, *In Search of Adam* (Houghton, 1955), p. 141.

17. Smith, G. Elliot, *The Evolution of Man* (Oxford University Press, 1924), pp. 61 and 77.

18. Dart, Raymond, *Adventures with the Missing Link* (Harper and Brothers, 1959), p. 215.

19. Keith, Arthur, "Darwin's Theory of Man's Descent as It Stands Today," *Science*, 66:1705:201, September 2, 1927, p. 205.

20. *Ibid.*, p. 205.

21. *Ibid.*, p. 207.

22. Shapiro, Harry L., Editor, *Man, Culture, and Society*. Chapter 1. (By Shapiro.), (Oxford University Press, 1956) p. 5.

23. Hooton, Ernest Albert, *Apes, Men, and Morons* (George Allen and Unwin, 1938), p. 105.

24. Howells, William, *loc. cit.*, p. 3.

25. Washburn, Sherwood L., "Tools and Human Evolution," *Scientific American*, 203:3:63, September, 1960, p. 63.

26. Rhodes, F. H. T., *The Evolution of Life* (Penguin Books, 1962), p. 252.

27. Stokes, William Lee, *Essentials of Earth History* (Prentice-Hall, 1960), p. 361.

28. Hall, Thomas S., *et al.*, *Life Science* (John Wiley and Sons, 1955), p. 450.

29. Hensill, John S., *The Biology of Man* (The Blakiston Co., 1954), p. 126.

30. Camp, Charles L., *Earth Song* (University of California Press, 1952), p. 73.

31. Livingstone, Frank B., "Rediscovering Man's Pongid Ancestor," *American Anthropologist*, 64:2:301, April, 1962, p. 301.

32. Eiseley, Loren, *The Immense Journey* (Random House, 1957), p. 111.

33. Eiseley, Loren, "The Time of Man," *Horizon*, 4:4:4, March, 1962, p. 4.

34. La Barre, Weston, *The Human Animal* (University of Chicago Press, 1954), p. 69.

35. Andrews, Roy Chapman, *Meet Your Ancestors* (The Viking Press, Edition of 1956), p. 17.

36. Quoted by William Straus Jr., *loc. cit.*, p. 208.

37. Zirkle, Conway, *Evolution, Marxian Biology, and the Social Scene* (University of Pennsylvania Press, 1959), p. 26.

38. Scheele, William, *Prehistoric Man and the Primates* (World Pub. Co., 1957), p. 24.

39. Straus, William L. Jr., *loc. cit.*, p. 208.

40. Linton, Ralph, *The Tree of Culture* (Alfred A. Knopf, 1957), p. 4.

41. Coon, Carleton, *The Story of Man* (Borzoi Books, 1954, Fourth printing), p. 11.

42. Ashley Montagu, M. F., *An Introduction to Physical Anthropology* (Charles C. Thomas, 1951), p. 102.

43. Ashley Montagu, M. F., *The Science of Man* (Odessy Press, 1964), p. 14.

44. Dorsey, George A., *Why we Behave Like Human Beings* (Harper and Brothers, 1925), p. 70.

45. Bates, Marston, *Man in Nature* (Prentice-Hall, 1961), p. 13.

46. Huxley, Julian, *The Wonderful World of Life* (Garden City Books, 1958), p. 36.

47. van der Horst, C. J., "A Human-like Embryo of *Elephantulus*," *Proceedings of the Zoological Society of London*, 117:2-3:333, 1947. See *Biological Abstracts*, 22:8:1982, October, 1948, Item 19666.

48. F. Wood Jones is famous for his theory that man evolved directly from tarsioids.

49. Eiseley, Loren, 1957, *loc. cit.*, p. 66.

50. Howells, William, *Mankind in the Making* (Doubleday and Co., 1959), p. 61.

51. *Ibid.*, p. 123.
52. Ward, Henshaw, *Charles Darwin* (Bobbs-Merrill, 1927), p. 304.
53. *Ibid.*, p. 300.
54. *Ibid.*, p. 300.
55. Hardin, Garrett, *Nature and Man's Fate* (Reinhart, 1959), p. 66.
56. Eiseley, Loren, 1962, *loc. cit.*, p. 4.

CHAPTER II

A BRIEF HISTORY OF
EVOLUTIONARY THOUGHT

It is well known that Aristotle influenced scientific thought for a long time, but it is not so well known that, although he lived in the fourth century before Christ, he influenced Christian theology even to recent times. This is because he influenced Augustine and others who tried to accomodate their interpretation of Scripture to certain of his views. Thus the influence of Aristotle, who in turn was influenced by another Greek philosopher named Empedocles, led to the introduction into Christian thought of a type of theistic evolution.

In examining the history of evolutionary thought one is impressed with the fact that the leaders of the evolution movement have been so largely anti-Christian. This includes Charles Darwin, although in his early years he professed to believe the Bible in its entirety. He prepared to become a "country clergyman," and he completed his theological training, but later in life he repudiated whatever faith he once had.

Bernard Ramm, who writes as a conservative Christian, says that Asa Gray, the American botanist who became a disciple of Darwin, was an evangelical Christian, but a closer look at the facts disposes of this notion. More difficult to explain is the fact, mentioned by Dr. Ramm, that Dr. James Orr, the noted conservative theologian of the latter part of the last century and the beginning of the twentieth, also entertained views of theistic evolution. Dr. Orr had the theory of evolution thrust upon him and he had to deal with it. He seems to have been convinced that the scientists had proved evolution to be true and that he had to do the best he could with it. He should not have capitulated so easily, and if he had not, he could easily have shown that the theory of evolution and the Bible are incompatible. Although the Bible gives a clear answer, we have something in addition which James Orr did not have, and that is a knowledge, based upon experience, that the espousal of the theory of evolution leads to compromises which in turn lead to liberalism, modernism, and a repudiation of the gospel of salvation through the atonement of Christ. The history of the last century has shown over and over that as the evolution theory is accepted by a society, Christian faith deteriorates. With the acceptance of evolution, the social gospel is substituted for the gospel of salvation by grace through the atonement of Christ by way of the cross.

In recent years a new thing has happened, and this is more dangerous to Christian faith than the attacks and ridicule of the evolutionists. Men of science who profess to be Bible-believing Christians are telling conservative Christian audiences that it is not only all right to believe at least a certain amount of evolution, but that it actually is necessary to do so. (This is accomplished by defining the term *evolution* in such a way that those who accept the definition become evolutionists in spite of themselves.) Surely this is indicative of a time of apostasy, as foretold in Scripture.

EMPEDOCLES

In the fifth century before Christ a Greek philosopher named Empedocles taught that parts of bodies were formed independently — heads without necks, arms without shoulders, eyes without their sockets — and were brought together into random arrangements by a force which he called love. Many of these arrangements of anatomical parts were so abnormal that they perished quickly. Others were less abnormal and were able to live for some time. There were individuals that had their heads on backwards. There were cattle with the faces of men and men with the heads of cattle. As the combinations which were less well suited to live perished, those which were best suited for survival persisted and are represented among the presently living animals and human beings.

Lest it be thought that such fantasy is irrelevant to the history of the theory of evolution, it must be pointed out that Professor Henry Fairfield Osborn, the eminent head of the American Museum of Natural History in New York City, said that Empedocles "may justly be called the father of the evolution idea."[1] He also attributed to Empedocles some knowledge of the particular theory of evolution for which Charles Darwin became famous, for he says that "in the ancient teachings of Empedocles we find the germ of the theory of the survival of the fittest, or of natural selection, and the absolute proof that Empedocles' crude hypothesis embodied this world famous thought is found in passages in Aristotle's *Physics*, in which he refers to Empedocles as having first shown the possibility of the origin of the fittest forms of life through chance rather than through Design."[2]

Professor Osborn is not alone in this evaluation of the importance of the ideas of Empedocles. Dr. Richard Swann Lull, Professor of Paleontology at Yale University, said in agreement, "Empedocles may be called the father of evolution."[3]

Dr. Benjamin Fuller of Harvard University said, "The fauna and flora, then, including human beings . . . are [according to Empedocles] the results of a true Darwinian evolution, the direction of which is explained entirely by chance, by the struggle for life, and by the survival of the fittest."[4]

Edward Zeller, the German philosopher and theologian, wrote a history of Greek philosophy which has gone through thirteen editions. He said that the attempt of Empedocles to explain the origin of living things on a mechanistic basis places him among the precursors of Darwin.[5]

Thus in the opinion of men of erudition, Empedocles deserves a place at the beginning of the history of evolutionary thought.

NOTES

1. Osborn, Henry Fairfield, *From the Greeks to Darwin*, 2d ed. (Charles Scribner's Sons, 1929), p. 52.
2. *Ibid.*, p. 54.
3. Lull, Richard Swann, *Organic Evolution*, rev. ed. (Macmillan, 1948), p. 6.
4. Fuller, Benjamin A. G., *History of Greek Philosophy. Thales to Democritus* (Henry Holt and Co., 1923), p. 195.
5. Zeller, Edward, *Outlines of the History of Greek Philosophy*, Eighth printing of the revised thirteenth edition (Meridian Books, 1960), p. 75.

ARISTOTLE

Aristotle taught that there is a continuous gradation of living forms from the lowest to the highest, culminating in man, and that this evolutionary sequence came about through an internal perfecting tendency. In contrast to the mechanistic belief of Empedocles, Aristotle believed that an intelligent Designer was responsible for planning the world.

Erik Nordenskiold, in his book *The History of Biology,* said of Aristotle's writings, "Here we find enunciated for the first time a really complete theory of evolution."[1]

In his *Introduction to Philosophy,* G. T. W. Patrick says, "Aristotle not only taught the doctrine of evolution, but he had, what Darwin lacked, a theory of its *causes.*"[2]

According to Professor Henry Fairfield Osborn of Columbia University and the American Museum of Natural History, the influence which Aristotle and Plato exerted on European thought as late as the early seventeenth century was greater than the influence of those who interpreted the Genesis account of creation literally.[3]

When Charles Darwin read a translation of a portion of the works of Aristotle, he commented that "Linnaeus and Cuvier have been my two gods . . . but they were mere schoolboys to old Aristotle."[4]

NOTES

1. Nordenskiold, Erik, *The History of Biology* (Tudor Publishing Co., 1935), p. 37.
2. Quoted by Oliver L. Reisner, *A Book that Shook the World,* Julian Huxley, Editor (University of Pittsburgh Press, 1958), p. 39.
3. Osborn, Henry Fairfield, *From the Greeks to Darwin.* 2d ed. (Charles Scribner's Sons, 1929), p. 105.
4. Darwin, Francis, Editor, *The Life and Letters of Charles Darwin* (D. Appleton and Co., 1896), Vol. 2. p. 427. (Letter to Dr. W. Ogle, February 22, 1882. This was two months before Darwin's death.)

AUGUSTINE

The figurative interpretation of the account of creation given in the Bible is not new. Professor Osborn says that it was Philo of Alexandria, in the first century of the Christian era, who first applied the allegorical method to the interpretation of the Old Testament.[1] This was the result of the influence of Greek philosophy. He goes on to say that Gregory of Nyssa, in the fourth century, began the movement which interpreted the Biblical account of creation in a partially naturalistic manner. This was completed by Augustine in the fourth and fifth centuries.

Aurelius Augustinus, or Augustine, Bishop of Hippo, is considered as the most eminent of the Latin Church Fathers, and he has been called the first "modern" man. His writings have deeply influenced theological thought to the present day. Henry Fairfield Osborn believes that Augustine and those who followed him expressed evolutionary views because they were influenced by the earlier Greeks. This is revealed in the commentaries on creation written by these theologians, "which accord very closely with the modern theistic conceptions of evolution."[2] He continues, "If the orthodoxy of Augustine [that is, orthodoxy from Osborn's point of view] had remained the teaching of the church, the final establishment of evolution would have come far earlier than it did, certainly during the eighteenth instead of the nineteenth century, and the bitter controversy between science and theology over this truth of nature would never have arisen." By "this truth of nature" Dr. Osborn means the theory of evolution. He believes that, if theologians had continued to follow the teachings of Augustine with respect to the origin of living things, theistic evolution would have been accepted from that time to the present, and no serious theological issue concerning evolution would have arisen.

To reconcile the views of Aristotle with Scripture, Augustine taught that, at a time when all things were in a state of confusion, God had already made all things potentially, but not actually. The objects of creation came about in due time through a series of natural causes instead of by creative acts. Thus Professor Osborn notes that Augustine "sought a naturalistic interpretation of the Mosaic record . . . and taught that in the institution of nature we should not look for miracles but for the laws of nature."[3] He quotes another writer as saying, "Augustine distinctly rejected Special Creation in favor of a doctrine which, without any violence to language, we may call a theory of evolution."[4]

The author of a college textbook, Relis Brown of Lawrence College, says it this way: "The great theologian Augustine reconciled Aristotle's concept of the gradual development of complex organisms from simple ones to the Genesis account of creation by suggesting that creation was potential and not actual. That is, the possibility of the development of complex animals was established when the universe began, but the realization of this potentiality followed only much later, after plants and simpler animals had gradually developed."[5]

Eldon J. Gardner of Utah State University says in his *History of Life Science*, "St. Augustine . . . favored an allegorical interpretation of the book of Genesis in the Bible and openly promoted an evolutionary concept as opposed to special creation."[6]

NOTES

1. Osborn, Henry Fairfield, *From the Greeks to Darwin,* 2d ed. (Charles Scribner's Sons, 1929), pp. 105, 106.
2. *Ibid.,* p. 11.
3. *Ibid.,* pp. 109, 110.
4. *Ibid.,* p. 110.
5. Brown, Relis B., *Biology* (D. C. Heath and Co., 1956), p. 475.
6. Gardner, Eldon J., *History of Life Science* (Burgess Pub. Co., 1960), p. 93.

FRANCISCO SUAREZ

Francisco Suarez lived from 1548 to 1617. The Jesuits consider him the greatest theologian their order has produced. It is said that he habitually studied seventeen hours a day, and his published writings fill twenty-three folio volumes. One of his books was burned in England and France because he declared that the Pope has the power to coerce kings.

Professor Osborn in his book *From the Greeks to Darwin* says that Suarez strongly opposed the views that Augustine taught about creation. He says that by promoting the concept of special creation Suarez was able to check the tide of evolutionary thought brought about by Augustine and subsequent theologians, and because of his influence the teaching of special creation dominated both theology and science up to the time of Darwin. Professor Osborn seems to be correct about this, although some have disagreed. Thus Suarez holds a very important place in the history of evolutionary thought.

The great tragedy of Suarez' life is interesting and instructive. Although he was highly honored for his wisdom and orthodoxy, and it is generally believed that his views represent "the very essence of orthodoxy"[1] from the Roman Catholic point of view, he was excommunicated by Pope Clement VIII. This disgrace, which ruined his health, came about because he wrote something which he thought was in accord with a decree of the Pope, but it turned out that he was mistaken. According to Roman Catholic doctrine, forgiveness of sins requires "absolution" pronounced by a priest. At that time there was a controversy as to whether or not confession could be made and absolution pronounced in cases where a man was dying and a priest could not be obtained in time. To settle the matter the Pope, in 1602, declared it to be a false, rash, and scandalous position for anyone to hold that "it is permitted sacramentally to confess one's sins by letter or messenger to an absent confessor and to receive absolution from that same absent priest."[2] Suarez interpreted this to mean that confession and absolution could not *both* be made in absentia, but he did not state this interpretation dogmatically. In fact he did just the opposite, for he said, "I submit this assertion to the judgment of the same Pontiff, together with everything else that is contained in this and any other works."[3]

But the Pope was very much displeased. In vain letters were addressed to him in behalf of Suarez. One pleaded with him to "honor and defend a man whose whole life is spent with such rare examples of virtue, with such constancy, with such glory to his order and for the service of the Church. . . ."[4]

In spite of all the pleas in Suarez' behalf, the blow was struck. "The rigorous and painful sentence of excommunication made an outcast of the champion of orthodoxy."[5] (*The Catholic Encyclopedia,* in its article on Suarez, does not mention his excommunication!)

It is said that now a priest will always give absolution to a dying man, even though it is not known whether or not he had any desire to make confession.[6] It is reported that a Catholic mother who lost a son in an airplane accident was greatly relieved when she met a priest who said that he had seen the wreckage from the window of a passing train and had given absolution to anyone who might be dying in it.

The real tragedy is that according to the Bible all of this is of no avail, for forgiveness in the sight of God comes only through accepting the death of the Lord Jesus Christ as the atoning substitute for the remission of our sins.

NOTES

1. Fichter, Joseph M., *Francis Suarez* (The Macmillan Co., 1940), p. 253. This book has the imprimatur, or approval, of Francis J. Spellman, Archbishop of New York.

2. *Ibid.,* p. 256.

3. *Ibid.,* p. 257.

4. *Ibid.,* p. 259.

5. *Ibid.*

6. *Ibid.,* p. 261.

MAUPERTUIS

Pierre Louis Moreau de Maupertuis was a man of remarkable genius. Through his brilliant work in showing that the sphere of the earth is flattened toward the poles, he provided the first proof that Newton's law of gravitation is correct. We tend to take the law of gravitation for granted, but at that time there was much opposition to it.

His greatest achievement was his discovery of the "principle of least action." Although intricate mathematical procedures are required in order to show what is involved in the principle, the gist of it is that any natural phenomenon is carried out in such a manner that the product of the time and energy involved is always a minimum. His work in this area was so far ahead of his time that it was not altogether appreciated until the advent of quantum mechanics. Three other mathematicians who later developed the principle have been erroneously credited with originating it.

The mechanics of Newton does not apply within the atom, but the principle of Maupertuis does apply there, and it has become the cornerstone of modern physics. Jerome Fee, writing in *Scientific American*, says, "It is not strange that the principle of least action is sometimes regarded as the greatest generalization in the realm of physical science."[1] In the technical sense used here, "action" is not relative, and Fee points out that "it is one of the few quantities which was left untouched by Einstein's theory."

Besides his genius in science and mathematics, Maupertuis seems to have excelled in philosophy. Bentley Glass of the Johns Hopkins University says that "in philosophy as in physical science, Maupertuis proved himself a powerful and original thinker."[2] Arthur O. Lovejoy, also of the Johns Hopkins University, has pointed out that Maupertuis anticipated Voltaire and several others in certain philosophical ideas.

Maupertuis anticipated Charles Darwin in a remarkable way a century before he published his *Origin of Species*. Bentley Glass says, "With certainty he must be ranked above all the precursors of Darwin."[3] Glass says that Maupertuis made "a beautifully clear statement of the survival of the fittest."[4] The principle of the survival of the fittest is equivalent to "natural selection," which is the basis of the theory of evolution which made Darwin famous.

Maupertuis also described evolution by mutations a century and a half before Hugo de Vries advanced his mutation theory. Furthermore, he realized that most mutations are deleterious, a fact which is somewhat embarrassing to evolutionists today. Darwin realized that his theory was weakened because he could not explain how variations suitable for evolution arose. In 1901 Hugo de Vries proposed the mutation theory to explain the origin of evolutionary differences, and at the present time the theory of evolution is based primarily upon mutations and natural selection, both suggested by Maupertuis long ago.

It is interesting to note that according to Glass, the reason Maupertuis proposed evolution through natural selection was that he had considered, and desired to refute, the argument for the existence of God from the apparent order and design seen in nature. This recalls how Darwin, a century later, endeavored to refute the teleological arguments of Paley, which he had formerly seriously considered. Evolutionists today are attacking the apparent evidences of God in nature with the substitution of evolution.

Shortly after the publication of Darwin's *Origin of Species* Gregor Mendel published his laws of inheritance, which were not well received at the time, but now are held to be basic to any consideration of evolution. Glass credits Maupertuis with discovering "virtually every idea of the Mendelian mechanism of heredity."[5]

Maupertuis enjoyed such contemporary fame as "has seldom been equalled," but today he is "practically unknown, or is remembered only as an object of ridicule and contempt."[6] In spite of his achievements, it is difficult to find his name in a history of science. The explanation of this strange circumstance is the fact that after a friendship of twenty years with Voltaire, during which time Voltaire wrote of him in most flattering language, this false friend suddenly turned against him with a vengeance. Maupertuis had a quarrel with a mathematician who said that Leibnitz had advanced the principle of least action in private correspondence before Maupertuis had published it. Leibnitz was deceased and the alleged recipient of the letter, one Henzi, had literally lost his head for treason in France. The letter could not be found and was officially declared spurious. Even if it had been genuine, the recognition as discoverer of this principle would still be due to Maupertuis, for according to the rules of priority it is the one who first publishes who gets the credit. But Voltaire sided against his former friend and used his pen to pile invective and ridicule upon him. He did it so effectively that the reputation of Maupertuis was ruined.

NOTES

1. Fee, Jerome, "Maupertuis and the Principle of Least Action," *Scientific Monthly*, 52:6:496, June, 1941, p. 496.
2. Glass, Bentley, Editor, *Forerunners of Darwin. 1745-1859* (The Johns Hopkins Press, 1959), p. 57.
3. *Ibid.*, p. 74.
4. *Ibid.*, p. 57.
5. *Ibid.*, p. 60.
6. Fee, Jerome, *loc. cit.*, p. 496.

ERASMUS DARWIN

The name of Charles Darwin is familiar to all, but probably few people today know anything about his grandfather, Doctor Erasmus Darwin. Dr. Darwin was a famous man in his day, both as a physician and as a writer. His renown was so great that the King of England, George III, invited him to be his personal physician. This honor was declined by Dr. Darwin. The reason he rejected this invitation from his king seems to have been, as C. D. Darlington of Oxford University has suggested, because he wished to devote his time to scientific writing.[1] The writings of Erasmus Darwin had to do with evolution, and they were well known at that time. They were translated into several foreign languages and were reprinted a number of times.

Professor Darlington has pointed out that Erasmus Darwin published the ideas for which his grandson later was given credit. He says, "As to the means of transformation, however [that is, the mechanism of evolution], Erasmus Darwin originated almost every important idea that has since appeared in evolutionary theory."[2]

Charles Darwin cited the famous essay on population by T. R. Malthus as the source of his inspiration for his natural selection theory, but Erasmus Darwin stated the principle of natural selection before Malthus wrote his essay. Darlington believes that Malthus got the idea for his essay from Erasmus Darwin,[3] and Conway Zirkle of the University of Pennsylvania presents evidence that Erasmus Darwin got the idea originally from Benjamin Franklin.[4] Loren Eiseley, also of the University of Pennsylvania, has come up with evidence that Charles Darwin really got his idea from William Blyth, a scientist who worked in India, and not from Malthus."[5] Both Darlington and

Eiseley believe that Charles Darwin cited Malthus as the source of his idea about natural selection because he did not wish the credit to go to another scientist instead of to himself. At any rate, Erasmus Darwin got no credit from his illustrious grandson. The only mention Charles Darwin made of his grandfather is in the *Historical Sketch* which he wrote for the third edition of his *Origin of Species*. He says, "It is curious how largely my grandfather, Doctor Erasmus Darwin, anticipated the views and erroneous grounds of opinion of Lamarck. . . ." It is also curious how Charles Darwin himself later espoused the same Lamarckian principles for which he criticized his grandfather.

The fame of Dr. Erasmus Darwin was brief, for even in his own lifetime public opinion turned against him. Garrett Hardin of the University of California at Santa Barbara attributes this to the growing evangelical movement led by John Wesley.[6] Today, as then, the gospel will discredit evolution or evolution will discredit the gospel.

The later life of Erasmus Darwin was clouded by scandal, and this is sometimes given as the possible reason why his grandson refused to mention him favorably.

If Erasmus Darwin had heeded the call of his king and had served him instead of devoting his time to evolutionary speculations, his life no doubt would have been more profitably spent.

NOTES

1. Darlington, C. D., *Darwin's Place in History* (Macmillan, 1961), p. 8.
2. Darlington, C. D., "The Origin of Darwinism," *Scientific American,* 200:5:60, May, 1959, p. 62.
3. Darlington, C. D., 1961, *loc. cit.,* p. 13.
4. *Ibid.,* p. 11, Footnote. Darlington cites Zirkle, 1941, who cites a paper published by Benjamin Franklin in 1775: *Observations Concerning the Increase of Mankind and the People of Countries.*
5. Eiseley, Loren, *The Firmament of Time* (Althenium Publishers, 1960) pp. 78 to 80.
6. Hardin, Garrett, *Nature and Man's Fate* (Reinhart and Co., 1959), p. 7.

LAMARCK

Jean Baptiste Pierre Antoine de Monet, Chevalier de Lamarck was the eleventh child of a poor but noble family. In compliance with his father's wishes he attended a religious school and was destined to become a Jesuit priest, but when he was sixteen years old his father died. He immediately left school, purchased an old horse, and rode off to war. He joined the army in the evening, and the following day he found himself in a battle in which all the officers of his company were killed. With less than one day's experience in warfare, he took charge, refused to retreat, and held the position until help arrived. His military career was very short, however, for he was soon forced to leave the army because of an injury he received when one of his companions playfully lifted him by the head.

For fifteen years he eked out a meager existence with mundane employment and studied plants on the side. As a self-made botanist he achieved fame and was honored by admission to the French Academy of Sciences. He compiled a catalog of the plants of France in which he introduced a method of identifying plants by *keys,* now common in taxonomic works, by which the identification of a specimen can be obtained through following a series of alternative contrasting descriptions.

After he had studied botany for twenty-five years and distinguished himself in that field, a political situation arose in France which caused him to be transferred from the area of botany to zoology. At the age of fifty he began studying zoology, and distinguished himself here even more than he had in botany. He ruined his sight by peering for long hours through his microscope. Finally he became totally blind and finished his work by dictating it to his daughters. Outliving four wives, he died in poverty and was buried in a common grave from which the bones were periodically removed to make room for others. No one knows where his remains are today.

Lamarck was the first person to produce a theory of evolution which was scientifically complete. Ernst Haeckel, one of the most aggressive proponents of evolution, said of Lamarck, "To him will always belong the immortal glory of having for the first time worked out the Theory of Descent as an independent scientific theory of the first order, and as the philosophical foundation for the whole science of biology."[1] His most notable work on evolution is his *Philosophie Zoologique,* which was published in the same year that Charles Darwin was born, 1809.

Lamarck was prone to making wild speculations. This ruined his reputation among his contemporaries, and his evolutionary views were not accepted by the other men of science. When Charles Darwin published his theory of evolution, he held Lamarck in contempt. But, strangely enough, as time went on he adopted more and more of the ideas of Lamarck, until some contend that he actually went further than Lamarck had gone in accepting the influence of the environment as a factor in evolution and heredity.

It was not until Charles Darwin became famous for his theory of evolution that the genius of Lamarck was appreciated. Darwin's fame roused interest in possible precursors, and this brought to light the important work of Lamarck in the field of invertebrate zoology, as well as Lamarck's views on evolution.

Lamarck has been much maligned because it is charged that he believed that animals evolved useful structures because of a process of "desiring" them. This hinges upon the interpretation of the French word *besoin*, as he used it. Some say that he had in mind no such implication in the use of this word.

Lamarck is more remembered today for his theory of "the inheritance of acquired characteristics" than for his vast contribution to the understanding of invertebrate zoology. The most commonly remembered of his illustrations is that of how the giraffes got longer and longer necks because they stretched higher and higher for foliage to eat as it became depleted near the ground. It should be remembered that Lamarck's and Darwin's theories as to how the giraffes got their long necks differ only in whether the length came about through stretching or through a perferential selection of those which happened to be born with the potentiality of growing longer necks than the average. Neither Lamarck's theory nor Darwin's explains how the animals which were not giraffes survived with their short necks, nor how the females survived with their necks about a foot shorter than the males, nor how the young giraffes with their much shorter necks managed to survive to adulthood.

The espousal of a theory of evolution leads to a repudiation of Scripture, and the case of Lamarck was no exception. In the book *Forerunners of Darwin*, Charles C. Gillespie quotes a French writer named Sainte-Bouve, who, he says, has best caught the spirit of Lamarck's philosophy. Sainte-Bouve says that Lamarck's "philosophical hostility [amounted] to hatred for the tradition of the Deluge and the Biblical creation story, indeed for everything which recalled the Christian theory of nature."[2]

Lamarck was a great and noble man in spite of his tendency to wild speculation. To know something of his life is to admire him, and at the same time to feel sympathy for him. But the fact is that his evolutionary philosophy led him to a "hatred . . . for everything which recalled the Christian theory of nature."

NOTES

1. *Collier's Encyclopedia,* 1967, Vol. 14, p. 275.
2. Glass, Bentley, Editor, *Forerunners of Darwin. 1745-1859* (The Johns Hopkins Press, 1959), p. 276.

ROBERT CHAMBERS

Evolution was first seriously brought to the attention of the general public from a scientific point of view in 1844, when Robert Chambers published his *Vestiges of the Natural History of Creation.* To protect himself from the reaction which he knew would result, he took great pains to conceal his identity as the author of the book. For a while there was a rumor that the author was Prince Albert, husband of Queen Victoria, and this helped to make the volume widely read. Although the truth about the authorship was not made known until after Chamber's death, suspicion that he had written it was strong enough to prevent him from becoming Lord Provost of Edinburgh in 1848.

Appraisals of the book from a religious point of view by contemporary reviewers varied from assertions that it was the work of a deeply religious man who did not contradict the writings of Moses and whose message was entirely consistent with Christian faith, to the opposite view. The fact is that it was a presentation of evolution, which therefore could not but oppose the writings of Moses and be inconsistent with the gospel of salvation by grace through the atonement of Christ. Its theology was deism, that is, the view that God started things going, established laws to keep them going, and then let the world go on by itself without further divine intervention. It seems hardly necessary to point out that this kind of theology is not Scriptural, for the Bible tells us that God has intervened many times in the affairs of men and will do so in the future. We believe He is intervening now, for we are admonished to pray, and there are answers to prayer.

Scientists of that day were critical of Chambers' book. Among those who were most critical was Thomas Henry Huxley. He did not accept evolution at that time, though he later became convinced of it because of Darwin's natural selection theory. He became Darwin's strongest defender against the anti-evolutionary forces and called himself "Darwin's bulldog." Professor Arthur Lovejoy, a Johns Hopkins Professor who gained fame through his studies in the history of ideas, says that Huxley became emotionally prejudiced against the *Vestiges* because of certain types of errors it contained which were of rather minor significance, and thus he did not appreciate the merit of the work as a whole.[1]

Professor Lovejoy expresses the opinion that Chambers' *Vestiges* presented sufficient evidence that it should have convinced the scientists of that day of the truth of evolution, and he believes that the fact that it did not do so is instructive in showing that "even in the minds of acute and professedly unprejudiced men of science, the emotion of conviction may lag behind the presentation of proof."[2] Human nature has not changed, and the scientists who are now committed to belief in the theory of evolution do not seem open to a serious consideration of the possibility that divine creation is a reasonable alternative to evolution through natural means.

Among those who were converted to belief in the theory of evolution through reading Robert Chambers' *Vestiges* were Ralph Waldo Emerson, the American essayest; Arthur Schopenhaur, the German philosopher; and Alfred Russell Wallace, the naturalist to whom credit is given as co-discoverer with Charles Darwin of the theory of natural selection, which is the basis of modern evolutionary theory. Professor Lovejoy attributed to Wallace's reading of the *Vestiges* a change in the orientation of his life, for he says that "from that time forward his mind was occupied with the problem of explaining the cause and *modus operandi* of evolution."[3]

The book was translated into German by Carl Vogt, who did not at the time believe in evolution. His motive in translating it was his conviction that the book was an attack upon orthodox Christianity, and he particularly praised it for this reason in the preface which he wrote for his translation.[4] He was later led to a belief in evolution through the writings of Charles Darwin, and he became a strong exponent of the theory.

Though the scientists of that day were not convinced by this work of Robert Chambers, it made a great impression on the laity. It went through twelve editions, twice as many as Darwin's *Origin of Species*. Darwin found it helpful to his own success in that it broke down prejudice against the concept of evolution, and he said, "In my opinion it has done excellent service in this country in calling attention to the subject, in removing prejudice, and in preparing the ground for the reception of analogous views."[5] It may not be amiss to mention here that Christian writers who are at the present time telling the conservative Christian public that now they may, or indeed must, accept a certain amount of evolution, are doing now what Chambers did then with his book, *Vestiges of the Natural History of Creation* — they are preparing the people to accept complete evolution, to the detriment of Christian faith.

An interesting side light on the life of Chambers is the fact that if he had not been present at the Oxford meetings where Thomas Henry Huxley and Bishop Wilburforce had their famous clash, that event would never have occurred. Huxley was determined to leave Oxford the day before, but Chambers persuaded him to stay. Hence, Huxley was present when the bishop made his speech and asked him whether he was descended from an ape on his grandfather's or grandmother's side.

Chambers ruined his health preparing a book which was his final publication. It was a collection of popular antiquities called *The Book of Days*. He never completely regained his health and died leaving unpublished a book he had begun on the life of Christ.

NOTES

1. Glass, Bentley, Editor, *Forerunners of Darwin. 1745-1859* (The Johns Hopkins Press, 1959), Chapter 13, By Arthur O. Lovejoy.
2. *Ibid.*, p. 356.
3. *Ibid.*, p. 362.
4. Stephen, Leslie, Editor, *Dictionary of National Biography* (Smith, Elder, and Co., 1887), Vol. 10, p. 24.
5. Darwin, Charles, Historical introduction to the third edition of *The Origin of Species*.

HERBERT SPENCER

On the ninth of November, 1882, a notable banquet was held in the city of New York. Only about two hundred people could be invited, and the popularity of the guest of honor was so great that an effort was made to keep mention of the banquet from the newspapers so as to avoid disappointing people who could not be invited. The speech which introduced the guest of honor extolled him as a man superior to all others of his generation, and even of all time, and included the following remarks: "We recognize in the breadth of your knowledge

. . . a greater comprehension than any living man has presented to our generation . . . in our judgment you have brought to the analysis and distribution of this vast knowledge a more penetrating intelligence and a more thorough insight than any living man has brought even to the minor topics of his special knowledge. In theology, in psychology, in natural science, in the knowledge of individual man and his exposition, and in the knowledge of the world . . . we acknowledge your labors as surpassing those of any of our kind."[1]

Some who received invitations were unable to attend the banquet, and they wrote letters praising the honored guest in extravagant language. The President of Columbia University said, "In revealing and demonstrating the laws which govern all progress, physical, moral, or social, he has himself contributed the most powerful impulse to the progress of the human race toward the good and the true that this or any other century has known. His philosophy is the only philosophy that satisfies an earnestly inquiring mind."[2] Oliver Wendell Holmes wrote, "We look with amazement upon the reach and compass of his vast triangulation of the universe."[3]

The recipient of all this adulation was Herbert Spencer, a peevish old man who had not had a sound night's sleep in twenty-seven years. Like Charles Darwin, he was a semi-invalid who lived to a good old age. Also like Charles Darwin, the excitement of even ordinary conversation could be too much for him. Though idolized as the greatest thinker of his day, he is now, less than a century later, a nearly forgotten man. Unlike the case of the forgotten Maupertuis, Spencer is forgotten because of the lack of real merit in his work.

Time ran out at the banquet before all the prepared speeches could be given. The next speech on the agenda was to have followed the toast: "Spencer's philosophy of evolution: the most original achievement in the history of thought."[4] In retrospect this seems quite amazing, for this event occurred twenty years *after* the publication of Darwin's *Origin of Species.*

In the ninth edition of the *Encyclopedia Britannica,* published in 1892, under the heading *Evolution,* Charles Darwin received about eight column-inches of space, while Herbert Spencer received about nineteen. In the text it is stated: "The thinker who has done more than anyone else to elaborate a consistent philosophy of evolution on a scientific basis is Mr. Herbert Spencer."

Whether there was any connection between Spencer's insomnia and the publication of the *Origin of Species* can only be surmised, though his sleeplessness began about the time of the appearance of Darwin's book. In the preface of his *Synthetic Philosophy* Spencer tells that in 1855, four years before the *Origin* appeared, he had suffered a disorder due to "overtax of brain." By 1860 he had spent most of his meager resources in publishing books which did not meet expenses. It was near the close of the previous year that the very wealthy Charles Darwin had published his *Origin of Species,* which sold out on the day of publication and brought its author much fame.

In March of 1860 Spencer issued a prospectus of a series of works which, when completed, would contain his views on evolution. At some later date he showed to a Mr. Edward Clodd some documents which disclosed that on the sixth of January, 1858, he had written a first draft of this prospectus.[5] On the basis of this first draft of a prospectus he tried to take credit for anticipating the work of Darwin!

Spencer's writings could be understood by the unlearned, and his influence helped popularize the idea of evolution. Although his views seemed very important at the time, the only contribution to evolution for which he is now remembered is his coining of the expression "survival of the fittest," which meant the same thing as Darwin's "natural selection." Darwin accepted Spencer's term as superior in some ways to his own.

Spencer's autobiography runs to 1268 pages. Under "religion" in the index there is given a reference to only one page,[6] although there are actually three pages devoted to this subject. He tells us that when he was a young man working on the railroad, his father wrote to him, calling his attention to religious matters and seeking a response. He says that he did not answer his father's letters because he could not say anything which would be satisfactory. He says that the "creed of Christiandom" was alien to his nature, and he tells of his rejection of the way of salvation as presented in the Bible. He also states that "To many, and apparently to most, a religious worship yields a species of pleasure. To me it never did so. . . ." And yet, as shown in the quotations already presented here, a man like this not only can be, but was, hailed by his followers as a great theologian and religious leader! "In theology . . . we acknowledge your labors as surpassing those of any of our kind." "His philosophy is the only philosophy that satisfies an earnestly inquiring mind."

When Spencer died, twenty-one years after Charles Darwin, he was not entombed in Westminster Abbey, where Darwin's remains lay. The reason was because of his anti-Christian sentiments. A half year later a request was made by a number of distinguished gentlemen that a memorial tablet be placed in the Abbey for him. This request also was refused on the grounds that the Abbey "as a place of Christian worship, could not appropriately receive the monument of a thinker who expressly excluded Christianity from his system of thought."[7]

NOTES

1. E. L. Y., Anonymous editor, *Herbert Spencer on the Americans and the Americans on Herbert Spencer* (D. Appleton and Co., 1887), p. 27.
2. *Ibid.*, p. 87.
3. *Ibid.*, p. 84.
4. *Ibid.*, p. 67.
5. Clodd, Edward, *Pioneers of Evolution* (Cassell and Co., 1907), pp. 183, 184.
6. Spencer, Herbert, *An Autobiography* (D. Appleton and Co., 1904), Vol. 1, p. 171.
7. Clodd, Edward, *loc. cit.*, p. 186.

CHARLES DARWIN

On the twelfth of February, 1809, Abraham Lincoln, the future distinguished President of the United States of America, was born in rural Kentucky. On the very same day, the twelfth of February, 1809, Charles Darwin, the future evolutionist, was born at Shrewsbury in England. This coincidence has inspired the comparison that while Lincoln freed men from physical slavery, Darwin freed men from the slavery of superstition. Spoken of in this way, the superstition from which Darwin is said to have freed men is nothing other than the tenets of the Holy Bible, and in particular the fundamental claims of the Christian faith.

The Lord Jesus Christ said of Himself, "If the Son therefore shall make you free, you shall be free indeed" (John 8:36). It was on this same occasion that He said, "You shall know the truth and the truth shall make you free" (John 8:32). This verse is probably misquoted and quoted out of context more than any other portion of Scripture. Cultists and liberals quote it freely and with enthusiastic approval, but quoted in context it condemns them. This statement was not made to the world in general, nor was it made about the knowledge of worldly facts or principles. It was made to those "which believed on Him." Furthermore, it had a condition, for He said to them, "If you continue in my word, then are you my disciples indeed; and you shall know the truth, and the truth shall make you free." In context, the Lord said to believers before the time of His sacrifice upon the cross that if they continued to believe according to His words to them, they would come to an understanding of the truth, and they would be freed from the penalty of sin through His vicarious and atoning death.

Evolutionists cannot very well accept the death of Christ as an atonement for sin, because according to the concept of the evolution of man from lower forms there is no need for an atoning Saviour. Instead of the origin of sin through a historic fall through disobedience of the first parents of mankind, man is improving from an animal status.

The preaching of the gospel has done more to free mankind from superstition than anything else has, as is well known to everyone who is acquainted with the work of gospel-preaching Christian missionaries, and yet the evolutionists seem to delight in saying that the acceptance of the theory of evolution has freed men's minds from superstition, meaning religious faith.

George Gaylord Simpson, who is perhaps the most outstanding evolutionist of our time, lived with the Lamarakoto Indians in South America. In his book, *This View of Life,* he briefly describes some of the superstitious beliefs of these Indians, and comments: "It is nevertheless superior in some respects to the higher superstitions celebrated weekly in every hamlet in the United States."[1] In his sight the basis for the superiority of their beliefs over Christianity seems to be that "Above all, they are not guilty of teleology." That is, they do not conceive of any purpose in the world.

Charles Darwin's maternal grandfather was Josiah Wedgewood, maker of the famous Wedgewood chinaware. His paternal grandfather was the famous Doctor Erasmus Darwin, whose views on evolution were known as "Darwinism" before Charles Darwin was born. Charles' mother died when he was eight years old, and he had very little recollection of her. His father was a highly successful physician who had no interest in religious matters. Charles seems to have had not only respect for, but also a certain amount of fear of his father.

As a young man Charles showed promise as he aided his father in his duties as physician, and later he went to Edinburgh to study medicine. But he took no interest in his studies and was a failure. This may be partially attributed to the uninteresting way the lectures were given and the effect of observing an operation in those days before the use of anesthetics. But it was largely due to the fact that he had come to realize that his father was going to leave him an estate which would make him independently wealthy for life. His chief delight was in hunting with dogs, and his father once said to him, "You care for nothing but shooting, dogs, and rat-catching, and you will be a disgrace to yourself and all your family."[2]

As a remedy for this situation, it was recommended that he take up the study of theology. He looked into the matter to see whether he could honestly subscribe to the creed of the Church of England. He found that he could, and he later wrote, "I liked the thought of being a country clergyman. Accordingly I read with care *Pearson on the Creed* and a few other books on divinity; and as I did not then in the least doubt the strict and literal truth of every word in the Bible, I soon persuaded myself that our creed must be fully accepted."[3] However, he later wrote in his autobiography that it had been illogical for him to profess that he believed what he could not understand and what he judged in his mature years to be unintelligible. It is evident that he had no real interest in theology, and the decision to study in this area was largely in obedience to his father's wish that he do something so as not to disgrace the family.

Gertrude Himmelfarb, one of Darwin's biographers, says of his father, "He respected neither the clergy nor his son enough to credit them with any profound religious convictions; and he was sufficiently aristocratic in his own sentiments to feel that, while he personally was superior to the irrational dogmas of religion, the masses of men required the stabilizing influence of a church —and in any event that his son required the stabilizing influence of a career."[4]

Gertrude Himmelfarb further comments that although the church at that time in England was the refuge of the talented and brilliant, it also rendered a service in "relieving despairing fathers of surplus sons."[5] She further remarks, "The final recourse of Victorian society for the maintenance of misfits and dullards was the church. Young men with no other discernable calling were graced with the highest calling of all."

Christ's College, Cambridge, where Charles Darwin went for his theological training, was not the wisest choice for a young man whose father deplored his interest in a sporting life. It is said that at this time the school was noted for gambling, drunkenness, moral laxity, and lack of discipline. The highest aspiration of the students was to be recognized as authorities on food and drink. One member of the faculty seems to have spent much of his time at the horse races, and a high official of the school is said to have never opened his mouth without an oath. This is the school where Darwin received his training for the Christian ministry.

Academic standards in those days were far different from those of today. The Professor of Astronomy and Geometry at Cambridge did not deliver a single lecture during the forty-two years of his tenure. A lecturer in mathematics, William Whewell, heard that a better position was to become vacant, namely the professorship in geology. With this in mind he took a three-month trip to Germany to learn something about the subject. He thereby qualified himself for the position, and received the appointment when it became available.

Darwin was influenced by the Reverend John Stevens Henslow, Professor of Botany, and came to be known as "the man who walks with Henslow." When Henslow became Professor of Botany he admitted publicly that he knew very little indeed about the subject.

Another professor who influenced Darwin was Adam Sedgwick, Professor of Geology. Upon his election to this position, Sedgwick declared: "I had but one rival . . . and he had not the slightest chance against me, for I knew absolutely nothing of geology, whereas he knew a good deal — but it was all wrong!"[6] To everyone's surprise, after he was elected Professor of Geology he made an effort to really learn something about the subject.

Darwin completed the requirements for his degree in theology, but later admitted that his time at Cambridge "was wasted, as far as the academic studies were concerned, as completely as at Edinburgh."[7] The following summer found him on a geological expedition in Wales with Professor Sedgwick, but his interest in geology at this time was very shallow to say the least, for he left the expedition and returned home in order to be ready for shooting on the opening day of the hunting season. He himself later wrote of this occasion, "at that time I should have thought myself mad to give up the first days of partridge-shooting for geology or any other science."[8]

He returned home in time to receive an invitation to travel as naturalist on the *Beagle,* which was sailing to make more accurate navigational charts. He very nearly did not go, and the history of the theory of evolution might have been rather different if he had remained at home. The post of naturalist had been offered to several others before him, but for one reason or another each was unable to accept. His father was strongly opposed to his going, but left a loop-hole in his objection, for he said that he would give his consent if one man of sound judgment thought it desirable that he go. An uncle met all of the father's objections, and young Charles was allowed to accept the invitation.

There was, however, still one more obstacle, for the captain of the ship, Robert Fitzroy, did not like the shape of Darwin's nose. He thought he could read a man's character by looking at his nose, and he did not like what he saw when he looked at Darwin. But Captain Fitzroy was persuaded to overlook the shape of Darwin's nose, and Darwin was accepted as the ship's naturalist.

The first volume of Lyell's *Principles of Geology* had just been published. It was this work of Lyell's which popularized and made acceptable to the men of science the view that all the agencies which produced geological changes in the past were the same which we observe today, such as local floods, earthquakes, landslides, and the like. In particular, Lyell's uniformitarianism denied the deluge of the time of Noah. This led directly to the development of the situation prophesied by Peter in his second epistle, where he wrote about scoffers in the last days who would reject the promise of the Lord's return, presenting as evidence their observation that "since the fathers fell asleep, all things continue as they were from the beginning of creation" (II Peter 3:3-6). Peter mentioned specifically that these people will willfully disregard the scriptural account of the flood which destroyed the life which was upon the earth.

Lyell's book contained facts which would be of importance to Darwin during his travels, and Professor Henslow recommended that he read it for that reason. However, he advised Darwin, "on no account to accept the views therein advocated."[9] But this advice was not heeded, and Darwin's acceptance of Lyell's theory marked the turning point in his life.

One of Darwin's biographers says, "Darwin's point of departure from orthodoxy on this voyage was, of course, his reading of the first volume of Lyell's *Principles of Geology.*"[10] Another biographer calls it "the book which influenced him more than any other."[11] Still another biographer remarks, "Possibly, without Lyell's *Principles of Geology,* Darwin would not have written his *Origin of Species.*"[12]

Darwin himself acknowledged his indebtedness to Lyell. He dedicated to Lyell his report of the voyage of the *Beagle* "as an acknowledgement that the chief part of whatever scientific merit this *Journal* and the other works of the author may possess has been derived from studying the well-known and admirable *Principles of Geology*."[13]

In 1844 Darwin wrote, "I always feel as if my books came half out of Lyell's brain, and that I never acknowledge this sufficiently . . . for I have always thought that the great merit of the *Principles* [*of Geology*] was that it altered the whole tone of one's mind. . . ."[14] At the time of Lyell's death in 1875 he said, "I never forget that almost everything which I have done in science I owe to the study of his great works."[15]

The most noteworthy stop on the expedition was the Galapagos Islands, on the equator, six hundred fifty miles from the west coast of South America. Here Darwin observed the birds which have come to be known as Darwin's finches, and it is often stated that his evolutionary ideas began here. David Lack, however, in his article on the finches in the *Scientific American* points out that Darwin did not mention the birds in his diary and mentioned them only briefly in his book on the voyage of the *Beagle*. It was not until a systematist named John Gould noted peculiarities in the finches that Darwin seemed to attach any significance to them, and commented on them in the second edition of his book. At any rate, much significance has since been attached to them, and Lack comments, "Thus obscurely, as an afterthought in a travel book, man received a first intimation that he might once have been an ape."[16]

The idea is that the birds got to the islands accidentally from the mainland, by the action of a storm or some freak of nature, and developed differently because they were isolated on separate islands. It is strange indeed, though apparently overlooked for convenience, that they would accidentally cross hundreds of miles of ocean and then remain isolated on small islands in sight of each other. If a storm carried them so far to sea, it is to be expected that sooner or later other storms would mix them up on the islands. William Beebe, the noted naturalist, did not believe the birds came to the islands by accident from South America, but that they came by way of a former land bridge from Central America.[17]

Darwin suffered considerably from seasickness on the voyage, and the illness he experienced during most of the rest of his life has frequently been attributed to the effects of the seasickness. Darwin himself rejected this explanation of his illness. As a young man he was very vigorous, and during the years of the expedition he displayed remarkable endurance. On one occasion in Patagonia he astonished his comrades with his stamina as they walked fifteen miles on a hot day without food or water. But one of his sons says that for nearly forty years he did not enjoy one day of the health of ordinary men.

His trouble has been attributed by various biographers to gout, eyestrain, glandular disturbances, heart trouble, psychological difficulties brought on by a dominating father, and to the bite of an insect in South America.

In recent times it seems to be rather generally accepted that the cause of his illness was mental rather than physical. As he tried one type of cure after another, each made him feel better for a short time, until the novelty of the experience wore off. The only thing that really brought relief was interesting work, while any unpleasantness made his symptoms worse. It seems more than a coincidence that his poor health began in 1837, the same year that he started the work which culminated, after much procrastination, in his book, *The Origin of Species*.[18]

The emotional strains which arose from this work may be grouped under three headings:

I. *Fear of criticism*. The idea of evolution was not a popular one at that time. His grandfather, Erasmus Darwin, had published evolutionary views and had been severely criticized for it. Robert Chambers published his *Vestiges of the Natural History of Creation* anonymously, but even though it was not proved during his lifetime that he was the author, the suspicion was sufficient to ruin his political ambitions.

In 1844, seven years after Darwin had begun his work on evolution, he broached the subject to a friend in the following words, "I am almost convinced (quite contrary to the position I started with) that species are not (it is like confessing a murder) immutable."[19]

When he finally published his book, he sent out presentation copies to various scientists with such notes as the following. ". . . how savage you will be, if you read it, and how you will try to crucify me alive."[20] "There are so many valid and weighty arguments against my notions, that you, or anyone, if you wish [to be] on the other side, will easily persuade yourself that I am wholly in error, and no doubt I am in part in error, perhaps wholly so, though I cannot see the blindness of my ways."[21] "I may, of course, be egregiously wrong; but I cannot persuade myself that a theory which explains (as I think it certainly does) several large classes of facts, can be wholly wrong; notwithstanding the several difficulties which have to be surmounted somehow, and which stagger me to this day."[22] "But I am perfectly well aware that you will entirely disagree with the conclusion at which I have arrived."[23]

II. *Desire for honor.* Although evolutionary papers published by men who were not scientists were being criticized unfavorably, there were men of science who were considering evolution seriously. Darwin was caught in a conflict between his fear of publishing and his desire to publish before some other scientist beat him to it. His friends urged him to publish before someone else robbed him of the honor of being first to present to the scientific world an acceptable theory of evolution. Although sympathetic biographers attribute the long delay to his thoroughness and desire to present all possible evidence, Darwin continued to procrastinate until forced to publish by receiving from Alfred Russell Wallace a letter which contained a perfect abstract of his own work. Darwin lamented that the neglected advice of his friends had not been heeded, for now he was honor-bound to give priority to another. His friends, however, persuaded him that under the circumstances the proper thing to do was to present a joint paper by himself and Wallace to the Linnaean Society. This was done, and Darwin published his *Origin of Species* the following year, 1859. Although Darwin made some statements which seem to indicate otherwise, he had a keen desire for recognition and honor.

III. *Religious convictions.* When Darwin sailed on the *Beagle,* his religious views were orthodox. Although he said that the change in his beliefs came so gradually that he suffered no distress, he must have had some inner conflict. His wife was very religious, and although they lived in harmony, this was a difference between them. Before Darwin married he asked his father's advice as to whether he should tell his future wife of his irreligious views, and his father advised against telling. Although he affirmed that acceptance of the theory of evolution need not interfere with religious convictions, he knew that it did in his own case and he knew there would be a strong reaction from religious people when his work became known.

In spite of Darwin's fears, the time was right. The book was a success, and the first edition was sold out on the day of publication. Reviews were of all sorts, from praise to condemnation. Of the early criticisms of the natural selection theory, the one which caused Darwin the most discomfort was by Fleeming Jenkin, a professor of engineering at Edinburgh University. Professor Jenkin argued logically, on the basis of Darwin's pre-Mendelian views of heredity, that a variation which should, according to Darwin, be important in evolution, would instead diminish in importance as its effect became further diluted in each successive generation. Professor C. D. Darlington of Oxford University says that this upset Darwin to such an extent that in successive editions of the *Origin of Species* he began to place more and more importance on the effects of the environment upon evolution. Professor Darlington points out that when Darwin's critics mentioned this, Darwin called to their attention something they had overlooked. In the first edition of the *Origin* he had prepared a line of retreat in case his natural selection theory was found untenable. "He now prudently took this line."[24] Thus Darwin retreated into the camp of Lamarck, whom he had despised, and put less reliance upon his natural selection theory.

Seven years before he died Darwin wrote a letter to his cousin, Francis Galton, in which he said, "If this implies that many parts are not modified by use and disuse during the life of the individual, I differ widely from you, as every year I come to attribute more and more to such agency."[25]

One of Darwin's admiring biographers goes so far as to attribute Darwin's change of attitude toward the influence of environmental factors to a desire on his part to make amends for the unkind things he had said about Lamarck, now deceased for nearly half a century.[26] Lamarck's theory of evolution was based upon the effects of the environment, and at first Darwin despised this and considered it to be in opposition to his own natural selection theory. But as his theory appeared to be found wanting as an explanation of evolution, he seemed to have no choice but to adopt more and more of Lamarck's views.

In an attempt to meet the need for an explanation of inheritance, and against the advice of his friends, Darwin published his pangenesis theory, which, as George Gaylord Simpson says, is now "charitably forgotten."[27]

Professor Darlington believes that in controversial areas Darwin became intentionally ambiguous, and that people with diametrically opposed views could thus read into his writing what they wished to see there. He concludes that Darwin "was able to put his ideas across not so much because of his scientific integrity, but because of his opportunism, his equivocation, and his lack of historical sense. Though his admirers will not like to believe it, he accomplished his revolution by personal weakness and strategic talent more than by scientific virtue."[28] In Darlington's opinion, Darwinism "began as a theory that evolution could be explained by natural selection. It ended as a theory that evolution could be explained just as you would like it to be explained."[29]

Professor Darlington is no admirer of Darwin as a man, but neither is he an anti-evolutionist trying to belittle him. Of natural selection he says with approval, "Here is a theory that released thinking men from the spell of superstition, one of the most overpowering that has ever enslaved mankind. . . ."[30] He further says, "We owe to the *Origin of Species* the overthrow of the myth of Creation, especially the dramatic character of the overthrow."[31]

Besides the criticism that the theory of natural selection was not true, there was also the charge that it was not new. When Darwin became famous, one author who tried to claim priority even had cards printed on which he announced himself as the discoverer of the principle of natural selection. Professor Darlington believes that Darwin's grandfather, Erasmus Darwin, "anticipated almost every important idea that has since appeared in evolution theory."[32] After Erasmus Darwin three physicians, William C. Wells, James C. Pritchard, and William Lawrence, according to Professor Darlington, "advanced explicitly and in detail the theory of natural selection."[33] Also a French scientist named Charles Naudin experimented with plants, attained results similar to those of Mendel, and proposed evolution by natural selection. The historically neglected Maupertuis had proposed evolution by natural selection a century before Darwin. Even in the sixth century Giorfano Bruno made a statement which sounds very much like natural selection: "Those elements of nature which are not suited for survival, and which have no adequate end, perish; others which have the right combination survive."[34]

Darwin claimed that he got the idea of natural selection from reading the essay on population by Thomas Malthus. As previously mentioned, it is believed that Malthus got the idea from Darwin's grandfather, Erasmus Darwin, and that he in turn got it from Benjamin Franklin. Some scientists believe Darwin really got the idea from a scientist in India, William Blyth, but preferred to give the credit to a non-scientist.[35]

All of this may be of little significance except that it shows something of Darwin's character which is different from the character given him by his biographers. Professor Darlington concludes that one of Darwin's vices was "a flexible strategy which is not to be reconciled with even average intellectual integrity. . . . Darwin was slippery."[36]

On the other hand, George Gaylord Simpson is an example of those who take the attitude that after all it was Charles Darwin and no one else who persuaded the scientists that evolution is a fact, and therefore it is he who deserves the credit.

As Darwin's fame grew, Captain Fitzroy of the *Beagle*, who nearly had not taken Darwin along because of the shape of his nose, became obsessed with the idea that he was to blame for the anti-Christian influence of the *Origin of Species*. If he had refused Darwin passage on the *Beagle*, all of this would not have happened. One morning he cut his throat and died a suicide.

For a long time there has been a rumor that shortly before his death Charles Darwin became a Bible-believing Christian. It is said that he confessed his conversion to a Lady Hope. Biographies of Darwin do not mention such an incident.

Darwin's wife was very religious, though a Unitarian, and she deplored such of his writings as seemed to her to put God farther off. She attended church regularly, had the children confirmed in the Church of England, and read the Bible to them. She questioned whether it was right to knit or go visiting by carriage on Sunday. She had parts of Darwin's autobiography deleted because of their irreligious emphasis, though they have since been restored. In other words, if Darwin had professed faith at the end of his life, she would have rejoiced and would not have suppressed the news.

In connection with the story of his conversion with Lady Hope, it is alleged that he said he regretted his evolutionary views, which were the immature thoughts of his inexperienced youth. This is definitely not true. Darwin was fifty years old when he published the *Origin of Species*, which brought him fame as an evolutionist. He was sixty-two when he published *The Descent of Man*, in which he discussed human evolution and expressed the opinion that man evolved from monkeys of the eastern hemisphere. The widely-circulated story that Darwin told Lady Hope that evolutionary ideas were the immature thoughts of his inexperienced youth either shows the spurious nature of the story or else it makes Darwin a liar.

After the publication of his theory, Darwin fought for evolution all his life and did not hesitate to mention his admiration of those who attacked the Bible and the church. For example he wrote in 1873, at the age of sixty-four, "Lyell is most firmly convinced that he has shaken the faith in the deluge far more effectively by never having said a word against the Bible than if he had acted otherwise. . . . I have lately read Morley's *Life of Voltaire* and he insists strongly that direct attacks on Christianity (even when written with the wonderful force and vigor of Voltaire) produce little permanent effect: real good seems only to follow the slow and silent side attacks."[37]

Darwin inserted the words "by the Creator" into the last sentence of the second edition of his *Origin of Species*. According to George Gaylord Simpson, Darwin added these words as "one of many gradual concessions made to critics of that book."[38] In a letter to Asa Gray, Darwin wrote, "If I have erred in giving to natural selection great power, which I am very far from admitting, or in having exaggerated its power, which is in itself probable, I have at least, as I hope, done good service in aiding to overthrow the dogma of separate creation."[39]

The only degree Darwin ever earned was in theology, and at the time he planned to become a country clergyman. In his autobiography, which he wrote for his children in his old age, he said of this intended career that it was never "formally given up, but died a natural death when on leaving Cambridge I joined the *Beagle* as naturalist."[40] He called the day he sailed with the *Beagle* his "second birthday." Since it was while on this voyage that he got his evolutionary ideas and his life was changed, this was a tragic substitute for the second birth of the Christian. (Speaking to Nicodemus, Christ said, "You must be born again," and explained that the second birth is a spiritual birth. John, chapter 3.)

Concerning his loss of faith while still a young man Darwin said in his autobiography, "I had gradually come by this time to see that the Old Testament from its manifestly false history of the world . . . was no more to be trusted than the sacred books of the Hindus, or the beliefs of the barbarian."[41] He continued, ". . . I gradually came to disbelieve in Christianity as a divine revelation."

In his autobiography he told his children that he lost his faith in Christianity as a divine revelation because he found differences in the Gospel accounts and because his observations of the laws of nature made miracles incredible. He concluded, "Thus disbelief crept over me at a very slow rate, but was at last complete. The rate was so slow that I felt no distress, and have never since doubted even for a single second that my conclusion was correct. I can indeed hardly see how anyone ought to wish Christianity to be true. . . ."[42]

Three years before his death he wrote to a student who inquired about his religious views, "Science has nothing to do with Christ, except insofar as the habit of scientific research makes a man cautious in admitting evidence. As for a future life, every man must judge for himself between conflicting vague probabilities."[43]

In the last letter he ever wrote, three weeks before he died, he expressed the opinion that the origin of life would be found to be a "consequence of some natural law."[44] In other words, he was denying the origin of life by divine creation.

Darwin was remembered as a kind and gracious man. One of his sons said that he never spoke an angry word to any of his children in his life.[45] One of his schoolmates at Cambridge remembered him as "preeminently good, just, and lovable; the most genial, warmhearted, gracious, and affectionate of friends; sympathetic with all that was good and true; hating everything that was false, vile, cruel, mean and dishonorable."[46]

A shipmate declared that "in all the five years on the *Beagle* Darwin was never known to be out of temper or to say one unkind or hasty word of or to anyone."[47] Another shipmate said that "Darwin was the only man he ever knew against whom he had never heard a word said, 'and as people, when shut up in a ship for five years are apt to get cross with each other, that is saying a good deal.' "[48]

An admiring biographer, George Dorsey, comments, "And so, somehow, we feel that we must agree with the old lady who, on being told that Darwin would go to hell for his wicked doctrines, exclaimed that God almighty could not afford to do without so good a man!"[49]

Concerning his understanding of Darwin's religious stand Dorsey says, "I have been called to account for saying . . . that Darwin died as he had lived, a Christian gentleman. . . . I know that Darwin made no 'profession' of Christianity. What I meant to say was that his life was Christlike, was what a Christian's life is supposed to be and so seldom is. . . . From the point of view of the modern fundamentalist, Darwin was not a Christian at all. He did not hate the things they hate, he had none of their blind intolerance, none of their so-called veneration for words, Books, Bibles, Creeds, Doctrines, and other fetishes."[50] Apparently Dorsey himself entertains too much hatred for fundamentalists to consider what the Scripture has to say about salvation. It is not a matter of anyone's opinion. The theme of the Bible is salvation through the atonement of Christ, accepted by the sinner as being for him. It is "not by works of righteousness which we have done" (Titus 3:5), for the best we can do cannot meet God's standard for righteousness. We have to have a Savior. Darwin's gracious nature was not sufficient to make him righteous in the sight of God, nor can anyone else expect to be righteous before God in his own merit.

Although a half century ago scientists were admitting that the Darwinian explanation of evolution is inadequate, today Darwin is very much in vogue again. Professor John Tyler Bonner, Head of the Biology Department at Princeton University, speaks for American biologists in general when he says, "In the hundred years since the publication of the *Origin of Species* our opinion of Darwin was never so high as it is now."[51]

In 1959, the year of the Darwin Centennial, a poll was taken by the University of Bridgeport, Connecticut, in which replies were received from 1,116 scientists and educators. The result of the poll showed that in the minds of these electors Charles Darwin ranked fourth among the greatest scientists of all time.[52]

Gamaliel Bradford, another of Darwin's biographers, sums up the situation for himself and some others as he says, "And it was Darwin, the gentle, the kindly, the human, who could not bear the sight of blood, who raged against the cruelty of vivisection and slavery, who detested suffering in men and animals, it was Darwin who at least typified the religious logic that wrecked the universe for me and for millions of others."[53]

In the end Darwin was interred with honors in Westminster Abbey. Herbert Spencer, who popularized evolution in England was denied burial there and also denied a memorial tablet on the grounds that he was anti-Christian. Darwin also was anti-Christian, although he was not so vocal about it as Spencer, if we accept his own account of his beliefs as written to his children in his autobiography and discount the story of Lady Hope.

The famous Julian Huxley makes a statement which is interesting and instructive in this regard. He says that "Darwin has become an intellectual hero in the Soviet Union," and goes on to say that Thomas Henry Huxley, Darwin's chief disciple and defender, "on the other hand, has never found such favor in Soviet Russia, *because of his refusal to adopt .an atheistic instead of an agnostic position*"[54] (italics added). In other words, the Communists recognized Darwin as an atheist, at least in Julian Huxley's opinion, and honored him for it.

In 1959, the year of the Darwin Centennial, the Communists honored Darwin with a medal and also with a postage stamp. The medal bears on the obverse an image of Darwin in profile, and on the reverse the *Beagle,* the ship on which he obtained his evolutionary views. The stamp bears his portrait.

It is a well-known fact that Karl Marx wished to dedicate his book *Capital (Das Kapital)* to Darwin, but that Darwin declined the honor. According to Gertrude Himmelfarb, in refusing to accept the dedication Darwin explained that it would pain certain members of his family if he were associated with so atheistic a book.[55]

Julian Huxley shows a reproduction of the title page of the copy of *Das Kapital* which Marx presented to Darwin. In the illustration the reader can read for himself in Marx' own hand: "Mr. Charles Darwin On the part of his sincere admirer Karl Marx London 16 June 1873. . . ."[56]

NOTES

1. Simpson, George Gaylord, "The World Into Which Darwin Led Us," *Science,* 131:3405:966, April 1, 1960, p. 967. (This is a chapter of his book, *This View of Life.*)

2. Barlow, Nora, Editor, *The Autobiography of Charles Darwin* (with original omissions restored), (Collins, 1958), p. 28.

3. *Ibid.,* p. 57.

4. Himmelfarb, Gertrude, *Darwin and the Darwinian Revolution* (Doubleday and Co., 1959), p. 39.

5. *Ibid.,* p. 39.

6. *Ibid.,* p. 47.

7. Barlow, Nora, *loc. cit.,* p. 58.

8. *Ibid.,* p. 71.

9. Darwin, Francis, Editor, *The Life and Letters of Charles Darwin* (D. Appleton and Co., 1888), Vol. 1, p. 60.

10. Glass, Bentley, Editor, *Forerunners of Darwin.* 1745-1859. Chapter by Francis Haber (The Johns Hopkins Press, 1959), p. 259.

11. Ward, Henshaw, *Charles Darwin* (Bobbs-Merrill Co., 1927), p. 66.

12. Dorsey, George A., *The Evolution of Charles Darwin* (Doubleday, Page and Co., 1927), p. 152.

13. Ward, Henshaw, *loc. cit.,* p. 67.

14. Darwin, Francis, Editor, *More Letters of Charles Darwin* (D. Appleton and Co., 1903), Vol. 2, p. 115.

15. Darwin, Francis, Editor, *Life and Letters, loc. cit.* Vol. 2, p. 374.

16. Lack, David, "Darwin's Finches," *Scientific American*, 188:4:66, April, 1953, p. 67.

17. *Encyclopedia Britannica*, 1957, Vol. 9, p. 968.

18. In his journal for 1837 he wrote, "In July opened first notebook on transmutation of species." *Encyclopedia Britannica*. 1962, Vol. 7, p. 66.

19. Darwin, Francis, Editor, *More Letters, loc. cit.*, Vol. 1, p. 40.

20. Darwin, Francis, Editor, *Life and Letters, loc. cit.*, Vol. 2, p. 12.

21. *Ibid.*, p. 14.

22. *Ibid.*, p. 15.

23. *Ibid.*, p. 12.

24. Darlington, C. D., "The Origin of Darwinism," *Scientific American*, 200:5:60, May, 1959, p. 60.

25. Darwin, Francis, Editor, *More Letters, loc. cit.*, Vol. 1, p. 360.

26. Dorsey, George A., *loc. cit.*, p. 219.

27. Simpson, George Gaylord, *loc. cit.*, p. 968.

28. Darlington, C. D., *loc. cit.*, p. 66.

29. *Ibid.*, p. 61.

30. *Ibid.*, p. 60.

31. *Ibid.*, p. 66.

32. *Ibid.*, p. 62.

33. *Ibid.*, p. 62.

34. Meyer, Frederick, *A History of Modern Philosophy* (American Book Co., 1951), p. 69.

35. See page 47, this book.

36. Darlington, C. D., *Darwin's Place in History* (Macmillan, 1961), p. 60.

37. Himmelfarb, Gertrude, *loc. cit.*, p. 368.

38. Simpson, George Gaylord, *loc. cit.*, p. 969.

39. This letter was written in 1861.

40. Barlow, Nora, *loc. cit.*, p. 57.

41. *Ibid.*, p. 85.

42. *Ibid.*, p. 87.

43. Dorsey, George A., *loc. cit.*, p. 261.

44. Simpson, George Gaylord, *loc. cit.*, p. 969.

45. Bradford, Gamaliel, *Darwin* (Houghton Mifflin Co., 1926), p. 197.

46. Dorsey, George A., *loc. cit.*, p. 43.

47. *Ibid.*, p. 58.

48. *Ibid.*, p. 58.

49. *Ibid.*, p. 271. This is originally from Grant Duff's *Diary*, 1896-1901, Vol. 1, p. 307.

50. *Ibid.*, p. 257.

51. Bonner, John Tyler, *The Ideas of Biology* (Harper, 1962), p. 45.

52. *A Progress Report of the University of Bridgport,* July, 1959.

53. Bradford, Gamaliel, *loc. cit.*, p. 247.

54. Huxley, Julian and H. B. D. Kettlewell, *Charles Darwin and His World* (Viking Press, 1965), p. 80.

55. Himmelfarb, Gertrude, *loc. cit.*, p. 364.

56. Huxley, Julian, *loc. cit.*, p. 80.

THOMAS HENRY HUXLEY

The outstanding converts to Darwinism who became Darwin's supporters, defenders, and interpreters to the people, were Thomas Henry Huxley in England, Ernst Haeckel in Germany, and Asa Gray in America. Herbert Spencer, the English philosopher, also popularized Darwin's works, but he was not a scientist.

Huxley called himself "Darwin's bulldog," and his eminent grandson, Julian Huxley, the biologist and evolutionist, is no doubt correct in saying that Thomas Henry Huxley was evolution's greatest protagonist.[1]

Professor Lovejoy of the Johns Hopkins University says that Huxley did not accept evolution from Robert Chambers because of an emotional bias.[2] Similarly Dr. Bibby, Huxley's biographer, asserts that the explanation of Huxley's defense of Darwin goes beyond his regard for scientific truth and is to be found in his emotional attachment to Darwin.[3] This is an interesting observation, especially since Dr. Bibby himself is committed to the evolutionary point of view and since the allegation is usually made that Christians base their beliefs upon emotions, while scientists are objective and unemotional, at least in their approach to scientific matters.

Although he lacked formal education, Huxley became an outstanding scholar. He was scrupulously honest. It was the honesty of a sincere humanism. To describe his position with regard to religion he coined the word *agnostic*. He was at unrelenting war with Christianity, and he said, "It is quite hopeless to fight Christianity with scurrility. We need a regiment of Ironsides."[4]

Recognizing that liberal Christianity has as its objective the laudable purpose of promoting morality, he was willing to cooperate with liberal clergymen, but even most of them opposed his views in those days. There were three notable exceptions to this. One was William Rogers, Rector of Bishopsgate, who was known as "Hang-theology Rogers." Another was Charles Kingsley, who wrote *Water Babies* in 1863. This well-known book is still in circulation, and it is the first book written for children which deals with evolution. The third liberal clergyman who agreed with Huxley's views was Frederick William Farrar, who gained such positions of influence as Chaplain to Queen Victoria, Speaker of the House of Commons, and finally Dean of Canterbury. Dr. Bibby says that Farrar "did much to help the reorientation of English education."[5]

An instructive, though tragic, example of the misapplication of words is afforded in the following. In 1881 Huxley was offered the position of Dean in a new school which was being started at South Kensington. He pointed out that a Dean in those days was customarily addressed as "The Very Reverend," and that this title would not be appropriate for him. However, he accepted the position. The mother of a certain potential student had misgivings about sending her son to a school where he would be under the influence of a man so irreligious as Professor Huxley. She was reassured, however, and permitted her son to enroll when it was explained to her that she was mistaken and everything was all right because Professor Huxley was a Dean. The young man was H. G. Wells. Whatever may have been the role of Professor Huxley in shaping the young man's life, his mother's worst fears were realized. In 1917 Wells published his blasphemous book, *God the Invisible King*. In it he said, "Never shall we return to the cross. By faith we disbelieved and denied. By faith we said of that stuffed scarecrow of divinity, that incoherent accumulation of antique theological notions, the Nicene deity, 'This is certainly no God.' "[6] In the next sentence he declared that he had found a god of his own making, but before his death he also gave up faith in that god and declared himself an atheist.[7]

Professor Huxley "saw the obvious religious implications of Darwinism and believed that there was no point at which science and theology could meet."[8] His biographer, Dr. Bibby, says that he regarded as honest and enlightened those who admitted that there is a conflict between Genesis and the science of his day, but he held in contempt those who "tried to keep a foot in both camps,"[9] that is, those who tried to reconcile evolution and Scripture.

Huxley was a member of the Metaphysical Society, and after lecturing to that august body on the problem of the nature of a frog's soul, he lectured on the resurrection of Christ. Being a staunch disbeliever in miracles, he held that Christ had not died on the cross and was still alive when entombed.[10] This was said to have been "the most notorious paper ever presented to the Society and the only one to which an additional evening was devoted for further discussion."[11] It was, however, so objectionable that even the editor of a prominent liberal periodical was alarmed and persuaded him not to publish it.

Agnostic as he was, deaths in the family were particularly difficult for him to bear. At the time of his mother's death he wrote to his sister, "I offer you no consolation, my dearest sister, for I have none." The death of his first son at an early age caused him much soul-searching, but he seemed to consider his unbelief a point of honor. He wrote to Charles Kingsley concerning the agnosticism which deprived him of hope and consolation, "I have searched over the grounds of my belief, and if wife and child and name and fame were all to be lost to me one after the other as the penalty, still I will not lie."[12]

He dreaded the thought of personal annihilation and felt horror at the thought that by 1900 he would be deceased and would, he believed, know no more about what would be going on then than he did in 1800, before he was born. He said he would rather be in hell than experience annihilation. "I had sooner be in hell a good deal — at any rate in one of the upper circles, where the climate and company are not too trying."[13] Even his views on hell were not Scriptural.

An event in the life of Huxley which has been widely publicized is his encounter with Bishop Wilburforce. His grandson, Julian Huxley, has called it "in some ways the most decisive event in the history of nineteenth century thought."[14] If there is any truth in this, it illustrates how emotionalism can take the place of judgment in influencing thought even in the highest civilization. At a meeting of the British Association for the Advancement of Science, Bishop Wilburforce made a speech attacking Darwinism. The fact is that he did not know enough about it to speak intelligently on the subject, and in spite of some coaching his ignorance was apparent. During the course of the address he turned to Huxley, who was sitting on the platform, and asked him whether he was descended from an ape on his grandfather's or grandmother's side. This was such a stupid statement that it does seem odd that no biographer has taken the trouble to point out that Huxley had four grandparents, including a grandfather and a grandmother on each side. Huxley immediately saw his opportunity, and according to his own account of the affair, he replied thus: "If then, said I, the question is put to me would I rather have a miserable ape for a grandfather or a man highly endowed by nature and possessing great means of influence, and yet who employs these faculties and that influence for the mere purpose of introducing ridicule into a grave scientific discussion — I unhesitatingly affirm my preference for the ape."[15]

In those days, more so than today, a speaker who could win a battle of wits made a great impression on the audience. Through this short speech Huxley achieved a tremendous victory for the Darwinian forces, although the whole thing had absolutely nothing to do with any evidence for or against evolution. It needs to be noted that unfortunately some others since that time who have desired to defend the Bible against the theory of evolution have merely brought discredit upon themselves and reproach upon their cause by making foolish statements after the manner of Bishop Wilburforce. Some scientists have also made foolish statements, but they are more easily overlooked by the public.

NOTES

1. Bibby, Cyril, *T. H. Huxley. Scientist, Humanist, and Educator* (Horizon Press, 1960), p. vii.
2. Glass, Bentley, Editor, *Forerunners of Darwin. 1745-1859* (The Johns Hopkins Press, 1959), Chapter 13.
3. Bibby, Cyril, *loc. cit.,* p. 78.
4. *Ibid.,* p. 253. Huxley's term "a regiment of Ironsides" is a military term here used figuratively. It is interesting to note that after the time of Huxley the Lord raised up a man named Harry Ironside as a *defender* of the faith.
5. *Ibid.,* p. 47.
6. Wells, H. G., *God the Invisible King* (Macmillan, 1917), p. 13.
7. Bales, James D., *Atheism's Faith and Fruits* (W. A. Wilde Co., 1951), p. 73.
8. Blinderman, Charles S., "Thomas Henry Huxley," *Scientific Monthly,* 84:4:171, April, 1957, p. 181.
9. Bibby, Cyril, *loc. cit.,* p. 83.
10. Blinderman, Charles S., *loc. cit.,* p. 180.
11. Bibby, Cyril, *loc. cit.,* p. 55.
12. *Ibid.,* p. 59.
13. *Ibid.,* p. 258.
14. Blinderman, Charles S., *loc. cit.,* p. 171, quoting from the book: *Julian Huxley on T. H. Huxley.*
15. *Ibid.,* p. 171.

ERNST HAECKEL

Ernst Haeckel, who became "the apostle of Darwinism in Germany," was doing research in Italy when he heard about Darwin's theory. Quickly converted to Darwinism, he advocated it at a scientific congress in Germany in 1863. The German men of science were not persuaded by his arguments, and it is reported that some expressed regret that such an unscientific matter could be discussed at a scientific gathering. Haeckel then resolved that if the men of science would not hear him, he would take the matter directly to the public. He held free public lectures in Jena, and attracted large audiences. He became the most popular zoologist in the country and converted many to belief in evolution.

He also adopted and popularized a philosophical system called *monism,* contending that matter cannot be interpreted aside from spirit, and vice versa. Another author who is also an evolutionist attributes Haeckel's later troubles to the fact that he made monism a substitute for religion.[1]

It is said that until it was pointed out to him that his evolutionary beliefs were contrary to the tenets of Scripture, he considered himself to be an evangelical and orthodox believer, accepting the literal truth of the Bible. But his evolutionary views eventually led him to become anti-Christian and to deny the existence of God. Erik Nordenskiold in his *History of Biology* says that the most striking feature of Haeckel's early letters is their Christian piety, "which contrast strongly with the hatred that Haeckel felt for Christianity in later years."[2]

The vehemence employed by Haeckel in his efforts to popularize the theory of evolution became a source of embarrassment to the other followers of Darwin, for they thought he might antagonize people to an extent that would harm their cause. However, the other disciples of Darwin seemed so moderate in comparison to Haeckel that much of the abuse which otherwise might have been received by them was concentrated upon him instead.

Haeckel made one of the missions of his life the promulgation of the recapitulation theory, which he called *the fundamental biogenetic law.* The essence of this is that during their embryonic development, organisms review the history of their evolutionary development. The form in which Haeckel taught this is quite untenable, and today even other forms of the theory have been largely abandoned by evolutionists. A scandal occurred when he was accused of falsifying his drawings of embryos to bring them into accord with his theory. He even went so far as to alter pictures of embryos drawn by someone else. A Professor Arnold Bass charged that Haeckel had made changes in pictures of embryos which he had drawn. Haeckel's reply to these charges was that if he is to be accused of falsifying drawings, many other prominent scientists should also be accused of the same thing, because in their drawings they sometimes leave out unimportant details and accentuate essential parts. Charles Singer comments in his *History of Biology*, "Haeckel was an admirable artist, whose imagination was ever prone to rule his brush."[3]

It seems nearly unbelievable, but it is a fact that in spite of the scandal which arose over Haeckel's drawings of embryos nearly a century ago, many *modern* college textbooks republish his drawings to illustrate the embryonic evidence in favor of evolution.

Like Herbert Spencer, Ernst Haeckel enjoyed immense popularity in his day, but he is no longer held in high esteem. Although he accomplished some important work, he wasted much of his time and talents with activities which have not endured. Professor H. H. Newman of the University of Chicago said several generations ago that scientists held the opinion that Haeckel's works "did more harm than good to Darwinism."[4]

Charles Singer in his *History of Biology* summarizes Haeckel's present status in the history of science thus: "His faults are not hard to see. For a generation and more he purveyed to the semi-educated public a system of the crudest philosophy — if a mass of contradictions can be called by that name. He founded something that wore the habiliments of a religion, of which he was at once the high priest and the congregation."[5]

NOTES

1. Wendt, Herbert, *In Search of Adam* (Houghton, 1955), p. 284.
2. Nordenskiold, Erik, *The History of Biology* (Tudor Publishing Co., 1935), p. 506.
3. Singer, Charles A., *A History of Biology*, rev. ed. (Henry Schuman, 1950), p. 480.
4. Newman, Horatio Hockett, *Evolution, Genetics, and Eugenics*, 3d ed. (University of Chicago Press, 1932), p. 30.
5. Singer, Charles A., *loc. cit.*, p. 480.

ASA GRAY

The great American botanist, Asa Gray, differed from the typical supporters of Darwin in that he professed Christian faith. Bernard Ramm, writing for a conservative Christian audience, puts Gray first in a list of evangelical Christians "who have espoused theistic evolution, and see no incompatibility between this acceptance and their

Christian faith."[1] Although Ramm says that he himself does not accept theistic evolution, he is making a point of assuring his readers that this position is not so bad after all, since evangelical Christians like Asa Gray found no incompatibility between theistic evolution and Christian faith.

Gray was one of the few intimates who knew about Darwin's views before the publication of the *Origin of Species.* Darwin wrote to him, July 20, 1857, "But as an honest man I must tell you that I have come to the heterodox conclusion that there are no such things as independently created species — that species are only strongly defined varieties. I know this will make you despise me."[2] But Gray did not despise him, and after a fuller understanding of Darwin's theory, Gray became one of his disciples.

In 1873 Gray called himself an "humble member of the Christian church," and said, ". . . as for orthodoxy, I receive and profess, *ex animo,* the Nicene creed for myself, though with no call to deny the Christian name to those who receive less."[3] He continued, "I dare say I am much more orthodox than Mr. Darwin; also that he is about as far from being an atheist as I am."[4] To the question, "Was Darwin an infidel?" Gray replied, "Can't say till you tell me what you mean by infidel — and perhaps not then."[5] Surely this is not the language of an evangelical Christian whose faith is in the atoning sacrifice of Christ upon the cross.

In the *Origin of Species,* Darwin had avoided the mention of human evolution, except by an allusion to it at the end of the book. But the *Origin* was so well received that he was encouraged to prepare and to publish *The Descent of Man,* which dealt with the problem of human evolution. He was somewhat fearful as to what Gray's reaction would be, because of Gray's professed orthodoxy. But Gray responded with a paraphrase of the words of King Agrippa to Paul, when Paul preached Christ to him. Agrippa said to Paul, "Almost thou persuadest me to be a Christian" (Acts 26:28). Gray said to Darwin, "Almost thou persuadest me to have been 'a hairy quadruped of arboreal habits, furnished with a tail and pointed ears.' "[6] In turn, W. H. Harvey, a European botanist, paraphrased Agrippa after reading one of Gray's pamphlets. "Almost thou persuadest me to be a Darwinite — not quite, but thou persuadest me to be a Grayite."[7] It is characteristic of the position which Gray took that it leads others in the direction of evolutionary belief and not in the direction of Christian faith.

Besides leading new converts to evolutionary beliefs, Gray's efforts in behalf of Darwinism were hailed by the liberals who were already believers in evolution, as aiding their cause. Charles Kingsley, the liberal theologian and evolutionist, wrote concerning the same pamphlet which had brought the comment from Harvey, "By far the best forward step in Natural theology has been made by an American, Dr. Asa Gray, who has said better than I can all that I want to say."[8]

Gray asserted "in season and out"[9] that Darwin had reintroduced teleology into natural history. This means that he believed Darwin had made a case for purpose or design in the biological world, in contrast to a world developed through chance, and this implies the intervention of God in nature. But Darwin and Gray did not agree about this, and the other prominent disciples of Darwin were strongly opposed to Gray's teleological views. His opponents won, and Gray "could not forget his sharp defeat on the design argument."[10] Dupree, Gray's biographer, concludes that "Gray knew he was making a joke when he said that Darwin had reintroduced teleology into natural history."[11]

In his later years Gray consented to give two public lectures at Yale University. The purpose of these lectures was to speak as a scientist and as a Christian to a confused public, and especially to theological students. Concerning this Dupree says, "The audience was now those conscientious people who had a yearning for both science and religion but who had somewhere become confused by all the diatribe. What they wanted was to see, not to hear or to reason with, but just to see a first-rate scientist who professed himself to be a theist and a Christian."[12] In the course of the lectures, Professor Gray gave his approval to the higher criticism of the Bible. He professed that creation was no less divine because it could be explained by natural causes. As to the origin of man, he said, "We do not know at all."[13] He seems to have anticipated modernism in saying that the Bible *contains* truth instead of *being* truth. His biographer recognizes it as a "light dismissal of Biblical authority,"[14] because Gray told his audience that the stream of Scripture "brings down precious gold; but the water — the vehicle of transportation — is not gold."[15]

Dupree states that Gray was not typical of orthodox Christian thinkers, for the aspersions cast by the theory of evolution upon the authority of the Scriptures "never bothered him," and when scientists could reach a consensus of opinion about something this "had clear priority over religion as a source of truth where the two entered the same territory."[16]

A study of the life and times of Asa Gray reveals what Ramm does not mention, namely, that Darwin used Gray as a weapon to combat those who objected to his evolutionary theory on religious grounds. Gamaliel Bradford, another of Darwin's biographers, has this to say: "In America Asa Gray, the great botanist, was a convert [to evolutionism] from the beginning and a most helpful disciple, and his aid was peculiarly welcome to Darwin, because Gray's eager orthodoxy was useful in conciliating many whose prejudices would naturally have been averse. Darwin repeatedly spoke of Gray as understanding his ideas better and expounding them more effectively than almost anyone."[17]

Ramm is using Gray the same way that Darwin did. He is presenting to Christians the view that after all evolution really is not so bad since an evangelical Christian like Asa Gray could also be an evolutionist.

It turns out that Asa Gray is a very questionable example of an evangelical Christian, but he is a good example of a person who has a Christian testimony and who is used by the evolutionists to influence other Christians to accept the theory of evolution.

NOTES

1. Ramm, Bernard, *The Christian View of Science and Scripture* (Wm. B. Eerdmans Publishing Co., 1955), pp. 264, 265.
2. Dupree, A. Humter, *Asa Gray* (Harvard University Press, 1959), p. 244.
3. *Ibid.*, p. 358.
4. *Ibid.*, p. 359.
5. *Ibid.*
6. *Ibid.*, p. 356.
7. *Ibid.*, p. 299.
8. *Ibid.*, p. 300.
9. *Ibid.*, p. 358.
10. *Ibid.*, p. 359.
11. *Ibid.*, p. 382.
12. *Ibid.*, p. 372.
13. *Ibid.*, p. 376.
14. *Ibid.*, p. 377.
15. *Ibid.*
16. *Ibid.*, p. 382.
17. Bradford, Gamaliel, *Darwin* (Houghton Mifflin Co., 1926), p. 121.

CHARLES KINGSLEY AND THE WATER BABIES

Charles Kingsley was an English clergyman who accepted evolution at once when Charles Darwin published his *Origin of Species.* He referred to Darwin as his "dear and honored master,"[1] and he reconciled Darwin's views with his own liberal theology by saying that "God's orthodoxy is truth; if Darwin speaks the truth he is orthodox."[2] He made evolution theistic by the remarkable and altogether unconvincing statement that "where there is evolution there is an evolver,"[3] implying that the evolver is God. He said, and it has been said many times since then, that the concept of a long evolutionary process is far grander than fiat creation.[4]

In 1863 Kingsley wrote *The Water Babies* for one of his children, who was four years old at the time, and it became a classic. Like Lewis Carroll's *Alice in Wonderland* and *Through the Looking Glass,* much of it is beyond the comprehension of children, and it is really a child's story for adults. It is a fairy tale which deals with ethics and religion and evolution. Following Charles Darwin's *Origin of Species* by only four years, it is, no doubt, the first juvenile book to deal with evolution.

In California there are forty-five cities that have a population of more than fifty thousand, and although the book is more than a hundred years old, all of these cities have it in the juvenile departments of their public libraries. It follows, then, that it may be found in public libraries all over the country. It is a delightfully-written book and its popularity is understandable. However, discerning Christians will find it disappointing, for although there are numerous references to the Bible, it does not express Christian beliefs. A critic who was an enthusiast for the works of Kingsley appraised it as glorious though rank heresy.[5]

Children who die of abuse or neglect are carried off by the fairies and become water babies, living in the water of streams and the sea. In order to merit what appears to be heaven (though some go there only for weekends) it is necessary for the water babies to do something which they do not like to do.

The hero of the story is Tom, a little chimneysweep who drowned. The unpleasant task he has to accomplish is to free his cruel former master, who drowned while poaching fish and is "serving his time" stuck in a chimney somewhere near the north pole. While on this mission Tom meets some former seamen, including Henry Hudson, who perished at sea and are "working out their time" as birds. After his rescue from the chimney through the efforts of Tom, his former master is assigned the job of keeping a volcano cleaned out to prevent earthquakes.

Reference is made to the evolutionary belief that life began in the sea and that all life came from that beginning, for he refers to the "salt water, which, as wise men tell us, is the mother of all living things." It is told in this story for young children that the elephant is first cousin to the coney of Scripture and second cousin to the pig. (To this day evolutionists consider elephants to be most closely related to the coneys and to the manatees and dugongs, which are completely aquatic.)

A fairy shows Tom and other water babies some pictures and tells a story which describes Darwin's natural selection theory. It shows how some creatures became adapted to living in the trees, and their feet became modified to grasp the branches.

One of Kingsley's biographers says that the example he set in his frank and fearless openmindedness with regard to evolution may have been his most valuable contribution to the cause of truth.[6] Another biographer says, "It is to men like him that the Church of England owed its continued existence when Darwin's book plunged orthodoxy into warfare with scientists."[7] The Lord said that the gates of hell will not prevail against His church (Matt. 16:18), and it is not through the efforts of men like Charles Kingsley that this prophecy will be fulfilled in maintaining the Christian church.

Kingsley was much criticized because of his unorthodox views, but the criticism decreased considerably when he became a chaplain of Queen Victoria. As one biographer puts it, "The religious and political views of the chaplain of the head of the Church and State could hardly be attacked as dangerously unorthodox."[8] But Christ is the Head of the church (Eph. 5:23) and anyone who teaches a gospel other than that of salvation by grace through the sacrifice of Christ upon the cross as the atonement for sin is not orthodox, even though he be the famous chaplain of a still more famous queen. Paul said, and he said it twice for emphasis, "But though we, or an angel from heaven, preach any other gospel to you than that which we have preached to you, let him be accursed. As we said before, so say I now again, If any man preach any other gospel than that which you have received, let him be accursed" (Gal. 1:8, 9).

NOTES

1. Kendall, Guy, *Charles Kingsley and His Ideas* (Hutchinson and Co., 1947), p. 136.
2. *Ibid.*, p. 137.
3. *Ibid.*
4. *Ibid.*
5. This is told by Kendall, *loc. cit.*, p. 118.
6. *Ibid.*, p. 135.
7. Martin, Robert Bernard, *The Dust of Combat* (Faber and Faber, 1959), p. 204.
8. *Ibid.*, p. 222.

ST. GEORGE JACKSON MIVART

Few indeed are the people to whom the name of St. George Mivart has any meaning today. However, his life and work have a definite bearing on the religious aspect of the evolution question. Also he has the distinction of being one of the very few persons with whom the mild-mannered Charles Darwin had a real quarrel.

At the age of sixteen, contrary to the wishes of his parents, Mivart became a Roman Catholic. Following a high mass he made a public profession which included the statement: "I do, at this present, freely profess and truly hold this true Catholic faith, without which no one can be saved." (However, it is a part of Roman Catholic belief that no one can be certain of salvation. Moreover, in recent times, in connection with the ecumenical movement, it is being stated by Catholics that people can be saved outside the Catholic Church.)

Jacob Gruber, Mivart's biographer, says that "even in his latter years when his devotion to Catholicism was demonstrated in his every act, it was the externals of the church — its rituals, its language, and its architecture — which chiefly concerned him."[1]

Mivart was an evolutionist. He was a close friend and a student of Thomas Henry Huxley, "Darwin's bulldog." He also knew Darwin personally and had the highest regard for him. But there came a time when he found that he could not attribute to natural selection the importance which the Darwinians attributed to it. He stated plainly his reason for this in a book called *On the Genesis of Species,* and he could not be ignored by the Darwinians because he was a scientist of considerable reputation. Darwin accused him of misquoting, but Alfred Russell Wallace, Darwin's friend and the co-discoverer of the theory of natural selection, assured Darwin that Mivart had not mis-quoted.

The relationship between Mivart and his former Darwinian friends became quite strained, but the real trouble came when Mivart wrote a review of some anthropological works and mentioned a publication of George Darwin, a son of Charles Darwin. He disagreed with the opinion of George Darwin that "divorce should be made consequent to insanity," and he expressed rather strongly his opinion of George Darwin's "encouragement of vice in order to check population."

Although Mivart later humbly apologized for having written this, and he really had no need to apologize for expressing his opinion in a review, his apology was not accepted. Charles Darwin wrote to Huxley that if he ever met Mivart he would "cut him dead."[2] He then wrote a letter to Mivart telling him that he would never communicate with him again, and he signed the letter with a very inappropriate "your obedient servant."[3]

One of Mivart's objectives was to show that evolution and Christianity are compatible. The Darwinians attacked him on this ground, although Darwin himself had said that evolution need not interfere with religion. Thomas Henry Huxley insisted that evolution *cannot* be reconciled with Christian faith. Charles Darwin then expressed delight that Huxley had "smashed" Mivart's theology.[4] (This was in 1871.)

While Huxley was contending that Christianity could not be reconciled with evolution, a mathematician turned philosopher named Chauncey Wright attacked Mivart's criticism of Darwinian natural selection by contending that "the principle of the theory of natural selection is taught in the discourse of Jesus with Nicodemus the Phari-see"![5]

Chauncey Wright tried to show that when Mivart distinguished between evolution and Darwinism, it was because of his inability to understand fully the matters concerned. This is interesting in light of the fact that a half century later, when the evolutionists were temporarily abandoning Darwinism, it was *they* who made a concerted effort to educate the public to the view that evolution and Darwinism are *not* the same. They even went so far as to accuse the anti-evolutionists of duplicity in failing to make a distinction between evolution and Darwinism. Darwin expressed appreciation and approval of Wright's efforts, though acknowledging that his writing was not very clear in parts.

Mivart made a blunder in taking Francisco Suarez as an example of a theologian whose principles favored reconciliation between evolution and Christian faith. Huxley quickly disproved Mivart's contention on this point.

Mivart complained that the Darwinians largely ignored his scientific objections, and made it a religious issue rather than a scientific one. In an essay which was a reply to Huxley, Mivart said, "It was not however without surprise that I learned that my one unpardonable sin — the one great offense disqualifying me from being a 'loyal soldier of science' — was my attempt to show that there is no real antagonism between the Christian revelation and evolution."[6]

Thus the Darwinians did not really answer Mivart's criticisms of natural selection. Indeed, Alfred Russell Wallace agreed with him, and wrote concerning Mivart's book *On the Genesis of Species*: "The arguments against natural selection as the exclusive mode of development are some of them exceedingly strong, and very well put, and it is altogether a most readable and interesting book. Though he uses some weak and bad arguments, and underrates the power of natural selection, yet I think I agree with his conclusion in the main, and am inclined to think it more philosophical than my own."[7]

St. George Mivart was a religious liberal, and he was a loyal Catholic — until that church began to interfere with his liberalism. This interference did not come until the close of his life. About the time of the publication of Darwin's *The Descent of Man*, Mivart stated that the evolution of man's body is in accord with Christian faith, so long as the origin of man's soul is accepted as an act of divine creation. As is the case with other liberals, he did not consider the acceptance of Scripture as particularly important, and he wrote to his friend Edmund Bishop, "As to the account of Creation, God need not have written such misleading words as 'and the evening and the morning were the first (second, third, etc.) day.' Neither need he have said that the grass and trees existed before the sun and moon! These statements are *absolutely* false. As to the Tower of Babel and the categorical description given of Noah's ark in the deluge: They are mere fables and quite divergent from objective fact. The account of the formation of Eve and of Adam, naming the animals who came for the purpose, are utterly incredible."[8] Quite significantly, his next statement is the question, "But if so, how about the account of the Fall . . .?" God's plan of salvation as given in the Bible is dependent upon the historicity of the fall of man from grace through willful disobedience as described in Genesis, and alternative views lead logically to the conclusion that Christ was a martyr instead of the Savior.

At the time of the publication of Mivart's view that the evolution of man's body is acceptable, if the soul be exempted, this seemed to much of the Catholic press as being so greatly superior to Darwin's theory that Mivart was greatly praised as a defender of the faith against materialistic theories. The general opinion of the Catholic theologians, however, seems to have been that it was heretical, and they expected his writings to be condemned. But to their surprise, five years and three publications later his opinion was given official approval when Pope Pius IX conferred upon him the degree of doctor of philosophy. His liberal views continued to be tolerated for a time during the reign of the next Pope, Leo XIII. He extended his evolutionary principles, and declared that through moral means the Catholic Church of the future would be the vehicle of the fulfillment of the prophecies of the kingdom of God on earth.[9]

Mivart's evolutionary teachings were not universally accepted, and the Reverend Jeremiah Murphy, writing with the backing of authority greater than his own, published an article in which he said that it is not possible for an orthodox Catholic to believe in the evolution of man — corporal or otherwise — since this belief is contradicted both by Scripture and by the Church Fathers.[10]

In 1893 Pope Leo XIII issued an encyclical which said in part, "It is absolutely wrong and forbidden, either to narrow inspiration to certain parts only of Holy Scripture, or to admit that the sacred writer has erred."[11] Jacob Gruber says that "within a few years the assertion of Scriptural infallibility condemned as erroneous the Mivartian theory of man's bodily evolution. One by one its advocates, faced with the abrupt ideological about-face, recanted."[12] M. D. Leroy, who had written a book in which he adopted Mivart's point of view, was called to Rome and told that his "thesis, after examination . . . by competent authority, has been judged untenable, especially in what relates to the body of man — being incompatible with the text of Holy Scripture and with the principles of sound philosophy."[13] By 1899, the year before Mivart's death, his first champion among the hierarchy of the church, Bishop Hedley, wrote his own recantation and stated that "the Mivartian theory . . . can no longer be sustained."[14]

Mivart himself was a rebel to the end, and during his last illness he wrote, "It is now evident that a vast and impassable abyss yawns between Catholic dogma and science, and no man with ordinary knowledge can henceforth join the communion of the Roman Catholic Church if he correctly understands what its principles and its teachings really are, unless they are radically changed."[15]

The situation has changed again since the days of Mivart's death, and now it is quite permissable for Roman Catholics in good standing with their church to believe exactly what Mivart taught about evolution.

Finally, in his life-long effort to liberalize the Catholic Church, Mivart held that the doctrine of hell is outmoded. His main objection to hell was that some people refused to join the Catholic Church because they did not wish to believe in hell. To modernize the church in this matter he wrote an article called *Happiness in Hell*. When this appeared in book form, it was placed on the "index" of forbidden books. However Mivart received an "authentic" statement which said that the ideas he expressed were not being condemned and that it is all right to hold these views, but that the times were not appropriate for the dissemination of such views.[16] Mivart "submitted" to this, but when *Happiness in Hell* was still listed on the "index" when it was released the year before his death, his patience was exhausted and he wrote a letter asking what fault was to be found with the article. Furthermore, he stated that, if he did not receive the requested information, he would withdraw his submission to having the article thus condemned. This, of course, was an act of insubordination.

The rebellious Mivart, although he knew that he was in his last illness, continued to make public denunciations of the Catholic Church. The inevitable result was excommunication.

On the first of April, 1900, Mivart died, and his friends sought in vain for permission to give him a Catholic burial, arguing that his actions had been the consequence of a diseased mind. There is, however, no evidence of any failing in his mind. To the end his mind was clear. On the day of his death he was to have been the guest speaker at a dinner given by the Author's Club. Ten days before this he wrote a letter of considerable length which, although quite heretical, was altogether rational. Among other things he declared, "St. John's account I put aside as ideal and fictitious. Of what we read in the Synoptics how much is *true* history? But if we accept most of it, it seems to me that certain parts are admirable, some teaching distinctly immoral, and other parts ignorant and foolish."[17] But by continuing to insist that his rebellion was due to a disease of the mind, his friends and relatives were able to achieve his reburial on church property four years later. There is no reason to believe that this helped him any any way, but it made them feel better.

NOTES

1. Gruber, Jacob W., *A Conscience in Conflict. The Life of St. George Mivart* (Columbia University Press, 1960), p. 11.
2. *Ibid.*, p. 110.
3. *Ibid.*
4. *Ibid.*, p. 89.
5. *Ibid.*, p. 77. Wright refers to the third chapter of the Gospel of John.
6. *Ibid.*, p. 97.
7. *Ibid.*, p. 77.
8. *Ibid.*, pp. 189, 190.
9. It is quite evident that Mivart's knowledge of prophecy was very superficial. It might also have been well for him to have made a study of the seventeenth and eighteenth chapters of Revelation.
10. Gruber, Jacob W., *loc. cit.*, p. 166.
11. *Ibid.*, p. 186.
12. *Ibid.*, p. 188.
13. *Ibid.*
14. *Ibid.*
15. *Ibid.*, p. 142.
16. *Ibid.*, p. 185.
17. *Ibid.*, p. 212.

THE SCOPES TRIAL

On the tenth of July in 1925 an unusual court trial got under way at Dayton, Tennessee. It was the first court trial ever broadcast by radio,[1] and it is reported that more words concerning it were cabled overseas than had been cabled previously about anything that had ever happened in America.[2] With the approval of his superiors, the defendant had agreed to proclaim himself a breaker of the law. The chief lawyer for the defense requested the jury to find the defendant guilty, so that the case could be carried to higher courts. Paradoxically, the Supreme Court of Tennessee upheld the rulings of the Dayton court but reversed the verdict. The reason for this reversal was a technicality which had nothing to do with the matter of evolution. The judge at Dayton had imposed upon the defendant the fine of one hundred dollars, which was the minimum possible under the law. The Tennessee Supreme Court held that a fine above the amount of fifty dollars had to be imposed by the jury and not by the judge. For this reason the defendant was declared innocent instead of guilty, and this reversal prevented the case from being appealed further.[3]

The circumstances which led to this peculiar trial began when the secretary of the American Civil Liberties Union in New York noticed a news item about a new Tennessee law which prohibited the teaching of evolution in tax-supported schools of the state. She called it to the attention of Roger Baldwin, director of the American Civil Liberties Union, and as a result that organization notified Tennessee newspapers that it would finance a trial if a teacher would cooperate by breaking the law. An item concerning this was read in a Chattanooga newspaper by George Rappelyea, a native of New York City who was employed in Dayton as a mining engineer. He persuaded both the county superintendant of schools and the head of the county board of education that it would be desirable to take advantage of the offer. Having obtained the consent of these dignitaries, he phoned John Thomas Scopes, the popular young football coach and a science teacher at the local highschool, and asked him to come to the drugstore.

As Scopes entered, Rappelyea was arguing the negative side of the question of whether the Bible should be taken literally. Rappelyea was the superintendant of a local Sunday school, but presently resigned this office. The pastor of the same church later offered his services as a witness for the defense, and as evidence of his fitness to serve in this capacity he declared that he did not think that the Bible had been "written in heaven, printed on India paper, sewed with silk, bound with calfskin, and tossed out the window."[4]

Although reluctant, Scopes agreed to comply with the plan and to admit that he had taught evolution after the anti-evolution bill had become law. Contrary to the usual accounts of the incident, Scopes did not agree to teach evolution and thus break the law as a test case. He has since admitted that to the best of his knowledge he never taught evolution.

Scopes was in no sense a crusader, as he is sometimes made out to be. He later remarked that "it was just a drugstore discussion that got past control."[5]

The recently adopted and highly slanted eighth grade textbook *Land of the Free* goes further in misrepresenting the basic facts about the Scopes trial than any other account which has come to the attention of this writer. The textbook says: "Then in 1925, a courageous teacher in Tennessee took a stand against the evolution law. John

Thomas Scopes, a teacher of science in the small town of Dayton, Tennessee, defiantly told his class about Darwin's theory. He was arrested and put on trial."[6]

Rappelyea wired the American Civil Liberties Union that they were ready to cooperate in Dayton, and the A.C.L.U. replied, "We will cooperate Scopes case with financial help, legal advice, and publicity."[7]

William Jennings Bryan, widely known as a Fundamentalist, became the leader of the prosecution. The other members of the prosecution included his son, William Jennings Bryan, Jr., and the Attorney General, A. T. Stewart. The defense was led by Clarence Darrow, notorious criminal lawyer and agnostic. The men who aided him were not sympathetic to the fundamentalist view of Scripture. Dudley Field Malone was a Roman Catholic and a divorce lawyer for the socially elite, himself divorced. Arthur Garfield Hays, an attorney for the American Civil Liberties Union, was a Jew.

From the outset and consistently, Darrow and his group wished to bring in expert witnesses to testify about evolution and the Bible. Also from the outset and just as consistently, Bryan and his men opposed this. William Jennings Bryan, Jr. pointed out that if a witness testified incorrectly about a matter of fact, he could be corrected and punished for perjury, but Darrow's witnesses would merely be expressing opinons. They could say anything they wished without fear of being charged with perjury and the trial would degenerate into a debate. The judge finally ruled that the expert witnesses would not testify in court, but he permitted statements by them to be read into the court proceedings for the benefit of the next court, following the appeal. But before this, the defense got one of its experts on the stand. This was Professor Maynard Metcalf of the Johns Hopkins University, a famous biologist. Asked to define the word *evolution*, he gave a definition which is hardly worthy of a freshman. He said: "Evolution, I think, means the change; in the final analysis I think it means the change of an organism from one character into a different character, and by character I mean its structure, or its behavior, or its function, or its method of development from the egg or anything else — the change of an organism from one set characteristic which characterizes it into a different condition, characterized by a different set of characteristics either structural or functional, could properly be called, I think, evolution — to be the evolution of an organism. But the term in general means the whole series of such changes which have taken place during hundreds of millions of years, which have produced from lowly beginnings, the nature of which is not by any means fully understood, the organism of much more complex character, whose structure and functions we are still studying, because we haven't begun to learn what we need to know about them."[8]

Besides the general confusion in this statement, Professor Metcalf introduced a specific point of confusion when he defined the development of an individual from an egg as an example of evolution. The word *evolution* has been used in this way, as it has also been used to describe improvements in mechanical devices, as "the evolution of the steam engine," but that was not what was being considered in this trial. He added confusion to confusion by testifying a little later that he had always been interested in "the evolution of the individual organism from the egg and also the evolution of organisms as a whole from the beginnings of life."[9]

Mr. Malone added his bit of confusion by saying that evolution never stops from the time a human being is a single cell, before prenatal development, until the end of his life, and he concluded from this that without the teaching of evolution, medical schools would be impossible. Mr. Hays, another member of the defense, also confused embryonic development with evolution.

Mr. Bryan was not confused about this, and he pointed out that a fourteen-year-old high school boy who had testified was not confused either. Mr. Hicks, another lawyer for the prosecution, also called the judge's attention to the fact that the issue was evolution and not embryonic development. Finally the judge asked Mr. Darrow directly whether he was contending for embryonic development from an egg or for the evolution of more complex forms of life from simple beginnings. Mr. Darrow replied that he was referring to the changes in animals from simpler forms up to man.

While he was on the stand, Professor Metcalf graciously volunteered a point in favor of the anti-evolution forces. He said that it is advantageous for single-celled green plants that live in the water to remain isolated cells, for they would not do so well if they formed groups of cells. However, if higher plants evolved from single-celled ancestors, as the theory of evolution demands, there must have been a time when single-celled plants *did* form aggregates of cells, contrary to their own best interests and to the best interests of the species. Darwinian natural selection should have prevented this. The principle of the survival of the fittest should have brought about the survival of the single cells and the extinction of the aggregates.

Another expert witness, whose testimony was not presented in court but was read into the record, was Professor Horatio Hockett Newman of the University of Chicago, another famous biologist. He opened his remarks with these words: "Evolution is merely the philosophy of change as opposed to the philosophy of fixity and unchangeability. One must choose between these alternate philosophies, for there is no intermediate position; once admit a changing world and you admit the essence of evolution."[10] He was saying that if you observe changes in the world, you are an evolutionist in spite of yourself. Since everyone who leads a normal life is aware of changes in the world, the implication is that belief in evolution is inescapable. This is adding more confusion to the confusion previously introduced by Professor Metcalf. Writers of some college textbooks have followed Professor Newman in presenting this point of view to young people, and even more amazingly, men who profess to be conservative Christians are now saying the same thing to the Christian public.

Professor Newman was a specialist in the study of twins. He said in his testimony for the Scopes case that identical twins are more alike than are brothers and sisters which are not identical twins, and these in turn are more alike than cousins. Members of a family have more genetic material in common, and so are more alike, than people of unrelated families. Individuals of the same race tend to be more alike than people of different races. He then said that if one admits this, there is no stopping place, and "it is logically impossible to draw the line at any level of organic classification."[11] In other words, if you have noticed that brothers and sisters have traits in common although they are not as much alike as identical twins, then in order to be consistent and not illogical, you must admit that a giraffe and a rattlesnake, or a peacock and a jellyfish, are also related, and the difference between their relationship and that between brothers and sisters in a human family is just a matter of difference of degree. He presents this not just to *illustrate* the concept of evolution, but as an *argument for* evolution! Again, the conclusion is that everyone who is consistent in his thinking is an evolutionist in spite of himself.

Another expert witness for the defense was Professor Fay-Cooper Cole, anthropologist of the University of Chicago. He testified that the way the neck joined the head in Neanderthal man and the position of the opening of the skull for the spinal cord "show conclusively that the head hung habitually forward." He also testified that the thigh bone and its joints "show that the knee was habitually bent and that this man walked in a semierect position."[12] Although some textbooks still say the same thing, it has been shown that these concepts about the appearance of the Neanderthal men are not true. (This is discussed in this book in the section called *Man.*)

Professor Kirtley F. Mather, Chairman of the Geology Department at Harvard University, testified that "there are in truth no missing links in the record which connects man with other members of the Order Primates."[13] This is so far from the truth that it should have made him eligible for the charge of perjury, but as William Jennings Bryan, Jr. had pointed out, if steps had been taken to do this, his statement would have been considered an opinion, and therefore exempt.

Mr. Malone said that the prosecution (that is, the anti-evolutionists) apparently thought that the evolutionists believe that man evolved from monkeys. He continued, "It is not the view, opinion, or knowledge of evolution held by the defense. No scientist of any standing today holds such a view."[14] William Jennings Bryan exploded this myth by quoting Charles Darwin's own words, from the sixth chapter of *The Descent of Man*: "The Simiadae then branched off into two great stems, the New World and Old World Monkeys; and from the latter, at a remote period, Man, the wonder and glory of the Universe proceeded." In spite of this, and other statements of the same sort made by Darwin and by subsequent scientists, we are repeatedly told to this day that only the uninformed and the ignorant believe that according to the theory of evolution man descended from monkeys or from apes.

Mr. Hays said that even if Scopes had taught that man evolved from monkeys, he would not have broken the law.[15] This statement is utterly absurd, but it illustrates very well how, when it suits their purpose, some people will actually use the sort of logic which one expects to find only in satirical cartoons. The law stated in part that "it shall be unlawful . . . to teach any theory that denies the story of Divine Creation of man as taught in the Bible, and to teach instead that man descended from a lower order of animals." Mr. Hays' contention was that since biologists use the same word, *order,* in a technical way in classification, and since men and monkeys are both classified as belonging to the Order Primates, men and monkeys belong to the *same* order, and hence the evolution of men from monkeys would not involve evolution from a "lower order of animals."

On the third day of the trial Mr. Darrow raised an objection to the custom of opening the court sessions with prayer. Since the trial involved a religious issue, he felt that opening with prayer was prejudicial to his side of the argument. The judge said that prayer would continue, since it was an established custom and not an innovation at this trial. One of the lawyers for the prosecution replied to Darrow's objection by saying that opening court with prayer could have no bearing on the question being investigated, namely whether or not Scopes was guilty. Another lawyer for the prosecution pointed out that Darrow's request for the omission of prayer was contrary to the contention which the defense had made when they said that Bible experts, if allowed to testify, would establish that the theory of evolution is not contradictory to the Bible and to Christian faith.

A petition was presented to the judge, requesting that if prayers continued, an opportunity be given to Unitarians, Jews, and Congregationalists to pray. The judge referred the matter to the local pastors' association, and as a result the court was opened the following day with the prayer of a Unitarian minister from New York City. The defense continued to protest the opening of court with prayer, and the courtesy was extended to them that their protest would be recorded automatically each day in the court proceedings without it being necessary for them to make repeated formal protests. Thus the evolutionists were not satisfied, but the religious liberals profited from the compromise.

The defense desired to show that the theory of evolution is in accordance with Scripture, but Mr. Darrow did not take the trouble to be logical or consistent. He said concerning the Bible, "We expect to show that it isn't in conflict with the theory of evolution."[16] He had just finished saying that "the Bible, in many ways, is in conflict with every known science." At another time he said, "Mr. Bryan says that the Bible and evolution conflict. Well, I don't know. I am for evolution anyway."[17]

In an attempt to show how unreliable the Bible is, Mr. Darrow bluffed shamelessly, with no concern about the reflection this would later have upon his personal honor. He said, "Are your mathematics good? Turn to I Elijah 2. . . ." (There is no such passage in the Bible.) Then he said, "Is your philosophy good? See II Samuel 3. . . ." (This chapter is a historical account of some events during the time of David.) Next he asked, "Is your astronomy good? See Genesis chapter 2 verse 7. . . ." (This verse is about the creation of man and has nothing to do with astronomy.) Finally he asked, "Is your chemistry good? See — well, chemistry — see Deuteronomy 3:6 or anything that tells about brimstone."[18] (This verse has nothing to do with chemistry or brimstone.)

Ray Ginger, who published an abridged account of the trial and who strongly favors the evolutionary side, gave a slightly different version of this and said of it, "Of course the references were hasty frauds, but serviceable enough."[19] Scopes said essentially the same thing in his book published a long time after the trial: "Darrow's references, spurious though they were, served his purpose of softening up the audience with specific references and then reverting to their applicability."[20]

The judge asked Mr. Malone, ". . . is it your opinion that the theory of evolution is reconcilable with the story of divine creation as taught in the Bible?" Mr. Malone answered, "Yes." He continued, "We have a defendant whom we can prove by witnesses whom we have brought here and are proud to have brought here, to prove, we say, that there is no conflict between the Bible and whatever he taught."[21]

As has been done ever since the days of Darwin, an attempt was made to exploit the testimonies of evolutionists who had a reputation as Christians. Scopes himself admitted recently concerning the witnesses, "They had been carefully selected, in order to prove that orthodox Christians also believed in evolution."[22]

One of these witnesses was Professor Maynard Metcalf, who had previously testified about evolution. He taught one of the largest Sunday school classes in the country and was ready to testify about the Bible. In his written testimony he said, "There is no conflict, no least degree of conflict, between the Bible and the fact of evolution, but the literalist interpretation of the words of the Bible is not only puerile; it is insulting, both to God and to human intelligence."[23]

Professor Mather, the geologist from Harvard, was also ready to testify about the Bible. He said, "The theories of evolution commonly accepted in the scientific world do not deny any reasonable interpretation of the stories of divine creation as recorded in the Bible. . . ."[24]

Mr. Hays read a statement written by Rev. Walter C. Whitaker, Rector of St. John's Episcopal Church in Knoxville, Tennessee. He was chairman of the committee which passed on the competency of new ministers for that denomination. He said, "As one who for thirty years has preached Jesus Christ as the Son of God and as 'the express image of the Father' I am unable to see any contradiction between evolution and Christianity."[25]

Again it was Mr. Bryan who understood why the Bible and the theory of evolution cannot be reconciled. He showed that according to the theory of evolution man has risen from lower forms of life and that if this is true, the Biblical account of the fall of man is denied. Hence, if evolution is true, there has never been a need for a Redeemer, and Christ was just a martyr. This is the center of the whole issue, and all the Bible experts the evolutionary forces could have produced would not have been able to make it otherwise.

The part of the trial which probably has been most publicized was the questioning of Mr. Bryan by Mr. Darrow. Mr. Bryan was a believer and he studied the Bible, but he really was not a Bible expert. He was under no obligation to take the witness stand, but he felt that if he did not it would be interpreted as an admission that the Bible could not stand under the attacks of non-believers. During this part of the proceedings Mr. Darrow said to him, "You insult every man of science and learning in the world because he does not believe in your fool religion."[26]

Mr. Darrow knew very little about the Bible, but he collected a number of questions with which to embarrass Mr. Bryan. Mr. Bryan was asked where Cain got his wife and he answered that he did not know. This was no doubt interpreted as an evasive answer, but the Bible does not give the answer in words. It is evident that Cain married a sister. The Bible says that Adam and Eve had both sons and daughters (Gen. 5:4) and Josephus, the great Jewish historian, says that Adam "was solicitous for posterity and had a vehement desire for children."[27] Mr. Darrow confused Mr. Bryan concerning the matter of whether Jonah was swallowed by a whale or by a fish. Mr. Bryan could not remember that in the New Testament in the King James version the word used is *whale*. He could hardly have been expected to know that in the original language the word does not mean whale as distinguished from fish, but rather it refers to a monster of the sea. He was asked a number of technical questions about the long day in the time of Joshua and about the date of the flood. He was even asked how many people were living in China five thousand years ago.

Mr. Darrow made some rather provocative remarks which caused the judge to say, "I hope you do not mean to reflect upon the court?" To this Mr. Darrow replied, "Well, your Honor has the right to hope." This was too much, and the judge cited him for contempt of court. This could have been very serious for Mr. Darrow, but when he apologized the following day, the judge freely forgave him.

One other apology was made during the trial. On one occasion when General Stewart of the prosecution had the floor, he was interrupted by Mr. Hays of the defense. He reminded Mr. Hays that he had the floor and asked him to keep his mouth shut. The next day he apologized for this discourtesy. The apology was accepted by Mr. Hays, who no doubt should have apologized to General Stewart for the occasion which caused the remark. Then Mr. Neal, another lawyer for the defense, said that General Stewart had been guilty of a grave discourtesy to another member of the defense. He was apparently referring to the fact that General Stewart had referred to Mr. Darrow as an infidel, which he was. The general replied that he apologized for unintentional rudeness but would not apologize for something which he had meant to say. Mr. Darrow presently made a lengthy speech in which he objected to the General's having called him an infidel. The judge asked General Stewart what he had to say about it and the general replied, "I think we are wasting a lot of valuable time."[28]

In contrast to this, William Jennings Bryan was repeatedly insulted and humiliated by Mr. Darrow, but he did not complain or retaliate. The first mention of Mr. Bryan during the trial was in a speech in which Mr. Darrow extended courtesies in a pleasant way to all the members of the prosecution except Mr. Bryan, who he said was the one "responsible for this foolish, mischievous, and wicked act,"[29] that is, the law which Scopes was accused of breaking. At the close of the trial, as the various participants were exchanging courtesies, Mr. Darrow said, "I want to say a word, I want to say in thorough sincerity that I appreciate the courtesy of the counsel on the other side from the beginning of this case, at least the Tennessee counsel. . . ."[30] Thus he took one last verbal slap at William Jennings Bryan, from Florida, and his son, from California. Mr. Bryan had just made a speech in which he emphasized that the importance of the trial was in bringing before the people an issue which would be settled sometime in the right way through evidence. He desired that the right should prevail.

In one speech Mr. Malone is reported to have said this: "We do not fear all the truth they can present as facts. We are ready. We stand with progress. We stand with science. We stand with intelligence. We feel that we stand with the fundamental freedoms in America.

We are not afraid. Where is fear? We defy it!" Then turning and pointing a finger at Mr. Bryan, he cried, "There is fear!" The report continues by saying that "the crowd went out of control — cheering, stamping, pounding on desks — until it was necessary to adjourn for fifteen minutes to restore order."[31]

It seems that Mr. Darrow became more popular with the crowd than Mr. Bryan, for Scopes later recalled, "My heart went out to the old warrior as spectators pushed by him to shake Darrow's hand."[32]

One correspondent wrote from Dayton, "A cartoon of Bryan, showing him in the guise of a monkey, has a great vogue here. The legend is, 'He denies his lineage.' Thousands are being sold in Knoxville and Chatanooga."[33]

A weekly magazine reported, ". . . as we go to press, he is still engaged in battling earnestly for organized ignorance, superstition, and tyranny. . . . He has illuminated vividly for the rest of us the essentially bigoted position of himself and his followers, and the degree of religious intolerance which they will undoubtedly enforce upon the country if they ever get the chance."[34]

Five days after the end of the trial Mr. Bryan died in his sleep. The man with whom he probably had his last conversation on earth said, "Four days after the trial ended I talked with him at some length, and he was even then quivering with hurt at the epithets which had been applied to him. He was a crushed and broken man."[35]

Under a dateline three days after his death another weekly magazine referred to him as ". . . the fraud which he is. . . ."[36]

William Jennings Bryan, though maligned and humiliated, was the hero of the Scopes trial. He demonstrated that he had a better basic understanding of evolution and of the Bible than his detractors had. When an eminent biologist confused evolution and embryonic development, Mr. Bryan set the record straight. When the opposition declared that no scientist of recognized standing believes that according to the theory of evolution man evolved from monkeys, Mr. Bryan pointed out Charles Darwin himself believed this, and that he said so in one of his books. When the evolutionary forces tried to show through the testimony of experts that the Bible and the theory of evolution can be reconciled, Mr. Bryan explained why this is not true. Mr. Darrow received the adulation of the crowd, but a sober examination of the record reveals ignorance and shamefully unworthy tactics on his part.

The jury deliberated nine minutes and found Scopes guilty of breaking the law. He was fined one hundred dollars, and it was understood that the case would be appealed. *The Baltimore Sun* offered to go bond for him and he accepted.

After his conviction, Scopes made a statement, which was the only thing he said during the trial: "Your Honor, I feel that I have been convicted of violating an unjust statute. I will continue in the future, as I have in the past, to oppose this law in any way I can. Any other action would be in violation of my ideal of academic freedom — that is, to teach the truth as guaranteed in our constitution, or personal religious freedom. I think the fine is unjust."[37]

According to Ray Ginger, after the trial Scopes confided to a newspaper man that something had worried him throughout the trial. The day the science lesson had been about evolution he had missed school, and so he had never taught evolution at all. He was worried because he feared he might be called to the witness stand. If he had been questioned under oath, he would have had to admit he was innocent.[38]

In an article in *Life* magazine Scopes is quoted as saying that he merely substituted for the biology teacher and commented, "I doubt very much that I taught his class evolution."[39]

In his book, *Center of the Storm,* Scopes says that in the drugstore discussion he was asked whether he had taught evolution while substituting for the biology teacher. His answer was, "We reviewed for final exams, as best I remember." His comment to the reader of the book is, "To tell the truth, I wasn't sure I had taught evolution. Robinson and the others apparently weren't concerned about this technicality. I had expressed willingness to stand trial. That was enough."[40]

In a television broadcast he has affirmed publicly that to the best of his knowledge he did not teach evolution. Thus he has apparently said on at least four different occasions that as far as he knows he never taught evolution.

When asked in an interview at the time of the trial whether or not he was a Christian, Scopes replied, "I don't know. Who does?"[41] He mentions this in his book and adds, "Anyone who would have answered this question in the affirmative probably had a different view of what it takes to be a Christian than I did. It has been my observation that anyone who is sure he is a Christian is likely to be mistaken."[42] Forty years after the trial, a convert to Roman Catholicism, he is quoted as saying, "I believe, but I reserve the right to doubt."[43]

Thus ended what has been called the world's most famous court trial. It has been said repeatedly that the anti-evolution forces won the trial but lost the case, and that since that time there has been no intelligent opposition to the theory of evolution. Even *Science,* the journal of the American Association for the Advancement of Science said in a news item thirty years after the trial, "Darrow may have lost his case, but he won a victory that has a permanent place in history."[44] This was said in apparent ignorance of the fact that Darrow wanted to lose the case and that he had requested the jury to find his client guilty, because he desired to carry the case to higher courts.

Professor Fay-Cooper Cole, anthropologist of the University of Chicago, has recounted his experiences upon his return to Chicago from Dayton.[45] He was called to the office of the president and was told that there had been considerable complaint about him because of his testimony concerning human evolution at the Scopes trial. He started to laugh, but the president told him it was no laughing matter. The University of Chicago was founded by Baptists, and there were more demands for his removal from the faculty than there ever had been for any other person. The board of trustees had considered the matter the day before. Professor Cole asked what the board had decided. In reply the president pushed a piece of paper across the desk to him. As he read the paper he found that the board had increased his salary!

Thus, as has been characteristic of many institutions of learning which were founded as Christian schools, a change was taking place. The University of Chicago with its associated divinity school was founded as "a great Christian university to counteract the materialism of the Middle West."[46] The Baptists were gathered at a national meeting when it was announced that Rockefeller offered to give $600,000 toward the founding of their school if they would raise $400,000. The entire assembly rose and sang the doxology. One leader exclaimed, "I scarcely dare trust myself to speak. I feel like Simeon when he said, 'Now, Lord, let thy servant depart in peace for my eyes have seen thy salvation'" (Luke 2:25-33). But such faith was premature, for modernism soon infiltrated into this Christian school. A professor at the divinity school dared to say, "The hypothesis of God has become superfluous in every science, even in that of religion itself." A Chicago secular newspaper commented on the situation: "We are struck with the hypocrisy and treachery of these attacks on Christianity. This is a free country and a free age and men can say what they choose about religion, but this is not what we arraign these divinity professors for. Is there no place in which to assail Christianity but a divinity school? Is there no one to write infidel books except professors of Christian theology? Is a theological seminary an appropriate place for a general massacre of Christian doctrines? We are not championing either Christianity or infidelity but only condemning infidels masquerading as men of God and Christian teachers."

The alleged reason why the American Civil Liberties Union sponsored the Scopes trial was because civil liberties were threatened. It is not easy to inquire into motives, but there is evidence that the alleged reason was not the real reason. On the first day of the trial a Chattanooga minister published in a local newspaper an extract from the report of the Lusk Committee of the New York legislature. It said in part: "The American Civil Liberties Union, in the last analysis, is a supporter of all subversive movements and its propaganda is detrimental to the best interests of the state. It attempts not only to protect crime but to encourage attacks upon our institutions in every form."[47]

Ray Ginger, in his abridged report of the Scopes court proceedings, says that one of the objectives of the American Civil Liberties Union at Dayton was to educate the public on evolution.[48] The trial was a great success in this regard. The effectiveness of one technique was illustrated at Dayton. When people are told over and over that they are backward and ignorant, it is natural for them to make an effort to counteract such aspersions, and the easiest way to do this is to fall into the trap which their adversaries have baited with the aspersions. In other words, in this case they are likely to endeavor to show that they really are broadminded and intelligent by professing an interest and even a belief in evolution.

Gordon McKenzie, a lawyer for the prosecution, speaking in behalf of the other members of the prosecution and in behalf of the county in which the trial occurred, said: "We have learned to take a broader view of life since you came. You have brought us your ideas — your views — and we have communicated to you, the best we could, some of our views. As to whether or not we like those views, that is a matter that should not address itself to us at this time, but we do appreciate your views, and while much has been said and much has been written about the narrow-minded people of Tennessee, we do not feel hard toward you for your having said that, because that is your idea.

We people here want to be more broadminded than some have given us credit for, and we appreciate your coming, and we have been greatly elevated, edified, and educated by your presence."[49] This speech was followed by applause by the people.

The foreman of the jury had this to say: "Personally I have always been open-minded on the subject of evolution and I will always be. What I want now is information on that important topic. Along with the other jurors I feel a deep disappointment that the scientific witnesses were not allowed to testify. It would have been an opportunity to find out something about how we come into the world."[50]

The foreman of the grand jury which indicted Scopes before the trial said that he believed in evolution because he could remember when cows produced milk which was inferior to that which he now fed to the hogs."[51]

A newspaper reporter interviewed the mothers of the two high-school boys who testified at the trial. One mother said she wanted her son to learn more about everything, including evolution. The other mother said she did not mind if they taught her son evolution "every day in the year. I can see no harm in it whatever."[52]

Issues are not always decided by evidences and facts. Mr. Darrow's ways won many of the townspeople to identify themselves with him instead of with Mr. Bryan. Ray Ginger notes that "the defense lawyers differed from the prosecution in smiling more readily, mixing more easily, and giving bigger tips to the telegraph messengers. The distinction was not lost on the townspeople of Dayton, and certainly helped to soften them for Darrow's subversion."[53]

A magazine said concerning the youth of Dayton, "They greeted Darrow as an infidel, found him an agnostic, acclaimed him more sympathetic, more tolerant, more kindly, and more Christian than the prosecution."[54]

The judge accepted from Mr. Hays copies of Charles Darwin's *The Origin of Species* and *The Descent of Man*.[55] This was accompanied by applause from the people. Mr. Hays reported that a minister requested from him a copy of Andrew White's *A History of the Warfare of Science with Theology*, to which he had referred during the trial. Andrew White was the first president of Cornell University, and his book is highly critical of Christian faith. Mr. Hays also announced that the drugstore where Scopes had made his decision to accept the offer of the American Civil Liberties Union would contain a circulating library of books on evolution.[56]

The A.C.L.U. controlled policies because it had offered to pay the costs. As Scopes says in his book, "The A.C.L.U. held the purse strings."[57] He says the A.C.L.U. paid his bill of $327.77. However, according to a news item in *Science*, "The $10,000 needed to finance the defense was raised chiefly through an appeal to members of the American Association for the Advancement of Science."[58]

In 1967 the state of Tennessee repealed the law under which Scopes was tried. The impetus for this seems to have been the desire to avoid embarrassment through publicity resulting from another lawsuit. A teacher had recently been expelled for teaching evolution, but later was reinstated. The teacher then filed a suit against the state, charging that the law interfered with academic freedom.

The state of Arkansas also has an anti-evolution law. This was declared unconstitutional in 1966. Again, the issue was academic freedom, and during the court proceedings the judge would not permit discussion of the matter on any grounds other than academic freedom. In 1967 the state Supreme Court of Arkansas reversed this decision of the lower court!

On November 12, 1968, the Supreme Court of the United States ruled that a law prohibiting the teaching of evolution in tax-supported schools is unconstitutional.

Accounts of the Scopes trial have been given to the public by men who do not understand the religious issues involved and who favor Clarence Darrow and his cause. Little has been said to the public in defense of William Jennings Bryan and the men who worked with him. He is still ridiculed and the position he took is very unpopular. Many who take the liberal and popular position on religious issues are welcoming enemies of the faith as Christian brothers and are fraternizing with those whose intention it is to destroy our liberties and our faith by any means they can employ.

NOTES

1. That the Scopes Trial was the first court trial broadcast by radio is stated in a number of places. See for example: Ginger, Ray, *Six Days or Forever* (Beacon Press, 1958), p. 103. *The Reader's Digest*. March, 1961, p. 137.

2. Mr. Bryan stated this after the close of the trial. It is recorded in: *The World's Most Famous Court Trial. A Complete Stenographic Report* (National Book Co., 1925), p. 316.

3. Grebstein, Sheldon N., *Monkey Trial* (Houghton Mifflin Co., 1960), p. 189.

4. Ginger, Ray, *loc. cit.*, p. 82.

5. *Ibid.*, p. 20. The Robinson Drug Store in Dayton is still in service. Although the interior is now modern, there is one oldfashioned table and four oldfashioned chairs. The table has a sign on it which reads: "At this table the Scopes evolution case was started. May 5, 1925."

6. Caughey, John W., *et al. Land of the Free* (Franklin Publications, 1967), p. 538.

7. Ginger, Ray, *loc. cit.*, p. 20.

8. *The World's Most Famous Court Trial, loc. cit.*, pp. 139, 140.

9. *Ibid.*, p. 136.

10. *Ibid.*, p. 263.

11. *Ibid.*, p. 266.

12. *Ibid.*, pp. 237, 238.

13. *Ibid.*, p. 247.

14. *Ibid.*, p. 115.

15. *Ibid.*

16. *Ibid.*, p. 146.

17. *Ibid.*, p. 282.

18. *Ibid.*, p. 84.

19. Ginger, Ray, *loc. cit.*, p. 108.

20. Scopes, John T., *Center of the Storm* (Holt, Rinehart, and Winston, 1967), p. 115.

21. *The World's Most Famous Court Trial, loc. cit.*, pp. 186, 187.

22. Scopes, John T., *loc. cit.*, p. 136.

23. *The World's Most Famous Court Trial, loc. cit.*, p. 252.

24. *Ibid.*, p. 248.

25. *Ibid.*, p. 223.

26. *Ibid.*, p. 288.

27. Josephus, Flavius, *Antiquities of the Jews*, Book 1, chapter 2.

28. *The World's Most Famous Court Trial, loc. cit.*, p. 99.

29. *Ibid.*, p. 74.

30. *Ibid.*, p. 317.

31. Cole, Fay-Cooper, "A Witness at the Scopes Trial," *Scientific American*, 200:1:120, January, 1959, p. 127.

32. *The Reader's Digest*, March, 1961, p. 144.

33. Hollister, Howard K., "In Dayton, Tennessee," *The Nation*. 121:3131:61, July 8, 1925, p. 61.

34. Anonymous, "The Week," *The New Republic*, 43:555:217, July 22, 1925, p. 219.

35. Milton, George F., "A Dayton Postscript," *Outlook*, 140:16:550, August 19, 1925, p. 551.

36. Krutch, Joseph Wood, "Darrow *vs.* Bryan," *The Nation*, 121:3134: 136, July 29, 1925 (Dateline of article, July 19), p. 136.

37. *The World's Most Famous Court Trial, loc. cit.*, p. 313.

38. Ginger, Roy, *loc. cit.*, p. 180.

39. *Life*, December 9, 1966.

40. Scopes, John T., *loc. cit.*, p. 60. See also p. 134.

41. Ginger, Ray, *loc. cit.*, p. 81.
42. Scopes, John T., *loc. cit.*, p. 83.
43. *Life, loc. cit.*
44. *Science*, 122:3157:23, July 1, 1955, p. 23.
45. Cole, Fay-Cooper, *loc. cit.*, p. 120.
46. Most of these facts are given by Rev. W. A. Criswell in an article called "The Curse of Modernism" published in *The Sword of the Lord*, October 2, 1964.
47. The *Times*, July 10, 1925; reprinted in the Knoxville *Journal*. See Ray Ginger, *loc. cit.*, p. 194.
48. Ginger, Ray, *loc. cit.*, p. 78.
49. *The World's Most Famous Court Trial, loc. cit.*, p. 316.
50. Ginger, Ray, *loc. cit.*, p. 179.
51. *Ibid.*, p. 73.
52. *Ibid.*, p. 123.
53. *Ibid.*, p. 115.
54. Hays, Arthur Garfield, "The Strategy of the Scopes Defense," *The Nation*, 121:3135:157, August 5, 1925, p. 158.
55. *The World's Most Famous Court Trial, loc. cit.*, p. 319.
56. Hays, Arthur Garfield, *loc. cit.*, p. 158.
57. Scopes, John T., *loc. cit.*, p. 67.
58. *Science*, 122:3157:23, July 1, 1955, p. 23.

JOHN DEWEY

John Dewey was born in 1859, the year of the publication of Darwin's *Origin of Species* and Marx's *Critique of Political Economy*. His early life showed no promise and his school work was mediocre. His scholastic transformation resulted from the chance reading of a book by Thomas Henry Huxley, Darwin's staunchest defender. Suddenly he led his class at the University of Vermont and won the highest grades in philosophy ever recorded in that school. As a graduate student at Johns Hopkins he is said to have shown promise but not brilliance. He lived a long life and became famous for his influence in American Education, where "his ideas influenced the lives of millions born in the twentieth century."[1]

He has been acclaimed as "typically American," and as "the foremost spokesman of democracy and science."[2] An anonymous writer in *The Johns Hopkins Magazine* says, "He became the spokesman of the humble American," and "He was a hero to children. He made their education living, creative, meaningful."[3]

The rector of the University of Peking said to him, "We honor you as the second Confucius."[4] The Turkish government offered him a special advisory position in its Ministry of Instruction. Lenin's widow requested him to come and teach in Russian Universities. "But Dewey never wavered from his vision of his own country as the favored setting for his bold and liberal ideas. The best qualities of his philosophy were intensely American: a love of freedom, humaneness, and an insistence upon equality of opportunity in the highest sense of the phrase. He moved his nation forward in its thought and gave new breadth to its ideology, and worked constantly to rescue democracy from burly sinners."[5]

Charles Frankel, Professor of Philosophy at the Johns Hopkins University, says, "Without vanity or pretentiousness, John Dewey made himself a spokesman for the best hopes of his generation. And to our generation he leaves the image of a man of unforced courage and honesty, living by choice in the mainstream of events, and yet rising above events to a coherent vision of what men might make of themselves. He helped us to see farther and to move more freely. It is to him as much as to anyone that we owe what belief we have that our own place in history can be an opportunity and not a fatality."[6]

All of this sounds very good, but before accepting the glorification of John Dewey as the hero of children, the spokesman for the humble American, and the foremost spokesman for democracy, it is necessary to know more about him and his views.

Professor Frankel makes some comments, and says, "To be for Dewey has been to be for progress, reason, and enlightenment. To be against him has been to be for God, the ancient values of our civilization, and the triumph of spirit over matter. . . . To his admirers Dewey was and is a representation of all that is most hopeful in American civilization. And to his detractors he was and remains a paradigm of some of the worst ills in our society."[7]

The terms *progress* and *democracy* sound fine, but these words may be used in different senses. Some who desire to undermine democracy use the word most freely. Dewey may have been innocent of any such desire, but from our perspective his discernment was poor indeed. One biographer says, "Dewey's praise for the educational accomplishments of the Lenin and Trotsky regime place him to the left of liberals in America."[8] He was the head of a commission that pronounced Trotsky "not guilty."[9] He was one of the founders of the League for Independent Political Action; he organized and led the American Committee for Cultural Freedom; for many years he was on the staff of *The New Republic;*[10] for many years he was also honorary president of the League for Industrial Democracy;[11] and he founded the Progressive Education Association.[12]

Dewey's interests obviously went beyond the field of education. James B. Conant, former president of Harvard University, who has made extensive studies in education, says, "Progressive education was clearly related to progressive politics."[13] He quotes Dewey: "But if one conceives that a social order different in quality and direction from the present is desirable and that schools should strive to educate with social change in view by providing individuals not complacent about what already exists and equipped with desires and abilities to assist in transforming it, quite a different method and content is indicated for educational science." Elsewhere Dr. Conant records his admiration for Dewey and continues, "If John Dewey hadn't existed, he would have had to be invented."[14]

Dewey based his philosophy upon *experience* as the ultimate authority in knowledge and conduct. This leads logically to the belief that human intelligence and the use of the scientific method can create the better society. This in turn leads naturally to the rejection of the supernatural element in religion, or in other words, to the rejection of God. He defined God as "the unity of all ideal ends arousing us to desire and action."[15]

Christian O. Weber in his book on the philosophy of education says, "Being 'religious' in Dewey's sense of the word does not require that one must believe in a supernatural realm and a deity. It does not imply the acceptance and practice of any form of worship or institutional religions. . . . Dewey offers his own point of view as a solution to the conflict between religion and atheistic belief. Dewey proposes, with the unbelievers, to reject all beliefs in supernatural realms and powers. Yet there will remain a way of life, freed from superstition, which Dewey considers may be called religious."[16]

Paul Arthur Schilpp of Northwestern University says that Dewey was the most thoroughgoing exponent of naturalism, which is a philosophy that is opposed to all forms of supernaturalism, and thus, of course, opposed to Christian faith. In 1951 Professor Schilpp said that naturalism had become "the main current of recent American thought, a current which has been largely directed by Dewey himself."[17]

Since Dewey rejected God, it is natural that he also abandoned Biblical standards of ethics. Professor Weber says, "Dewey rejects all views which regard moral values as being absolute, eternal, and having *a priori* validity. Moral values are subject to perpetual *reconstruction* as required by increasing knowledge and social change."[18] (This is "situation ethics.")

This is the philosophy of the man whose ideas have "influenced the lives of millions born in the twentieth century."

In view of all this it comes as no surprise that Dewey was an evolutionist. Professor Frankel says that when Dewey was at Johns Hopkins, Fascism and Communism were not yet issues, but "the great issue that had to be absorbed into Western thinking was the theory of evolution."[19]

According to Professor Weber, "Dewey was the first philosopher of education to make systematic use of Darwin's ideas."[20] This in itself, considering the great influence Dewey had over education, earns him a place in the history of evolutionary thought.

Professor Frankel complains that Dewey failed in his writings to clarify where he stood on issues political, ethical, and educational. He says that Dewey "was an innovator in education whose views about progressive education are still a legitimate subject for debate."[21] Others have said much the same thing, but it appears to be largely quibbling, for Dewey's leadership in what has become known as progressive education is unquestionable.

Outstanding among Dewey's disciples were George Counts and Harold Rugg. Counts produced a seventeen-volume study on American education, which contained the following typical recommendation: "Cumulative evidence supports the conclusion that in the United States, as in other countries, the age of individualism and lassez-faire in economy and government is closing and a new age of *collectivism* is emerging."[22] Harold Laski, who later became head of the British Fabian Society, commented on this work: "At bottom, and stripped of its carefully neutral phrases, the report is an educational program for a Socialist America."[23]

Counts also translated into English a Communist textbook, and in the foreword he said, "A single glance at the contents of the book convinced me that here was a document of rare quality. Practically every page carried the work of genius. It presents the major provisions of the [Russian] Five Year Plan with extraordinary clarity and charm — but perhaps most important it reveals the temper of the [Communist] revolutionary movement and the large human goals toward which it is consciously building. . . . This translation is designed to acquaint adults, teachers, and educators, with a phase of the Russian experiment which in the long run may prove to be far more important than those sensational aspects of the revolutionary struggle which are emphasized in both the daily press and even more serious publications."[24]

Counts later became disillusioned with Communism, but his seventeen-volume study of education called for a new era in textbooks and teaching ideas. Harold Rugg took charge of this. He went too far too fast in downgrading American heroes, attacking the Constitution, and propounding an anti-religious bias. John Stormer, who wrote *None Dare Call it Treason,* brings the situation up-to-date and quotes from current history textbooks. He says, "Through the combined actions of the Communists and the disciples of Dewey, Counts, Rugg, and other *Frontier Thinkers,* many of our schools have become institutions for producing the 'new social order.' " Mr. Stormer says that of course this is not true everywhere, due to the actions of alert school boards and parents. But because of this "the 'progressivist' thinkers are actively advocating a massive program of federal aid to education which would ultimately remove control of the schools from the local level and transfer it to Washington."[25]

Dewey's philosophy is *pragmatism.* To the non-professional philosopher the essence of pragmatism appears to be that whatever works is right and true. The criterion of truth is expediency. Pragmatism denies absolute values. It is a natural outgrowth of an atheistic, evolutionary, view of life.

The present writer remembers a college professor in the Department of Philosophy who was explaining pragmatism to a group of college students and illustrated it by saying that if a housemaid while dusting accidentally knocked over and broke an expensive vase, if she could convince the lady of the house that the vase was knocked over by the cat, then it really *was* the cat that did it. Other philosophers might not agree that successful lying comes under the category of pragmatism, but this example has remained in the mind of at least one impressionable college freshman for many years.

The pragmatic school of philosophy arose and flourished under the leadership of William James and John Dewey. James credited its origin to Charles S. Pierce, but Pierce repudiated pragmatism when he saw where it was leading.

The New Funk and Wagnalls Encyclopedia says that according to the pragmatic point of view "the test of the truth of a thing is its practical utility."

Collier's Encyclopedia says, "All pragmatists come together on a number of fundamental principles. . . . among these principles are . . . the repudiation of anything as absolute or fixed or final, either in human nature or nature. . . ." It further says that in pragmatism the judgment of every value, such as the true and the false and the good and the bad are based upon the consequences to the individual.

It seems that perhaps the old college professor really was correct in his illustration of pragmatism. Incidentally, he himself was a pragmatist.

Dr. Max Rafferty, California Superintendant of Schools, believes that the decline of absolutes as the bases of standards is responsible for the growth of such evils as public immorality, juvenile delinquency, and vandalism. When asked whether these evils have a "common denominator," he answered, "Yes. They have one thing in common, and that is what I call 'the decline of the absolute' in this country."[46]

If it is correct that pragmatism is the philosophy that that which works is right and true, and if it is also correct that pragmatism has led to delinquency and vandalism and to acceptance of the idea that deceit is all right if the individual practicing it does not get caught, then pragmatism condemns itself, for it does not work.

NOTES

1. Anonymous, "Profile of a Visionary," *The Johns Hopkins Magazine,* 11:3:3, December, 1953, p. 3.

2. Rathe, Anna, Editor, *Current Biography,* 1944 (The H. H. Wilson Co., 1945), p. 156.

3. Anonymous, *loc. cit.,* p. 4.

4. *Ibid.,* p. 6. The other information presented in this paragraph is from the same source.

5. *Ibid.*

6. Frankel, Charles, "John Dewey: Where He Stands," *The Johns Hopkins Magazine,* 11:3:7, December, 1959, p. 23.

7. *Ibid.,* p. 7.

8. Rathe, Anna, *loc. cit.,* p. 158.

9. Anonymous, *loc. cit.,* p. 6.

10. Rathe, Anna, *loc. cit.,* p. 159.

11. Ratner, Sidney, "A Salute around the Globe," *Saturday Review of Literature,* 42:47:18, November 21, 1959, p. 53.

12. Stormer, John A., *None Dare Call It Treason* (Liberty Bell Press, 1964), p. 102.

13. Conant, James B., *The Education of American Teachers* (McGraw-Hill, 1963), p. 114.

14. *Time*, 74:11:70, September 14, 1959, pp. 71, 72.

15. Rathe, Anna, *loc. cit.*, p. 159.

16. Weber, Christian O., *Basic Philosophies of Education* (Reinhart and Co., 1960), p. 258.

17. Schilpp, Paul Arthur, *The Philosophy of John Dewey*. 2d ed. (Tudor Publishing Co., 1951), p. 491.

18. Weber, Christian O., *loc. cit.*, p. 257.

19. Frankel, Charles, *loc. cit.*, p. 19.

20. Weber, Christian O., *loc. cit.*, p. 252.

21. Frankel, Charles, *loc. cit.*, p. 20.

22. Stormer, John A., *loc. cit.*, p. 102.

23. *Ibid.*, p. 102.

24. *Ibid.*, p. 103.

25. *Ibid.*, p. 122.

26. *Christian Victory*, July, 1964, p. 5.

PIERRE TEILHARD DE CHARDIN

One of the most controversial figures of our time is Pierre Teilhard de Chardin, scientist and Catholic priest, who died in 1955. Such outstanding scientists as Julian Huxley and George Gaylord Simpson praise him highly, although his fame has come from his philosophical and theological writings and not from his scientific work. These writings are so heretical that the Roman Catholic Church forbade their publication during his lifetime and removed him from his teaching position. But within ten years after his death the situation became very different.

At the Brussels World Exposition his portrait was hung among portraits of the great men of our time in the Vatican Pavilion.[1] A seminar about him has been conducted at Fordham University, a Roman Catholic university in New York City, by a professor who said, "Teilhard will become the Church's new philosophical system."[2] It is reported that an expert on the Second Vatican Council predicted that the outcome of that council "will either reflect the Teilhard spirit or it will accomplish nothing of importance."[3] Twenty-seven Roman Catholic scholars spent five weeks in an intensive consideration of the writings of Teilhard, and it is reported that they concluded with "the feeling that Teilhard's thought may ultimately lead to the most radical re-dressing of Catholic philosophy since Saint Thomas Aquinas introduced Aristotle into the medieval church seven centuries ago."[4]

As a boy of six or seven Teilhard began to collect objects of metal, such as nails and discarded cartridge shells, and worshipped them as idols. He later confessed that despair overwhelmed him when he discovered that iron rusts, and to console himself he searched for more durable idols. He did not subsequently admit the folly of this, nor did he repudiate this idolatrous worship. On the contrary, he declared as an adult that his entire spiritual life seemed to him to be a development of this childhood belief.

Evolution is the heart of Teilhard's philosophy, and Roman Catholic theologian Petro Bilanick says, "From Teilhard on, theologians cannot ignore evolution in their thoughts or works."[5] One biographer says that Teilhard's central theme is that "evolution is a general condition to which all theories, all hypotheses, all systems must bow, and which they must satisfy if they are to be thinkable and true. Evolution is the light illuminating all facts, a curve that all lines must follow."[6] In an essay Teilhard described Christ as a presence irradiating evolution.

At the Twentieth Annual Convention of the American Scientific Affiliation Robert J. O'Connell, a Jesuit priest who greatly admires him, gave a talk on Teilhard. He told the delegates to the convention that one of Teilhard's main emphases was to allay the fears that theologians may have for evolution and "to show how splendidly the Christian view coheres with the evolutionary view of man and the world." The talk was published in the *Journal of the American Scientific Affiliation* for September, 1966.

According to Teilhard, evolution started with inanimate matter at a point which he calls *Alpha*, and it is now converging to a point which he calls *Omega*. Omega is the culmination of all evolution, inanimate, animate, and spiritual, and it is equivalent to God. The force which is drawing everything to this convergence at Omega is love. He says that this love draws even inanimate objects, and that it is more fundamental than the love of wife, of children, of friends, or of country.[7] He holds that eventually all mankind, individually and collectively, will achieve perfect union with God.

His description of the ultimate, translated from French into English, is as follows: "Now when sufficient elements have sufficiently agglomerated, this essential convergent moment will attain such intensity and such quality that mankind, taken as a whole, will be obliged . . . to reflect upon itself at a single point; that is to say, in this case, to abandon its organo-planetary foothold so as to pivot itself on the

nscendent center of its increasing concentration. This will be
nd and the fulfillment of the spirit of the earth."[8]

people, including notable ones, are praising Teilhard's writings
is might cause one to hesitate in calling such writing utter
how can one do otherwise?

nday, 1955, Teilhard was commenting on the splendor
he fell to the floor unconscious. When he regained
id, ". . . But what happened? I don't remember
ne it is terrible."[9] He died before a physician
led.

being prepared which will make Teilhard's
Communists, and it will have a preface
ook called *God Is Dead.* Concerning
was fond of saying" that "a synthesis
the Marxist 'God-up-ahead' is the
lay 'in spirit and in truth.' "[10]

Convention of the American
urope, both Christians and
bridge this century offers
opposing views."

virtue of the whole
ndissolubly bound
Gospel than ever
ore real, more
c magazine
e a close
of the
aint's
a

"entist," *Com-*

World," The

Catholic World,

brings us back to the
at a force which he
This is called the first

of Man (Harper and

30, July, 1962, p. 480.

Flight from Time," *Catholic*

371.

AN SCIENTIFIC AFFILIA-

Christian faith cannot avoid the
erican Scientific Affiliation. This
fluence on Christian teachers of

the
or em-
sents *any*

other gospel than that of salvation by faith in the atonement of
Christ, he is to be accursed (Gal. 1:8, 9). The writer concludes: "The
answer to the problem and controversy over Teilhard de Chardin is
not easy, nor is there any ready-made solution. It will take patient
serious, and courageous study along with the prudence of a Solomon
separate the wheat from the chaff. But the results thus far
tained clearly indicate that the effort is well worth while."[14] To
even a most humble person can say with boldness on the author'
the Holy Bible: "Nonsense!" A child who has accepted Christ
Savior can cut with a single stroke the Gordian knot over wl
these eminent philosophers and theologians labor so hard and
lessly.

NOTES

1. Stern, Earl, "A Great and Controversial Priest and Sci
monweal, 71:14:400, January 1, 1960, p. 400.
2. Kobler, John, "The Priest Who Haunts the Catholi
Saturday Evening Post, October 12, 1963, p. 44.
3. Ibid., p. 43.
4. Barns, J. Edgar, "God Up Above — Or Up Ahead?"
191:1141:23, April, 1960, p. 30.
5. Newsweek, August 31, 1964, p. 70.
6. Kobler, John, loc. cit., p. 44.
7. In a sense the circuit is now complete, and this
early Greek philosopher Empedocles, who taught t
likened to love brought together various objects.
statement of a theory of evolution.
8. Teilhard de Chardin, Pierre, The Phenomen
Brothers, 1959), p. 287.
9. Kobler, John, loc. cit., p. 50.
10. Burns, J. Edgar, loc. cit., p. 26.
11. Anonymous editorial, America, 107:15:4
12. Ibid., p. 480.
13. Francoeur, Robert T., "For Teilhard, N
World, 193:1158:367, September, 1961, p.
14. Ibid., p. 373.

THE POSITION OF THE AMERI
TION

A discussion of evolution and
matter of the position of the A
organization has had a wide

science, and through these teachers and through the book *Evolution and Christian Thought Today,* a wide influence on the conservative Christian laity.

A statement printed inside the front cover of the *Journal of the American Scientific Affiliation* says that the purpose of the organization is "to study those topics germane to the conviction that the frameworks of scientific knowledge and a conservative Christian faith are compatible." As stated on convention programs, the American Scientific Affiliation is "a group of Christian scientific men, devoting themselves to the task of reviewing, preparing, and distributing information on the authenticity, historicity, and scientific aspects of the Holy Scriptures in order that the faith of many in Jesus Christ may be firmly established."[1]

The original statement of faith, which was signed by those who became active members, included the following words: "I believe that the Bible is uniquely inspired by God, is inerrant in the original writings, and that it gives me a true revelation of God. . . . In view of the great amount of manuscript material available for checking the accuracy of the text of the Scriptures as preserved through the ages, I consider its present text to give reliable evidence of the exact words of the original Scripture save where clear manuscript evidence shows that an error of transmission has occurred. This Bible I accept as my final authority in matters of faith and conduct."[2]

By 1955 dissatisfaction was felt with the constitution of the organization, and still more dissatisfaction was felt with the doctrinal statement. In March of that year an editorial appeared in the *Journal* announcing that the president had appointed a committee to study the matter of changing the doctrinal statement. It was asserted that this did not imply any objection to doctrines specifically mentioned in the statement. The desire for change was a matter of expediency, for it was felt that the doctrinal statement was "a hindrance to the development we should be experiencing."

It was charged that the statement of faith caused some prospective members to refuse to join. This is a strange reason to give, for the purpose of such a statement is to screen out persons who are not in accord with it. Another reason given was that judging by the experience of another group which was refused on-campus meetings at a major university, the doctrinal statement would constitute a barrier between the A.S.A. and other institutions.

In the next issue of the *Journal*, June, 1955, Irving W. Knobloch, who writes a regular feature for this magazine, discussed three views of evolution. The first is the view that the species of animals and plants now living have come unchanged from the time of the original creation. (This view is frequently ascribed to anti-evolutionists, although to do so is altogether unfair. Those who make this charge are in a position to know very well that the scientists who are specialists in classifying animals and plants are constantly "splitting" some species into a greater number and "lumping" others into fewer. The idea that anti-evolutionists must believe that species as recognized by the evolutionists were created as such is a popular "straw man" which the evolutionists set up and then boldly knock down. If the scientists keep changing their minds as to what is a species and what is not a separate species, so that the number of species keeps changing, how can they honestly say that anti-evolutionists must believe that each species was created separately? It is illogical and it is ridiculous.)

The second view he mentions is total evolution, as accepted by the evolutionists. Although he does not hold this position, he says that in fairness to this point of view it must be said that animals and plants have changed. As examples to illustrate this he says that whales have probably lost limbs they once had for walking on land, and he cites the case of the serpent in the third chapter of Genesis. The case of the serpent mentioned in Genesis has nothing to do with evolution. On the other hand, it seems to require a great deal of evolutionary faith to believe that whales lost limbs they had had for walking on land. A little further on he discloses that he accepts evolution within the phylum. The phyla are the largest or most inclusive categories within the animal kingdom. For example, all creatures with bones, as well as some others, belong to the same phylum. We belong to the same phylum as fish. Although he says that he does not accept total evolution, he says that the ultimate proof of evolution "will have [not would have] severe consequences for those holding the fundamental beliefs of the Christian faith."

The third position he discusses "allows for evolution of certain created types; how many and of what kind no one knows." In accordance with his previous statement about the phyla he suggests that the *kinds* of Genesis may have been phyla. And then, for a man who has signed the statement of faith, Professor Knobloch makes the amazing statement that the "main flaw" in this view is that "it requires faith enough to believe in a creation of some plants and animals."

Although he has said that he does not hold the second view, or total evolution, he says that this second view is more in accord with the facts *"as we know them today"* (his italics) than the other views.

In the *Journal* for December, 1963, Dr. Knobloch, still writing his regular column, says: "The theory of evolution is a grand concept and one that the working scientist must adopt. . . . It does seem logical to the Christian that God played some part in the formation of the universe, but the exact methodology is uncertain. . . . Some of us are relatively good, and some of us are vile. Our vileness may be due to sin or it may be due to our animal inheritance. No one really knows."

Commenting on an article by Dr. Russell L. Mixter, Dr. J. Frank Cassel, a frequent contributor to the *Journal*, writes in the issue of December, 1959, "Thus in fifteen years we have seen develop within the A.S.A. a spectrum of belief in evolution that would have shocked all of us at the inception of our organization." He expresses the opinion that membership in the A.S.A. by that time was represented by four main types of people: (1) those less well informed than the others (note the implication of this) who protest the change, (2) those who react by expressing themselves less frequently on scientific matters, (3) those who are less active in the affairs of the A.S.A, and (4) those who remain active and express their convictions together with the challenge, "If you have a better approach please tell me quickly for this one of mine has been bought at great price to my peace of mind."

In the June, 1960, issue of the *Journal* there is an article by Irving A. Cowperthwaite called "Some Implications of Evolution for the A.S.A." Dr. Cowperthwaite says, "Naturally, if evolution has become established beyond a reasonable doubt, we must accept it even though it seems that we have to make an 'agonizing appraisal' of our interpretation of Scripture." He points out some of the difficulties in trying to harmonize evolution and Scripture, and although he suggests possible answers, he confesses that the suggested answers are not adequate. He then asks the question, "If evolution is now a solidly established scientific law which must be accepted and if evolution cannot be harmonized with the Biblical story, then what is to be our attitude toward the Bible?" The paper concludes with the words: "No solution to the problem of fitting acceptance of evolution into the framework of traditional A.S.A. beliefs regarding the harmony of science and Scriptures has been found in the course of this study.

It is therefore necessary to conclude this discussion with a question instead of an affirmation. Is harmonization possible, and if so, how?"

Dr. J. Frank Cassel undertakes to answer this in the same issue of the *Journal*, and he throws his weight in favor of evolution by saying, "As we began seriously, critically, and objectively to examine the data of evolution, we became less and less convinced of its refutability." He proposes theistic evolution, and then says of the Biblical account of creation, "On the other hand, I can say that this is a beautiful account of the birth of mankind — that 'Adam' was not 'a man' but 'man, the species,' and that 'woman' is of the same nature and 'flesh' as man." He continues, "Again the Adam-Eve sequence can be explained as spiritual. Whether this is true or a dodge is, of course, an academic question, for is it not the spiritual message which God seeks most to impart to us? Then why worry about what passages are to be interpreted literally and which figuratively. Look, rather, to God to reveal Himself more fully and most directly to you from each passage according to your need." Professor Cassel knows in whose camp he stands, for his next sentence is, "Do I sound neo-orthodox here? I can't help it. . . ."

This issue of the *Journal* also contains a letter by H. Harold Hartzler, then president of the A.S.A., in reply to Dr. Cowperthwaite. President Hartzler says, "I have read your paper over carefully and have done considerable thinking on it since that reading. I have been attempting to find a mature Christian person in this vicinity with whom I might discuss your paper. I must say, as of now, I have not found such a person. I certainly do agree with you that the Biblical account clearly implies man as a special creation of God; and furthermore that this climaxes His creative work. Personally I hold to the point of view that evolution does not have the answer here. However, we must reserve final judgment on this point until we have more evidence." He adds, "Concerning the matter of the antiquity of man, I must say that I do not see any possible difficulty between the Biblical account and the theory of evolution." Dr. Cowperthwaite concluded that evolution and Scripture cannot be harmonized, but president Hartzler tells him that "there are many who say that this simply is not so. This has been brought out at a number of A.S.A. discussions." Concerning the view that the account of creation is written in figurative and picturesque language and not meant to be taken literally, Mr. Hartzler says, "I am quite sure that this is the attitude of a number of A.S.A. members," and adds that "we must be very cautious and indeed quite charitable with those who take this point of view."

In the year of the Darwin Centennial, 1959, the A.S.A. put out its book *Evolution and Christian Thought Today*, edited by Dr. Mixter. As the book was written by a number of A.S.A. members and was published under the auspices of the A.S.A., it represents the A.S.A. point of view. The reader will find evolution rather taken for granted. For example, "Many authorities believe that interspecific hybridization has played an important role in evolution. The list of hybrids in the appendix, incomplete as it is, confirms their opinion. If hybridization plays only a minor role in evolution, as some maintain, it is very strange indeed that there are so many vigorous, fertile hybrids in existence today. . . ."[3]

James O. Buswell III says in italics that there are no data which conflict with the Genesis account as interpreted in the context of the author's language and culture. This denies authorship by divine inspiration.[4]

A popular book on human evolution written after the publication of the A.S.A. book contains a very interesting comment. The author says, "There is a kind of epilogue to the Scopes Trial story. In 1959 there appeared a book called *Evolution and Christian Thought Today*. . . . The book is a collection of essays by scientists who regard themselves as 'conservative Christians.' One of the contributors was George K. Schweitzer, Associate Professor of Chemistry at the University of Tennessee. In his essay, Dr. Schweitzer wrote that the Biblical story of creation was intended to tell us who created the universe, not how it was created. Modern research, he said, has shown that the early chapters of Genesis should be interpreted 'poetically and allegorically,' not literally. No one in Tennessee called for Dr. Schweitzer's arrest."[5]

The Tennessee law under which Scopes was arrested has since this time been repealed, but even before the repeal Dr. Schweitzer could not have been arrested for his contribution to this book. The law forbade the teaching in tax-supported schools that human beings evolved from lower forms of life. The significant thing about this book is that an evolutionist expresses the opinion that a contributor to the book *Evolution and Christian Thought Today* presented the position of the evolutionists so clearly that he would be eligible for arrest because the law under which Scopes was convicted was still on the books at that time.

Of course it is true that anti-evolutionary material can be found in writings of members of the A.S.A. There are members who are strong creationists. Some say it is unfair to point out examples of the evolutionary writing without mentioning material that is not evolutionary. But the point is that members sign a statement of faith which would lead one to believe that *all* writings of the members dealing with the matter of evolution would be anti-evolutionary. Instead of this there is a strong trend toward the acceptance and teaching of evolution. And as previously mentioned, J. Frank Cassel admits in the *Journal of the American Scientific Affiliation* that those who oppose this trend have become less active and have a less effective voice in the affairs of the A.S.A

In a poll of A.S.A. members, opinion was requested concerning the following statement: "All the living forms in the world have been derived from a single form of life." From the membership of the A.S.A. 490 questionnaires were returned. Thirty-eight members, or 7.7% of those who returned the questionnaire did not think this a matter of sufficient importance to answer or preferred not to commit themselves about it. Of those who answered this part, 20 (4.4%) agreed, 295 (65.3%) disagreed, and 137 (30.3%) gave a "qualified answer."[6]

Let us see what these figures mean. The 4.4% who agree with this statement go as far or further than Charles Darwin, for he postulated that all forms of life on earth came from one or a few simple forms and they are willing to say it was from one. Again, this demonstrates that the signing of statements of faith can be meaningless in some cases. It appears that those who gave a "qualified answer" agree at least to some extent. Thus those who agree and those who give a qualified answer represent 34.7% of the sample, or about a third of the membership.

What about the 65.3% who disagree? They include the creationists and the "progressive creationists." It is not possible to distinguish them by their answer to this question, but we already know that it is the "progressive creationists" who are most vocal and are most active in directing the policies of the organization. The "progressive creationists" classify themselves as creationists. Thus this poll indicates that now about a third of the membership accepts more evolution than the "progressive creationists" do.

NOTES

1. Cassel, J. Frank, "Species Concepts and Definitions," *Journal of the American Scientific Affiliation*, 12:2:2, June, 1960.
2. *American Scientific Affiliation.* Descriptive booklet put out by the A.S.A., p. 7.
3. Mixter, Russell, L., Editor, *Evolution and Christian Thought Today* (Wm. B. Eerdmans Pub. Co., 1959), p. 103.
4. *Ibid.*, p. 184.
5. Silverburg, Robert, *Man Before Adam* (Macrae Smith Co., 1964), p. 228.
6. This information was received in private correspondence from a person who has held high office in the A.S.A. I was given only this one statement from the poll and the replies made to it.

EVOLUTION AND EDUCATION

In 1924 Professor William Patten of Dartmouth College published an article called, "Why I Teach Evolution."[1] It is very unlikely that an article on this subject would be accepted for publication at the present time, for it would be said that the teaching of evolution is no longer an issue. In those days there was still sufficient anti-evolutionary sentiment that Professor Patten could open his article with the statement: "It is often said that the moral and religious effects due to the teaching of evolution are disasterous; and even if this is not the case, that evolution in itself is not a suitable diet for college freshmen."

Professor Patten disagreed with the attitude which he said was common in 1924, and he presented three reasons why he taught the students evolution: (1) Evolution is accepted by practically all biologists. (2) The teaching of evolution is "the only way to bring back a living God into those fields of human thought and experience from which the teachings of 'high-brow' philosophy and 'low-brow' religion are excluding Him with extraordinary thoroughness and rapidity." (3) The methods by which evolution comes about exemplify the ideal methods of democracy and Christianity in successful operation on a universal scale.

Thus two of his three reasons are associated favorably with Christian faith. But it is rather evident that Professor Patten did not think of Christian faith as it is defined in the present discussion — as the faith which the sinner exercises when he accepts Christ's death upon the cross as the atonement for his sins, admitting that he himself cannot merit salvation through his own efforts. Indeed, Professor Patten would most likely have called this "low-brow" religion. He said, and he repeated it for emphasis, that "there is no difference between that which is vital in science and what is vital in religion." He concluded his article with the remarks: "For young and old, for highbrow and lowbrow, the study of evolution makes life more significant and more beautiful. It justifies our faith and fortifies our ideals. It makes God a more imminent reality. It helps all of us to understand the purpose of life, and how to accomplish it. That is why I teach evolution."

Besides his naivete in regard to the relationship between evolution and the ideals of democracy, Professor Patten displays a complete lack of understanding of the fundamentals of the Christian faith. He is not unique in the point of view he expresses. A number of textbook writers have endeavored to show the student that the acceptance of evolution is not detrimental to faith. Professor Paul Amos Moody of the University of Vermont, in his textbook *Introduction to Evolution*, writes an open letter to the students, in which he professes to believe in the Creator because of the evidence of design in the universe. He says, "The more I study science the more I am impressed with the thought that this world and universe have a definite *design* — and a design suggests a *designer*. It may be possible to have a design without a designer, a picture without an artist, but *my* mind is unable to conceive of such a situation."[2] Recognizing the Creator through the evidences of His creation is commendable, but it does not go far enough. Unless the implications of this design are carried to the conclusion which is the theme of the Bible, the mission of the Savior is not understood, and the way of salvation is not perceived. Professor Moody takes the details of creation very lightly and tells the student: "Yes, the first chapters of Genesis are great religion. Why worry about the fact that they are not valid science?"[3] He asks the question, "What is the influence of evolutionary thinking upon our ideas concerning man himself?" He answers this question as follows: "Succinctly, it changes our viewpoint so that we regard man no longer as a 'fallen angel' but instead as a 'risen animal.'" He continues, "Some people, mostly of an older generation, are sincerely distressed by this changed viewpoint. For them there was comfort in the thought that man once was perfect, and that his principal task is to regain that perfect state."[4] In saying these things Dr. Moody displays his ignorance of the Bible and Christian faith. Men never were angels.

Christians do not find comfort in the thought that man was once perfect, but their comfort is in the fact that they are redeemed by the sacrifice of Christ, and are thereby made perfect in the sight of God, though they could never achieve this through their own efforts. Furthermore, Christians do not believe that they have a task to accomplish in regaining a perfect state. Through accepting Christ not only as Savior but also as Lord, they endeavor to lead a life pleasing to Him, but their perfection in the sight of God is through Christ's merits and not through their own deeds or accomplishments.

Textbooks in the life sciences at the college level teach evolution as a fact. When an author mentions the implications of evolution to Christian faith, it is generally similar to that of Professor Moody in his textbook of evolution. Professor M. W. de Laubenfels of the University of Hawaii discusses the problem at greater length than is done by most textbook authors. He tells the students that there is no evidence against evolution,[5] and that there is evidence of a creator. He concludes that "a thoughtful person finds overwhelming assurance of harmony between the ideas of evolution and creation; some people wisely speak of 'creation by evolution.' "[6]

This kind of writing has become rather common among evolutionists who are not atheistic in their approach to the subject, and it may confuse or deceive those who do not understand it. Ever since Charles Darwin added a sentence about the Creator to the end of the second edition of his *Origin of Species,* this technique has been used to make the idea of evolution palatable to the religious reader.

Professor de Laubenfels believes in the Creator, but according to him the process of creation was such that human beings could develop from opossums, for he says, "An opossum does not climb a hill to see a beautiful sunset, nor is an opossum here concerned about the welfare of opossums in South America. Evolution has made out of the opossum a being that writes sonatas, and yearns for the welfare of beings miles away."[7] (It is to be assumed that he knew he was writing loosely, for evolutionists do not believe that human beings evolved from oppossums.)

To illustrate for the students the position of anti-evolutionists, Professor de Laubenfels gives an example which is utterly absurd and irrelevant. "Several years ago a party was being shown through Yellowstone National Park. The guide in charge was showing the magnificent view of Yellowstone Canyon. He told how it had changed in the eighteen years he had been exhibiting it. The wall was worn down in some places, the forest had moved up in another place, the river had changed its course. A lady tourist finally rose in wrath to protest. Her words were to this effect. 'You atheist, you! You are evidently one of those infidels who believe in evolution. How dare you stand there and tell us that this canyon is not exactly as God created it!' "[8] The professor displays his complete lack of understanding of the problem by his next sentence, which is, "There is the case against evolution!" There may be lady tourists who do not understand either, but at least they do not publish books on the subject. There is no comparison between the changes in Yellowstone Canyon due to rock-slides, erosion, and the like, and the kind of changes which would, as the professor alleges, transform marsupials into human beings.

Some writers of science textbooks make slurring remarks about Scripture. Lorus and Margery Milne of the University of New Hampshire say that attempts of earlier biologists to defend the *status quo* (that is, to defend creation as opposed to the theory of evolution), "seem comical from our present knowledge, but at the time they were in dead earnest. First they began by quoting the authorized King James translation of 'The First Book of Moses, called Genesis.' "[9] On the following page they make an attempt at reassuring religious students by saying that since the theory of evolution does not explain how things *began,* "the need for a Creator is not reduced a whit."

Evolutionists look upon man as an animal. It is true that anatomically and physiologically the human body has structures and functions comparable to those of the animal. A great deal about human heredity has been learned by breeding fruit flies. Much about human physiology has been discovered through the study of guineapigs and rats. However, the term "man and other animals" has become so common that it appears to be used for the purpose of indoctrination. In his textbook, *Biology: Its Principles and Implications,* Professor Garrett Hardin of the University of California at Santa Barbara uses the expression "man and other animals" and its equivalent no less than twenty-six times.[10] This amounts to brainwashing, where the student is led to accept something as a fact merely because he hears it so often or sees it in print so frequently. As a rose by any other name would still have the same fragrance, so man is what he is no matter what he is called. However, what he is called can make a great difference in his way of thinking about himself, and if students are indoctrinated with the concept that man is "another animal," the task of winning reluctant ones to accept the evolutionary point of view will be greatly facilitated.

With the exceptions of Cornell and Johns Hopkins, the older institutions of higher learning were founded as Christian schools, but most of them have lost their Christian testimony. There have been a number of reasons for this, but in view of the repeatedly observed phenomenon that evolutionary teaching and a strong Christian testimony will not thrive together, it appears that the introduction of evolutionary teaching in these institutions was in a significant measure responsible for the decline in Christian faith.

Ohio Wesleyan University will serve as an example to illustrate how a Bible-centered Christian school can gradually be transformed into one which is liberal and only nominally Christian.

Founded in 1842, before the theory of evolution was an issue, Ohio Wesleyan was not a theological school. Of the twenty-seven men who comprised the first five graduating classes, only four became ministers of the gospel. The school day was begun with prayer, and revivals were characteristic. In 1860 the YMCA at Ohio Wesleyan is said to have ranked first in size among all the college YMCA groups of the United States, and to have had "more influence on the life and work of this college than all other organizations combined."[11] (In those days the YMCA had not yet become theologically liberal.)

Biological science and geology were combined into one department of learning in 1871, twelve years after the publication of Darwin's *Origin of Species*. The department was headed by Edwin T. Nelson, the first member of the faculty to hold the Ph.D. degree. On the matter of evolution, Professor Nelson was said to have been noncommittal in public. In 1872 he gave a chapel talk on the harmony of science and Scripture. The following year he lectured on this subject in the classroom, and it is reported by students that "he quietly helped them in their personal intellectual adjustments along this line."[12] An alumnus said, "He let us interpret the first chapter of Genesis in our own way."[13]

In 1879, twenty years after the publication of the *Origin of Species* and about a dozen years before evolution was taught in the classroom at Ohio Wesleyan, a graduating senior presented a commencement address on the subject, "Evolution from a Theistic Viewpoint."[14] This was Cyrus B. Austin, who later became Professor of Mathematics and Vice President of the school. He was also Dean of Women for forty years. (Not a printer's mistake.)

James Whitford Bashford became President in 1889. Before coming to Ohio Wesleyan it had been his intention to become a Unitarian Minister. He brought liberalism to the school, but it was integrated with traditional Christianity. Henry Clyde Hubbart, in his history of the college, says, "although a vigorous administrator and scholar as well, Bashford's dominant interest was in interpreting life's meanings to students, and in stirring the depths of their religious natures. For that day a liberal of the advanced type, accepting the theory of evolution and the findings of Biblical criticism, he was nevertheless an ardent evangelist."[15] Of his administration Hubbart says, "In a spirit of great optimism horizons widened, late nineteenth century Christian liberalism became enthroned in the classroom, laboratory, chapel, and the new experimental and Darwinian science came in; all this intellectual advance, however, being cast in the frame of zealous evangelistic religion."[16]

One of Bashford's friends is quoted as saying, "If Bashford's views were widely known, some would think that he was tearing everything to pieces."[17] It is most likely that if the constituency of the college had been warned at this time about the trends that were developing in their school, they would not have believed it, and would have defended the administration and the faculty.

According to Hubbart, "The modernization of the college that came under President Bashford brought no greater change than in the field of biology. The third period of science was ushered in. In 1891, Bashford brought Edwin G. Conklin (Ohio Wesleyan, 1885; Ph.D., Johns Hopkins, 1891) as Professor of Biology, Nelson becoming Professor of Physiology and Geology. . . . Here only three years, Professor Conklin introduced modern biology and exerted great influence . . . evolution was accepted and taught in the classroom."[18]

From Ohio Wesleyan, Professor Conklin went to Princeton University, where he became one of the nation's leading biologists. His place at Ohio Wesleyan was filled by Edward L. Rice, who came with a definite understanding with President Bashford that he was free to teach evolution.[19]

Professor William G. Williams, teacher of language, literature, and grammar, was a highly respected, intelligent man of great integrity. He was a member of the faculty for the remarkable period of fifty-seven years. The writer of the history of the school's first hundred years says that he was a born-again Christian. He did not mind expressing his feelings, for when he was displeased by a speech made by the President in a faculty meeting he arose and said, "It is no part of my duty here, I think, to spend time listening to such objurgations."[20] Thereupon he took his hat and walked out of the room. However, he took no stand with regard to the developing trend in evolutionary thought on the campus. He said, "I am too old to change my opinion, but I like to hear what the younger men think."[21] He did not seem to recognize a danger in the trend.

It seems that the only person of note who took issue with the theory of evolution was Lorenzo Dow McCabe, Professor of Philosophy and acting President of the school 1873-1876 and 1888-1889. He called it the "pernicious doctrine of evolution," and Hubbart reports that it received his "blasting condemnation."[22]

Mr. Hubbart sums up the situation in these words: "Throughout the years the men in the science departments have been sincere believers, and almost without exception active members in the various churches. They have helped undergraduates build their newly acquired science into a Christian philosophy of life, and have been unhampered by any official meddling with either their beliefs or their teaching."[23] Professor Conklin became the most famous of the science teachers, and Mr. Hubbart could hardly have failed to consider him when making this statement about the men in the science departments being sincere believers. However, the same year that Hubbart's history of the college was published (1943), Professor Conklin's book *Man, Real and Ideal* was also published. It is based upon a series of lectures delivered some years before.

Professor Conklin was the first to teach evolution in the classroom at Ohio Wesleyan, and his book, of course, is written from the evolutionary point of view. He says, "Man is one of nearly a million known species of animals that have appeared, flourished, and in many cases disappeared during a thousand million years past. The human species, like all other species, has come into being by natural evolution and not by supernatural creation. In both phylogeny [evolutionary development] and ontogeny [embryonic development] body, mind, and morals have been developed by natural processes."[24] He expressed the opinion that "the lesson of evolution is full of hope for the future, a real 'gospel' to a distracted world."[25]

His philosophy leads to the conclusion that the value of prayer is merely the subjective influence that the prayer has upon the one who prays. He said that there are two kinds of results which can be gained from prayer: prayer may direct the attention of the individual to needs which can be met through human effort, or, if this is impossible, prayer may produce a spirit of resignation to the inevitable. The best example of the former, he said, is the Lord's prayer, "in which every petition can be answered by man himself, if sufficiently strengthened and inspired."[26] He said that the best example of the second kind of prayer is the prayer of our Lord in Gethsemane, where He prayed, "O my Father, if it be possible, let this cup pass from me; nevertheless, not as I will but as Thou wilt." Professor Conklin concluded that as the Lord prayed this prayer three times with increasing resignation to the inevitable, "He then went bravely to His trial and crucifixion." Such statements, of course, merely reveal how little the professor knew about the matters concerning which he chose to expound.

Professor Conklin defined the religion of the scientist thus: "What kind of religion does science leave to man? Not one of superstition, mythology, and magic, but one of nature, order, humanism. The religion of science must be based on the solid ground of reality, but it must reach up into the atmosphere of high ideals. Its God is not a person after the manner of men, who stands outside of nature and now and then interferes with its workings [as in working miracles and answering prayer], but rather the God of science is 'eternal process marching on' through the evolution of galaxies and solar systems, of earth and life and man, of emotions, intelligence, and reason, of society, ethics, and religion, of ideals of truth, beauty, goodness, of human asperations for freedom, justice, and peace. This is the eternal God that science sees in all nature."[27] But this is not the God of the Bible. This is a manmade god existing only in the human imagination.

In spite of his optimism in a future controlled by evolution, Professor Conklin has no consolation to offer for "the reality of death." He says, "Saints, prophets, philosophers, and poets have found a way of escape from the reality of death through faith in immortality of the soul. In this faith Saint Paul said, 'O death, where is thy sting? O grave, where is thy victory?' . . . this is a glorious faith, a conquering hope, which I would gladly share, but I am not aware of any sound scientific evidence in favor of this belief."[28]

This is the man who introduced the teaching of evolution at Ohio Wesleyan.[29]

The revivals for which Ohio Wesleyan was noted in its early days flourished on into the administration of President Bashford. "Glorious" revivals are said to have occurred during his tenure of office, although liberal teachings were being introduced at the same time. The revival meetings were dignified and spiritual, and it was reported in 1881 that "the meetings could not be accused of injury to scholarship or good behavior."[30]

In 1886 it was recorded that "the meetings have been unusually quiet and impressive; the results will be lasting; the necessity of regeneration has been presented with wonderful calmness and clearness."[31]

By 1896 a division among the students was evident at times of revival. Besides the influence of the liberal element, there was a tendency toward excesses on the part of some others.

It is said that after 1905 the emphasis changed somewhat. The meetings which were held were not of the nature of revivals. Meetings of a different sort were continued until around 1929. Hubbart comments that the revival was abandoned about the same time church attendance was no longer required and sororities and dancing were introduced.[32]

Prayer had been offered publicly on the day the college opened, November 13, 1844, and this practice was continued daily until 1935. Hubbart remarks that "beginning as early as 1920 or even before, however, the service came to lose some of its devotional emphasis, and to take on an eclectic quality, with still, at times, a considerable religious element, but with secular, educational, or entertainment features coming to the fore, such as lectures, musical chapels, or college shows. . . . In 1935 the college catalog displaced the words 'daily devotional service' with the words 'daily assembly.' "[33]

The *Ohio Wesleyan Magazine* for June, 1963, reports that on April 6 of that year the college was host to about a thousand leading scientists and educators who met to discuss "the extent to which man may some day be able to control development of his own species." This symposium on evolution and genetics was part of a program for the dedication of a new science building. One of the men honored in the dedication was Dr. Edward L. Rice, who succeeded Professor Conklin, and who was hailed in the article as "one of the pioneers in teaching evolution." Speakers at the symposium "outlined findings in the past decade which have led scientists to believe control of heredity and evolution may eventually be possible by technical means."

This is the history of a trend in the case of one particular institution of higher learning, but it is paralleled by many others, and this trend to apostasy appears to be continuing with increasing momentum.

As is seen in this example, there are other factors which also are involved, but the losing of its Christian testimony by a school is paralleled by its increasing acceptance of evolutionary theory.

Prayer and eternal vigilance are the price for those who do not wish to follow where the others have gone. There are two chief sources of difficulty confronting the leadership of those schools which would not succumb to evolutionary teaching. 1. There are a number of Christian men of science who are teaching a modified form of evolution. Their influence is breaking down resistance to the acceptance of evolution in some degree, and as a result administrators as well as teachers are not recognizing the danger signals. 2. As schools increase their offerings because of larger enrollments and to meet the demands for academic excellence, it becomes ever more difficult to obtain qualified faculty members who take a clear stand in opposing evolution.

Christian schools which appear to be in transition between an anti-evolutionary stand and a position where the teaching of evolution is accepted, tend to be quite sensitive to criticism. It is affirmed by them that any criticism in this regard is false and scandalous. It is said that it cannot be true because the members of the faculty sign a statement which makes it impossible.

A professor of a certain Christian school appeared on a popular television program in a debate on evolution. He debated on the side *for* evolution, teamed with a chain-smoking biologist of a secular school, and against two men from another Christian school who took the side against evolution. He appeared on the program in the name of the Christian school where he taught and the event was advertised before the time of the program. Since it was altogether public, there seemed to be no reason why it should not be used as an example here, with the name of the school. However, as a matter of courtesy, the paragraph mentioning this was sent to the president of the school for his comment.

The vehemence of the request not to mention the name of the school in connection with this event was unexpected in light of the publicity involved in the program itself. There followed a series of communications over the matter of what evolution really is. Two important matters remained unanswered though asked repeatedly during the course of this correspondence. (1) Why is it so important what the critic means by the term *evolution,* when the really important thing in this case is what the professor who appeared on the program meant by it and what the viewing public thought he meant? (2) Why is it so scandalous to mention the name of the school in reporting the fact of the broadcast in a discussion of evolution and education when the school was not embarrassed by the broadcast itself?

This is not a unique case. It is typical. It is important because it illustrates the difficulties encountered by anyone, whether an outsider or an insider, who tries to keep a Christian school from making the transition from a strong Biblical stand to a modernistic position. When the danger signs begin to appear they are disregarded. Anyone who calls attention to them finds his effort is not appreciated. As things progress and the signs become more clear, criticism is met with strong denials, accusations of persecution, and aspersions as to the motives of the one making the criticism. The final stage is the accomplished fact of the institution gone theologically liberal. All along the way those who desire the school to retain the stand for which it was founded are not allowed to speak freely, while those on the opposite side, who are making the innovations that are leading the school in the new direction, are honored and allowed to speak freely. It is only during the time that the school is sensitive to criticism that there is any hope of accomplishing anything of value through discussion or criticism. When the time comes that the school is no longer sensitive it is too late. But while discussion and criticism might still be of value they are considered un-Christian and unethical. Thus when the trend has begun, those who desire to liberalize a school have a great advantage.

In the secular schools the situation is different. How much evolution is taught and whether it is called evolution or something else depends merely upon the trend of the times.

H. J. Muller, the noted late geneticist and Nobel Prize winner of Indiana University, complained in 1957 that the teaching of evolution was given scant attention in the grade schools and high schools. He expressed the opinion that unless evolution becomes an integral, fundamental part of the average American's way of thinking and outlook of life, then "we only deserve the fate of sheep, which a sheep-like behavior will bring."[34]

In his opinion we can maintain our position as the dominant species of the earth only if we keep a careful watch over other living things and control long-term processes which tend to bring about changes in other creatures and in ourselves. He believes that in order to do this we must understand the mechanism of evolution. But for centuries even the wisest men knew nothing about the mechanism of evolution and most of them did not even believe in evolution. It does not seem to follow that it suddenly must be so very important for everyone to have an evolutionary view of life in order to keep other species from gaining superiority over us. However, much progress has been made toward the teaching of evolution as a fact in the grade schools, and those who agree with professor Muller should now be pleased.

A fourth-grade textbook (The Macmillan Science-Life Series, Book 4, Revised Edition), recently in use in California public schools and elsewhere, contains the following: "Scientists believe that the first animals on earth were one-celled animals, like the ameba. From these all other kinds of animals have developed. The newest animals are human beings."

In the science series which has been adopted for use in California starting in 1967 (*Concept in Science,* Harcourt, Brace, and World publishers), the transition is being made from the use of the words *change* and *develop,* meaning *evolve,* to the direct use of the words *evolve* and *evolution.* Parts of the teacher's editions for the first grade and fifth grade texts are identical. The teachers are told, "Living things are in constant change. The universe changes; the Earth changes; the single organism and the species change over the ages. The concepts of adaptation over the ages, divergence in form, convergence in geographical isolations, and evolution are within the purview of this conceptual scheme. . ."

There is a point in the fifth-grade text where the teacher is told, "You may recognize that the term *change,* which is used in discussing the development of living things, means that more complex organisms have evolved from simpler organisms during the two-or-more billions of years of life on earth. Our present-day biological forms have evolved because of their ability to survive in changing environments. The mechanisms of biological evolution are based upon complex understandings of the interaction of heredity and environment. Why any organism exists today — why we exist — is rooted in many biological changes and adaptations. If this understanding is firmly grasped, the use of the term *evolution* may have value at this point in the child's development." So now there will be no more need to hedge with other words, and the word *evolution* may be used directly to the children in the fifth grade.

The term *change* is repeated with a regularity that suggests "brain-washing." It is used thirty times on one page of the teacher's edition for the first grade book. The teacher is told, "The only constant is change itself."

The fifth-grade children are told three times in twenty-seven pages that the higher forms of life come from the one-celled forms. They are encouraged to do some evolutionary speculating themselves. They are told that sharks have skeletons of cartilage and cod fish have skeletons of bone. They are then asked to think which came earlier, sharks or cod-like fish. They are given a hint: in an individual's development, cartilage develops first and later it becomes bone. From this information the children are supposed to conclude that sharks evolved first. But there are at least three things wrong. Cartilage does not *become* bone, it is *replaced* by bone. So many contradictions and inconsistencies have been found in the idea that individual development shows the order of evolutionary development that it has been abandoned by outstanding evolutionists. Finally, the evolutionists no longer believe that sharks evolved before the bony fish.

The BSCS (Biological Sciences Curriculum Study) high school biology textbooks, well known as the Yellow, Green, and Blue Versions, represent a new departure in textbooks and they are thoroughly evolutionary in their approach to the subject. The lead article in the December, 1967, issue of *The American Biology Teacher* is called "The Centrality of Evolution in Biology Teaching." It was written by Professor Bentley Glass, who was BSCS Chairman. He says that there is still sufficient anti-evolutionary sentiment in the country that some publishers are reluctant to accept for publication books which promote the theory of evolution. But he tells that the BSCS had no such problem. They had no fear of public opposition and they had no worry as to whether their work would be a commercial success or not. It would seem that this could be so under only one circumstance, and George Gaylord Simpson confirms this on page 41 of his book *This View of Life*. He says that the books were subsidized by the federal government!

Loren Eiseley of the University of Pennsylvania can always be counted on to say something in an interesting and unusual way. He himself is an evolutionist and a teacher of evolution, and here is how he describes the relationship between the student and the teacher. "The student asks you, as a child his mother, 'Where did I come from?' 'Son,' you say, floundering, 'below the Cambrian there was a worm.' Or you say, 'There was an odd fish in a swamp and you have his lungs.' Or you say, 'Once there was a reptile whose jaw bones are in your ears.' Or you try again, 'There was an ape and his teeth are in your mouth. Your jaw has shrunk and your skull has risen. You are a fish and reptile and a warm-blooded, affectionate thing that dies if it has nothing to cling to when it is young. You are all of these things. . . . You began nowhere in particular. You are really an illusion, one of innumerable shadows in the dying fires of a mysterious universe. Yesterday you were a lowbrowed skull in the river gravel; tomorrow you may be a fleck of carbon amid the shattered glass of Moscow or New York."[35]

NOTES

1. Patten, William, "Why I Teach Evolution," *The Scientific Monthly,* 19:6:635, December, 1924.

2. Moody, Paul Amos, *Introduction to Evolution.* 2d. ed. (Harper and Brothers, 1962), p. 514.

3. *Ibid.,* p. 513.

4. *Ibid.,* p. 518.

5. de Laubenfels, M. W., *Life Science* (Prentice-Hall, 1949, Printing of 1950), p. 382.

6. *Ibid.,* p. 387.

7. *Ibid.,* p. 386.

8. *Ibid.,* p. 382.

9. Milne Lorus J. and M. J. Milne, *The Biotic World and Man* (Prentice-Hall, 1952), p. 461.

10. Hardin, Garrett, *Biology: Its Principles and Implications* (W. H. Freeman and Co., 1961), pp. 200, 276, 287, 320, 357 (twice), 358, 367, 374, 380, 407, 410 (twice), 416, 420, 437, 467, 476, 477, 512, 513, 519, 544, 550, 558, 607. This includes two references to "nonhuman animals," implying that there are also human animals.

11. Hubbart, Henry Clyde, *Ohio Wesleyan's First Hundred Years* (W. B. Conkey Co., 1943), p. 319.

12. *Ibid.,* p. 253.

13. *Ibid.*

14. *Ibid.,* p. 72.

15. *Ibid.,* p. 95.

16. *Ibid.,* p. 87.

17. *Ibid.,* p. 95.

18. *Ibid.*, p. 247.
19. *Ibid.*, p. 253.
20. *Ibid.*, p. 83.
21. *Ibid.*, p. 253.
22. *Ibid.*, p. 80.
23. *Ibid.*, p. 253.
24. Conklin, Edwin Grant, *Man, Real and Ideal* (Charles Scribner's Sons, 1943), p. 148.
25. *Ibid.*, p. xi.
26. *Ibid.*, p. 202.
27. *Ibid.*, p. 203.
28. *Ibid.*, p. 179.
29. This is the same Professor Conklin who is quoted in *The Reader's Digest*, January, 1963, under the heading *Nine Scientists Look at Religion.* He said, "The probability of life originating from accident is comparable to the probability of the unabridged dictionary resulting from an explosion in a printing shop." This sounds good, and it is remarkable that a man with his background would say this, but to take it out of context and to represent it as the statement of an anti-evolutionist is a grave error.
30. Hubbart, Henry Clyde, *loc. cit.*, p. 317.
31. *Ibid.*, p. 317.
32. *Ibid.*, p. 314.
33. *Ibid.*, p. 308.
34. Muller, H. J., "Man's Place in Living Nature," *Scientific American*, 84:5:245, May, 1957, p. 245.
35. Eiseley, Loren, "The Time of Man," *Horizon*, 4:4:4, March, 1962, p. 6.

EVOLUTION AND THE CHURCH

As the theory of evolution has become more and more accepted, modernism has increased within the nominal Christian church. With the growth of belief in an animal ancestry for man, faith in salvation through the atonement of Christ has declined. This is to be expected because belief in an evolutionary development of man from lower forms prevents a belief in the historicity of the Biblical account of the fall of man from a state of innocence because of disobedience. It makes Christ a martyr instead of the Savior.

One Sir Richard Gregory is reported to have written an epitaph for himself:

My grandfather preached the gospel of Christ
My father preached the gospel of Socialism
I preached the gospel of Science[1]

In 1891 an Episcopal clergyman named Howard Mac Query, who accepted evolution and had very liberal theological views, wrote, "Moreover, I felt that it could be only a few years, at most, before such views as are advocated in this volume would be pretty generally accepted by the Church; for, whether they be true or false, they are being taught in all the leading educational institutions of the land; and the rising generation, which will furnish religious, moral, and intellectual teachers to the next, is being thoroughly imbued with such teaching."[2]

The march to modernism by the nominal Christian church has been speeded by the oft-repeated claim that there is no real conflict between evolution and Christian faith. It is said that evolution does not account for the ultimate cause, and that therefore there is room for God as this ultimate cause. Those who say this do not realize that the issue is not over the provision of a loophole which may be labeled *God,* but over salvation from the penalty for sin. Many say that the conflict between evolution and Christian faith is just a misunderstanding, but they themselves do not understand what the issue is. It is not just a difference of opinion as to whether creation was rapid or long and drawn out through theistic evolution. The issue is this: was Christ what He claimed to be or was He an imposter; was His death the atonement offered to the people of a fallen race or was it the early martyrdom of a teacher ahead of His time? The answer obtained from the Bible and the answer derived from evolution are different and irreconcilable.

It is natural that when scientists who do not understand the issue and who are not particularly interested in the Christian religion consider this matter, they base their arguments on statements made by modernistic leaders of the nominally Christian church. The position of these men accommodates the views of the evolutionists, and evolution and modernism each lend prestige to the other.

James McCosh, while President of Princeton University, said that, if Christian ministers insist that Christian faith and the theory of evolution are incompatible, the result will be that people will be driven away from accepting Christian faith. This assertion has been repeated many times since then. But if he is right, the end result will be the same either way as far as Christian faith is concerned. If it is true that the denial of evolution drives people from accepting Christian faith, and if it is also true that the acceptance of evolution prevents people from having Christian faith, then the people to whom this applies would not be Christians no matter what course is taken. But if the denial of evolution drives away only those who would not be able to accept the Christian faith anyhow, because of their evolutionary beliefs, while the acceptance of evolution denies Christian faith itself, it is far better to repudiate the theory of evolution, and by so doing drive away only those who would not have faith anyway.

We know from prophecies in the Bible that a time of great apostasy and a falling away from the faith is to come. The effect of evolutionary teaching is apostasy. The teaching of the theory of evolution is an important factor in the growing apostasy. Discerning believers will proclaim the gospel of salvation by grace through the atonement of Christ, and warn against false teaching which is contrary to Scripture.

NOTES

1. Quoted by Warren Weaver, *Eternity,* July, 1959, p. 17.
2. MacQuery, Howard, *The Evolution of Man and Christianity,* Revised edition (D. Appleton & Co., 1891), p. xix.

Chapter III

SCIENCE AND RELIGION

The basic conflict between science and Christian faith is not over the theory of evolution, but over the scientific method.

The scientific method is essentially a way of learning through repeated observations, or experiences. Instead of waiting for experiences to present themselves, the scientist sets up conditions which result in the kinds of experiences he is interested in observing with regard to some phenomenon he wishes to investigate. These are experiments.

The scientific method is based upon the principle of the uniformity of nature, which means that under the same circumstances the same cause will always produce the same effect. Generally this is true. If it were not, we would live in a capricious world, never knowing what to expect next. But the trouble comes when the scientist applies this principle to all of life. If the principle of the uniformity of nature always holds true, there can be no miracles, no supernatural acts of God, and indeed no God.

Science has accomplished so many wonderful things that many people have been led to accept the scientific method and the principle of the uniformity of nature as basic to their philosophy of life, culminating in the denial of miracles and of a personal God. There is no doubt that much of the scepticism, agnosticism, and atheism in the civilized world is attributable to an extrapolation of the concept of the uniformity of nature beyond the laboratory and into all of life.

The prophet Elisha told Naaman the Syrian by the authority of God that if he would dip himself seven times in the river Jordan he would be cleansed of his leprosy. He dipped himself seven times and was immediately cleansed (II Kings 5). This was a miracle. It is not a scientific way of dealing with leprosy. It is not repeatable. If it were repeatable, lepers would even now be going to the Jordan to be cleansed by dipping themselves seven times.

Much of what constitutes evidence for evolution is not repeatable and cannot be investigated by the scientific method. Therefore it is believed by some that the theory of evolution should be considered under the heading of philosophy instead of science. However, it is generally taught as science, and students and the public are constantly being told that all reputable scientists accept it as a fact.

In this age of scientific enlightenment, people who fear the effect of science upon religion are considered backward indeed, but the fact is that there are grounds for such fear. Furthermore, scientists themselves have been guilty of provoking the fear. As the scientific method came into prominence, it was the boast of many scientists that science would explain everything and nothing would be left to religion. Although some college textbooks assure the student that science cannot explain the ultimate cause and that therefore it will not displace God, the fact is that scientists are trying to explain the origin of life and everything else. It is now boldly stated in articles for the public that scientists are endeavoring to take upon themselves the role of God.

Neal D. Buffaloe, Professor of Biology at Arkansas State Teachers College, reminds us that "during the latter portion of the nineteenth century, the rift between biology and religion became so great that in most civilized countries an attitude of 'science or religion, God or evolution' prevailed. This rift has not entirely healed in the minds of a great many people, and to them, even the word 'science' may be associated with complete rejection of religion."[1]

Arthur Keith, the noted English anthropologist, said, ". . . it is the duty of theologians not to expect scientific men to modify their facts to fit religious views, but that religion must be modified to fit man's changing needs, and to be in keeping with the truth as revealed in scientific inquiry."[2] A few years later this same Professor Keith wrote concerning the theory of evolution, "By this new knowledge my youthful creed was smashed to atoms. My personal God, Creator of Heaven and Earth, melted away. The desire to pray — but not the need — was lost; for one cannot pray to an abstraction."[3]

A biologist from the University of California at Los Angeles says, "In my opinion, it is never fitting for a true scientist to deviate from the natural cause explanation. If some god can create new genes out of nothing at will, then there is no point in any of us seeking the basis of life."[4] He will not consider the possibility that God created; that would spoil his scientific approach to the problems of life.

It is sometimes said that the theory of evolution must be accepted merely because it is scientific (although it may really be a philosophy), while if creation had occurred, that would not be scientific. This is false logic. If detectives worked on this principle when trying to solve a crime, they would ignore a person who confessed that he did it. They would say that this is not a scientific way to solve a crime. They must find clues and pursue them in a scientific manner. But even if they used so illogical an approach they might in the end find that the person who made the confession really had done what he said he did, but the evolutionary scientists have already ruled God out and will not consider the possibility that He did create.

It is not only the works of God which are rejected because they are not subject to the scientific method, but also the works of Satan and his demons. Because of the influence of science, most people today do not believe that demons exist or that demon activity is a reality. The fact that the Bible states plainly that there are demons does not impress these people, and they consider demon activity to be merely imagination and superstition.

It is said that science has freed mankind from the fear of evil spirits, but the fact is that it is the influence of the gospel of Jesus Christ which has freed men from the fear of demons.

Because the evil spirits, or demons, have wills of their own, they cannot be counted on to react always the same way under the same circumstances. Thus diabolical activities do not lend themselves to investigation by the scientific method. Because ignorant people have ascribed to the work of demons natural phenomena which they could not understand, and because spirit phenomena can to a certain extent be counterfeited by charlatans, and because witch hunts have run to excesses, demon activities are lightly dismissed as superstitious inventions of ignorant and uncritical people. It does not, however, require a superior intellect to see that none of these are valid arguments against the reality of demons and diabolical activities.

It is frequently said that science and the Bible are complementary revelations of God and that therefore there can be no conflict between them. It is maintained that since the Bible is not a textbook of science, the scientists should be taken as authorities in matters relating to science, and the Bible should be the authority in matters of a spiritual nature. This is the "double revelation theory." The meaning is that God has given man two revelations, one through nature and the other through the Bible.

Henry Ward Beecher, the eminent liberal preacher, published a sermon in 1885 on "The Two Revelations," and dedicated himself to promoting this double revelation theory. The opening sentence of his sermon was, "That the whole world and the universe were the creation of God is the testimony of the whole Bible . . . but how he made them — whether by the direct force of a creative will or indirectly through a long series of gradual changes — the Scriptures do not declare." Beecher was convinced that the latter method was the one the Lord used and that it required many millions of years. He told his congregation that the Bible does not tell the *method* by which God created, and that the method was through an evolutionary process. This is the same message which is being given today by some men who profess to be Bible-believing Christians.

Information about creation can come only through revelation, for it is beyond the scope of the scientific method. Attempts to look at creation scientifically leads to an acceptance of the double revelation theory, which in turn leads to an acceptance of evolution.

NOTES

1. Buffaloe, Neal D., *Principles of Biology* (Prentice-Hall, 1962), p. 317.
2. Keith, Arthur, *Concerning Man's Origin* (Watts and Co., 1927), p. viii.
3. Keith, Arthur, "Faith or Science?" *Forum,* April, 1930.
4. Hinton, T., Letter, *Journal of the American Scientific Affiliation,* 7:4:14, December, 1955.

TELEOLOGY

Science, the journal of the American Association for the Advancement of Science, for December 5, 1958, carries an article which begins: "Each of us is for good and against evil."[1] This is a rather unusual beginning for an article in a scientific journal. However, the reader is naturally inclined to respond with whatever his vocabulary contains for the equivalent of *Amen!* But in our day and generation it is necessary to be cautious before endorsing a statement which is even as apparently straightforward as this. The author's next sentence is: "For most teachers of science, teleology and anthromorphisms are not issues to be debated but to be deplored — we stand against the evil."

In deploring and standing against the "evil" of teleology, he is deploring, opposing, and calling evil the concept of *purpose* in the world. A Bible-believing Christian cannot take such a position. God created with a purpose, and His purpose in creation continues.

Calling teleology evil leads to the conclusion that a concept of God acting in nature is evil. The author of the article does take that position, for he says that he finds objectionable non-rigorous language habits in teaching which may imply "the activity of a supernatural being." Note that by calling this a non-rigorous language habit, he implies that teachers would not *intentionally* imply any divine activity, but would do so only by careless habits of speech. He further clarifies this by saying that a teacher should not say anything about natural law, for this might cause some students to conclude that if there is natural law, there should also be a law-Giver, and that would be bad!

The answer to the author's use of the terms *good* and *evil* is found in Isaiah 5:20. "Woe unto them that call evil good, and good evil."

By quoting from current textbooks, the author of the article illustrates his contention that the writers of textbooks are unduly careless in making teleological implications. For example he quotes as follows from a textbook: "One purpose of food is to act as a fuel for our bodies, supplying us with heat and muscular energy."[2] According to him it is unfortunate that the writer of the textbook said that food has a purpose. He recommends that teachers say that some plants *accumulate* starch, not that they store starch, because the latter may connote a purposeful laying away of something for the future. He urges teachers to refrain from saying that hydrogen and oxygen combine *to* form water. The proper way to say it is that hydrogen and oxygen combine *and* form water. To say that they combine *to* form water has teleological implications. He denies that this is quibbling, because, he says, if a teleological interpretation of a statement is possible, some students will make it. Even though it seems obvious to the teacher that this is merely a convenient way of saying something with no teleological implications intended, if it *can* be misunderstood, it *will* be misunderstood by some.

If a science teacher writing in a scientific journal can assume that other science teachers basically agree with him in being anti-teleological, and can so strongly urge them to bend over backward to avoid the slightest appearance of giving a teleological interpretation of anything, how much more careful should Christian teachers be to keep from using language which contains evolutionary implications! However, Christian writers and speakers are now doing just the opposite, and are telling students and adults that it is now not only all right to accept a certain amount of evolution, but that it is impossible to do otherwise.

Four scientists who did not altogether agree with the author of the article wrote letters to the editor of the journal.[3] Only one of the four disapproved of the atheistic implications. George Gaylord Simpson pointed out that Charles Darwin, "the very arch-hero of anti-teleology," made teleological statements, and he evidently did it purposely and not carelessly. Dr. Simpson also made another interesting observation. To follow the rigorous anti-teleological phraseology urged in the article, one would have to say that the sea turtles go ashore *and* lay their eggs, and not that they go ashore *to* lay their eggs. To avoid any purpose in the turtles' going ashore leads to another unintentional implication — that a remarkable coincidence always occurs, and the turtles *just happen* to be ashore at the time when they lay their eggs. Of course, there is no coincidence of this kind. Sea turtles go ashore when it is time for them to lay their eggs and they lay them on the land. Sea turtles of some species do not go ashore at any other time.

In the first chapter of Romans the apostle Paul says that the working of God is so obvious in nature that even the heathen are without excuse for their idolatry. That being so, how much more are we without excuse when we know so much more than the heathen did in those days. A Christian cannot help taking a teleological view of the world, though a Christian who is a scientist assumes uniformity in the laboratory, for he is not expecting his research to be influenced by a miracle.

A member of the American Scientific Affiliation expresses the opinion in a book review that "as science finds explanations, and as the fossil record becomes more complete, one's God, in a sense, becomes smaller and smaller."[4] But "explanations" will never diminish the evidences of the works of God in nature. Indeed, a scientific "explanation" may reveal a marvellous phenomenon to be even more wonderful.

Charles Darwin did a considerable amount of research on carnivorous plants, but even the Venus fly trap with its leaves that snap shut like a bear trap and the utricularia with its elaborate under water box trap did not bring him to accept a teleological view. It is not to be expected that any presentation of a collection of some of the amazing phenomena of nature will influence those whose minds are closed to a teleological explanation. Yet it would be amiss to omit the mention of a few of the marvels of creation.

Besides the well-known carnivorous flowering plants, a number of molds are adapted to capturing animal prey. Joseph J. Maio of the University of Washington School of Medicine says that many of the molds are so specialized that they are able to trap only one species of animal. He comments, "How they evolved their predatory habits and organs remains an evolutionary mystery."[5] The most unusual of these traps is a ring of three cells attached to the filament of the mold. When a nematode worm pushes its head inside the loop, the ring inflates in less than a tenth of a second, securely holding the worm in this three-celled collar. If a worm touches the *outside* of the ring nothing happens; if the loop inflated when touched from the outside it would catch nothing. After capturing its prey, the mold grows filaments into its body, utilizing the tissues of the worm for food. As in the case of the archer fish (mentioned in connection with Darwin's natural selection theory) the spectacular manner for which it is adapted for obtaining food is not a necessary way for it to obtain its nourishment. The mold can live very well on vegetable matter, and trapping nematodes is a sort of luxury. Another remarkable feature of this strange phenomenon is that the nematodes themselves induce the mold plants to develop the rings. When nematodes are absent from the soil, the molds do not develop the rings, but in the laboratory the plants will develop the rings even if given water in which nematodes have lived. The worms apparently secrete some chemical substance which induces the mold plants to develop the three-celled rings. This, of course, does not "explain" how the plants obtained the ability to produce such traps.

The cells in the honeycombs of the bees are marvels of engineering. In 1859 Darwin corresponded with a Cambridge professor named William H. Miller about some measurements of the cells made by bees. He wrote to Professor Miller, "Your letter actually turned me sick with panic."[6] This was not a scientific attitude, and it was for the same reason that Darwin said he felt sick when he thought of an eye or of a feather in the tail of a peacock. He could not explain these things by his theory of natural selection. He no doubt would have felt sick again if he had known that bees can fly around obstacles in a circuitous route, and then compute the direction to the place where they have been. Karl von Frisch says, "That they are able to fly by an indirect route and yet reconstruct the true direction without the aid of ruler, protractor, or drawing board, is one of the most wonderful accomplishments in the life of the bee and indeed in all creation."[7]

Birds are not noted for intelligence, but some of them do amazing things. It is indeed a marvel how birds find their way unerringly when migrating long distances, and how many kinds can return to their nesting sites when experimentally displaced hundreds and even thousands of miles from their nesting grounds. Six hundred years before the birth of Christ the prophet Jeremiah wrote about the migration of birds, and said, "Yea, the stork in the heaven knoweth her appointed times; and the turtle [dove] and the crane and the swallow observe the time of their coming: but my people know not the judgment of the Lord" (Jer. 8:7). But even in comparatively recent times the mystery of what happens to certain kinds of birds during the winter has been explained by such fantastic ideas as these: the kinds of birds which are not seen in the winter have merely changed into the kinds which are seen; they hibernate in the mud at the bottoms of ponds; they fly to the moon and reside there.

By marking birds, their migrations can be studied. The way adult birds fly unerringly for long distances, often over open ocean, is remarkable, but even more amazing is the feat performed by inexperienced young birds. Many shore birds leave for the south before their young are able to make the trip. A few weeks later the young birds, which previously have never been away from the nesting area, take off and fly unerringly to the wintering grounds of their species, meeting there their elders who arrived several weeks previously.

Various theories have been proposed to explain how the birds are able to perform their incredible feats of navigation. It was suggested that some of them orient themselves by the stars, but this seemed so fantastic that it was not considered seriously until recently. To test the ability of certain warblers to orient by the stars some German scientists raised the birds "in completely closed, sound-proof chambers where they lived in the illusion of eternal summer, year in and year out."[8] Yet at the time of year when the species was about to migrate, the caged birds became restless. A bird placed in a cage with a glass top and located in a "planetarium" which was evenly illuminated would not orient, but when the artificial sky was flashed upon the domed ceiling, the bird would invariably take a position oriented in the direction which the birds in nature were flying — south east. As the artificial sky was moved to match the appearance of the real sky to a bird flying in the direction that the caged bird was oriented, the bird would maintain this position until its apparent position matched the region of the mouth of the Nile river, then it would change its orientation to south, as the birds in nature turned south to follow the Nile. On one occasion the scientists suddenly shifted the artificial sky so that it represented a change of time of five hours and ten minutes. The investigator reports, "The bird at once showed that it was deeply disturbed. It looked excitedly at the unfamiliar sky and for almost a full minute stood irresolutely. Then it suddenly turned and took wing in the westward direction." Somehow this bird which had been raised in an artificial environment figured out in less than a minute where on earth it should be according to the appearance of a strange sky, and oriented itself to go back to where it really was. As the scientists adjusted the artificial sky, the warbler continued to orient in a homing direction until nearly back to the place where the artificial sky matched the real sky, and then it oriented south east in the direction of its normal migration from that area.

Some of the actions of birds are very stereotyped. Jean George tried in vain to raise a young herring gull without realizing this at first. The bird refused to eat, and food forced down its throat was thrown up again. In nature young herring gulls must tap a red spot on the beak of the parent to be fed. If the young bird fails to do this, the parent will not feed it. When a dab of red color was applied to the author's thumb and held over the young gull, he eagerly struck at the spot and opened his mouth wide for food.[9] This is a strange situation to come about through natural selection.

Bats avoid obstacles and catch insects in flight by emitting high-pitched squeaks and receiving the echo. These sounds are inaudible to the human ear, but some moths can hear them at a distance of at least a hundred feet. Upon hearing the bat, the moth immediately begins performing avoiding reactions. Moths of the family Noctuidae are frequently infested by a kind of mite which lives in the ear, destroying the hearing. If the moths were unable to hear the bats, they would more readily fall prey to them, and the mites would also perish. The mites infest only one of the moth's ears, leaving the other intact. In more than ten thousand infested moths examined, only two had mites in both ears. Although more than ten females and their progenies have been found overcrowding one ear of a moth, the other ear was free of mites and intact. Experimentally nine mites were placed at various points on a moth. Within a short time they had all established themselves in the same ear. Even when a mold began to grow there, making the ear unsuitable for the mites, they swarmed over the head and thorax of the moth but left the other ear unharmed.[10]

Jellyfish and polyps have stinging capsules called nematocysts, which are used both in defense and in the capture of food. They are complicated in structure, and Thomas A. Stephenson, Professor of Zoology at University College, Wales, considers them to be "among the most extraordinary structures to be found in the animal kingdom."[11] But as a defense mechanism they are ineffective against certain sea slugs. The sea slugs not only attack and eat the animals, but they do it without causing the nematocysts to explode. Even more amazingly, the slug can transfer the unexploded capsules from its digestive tract to special sacks in its skin, where they are kept in readiness to explode in defense of the slug should danger threaten. Some of the jellyfish and polyps produce several kinds of nematocysts, and some slugs have the ability to sort out the different kinds and retain for their own use only the more powerful ones, digesting the others with the rest of their food.[12]

The larva of a certain kind of fly feeds on olives. It seems that certain bacteria are necessary to enable the fly to digest the juices of the olive. The fly has at least two adaptations, both of which are necessary to maintain the flies as a species. The larvae have pockets in the esophagus to accommodate the bacteria. The adult female flies have special organs in the oviducts to provide a supply of the proper bacteria to the next generation of flies.[13]

Douglas Dewar, who was not an evolutionist, tells about the remarkable life history of a butterfly named *Maculinea arion*. The eggs are laid on a plant, and after feeding on the plant for several weeks the young caterpillar makes its way to the ground. In order to complete its life cycle, it must meet a certain kind of ant. If and when it meets such an ant, the ant strokes it with its antennae, and the caterpillar exudes a sweet fluid from a special gland on its tenth segment. The ant likes this substance and carries the caterpillar home to its nest. There the ants drink the sweet fluid exuded by the caterpillar, and the caterpillar feasts on larval ants. It winters in a special cavity of the ant's nest, and in the next season it continues eating young ants. Finally in June the time for its pupation arrives, and when it emerges from the pupa as an adult butterfly, its wings delay opening while it crawls through the passages of the ant nest to the outside. When the wings are spread and ready, it flies away to establish more of its kind on the proper kind of plant to start the cycle all over again.[14] It will be noticed in the case of this butterfly, as in the case of some beetles, that the ants cherish a luxury item to the injury of themselves as a species.

It is now well known how the yucca plant and the pronuba moth are dependent upon each other. The moth has been fertilizing the plant in a remarkable way for untold centuries before human beings even suspected that most flowering plants need to be fertilized to set seed. Year after year the moths went about their business fertilizing the flowers while botanists speculated about the function of stamens, and suggested such ridiculous things as the possibility that they served to ventilate the flower. The moth takes pollen from the anther of a stamen, rolls it into a ball, and carries it to another flower, where it places the pollen upon the stigma of the pistil. The moth then lays its eggs in the ovary of the pistil. Thus the yucca is able to develop seeds, and the larvae of the moth are nourished as they eat the developing seeds. But the larvae mature before they eat all the seeds, and so a sufficient number of seeds are spared to produce more yucca plants.

There are many amazing adaptations on the part of plants, particularly among the orchids and legumes, for insuring fertilization by insects. Some flowers are adapted to fertilization by the wind, and generally they lack showy petals and produce no nectar. Other flowers are consructed in such a way as to prevent fertilization by wind or insects, and they fertilize themselves. Still others set seed without fertilization.

There is a spider which builds a dome-shaped, air-tight web beneath the surface of the water and then fills it with air by carrying bubbles down to it from the surface. There are spiders which catch prey by "lassoing" it with a sticky ball of webbing attached to the end of a thread.

There seems to be no end to the marvels of creation, and no doubt there are many more that are not known than there are those which have come to the attention of scientists. But neither any one of them nor all of them together will convince those who would explain all by evolution. Perhaps this is not surprising, for even God's chosen people, who had personally witnessed many remarkable miracles, made a calf of gold at the very time when they knew Moses was on the mountain talking to God; and they worshipped the calf as representing gods which had brought them out of Egypt. But people today are without excuse, as the Israelites who made the calf were without excuse, for, as Paul said, even the heathen people of his day were without excuse for their idolatry because the acts of God are so clearly manifest in nature.

Refusing to accept a plan or purpose in the world leads naturally to the denial of the sovereignty of God. It leads also to the conclusion that man was an improbable outcome of an evolutionary diversification instead of a special creation in the image of God.

George Gaylord Simpson, one of the most renowned evolutionists of our day, says concerning the evolutionary interpretation of the production of man, "As applied to mankind, that interpretation shows that we did not appear all at once but by an almost incredibly long and slow progression. It shows too that there was no anticipation of man's coming. He responds to no plan and fulfills no supernal purpose. He stands alone in the universe, a unique product of a long, unconscious, impersonal, material process, with unique understanding and potentialities. These he owes to no one but himself, and it is to himself that he is responsible. He is not the creature of uncontrolable and undeterminable forces, but his own master. He can and must decide and manage his own destiny."[15]

Loren Eiseley, Professor of Anthropology at the University of Pennsylvania, says that man "did not have to be any more than a butterfly or a caterpillar. He merely emerged from that infinite void for which we have no name."[16]

It is to positions like this that anti-teleological views lead.

In 1794 William Paley published his famous *Evidences of Christianity*. It had gone through twenty-five editions by 1816. His teleological arguments impressed the young Charles Darwin when he was considering whether to take up theology for a career. Darwin later changed his point of view and became a leader of the anti-teleological movement. Professor Kerkut informs us that this book was required reading at Cambridge (where Darwin got his theological degree) and that students had to pass a test on its contents until the year 1927. At this time, when the requirement was abandoned, some professors were still favoring the practice of requiring that the students read the book, though their reason for this may be surprising. They said, "For in this way the student will be forced to realize just how weak the evidence in favor of Christianity really is"![17]

NOTES

1. Bernatowicz, A. J., Teleology in Science Teaching, *Science*, 128: 3336:1402, December 5, 1958.

2. Krauskopf, K., *Fundamentals of Physical Science* (McGraw-Hill, 1953), p. 384.

3. *Science*, 129:3349:129, March 6, 1959.

4. Robertson, D. S., Review of *The Transformist Illusion, Journal of the American Scientific Affiliation*, 12:3:91, September, 1960.

5. Maio, Joseph P., "Predatory Fungi," *Scientific American*, 199:1:67, January, 1958, p. 68.

6. Darwin, Francis, Editor, *More Letters of Charles Darwin* (D. Appleton and Co., 1903), Vol. 1, p. 122.

7. von Frisch, Karl, *The Dancing Bees* (Harcourt, Brace, and Co., 1955), p. 125.

8. Sauer, E. G. F., "Celestial Navigation by Birds," *Scientific American*, 199:2:42, August, 1958.

9. George, Jean, "The Sociable Sea Gull," *Reader's Digest*. August, 1963, p. 109.

10. Treat, A. E., "A Case of Peculiar Parasitism," *Natural History*, 67: 8:366, August, 1958. J. L. Cloudsley-Thompson, *Animal Behavior* (Macmillan, 1961), p. 112.

11. Stephenson, Thomas A., *Encyclopedia Britannica*. "Coelenterata," 1957, Vol. 5, p. 938.

12. See J. A. Colin Nichol, *The Biology of Marine Animals* (Interscience Publishers, 1960), p. 375.

13. See Marston Bates, *The Nature of Natural History* (Charles Scribner's Sons, 1950), p. 130.

14. See Douglas Dewar, *The Transformist Illusion* (Dehoff Publications, 1957), p. 259.

15. Simpson, George Gaylord, *Life of the Past* (Yale University Press, 1953), p. 155.

16. Eiseley, Loren, "The Time of Man," *Horizon*, 4:4:4, March, 1962, p. 10.

17. Kerkut, G. S., *Implications of Evolution* (Pergamon Press, 1960), p. 2.

FAITH

Evolutionists commonly say with an air of depreciation that Christians depend on faith while the evolutionists have facts. The fact is that evolutionists also depend on faith, while Christians also have facts. Since evolutionists and Christian anti-evolutionists both have facts and both depend upon faith, the final question is: Upon what will *you* place *your* faith?

In the first place, as previously mentioned, most evolutionists have faith in the uniformity of nature, which excludes miracles and other manifestations of supernatural acts of God. They have faith that all life on earth could have come about and did come about through the interaction of blind forces acting upon the kinds of material which were available before there was any life.

W. W. Wheeler, the great entomologist, said concerning faith in supernatural acts of God versus natural causes in evolution, "There is no question as to which of these explanations [supernatural or natural] the scientist and philosopher must prefer, for as Joseph McCabe [a strongly anti-Christian philosopher and former Catholic priest] says, 'no plea for the supernatural origin of anything is valid so long as there is a possibility of a natural explanation of its origin.'"[1]

George E. Hutchinson, Professor of Zoology at Yale University, goes even further and says that if there is no choice, instead of accepting the supernatural acts of God, the scientist may have to assume that there have been changes in the laws of nature. "The conditions under which life could originate can be analyzed into a number of geochemical questions which are probably ultimately soluble. When their solution is effected, experimental models could be set up initiating the most probable primitive conditions. Some attempts of this sort have of course been made, but no positive results of very great interest have been obtained. *If the results are persistently negative, it may be necessary to fall back on some hypothesis as to secular change in the laws of nature. . . .*"[2] (Italics are not in the original.) One of Darwin's biographers said that Darwin always gave God a chance, but modern evolutionists like Professor Hutchinson do not give God a chance.

The scientific method is an inductive method, based upon repeated observations. When a scientific explanation of a phenomenon is sought, the ultimate answer is that one event is assumed to be the cause of another because the one is always observed to follow the other. A possible uncertainty remains as to whether a certain event will always follow another just because it has always been observed to do so in the past. To believe that it will do so involves an element of faith.

The scientific method may be illustrated by an experiment which is one of the most famous of all time. When Louis Pasteur perfected a vaccine against the dreaded disease of anthrax, the first such vaccine ever made, his adversaries challenged him, and he agreed to a public experiment. The basis for Pasteur's hopes for demonstrating the effectiveness of his vaccine was fourteen successful trials in his laboratory. Since it had happened this many times in the laboratory, he had sufficient faith that it would happen again that he accepted the challenge. The experiment began on April 28, 1881, at Pouilly de Fort in France. Much was at stake. Anthrax killed large numbers of domesticated animals and also it was fatal to human beings. Also, if Pasteur proved to be right, the germ theory of disease would be established and the classical theories of medicine would be outmoded. In the experiment thirty-one animals were vaccinated and twenty-nine were not. Then all of them were inocculated with anthrax germs. Pasteur himself became uneasy at this stage of the experiment, and questioned whether he should have made more than fourteen test runs in the laboratory before announcing the vaccine. But soon all the animals which had not been vaccinated showed symptoms of anthrax, and within two days nearly all of them had died. None of the vaccinated animals developed symptoms of the disease.

The eminent George Gaylord Simpson says concerning the inductive nature of the scientific method, "The concept of 'truth' in science is thus quite special. It implies nothing eternal and absolute but only a high degree of confidence after adequate self-testing and self-correcting."[3] Professor Simpson says further that "above the level of triviality there is hardly any scientific subject on which agreement is literally universal."[4] He says that the most fundamental reason for disagreement in science is the inherent impossibility of complete certainty. He points out that "*one* fact may disprove a theory and not *all* facts can be observed; therefore an investigator cannot completely discard the possibility that a discrepant phenomenon may occur." He further points out that "in any complex situation the data are rarely so complete that only *one* explanation can conceivably be correct." In other words, there are likely to be rival theories.

If these things can be said about science in general, it is evident that they apply much more to something like the theory of evolution, which cannot be tested directly by the scientific method. Dr. Simpson, himself a renowned evolutionist, says in the same article, "Sometimes theories go beyond that which is testable, by means now available, at least. Such aspects of theories are, for that reason, not scientific in fact, and the disagreement is in the field of philosophy and not of science." He adds parenthetically that he believes it is essential for scientists to philosophize, but they should know when they are doing it. It is interesting to note in this paper that Dr.

Simpson says that theology now comes within the scope of science, and he classifies it under the heading of "animal behavior."

Many phenomena have been observed so regularly to occur under certain conditions that they are taken for granted, and it is not realized that faith in the uniformity of nature is being exercised. But the situation is quite different with regard to the theory of evolution, for many alleged phenomena in the evolution of life are mysterious, and to accept them requires faith.

Professor J. Arthur Thompson, Professor of Natural History at the University of Aberdeen, expressed faith in the theory of evolution in this strange way: "It stands more firmly than ever, except that we are more keenly aware than in Darwin's day of our ignorance as to the origin and affinities of the great classes. But, frankly, the only scientific way of looking at the present-day fauna and flora is to regard them as the outcome of a natural selection."[5]

The evolutionary derivation of animals with backbones from animals without backbones has always been a difficult problem. John M. Taylor, Professor Emeritus of Biology at Amhurst College, said, "How some ancient ancestor had succeeded in developing bone, in many respects the most marvellous tissue of our bodies, is beyond my comprehension. He did it."[6] Concerning the evolution of vertebrates from invertebrates, Professor Hooton of Harvard said, "All this is complicated, obscure, and dubious. Anyway there evolved from the invertebrates a tribe of animals that, by hook or by crook, had acquired backbones."[7]

Professor Hooton also points out that "As a matter of fact, every phylum except the molluscs has been suggested as the ancestor of the vertebrates."[8]

Professor William Patten of Dartmouth was noted, among other things, for deriving the vertebrates and ourselves from the spider group. Concerning this, William K. Gregory of the American Museum of Natural History commented, "According to Professor Patten of Dartmouth, the vertebrates were derived from the arachnid stem. . . . But if these disagreeable creatures are our remote relatives, then the highly developed head which they had acquired after so many millions of years of struggle all had to be largely made over when the vertebrate stage of organization was reached. They had to sacrifice their elaborate leg-jaw apparatus, their very mouths were stopped and a new mouth and jaws formed, their eyes were turned upside down and inside out, and a new set of swimming organs had to be developed."[9] Either Professor Patten had much faith in evolution or else he was unaware of the problems which Dr. Gregory pointed out.

A generation or so ago the earthworm group was favored as ancestors of the vertebrates, and certain aspects of the human body were said to indicate that we evolved from an ancestor which had repeated similar segments, like an earthworm. Now the starfish group is favored. This group does not have repeated segments as the earthworms do, but other features are used for comparison, and the segments are forgotten.

It takes faith to believe that land animals evolved from fish. Professor Hooton says, "Just how fins developed into limbs is still a mystery — but they did."[10]

In making a case for the evolution of "true land animals" from amphibians, perhaps the most difficult feature to explain is the origin of the egg suited for hatching on land. Such an egg must have a number of features which are very different from the eggs of fishes and amphibians. Professor Alfred Romer of Harvard considers this, and says that a supernatural agency (God) is not necessary to explain the origin of an egg of this kind. His explanation is that aquatic animals acquired lungs because lungs have an advantage while the animal is still in the water; they developed limbs in the place of fins because limbs are advantageous even while the animals still dwell in the water; and they developed eggs which could be laid on land, because this also had an advantage.[11] He does not intend this to sound like Lamarckism, but it does sound somewhat that way, and Lamarck was criticized by those who interpreted his writings to imply evolution through a need or "desire" for certain adaptations. At any rate, Professor Romer's explanation seems to require a certain amount of faith.

The impression is frequently given that birds are so much like reptiles that the evolution of birds is no problem at all. But J. Arthur Thomson admits difficulties and acknowledges a need of faith, as he says, "Our frankness in admitting difficulties and relative ignorance in regard to the variations and selections that led from certain dinosaurs to birds cannot be used by any fairminded inquirer as an argument against the idea of evolution. For how else could birds have arisen?"[12]

George Gaylord Simpson lists five hypotheses which may be considered in seeking an explanation of the origin of horses.[13] One of these hypotheses is that a pair of animals known as condylarths "suddenly gave birth to a litter of Dawn Horses." Concerning this he says, "In the nature of things this hypothesis cannot be ruled out categorically and some respectable scientists support it. Nevertheless it is so improbable as to be unacceptable *unless we can find no hypothesis more likely to explain the facts.*" (Italics are not in the original.) He is saying that if he cannot find a hypothesis better than one which he considers to be essentially unacceptable, he is willing to accept the unacceptable one.

Roy Chapman Andrews of the American Museum of Natural History had such faith in Dr. Franz Weidenreich, the anthropologist, that when Weidenreich published the view, contrary to that held by others, that the Java man, *Pithecanthropus erectus,* was our direct ancestor, Andrews said, "It is comforting to know who was one of our most remote ancestors and that we need no longer wear the bar-sinister across our escutcheons."[14]

One could go on citing examples of the kind of faith evolutionists have. This kind of faith goes far beyond the previously-mentioned faith in the uniformity of nature, which is basic to the scientific method.

In 1921 the British botanist D. H. Scott, said, "A new generation has grown up which knows not Darwin. Is even then evolution not a scientifically ascertained fact? No! We must hold it as an act of faith because there is no alternative."[16]

T. Christie Innes wrote a tract called *Darwinism: Faith or Science?* Below are some statements he collected which were made by evolutionary scientists.

William Bateson, Professor of Biology at Cambridge University, said, "We have the impression that it is only by extraordinary acts of faith that biologists can suppose that the actual progress of life can be explained in the terms they adopt!"[17]

D. M. S. Watson, Professor of Zoology in London University, said, "Evolution is a theory universally accepted, not because it can be proved to be true, but because the only alternative, 'special creation,' is clearly impossible."[18] This is quoted from the presidential address before the British Association for the Advancement of Science.

A Professor A. P. Kelly is quoted as having said, "One of my university students said to me, 'We are determined to believe evolution, not because it is true nor that we believe there is any evidence for it, but because it has become the symbol of our liberalism.'"[19]

W. T. Calman of the Zoology Section of the British Museum said,

"We all, even the youngest of us, profess to accept the doctrine of evolution, if only as a convenient weapon with which to meet the fundamentalists."[20]

As Professor Hooton said, all of this is very confusing. But one thing is clear. Evolutionists *do* exercise faith.

NOTES

1. Mason, Frances, Editor, *Creation by Evolution*, (Duckworth, 1934), p. 211.

2. Hutchinson, George F., *Encyclopedia Britannica*, "Biology," 1957, Vol. 3, p. 601.

3. Simpson, George Gaylord, *Notes on the Nature of Science* (Harcourt, Brace, and World, 1962), p. 11.

4. *Ibid.*, p. 7.

5. Thomson, J. Arthur, *The Outline of Science* (G. P. Putnam's Sons, 1922), Vol. 2, p. 365.

6. Tyler, John M., *The Coming of Man* (Marshall Jones Co., 1925), p. 28.

7. Hooton, Ernest Albert, *Up from the Ape* (Macmillan, 1947), p. 57.

8. *Ibid.*, p. 56.

9. Gregory, William K., *Our Face from Fish to Man* (G. P. Putnam's Sons, 1929), p. 7.

10. Hooton, Ernest Albert, *Apes, Men, and Morons* (G. P. Putnam's Sons, 1937), p. 78.

11. Romer, Alfred S., "Origin of the Amniote Egg," *Scientific Monthly*, 85:2:57, August, 1957.

12. Thomson, J. Arthur, *loc. cit.*, p. 368.

13. Simpson, George Gaylord, "The Great Animal Invasion," *Natural History*, 49:4:206, April, 1942.

14. Andrews, Roy Chapman, *Meet Your Ancestors* (The Viking Press, 1945), p. 73.

15. Howell, A. Brasier, *Aquatic Animals* (Charles C. Thomas, 1930), pp. 34, 35.

16. Scott, D. H., "Presidential Address," *Nature*, 108:2709:153, September 29, 1921.

17. Bateson, William, *The Limitations of Science* (Chatto and Windus, 1933), p. 200.

18. Watson, D. M. S., London *Times*, August 3, 1929.

19. Betts, E. H., "Evolution and Entropy," *Journal of the Transactions of the Victoria Institute*, 76:1, 1944, p. 23.

20. *Proceedings of the Linnean Society*, 147th Session, p. 145.

FANTASY

Nominal Christian organizations are declaring more and more that the Scriptural account of creation is a myth or fable. Defending the

Bible has become so unpopular that anti-evolutionary writing needs to be heavily documented. On the other hand, evolutionists may glibly make all sorts of extravagant and fantastic statements without fear of contradiction or ridicule.

Professor William Etkin of the College of the City of New York says in the college textbook he wrote, "We are but fish made over, and, although the job of alteration is a good one, the original plan shows through here and there somewhat like the original design of a house that has been remodeled."[1]

Professor William Howells, writing while at the University of Wisconsin, agreed with this, and said, "Man . . . is a modified fish."[2]

Professor William K. Gregory of the American Museum of Natural History and Columbia University thinks it is very important that we be aware of our ancestry from the fish. He says, "How much arrogance, deceit, and wickedness would have been spared the world, if man had realized that even the most imposing human faces are but madeover fishtraps, concealed behind a smiling mask, but still set with sharp teeth inherited from ferocious pre-mammalian forebears."[3] This flight into fantasy is spoiled by statistics which show that wickedness is increasing faster than population growth, although our evolution from lower forms is accepted more widely today than at any time in the past.

As Associate Professor of Anthropology at the University of Wisconsin, William Howells published a book on evolution called *Mankind So Far*. Of the tree shrew, a small mammal, he wrote, "There is no difficulty in showing, in full detail, that a primitive insectivore is a hairy, four-footed, air-breathing, warm-blooded, live-bearing, tree-going fish."[4] Twelve years later, as Professor of Anthropology at Harvard University, he rewrote the book as *Mankind in the Making*. By this time it was decided that tree shrews are primates instead of primitive insectivores, but otherwise he liked the statement so well that he included it again with very little change: "We can plainly see that a tree shrew is a hairy, four-footed, air-breathing, warm-blooded, live-bearing, tree-going fish."[5]

Professor J. B. S. Haldane of the University of London sees clearly a stage in evolution somewhat earlier than typical fish, and says, "The following stages in human ancestry are quite clear. Four hundred million years ago our ancestors were fish (if you can call them fish) without lower jaws or paired fins."[6]

As already mentioned, evolutionists now believe that our closest relatives among the invertebrates are members of the starfish group. Back in 1925, George A. Dorsey of the University of Chicago and the American Museum of Natural History said that the fact that our system of numbers is based upon *ten* may be due to our invertebrate ancestry. He said, "Possibly our decimal system is due to the five-fingered hands inherited from a starfish ancestor."[7] This is indeed quite a flight into fantasy, and a remarkable statement for an evolutionist to make. Although we are said to be most closely related to the starfish group, this does not mean that evolutionists believe we had starfish for ancestors. An evolutionist would say that starfish are far too specialized to be in our line of ancestry, and that we and the starfish both descended from some common more generalized ancestor. It is assumed that this ancestor had bilateral symmetry, as we do and as the larva of a starfish does, and not radial symmetry like a starfish. The radial development of the starfish is thought to have come about *after* they diverged from our line of descent. Thus the five-parted body of the starfish has nothing to do with the five digits at the extremities of the appendages of our bilaterally symmetrical bodies.

A temporary defeat may, in the end, be a real advantage. Professor Eiseley tells us that when our ancestors came down out of the trees the first time, they were chased back up again by the rodents. This was fortunate, for if they had stayed on the ground, all of their descendants would have been four-footed animals, and human beings never would have evolved. He says, ". . . through several million years . . . the primate order, instead of being confined to the trees, was experimenting to some extent with the same grassland burrowing life that the rodents later perfected. The success of these burrowers crowded the primates out of their environment and forced them back into the domain of the branches. . . . Our ancient relatives, it appeared, were beaten in their attempt to expand upon the ground. . . . The shabby pseudorat [that's our ancestor] . . . had ascended again into the green twilight of the rain forest. The chatterers with the ever-growing teeth [that's the rodents] were his masters. The sunlight and the grass belonged to them. It is conceivable that except for the invasion of the rodents, the primate line might even have abandoned the trees. We might be there on the grass, you and I, barking in the highplains sunlight."[8]

Since we live on the ground, Professor Eiseley and the other evolutionists must bring our ancestors down from the trees. Carleton

Coon, Professor of Anthropology at Harvard University, says that having arrived at the monkey stage in the evolutionary process, our ancestors were forced to the ground because of the disappearance of forested areas. With the disappearance of the trees, our ancestors were deprived of their former food of fruits and seeds, and had to subsist on grubs and meat left by the larger predators. "Somewhere in the tropical regions of the earth, probably in Africa, a band of large monkeys lived in a forest. Every morning at daybreak they awoke, and the males began calling to their families to follow them to the feeding grounds. [This sounds as if it ought to start out, "once upon a time."] There they spent most of the day, picking fruit, peeling and eating it, and robbing bird's nests of their eggs and their fledglings. As time went on, however, the fruit became scarcer, and when the monkeys tried to move to another part of the forest they found their way blocked. Every way they turned they came to the edge of the trees, and all about them was grass. They were trapped. As the fruit and fledglings failed them, they had no choice but to climb down to the ground. In their frantic search for food they learned to lift up stones to collect insects and grubs. . . . After a while, however, the climate changed once more and the forest crept back over the plain. Some of the descendants of the monkeys that had learned to walk upright went back to the forest, where they became the ancestors of the apes. Only those upright ones that stayed out in the open grew to be men."[9]

Professor Eiseley brings us down from the trees as apes instead of as monkeys, and in a situation just the opposite of the one previously described. He says that it was because of the *abundance* of fruit that our ancestors were able to survive on the ground. "On the edge of the forest, a strange, old-fashioned animal still hesitated. . . . He had a passion for lifting himself up to see about, in his restless, roving curiosity. He would run a little stiffly and uncertainly, perhaps, on his hind legs, but only on those rare moments when he ventured out upon the ground. . . . He was a ne'er-do-well, an in-betweener. Nature had not done well by him. It was as if she had hesitated and never quite made up her mind. Perhaps as a consequence he had a malicious gleam in his eye, the gleam of an outcast who has been left nothing and knows he is going to have to take what he gets. One day a band of these odd apes — for apes they were — shambled out upon the grass; the human story had begun. Apes were to become men, in the inscrutable wisdom of nature, because flowers had produced seeds and fruits in such tremendous quantities that a new and totally different store of energy had become available in concentrated form."[10]

Professor Eiseley summarizes the history of the two-hundred-inch telescope on Mount Palomar as follows. "A billion years have gone into the making of that eye; the water and the salt and the vapors of the sun have built it; things that squirmed in the tide silts have devised it."[11] He repeats his confidence in the evolutionary powers of nature by saying, "It gives me a feeling of confidence to see nature still busy with experiments, still dynamic, and not through or satisfied because a Devonian fish managed to end as a two-legged character with a straw hat."[12]

He sees no purpose in the evolution of man from the fish, but he feels compassion because of the discomfort suffered by the fish as it first came to land from the water. "Do not look for the purpose. Think of the way we came and be a little proud. Think of this hand — the utter pain of its first venture on the pebbly shore."[13] If we had to depend on a fish for our existence, and if the pain in coming out of the water had been so great, the fish would not have come out but would have flopped back into the water, and we never would have been. But the One who made us also suffered for us. He permitted His hands to be pierced in crucifixion that we might be redeemed and be with Him eternally. Evolutionists cannot believe this because evolution denies the historicity of the fall of man through disobedience, which made redemption necessary.

Concerning a catfish which he found trapped in the ice, Professor Eiseley says, "He lived with me all that winter. . . . One night when no one was about, he simply jumped out of his tank. I found him dead on the floor next morning. . . . 'Some of your close relatives have been experimenting with air breathing,' I remarked, apropos of nothing, as I gathered him up. 'Suppose we meet again up there in the cottonwoods in a million years or so.' I missed him a little as I said it."[14]

NOTES

1. Etkin, William, *College Biology* (Thomas Y. Crowell Co., 1950), p. 487.

2. Howells, William, *Mankind So Far* (Doubleday and Co., 1944), p. 18.

3. Gregory, William D., *Our Face from Fish to Man* (G. P. Putnam's Sons, 1929), p. 153.

4. Howells, William, *loc. cit.*, p. 107.

5. Howells, William, *Mankind in the Making* (Doubleday and Co., 1959), p. 123.

6. Haldane, J. B. S., *What Is Life?* (Boni and Gaer, 1947), p. 79.

7. Dorsey, George A., *Why We Behave Like Human Beings* (Harper and Bros., 1925), p. 76.

8. Eiseley, Loren, *The Immense Journey* (Random House, 1957), p. 8 ff.

9. Coon, Carleton, *The Story of Man* (Borzoi Books, 1954, 4th printing, 1958), p. 11.

10. Eiseley, Loren, *loc. cit.*, pp. 74, 75.

11. *Ibid.*, p. 45.

12. *Ibid.*, p. 47.

13. *Ibid.*, p. 7.

14. *Ibid.*, pp. 23, 24.

OBJECTIVITY

Some time ago a popular film was produced to enlighten Christian young people on the subject of evolution. It strongly portrayed scientists as honest and objective in their appraisal of evidence for and against theories in general and the theory of evolution in particular. But scientists have the weaknesses of other human beings, and for some reason they become more emotional about the matter of evolution than about anything else that comes under the heading of science. In writing about evolution, scientists make extravagant statements such as chemists and physicists would never do in their fields. A number of them feel it desirable or necessary to make disparaging statements about the Bible. Biologists in the classroom have threatened to give low grades or to fail students who did not profess to accept the theory of evolution.

Discussing the Swanscombe skull, Professor Keith said that it is more modern in appearance than would have been expected, considering the location where it was found. He further says that if such discoveries are in accord with expectations, no one doubts their significance; but if they are not in accord with expectations they are doubted or even rejected. Of the Galley Hill skull he says that either it is of "Chellean time" or else the geological record is at fault, and comments, "Modern authorities [this was in 1929], almost without exception, when faced with this alternative, reject the geological record, preferring to believe in the rapid mutability of the human body and the recent evolution of modern man."[1] Since that time there has been another change of view on this matter, but human nature has not changed and scientists cannot always be relied upon for expressing objectivity.

Professor Keith also said, "If human remains were found in one of the older Pleistocene deposits, and they proved to be modern in size and shape, they were rejected as spurious antiques, no matter what the state of their fossilization might be. On the other hand, if these remains proved unmodern in character, then they were accepted as genuinely old, even if only imperfectly fossilized. It seemed to me then, as it does now, that, in this matter, the geologist's dice were so heavily loaded that it was scarcely possible for modern man to have a fair throw."[2]

Professor Loren Eiseley of the University of Pennsylvania says of the Foxhall jaw: "At all events after it had passed under many eyes, interest waned, *largely because the jaw was modern in appearance.* . . . Since there was nothing about it that the anatomist would surely regard as primitive, interest quickly faded. Only time will tell how many other ancient human relics have been discarded simply because they did not fit a preconceived evolutionary scheme."[3]

Professor Franz Weidenreich of the University of Chicago tells that the anatomist J. Kollmann did not accept *Pithecanthropus* as belonging to the line of human evolution when other evolutionists did accept it, because he had a theory that our ancestors were small, while *Pithecanthropus* was tall. Dr. Weidenreich comments, "This is a striking example of the extent to which paleontological facts are disregarded and replaced with purely speculative constructions when the evolution of man was the topic and when facts did not agree with preconceived ideas."[4]

J. S. Weiner of Oxford University said, "For instance the Galley Hill skull, which was discovered as long ago as 1888 in the Thames valley was apparently attributable to the end of the long second interglacial period. But this and other such finds were then unacceptable largely because the general opinion at that time would not admit the appearance of *Homo sapiens* earlier than Neanderthal man's."[5]

Professor Weidenreich also discusses the way Thomas Henry Huxley arranged skeletons for an illustration. He says, "But Huxley placed more emphasis on similarities in his illustration than on dissimilarities, because he wanted to show that the organization of the human skeleton is, in principle, that of an anthropoid. Therefore he depicted the great apes in an 'erect' position but man in a not completely erect one."[6]

Professor Romer, the outstanding comparative anatomist of Harvard University, says concerning the early decades of the present century, "There remained, however, a large number of Paleozoic fossils . . . which did not fit well into the general evolutionary picture nor into any familiar group. . . . A common solution was to ignore them. . . . They were in general treated rather as appendages to the recognized groups, as undesirable excrescences on an otherwise well-rounded evolutionary structure. . . . The evolutionary story is not the simple one which we have believed; and much of it was, it would seem, erroneous."[7]

The scandal connected with Ernst Haeckel's falsifications of the drawings of embryos in order to support his recapitulation theory is well known. Concerning this recapitulation theory, Professor Alfred Huettner of Queens College said, "At its most dominant period its ever accumulating 'exceptions' and defects were diligently overlooked. . . ."[8] Concerning Haeckel's blastea-gastrea theory, which was an important part of his recapitulation theory and which has been presented in textbooks ever since the early days of Darwinism, Professor John Tyler Bonner of Princeton University says, "We may have known for almost a hundred years that Haeckel's blastea-gastrea theory of the origin of the metazoa [that is, the many-celled animals] is probably nonsense, but it is so clear-cut, so simple, so easy to hand full-blown to the student."[9]

Opinions about some of these things may still change, but the point is that when it comes to evolution, scientists are not all objective or even honest in their approach to the problems.

NOTES

1. Keith, Arthur, *The Antiquity of Man* (Williams and Norgate, 1929), Vol. 1, p. 266.

2. *Ibid.*, p. xi.

3. Eiseley, Loren, *The Immense Journey* (Random House, 1957), p. 18.

4. Weidenreich, Franz, *Apes, Giants, and Men* (University of Chicago Press, 1946), p. 47.

5. Weiner, S. J., *Man's Ancestry. New Biology* #5, 1948, p. 87.

6. Weidenreich, Franz, *loc. cit.*, pp. 6, 7.

7. Romer, Alfred S. "The Early Evolution of Fishes," *Quarterly Review of Biology*, 2:1, March, 1946, p. 35.

8. Huettner, Alfred F., *Comparative Embryology of the Vertebrates*, Rev. ed. (Macmillan, 1949), p. 5.

9. Bonner, John Tyler, Review of: *Implications of Evolution*, by G. A. Kerkut, *American Scientist*, 49:2:240, June, 1961, p. 242.

CHAPTER IV

APPROACHES TO THE THEORY OF EVOLUTION

I. ATHEISTIC EVOLUTION

It is not intended to mean or to imply that the evolutionists quoted here are atheists or even agnostics, though some of them may be. What is to be considered is the atheistic approach to the problem of evolution. Information about the theory of evolution found in scientific literature is almost entirely from an atheistic point of view, in the sense that acts of God are not taken into consideration.

When performing his experiments in the laboratory, the scientist has faith in the uniformity of nature and believes that anyone repeating his work anywhere and at any time under the same conditions will get the same result. Thus scientists can discuss their research without referring to God. But discussions about evolution are different. No one but God was there when life began. Most of the evidence of evolution is circumstantial and cannot be repeated. Laboratory experiments which deal with evolution are limited to changes of such kinds as cannot be shown to have been able to produce more complex forms of life from simpler forms.

It is the opinion of evolutionists, expressed over and over, that only the uninformed, the ignorant, and the bigoted do not accept evolution as a fact. This has been repeated so many times that people are afraid of being called ignorant if they express any doubts about the truth of evolution.

Although any public library will yield quantities of statements affirming that the biologists consider evolution to be an established fact, it is possible to find statements to the contrary. For example, the following statement occurs in a book written by Ernst Mayr and others. Professor Mayr is of the University of California and the American Museum of Natural History. He admits: "Every one of the

164

sources of information on phylogeny [evolution] that has been used in the past has its limitations and pitfalls. This is true of genetics, physiology (including serology), embryology, and zoogeography. It is even true of paleontology, because there are several interpretations possible for many fossil remains, particularly if they are incomplete."[1] Dr. Alan Boyden of Rutgers University says, "Actually we shall never be able to prove the common ancestry of all animals, and therefore we have no right to state as a fundamental principle what must always remain an assumption."[2]

Professor Theodosius Dobzhansky of Columbia University says, "It would be wrong to say that the biological theory of evolution has gained universal acceptance among biologists or even among geneticists. . . . Its acceptance is nevertheless so wide that its opponents complain of inability to get a hearing for their views."[3]

Two interesting, though not typical, statements which show to what extremes scientists can go on the matter of evolution are the following. C. H. Waddington of Oxford University said that evolution now enables us to give an exact definition of the terms *right* and *wrong* — right being that which helps and wrong that which hinders evolution.[4] Calvin S. Hall of Western Reserve University said, "You may question, of course, whether rat intelligence is the same as human intelligence, but if you do put the question you are really not an evolutionist, and therefore your views deserve little serious consideration."[5] It would hardly be possible to formulate a sentence less worthy of inclusion in a scientific journal.

Following is a selection of more typical statements.

Horatio Hockett Newman of the University of Chicago said, "There is no rival hypothesis except the outworn and completely refuted idea of special creation, now retained only by the ignorant, the dogmatic, and the prejudiced."[6]

William Howells of the University of Wisconsin said, "The 'theory of evolution' is an overworked term, in the popular usage, and unfortunate besides, since it implies that, after all, there may be something dubious about it. Evolution is a fact, like digestion."[7]

William Patten of Dartmouth wrote, "Evolution itself has long since passed out of the field of scientific controversy. There is no other subject on which scientific opinion is so completely unanimous. It is the one great truth we most surely know."[8]

Gordon Alexander of the University of Colorado said, "The proofs of evolution are not merely adequate; they are overwhelming. The fact of organic evolution is a part of the thinking of every individual who may properly call himself a biologist."[9]

Gilbert M. Smith of Stanford University wrote, "No one who, since the publication of [Darwin's] *Origin of Species* in 1859, has impartially investigated this evidence has questioned the validity or the usefulness of the idea of continuous evolution."[10]

Michael F. Guyer of the University of Wisconsin said, "The fact that every biologist who understands the exhaustive study of the evidence comes to the conclusion that living organisms do exhibit such evolutionary relationships surely indicates the reliability of the conclusion. If we cannot take the word of the specialist in his own field, whose word can we accept?"[11]

Paul Weatherwax of Indiana University said, "The doctrine is no longer questioned by any biologist."[12]

Edwin Grant Conklin of Princeton University said essentially the same thing, "The fact of evolution is no longer questioned by men of science."[13]

Marston Bates of Harvard University complained, "Most books on evolution take up a lot of space with the review of the evidence that some process of evolution has taken place. There is no more question of this among contemporary scientists than there is of the relative movements of the planets within the solar system. . . ."[14]

One could go on, seemingly endlessly, quoting scientists and authors of textbooks of biological science to the effect that evolution is a fact and all scientists accept it as such.

Although Darwin's fame came quickly, he did not convince the men of science as rapidly as we have been led to believe. His friend and geology teacher, Adam Sedgwick, was not converted to a belief in evolution by Darwin's *Origin of Species*, and he wrote of it: "We venture to affirm that no man who has any name in science, properly so-called . . . has spoken well of the book, or regarded it with any feelings but those of deep aversion. We say this advisedly, after exchanging thoughts with some of the best-informed men in Britain."[15]

Nearly thirty years after the publication of the *Origin of Species*, on the fifth of March, 1888, another Sedgwick, William T. Sedgwick, Professor of Biology at the Massachusetts Institute of Technology, wrote a letter to Edward S. Morse, Director of the Peabody Academy of Science. Professor Morse had on many occasions written and lectured in defense of the theory of evolution, and Professor Sedgwick wrote him concerning a future lecture. In the final paragraph of the letter he said, "I find in short that with these vigorous attacks upon Darwinism and no defenders, our cause bids fair to middle, as it has already mystified a lot of the 'laity.' For heaven's sake then do give them a little sound evolutionary doctrine and don't fail to say, 'as is agreed by all but a very few.' Let us not have Darwin trodden on without at least an answer."[16]

Thus about thirty years after the publication of the *Origin of Species* a lecturer on evolution was urged to tell the people that the truth of the theory of evolution was at that time accepted by all but a very few, although it was at the same time admitted that this was not so.

The essence of atheistic evolution is that evolution is a fact and that the evolution of living creatures can be explained apart from the concept of God. Some postulate that the evolutionary process was initiated by a force of some kind, which may be referred to as God or called by some other name.

George Gaylord Simpson strongly objects to the idea that atheistic evolution means evolution by *chance*. Julian Huxley implies the same thing. They point out that natural selection is a directive force. Nature *selects* the best from among chance mutations, the term *best* referring to those most suited to the environment in which they find themselves, so that they are somewhat more likely than others to reach the age of reproductive maturity.

NOTES

1. Mayr, Ernst, *et al., Methods and Principles of Systematic Zoology* (McGraw-Hill, 1953), p. 42.

2. Boyden, Alan, "Systematic Zoology; A Critical Appreciation. Part I. Systematic Serology and Its Relation to General Biology." *Physiological Zoology,* 15:2:109, April, 1942, p. 117.

3. Dobzhansky, Theodosius, "Evolutionary and Population Genetics," *Science,* 142:3596:1131, November 29, 1963, p. 1134.

4. Waddington, C. H., Cited by R. E. D. Clark, *Darwin Before and After* (Paternoster Press, 1958), p. 121.

5. Hall, Calvin S., "The Inheritance of Emotionality," *Sigma Xi Quarterly,* 26:1, March, 1938, p. 19.

6. Newman, Horatio Hockett, *Evolution, Genetics, and Eugenics* (University of Chicago Press, 1932, Printing of 1939), p. 51.

7. Howells, William, *Mankind So Far* (Doubleday and Co., 1947), p. 5.

8. Patten, William, "The Ways of Men, Apes, and Fishes," *Scientific Monthly,* 31:4:289, October, 1930, p. 290.

9. Alexander, Gordon, *General Biology* (Thomas Y. Crowell, 1956), p. 808.

10. Smith, Gilbert, *et al.*, *A Textbook of General Botany*, 4th ed. (Macmillan, 1942), p. 630.

11. Guyer, Michael F., *Speaking of Man* (Harper and Bros., 1942), p. 302.

12. Weatherwax, Paul, *Plant Biology* (W. B. Saunders, 1942), p. 370.

13. Conklin, Edwin Grant, *Man, Real and Ideal* (Charles Scribner's Sons, 1943), p. 28.

14. Bates, Marston, *The Nature of Natural History* (Charles Scribner's Sons, 1950), p. 222.

15. Clark, R. E. D., *loc. cit.*, p. 49.

16. Dexter, Ralph W., "An Early Defense of Darwinism, *"The American Naturalist*, 93:869:138, March-April, 1959.

II. THEISTIC EVOLUTION

Theistic evolution is as old as the acceptance of evolution by the nominal Christian church. Those who hold this position consider evolution to be a fact, but they believe that it has been divinely directed instead of coming about through natural processes. It is frequently said by those who advocate theistic evolution that it is a grander concept to think of God working in this way than to think of Him producing living creatures by fiat creation. However, what is important is what the Bible says, and not what men may think is grander.

Theistic evolution contradicts the Bible both historically and doctrinally. As to the historical approach, there is one fact which should forever settle the matter for Bible-believing Christians. There is a fact which cannot possibly be wrested and fitted into an evolutionary interpretation. It is expressly stated in Scripture that Eve was formed from a portion of the side of Adam, which the Lord removed for that purpose. This is usually said to be a rib, for the term is so translated in the King James version of the Bible. Since the Bible plainly states that the first woman was formed from a part taken from the side of the first man, we are given a detail of creation which cannot be forced into any theory of evolution.

Denying the historical accuracy of the Bible in the account of creation leads to a doctrinal position known as *modernism*. If men evolved from the beast, the sin nature is an inherited animal characteristic and cannot be due to the fall of man through disobedience.

This denies the need of a Redeemer, and thus the atonement of Christ is neglected or denied.

Theistic evolution is accepted by the liberal Christian church, but it is now also invading the conservative evangelical fold. As an illustration, let us consider the book *Science Returns to God*, by James H. Jauncey.[1] The author professes that his view of the Bible is "the traditional, or conservative, view which claims that the Bible in its entirety is the word of God and, as such, is accurate in everything that it says in every branch of knowledge, including science and history."[2]

Concerning the problem of Christian faith versus the theory of evolution he says, "However, there is evidence on every hand that the conflict seems to be disappearing. There are a great number of biologists who at least tentatively believe in evolution, but who nevertheless are active members of Christian churches and find no problem at all. The general attitude is that even if evolution were to prove true, instead of making God unnecessary, it would merely show that this was the method God used."[3] This, of course, is theistic evolution. It is evident that if the conflict is disappearing in this manner, it is disappearing because more and more people are taking evolutionary views for granted.

At another place in the book he says that "this kind of thinking would consider the evolutionary process as the means that God is using. The point that the author wishes to make here is that even if the origin of man from the evolutionary hypothesis were proved to be correct, there still would be no insoluble difficulty for the Christian interpreter."[4] Thus, as an expert in science and as one who professes to take the conservative Christian view of the accuracy of the Bible, he tells his audience that it does not matter whether or not man came into being through the process of evolution.

Finally he says, "Neither do Bible texts often quoted against evolution give us a decisive answer. For instance, in Genesis 1 it constantly refers to each act of creation of living things to be 'after his kind.' But this gives no problem to the evolutionist because it refers to the finished act. . . . That there are differences in the completed acts nobody denies. But this gives us no guidance on what happened before this. Apparently the answer to the riddle will ultimately have to come through science."[5] Evolution requires a method which must be explainable, but creation requires none, just as a miracle requires no explanation. If living things were created, as the Bible says they were, there is no riddle to solve and there is no answer to be sought through science.

Attempts to explain creation lead naturally to attempts to explain the miracles. This further leads to attempts at discrediting other supernatural elements of the Bible, and when this is done there is nothing left but the tenets of modernism. The author of the book under consideration points out that it is a perilous procedure to try to find scientific explanations for miracles. He explains this by saying that by the time an apparently satisfactory scientific explanation has been made, the scientific evidence upon which the reconciliation has been made may no longer be considered valid, and "the result is to bring fresh discredit upon the miracle."[6] It seems evident, however, that this should bring discredit upon the miracle-explainer and not upon the miracle. But even after this warning, the author himself proceeds to offer explanations for miracles.[7]

At the time of the Exodus the Lord slew the first-born of the Egyptians, both of men and of cattle. The Israelites were spared because they put the blood of the passover lamb above and on the sideposts of their doors (Ex. 11:4-7, 12:21-30). The author says, the death of the firstborn "could have been caused by a number of diseases."[8] However, he makes no attempt to answer the obvious question: What diseases would selectively kill just the *firstborn* of men and of cattle, and would spare the firstborn of families which had sprinkled blood around their doors?

He offers three suggestions concerning the axhead which the prophet Elisha caused to float after it had been lost in the Jordan river (II Kings 6:1-7).[9] First of all, he says that its ability to float would depend upon its composition, and that we do not know of what material it was made. The Bible says it was made of iron (II Kings 6:6).[10] If it had been made of something which would float, there would have been no problem in the first place. Next, he says that minerals or other chemicals in the water might have caused sufficient buoyancy. But if there had been sufficient buoyancy to float it, there would have been no problem. Also, it is to be remembered that it fell into the Jordan, which is fresh water, while even the Dead Sea, with its high chemical content, will not float anything as dense as aluminum, much less iron. Last of all, he says that rapidly moving water can bring heavy objects to the surface. But if this had been the case, the axhead would have been far downstream in a short time, while the Bible states that the Prophet asked where the axhead had fallen into the water, threw a stick into the water at this spot, and the axhead came to the surface.

Professor Jauncey says that as science advances, many of the difficulties in understanding miracles becomes less, and as an example he cites the case where the Lord Jesus appeared to His disciples in a room where the doors were closed (John 20:19). A few generations ago a door was thought of being solid, while "now we know it is mostly space anyway,"[11] since the discovery of the molecular composition of matter. But knowledge about the atomic structure of matter does not make it any easier for a person to pass through a closed door than it was before we had this knowledge. A chicken wire fence has less matter and more empty space than a door, but neither a man nor a chicken can pass through such a fence.

Attempts to explain the miracles of the Bible on a naturalistic basis or to make them seem more credible to those who wish to avoid a belief in the supernatural acts of God will only encourage such persons to continue in their theological liberalism instead of leading them to an acceptance of the miracles and to a saving knowledge of the Lord Jesus Christ.

A century ago, in the days of Darwin, an ordained minister named James Maurice Wilson held the office of Canon of Worcester and was at the same time a teacher of science. In his discussion of the transformation that the theory of evolution brought upon his life, he states very clearly the issues which confuse many today, and his attempt to reconcile evolution with Christian theology led him directly into modernism.

He wrote, "The evolution of man from lower forms of life was in itself a new and startling fact, and one that broke up the old theology. I and my contemporaries, however, accepted it as a fact. The first and obvious result of this experience was that we were compelled to regard the Biblical story of the Fall as not historic, as it had long been believed to be. . . . But now, in the light of the fact of evolution, the Fall, as a historic event . . . was excluded and denied by science. . . . If there is no historic Fall, what becomes of the redemption, the Salvation through Christ? How does Jesus save His people from their sins?"

Thus he shows precisely how evolutionary belief attacks basic Christian doctrine. He goes on to show how modernism builds its un-Scriptural faith in an effort to reconcile evolutionary doctrine with the Bible. "How does Jesus save His people from their sins? *He makes them better.* . . . The relinquishment of the old attempted explanations of 'the atonement' has not robbed the Cross of any of its significance or power in the salvation of man. If salvation by the Cross has now come to mean for Christian men salvation from sin itself, not from the *penalty* of sin, 'salvation' has become more real, more verifiable, than before. It is the sins of the world and our sins that He who died on the Cross is taking away, by making us better. [This is not at all Scriptural.] Salvation is not then thought of as an escape from hell, but as a lifting us all out from living lives unworthy of us. Religion so conceived is not the art of winning heaven, but the effort to become better and to work with God."[12]

Here have been illustrated two approaches to evolution from a theistic point of view. One author considers himself a conservative Christian in good standing, and tells his readers that evolution may be the means by which God did His creating. He ignores the problem of what evolution does to Christ's atonement for sin. The other author is very much aware of what his evolutionary belief has done to his former belief in the atonement. In dealing with the problem, the only solution he finds is in accepting a modernist theology.

No matter what the approach, theistic evolution leads logically to modernism.

NOTES

1. Jauncey, James H., *Science Returns to God* (Zondervan Publishing House, 1961).
2. *Ibid.*, p. 25.
3. *Ibid.*, p. 20.
4. *Ibid.*, p. 49.
5. *Ibid.*, p. 56.
6. *Ibid.*, p. 41.
7. He believes that miracles are governed by natural law and that supernatural events, that is, miracles, "are merely natural events being used by God to bring about His purposes" (page 39). His logic is as follows: If it is necessary for God to break natural laws in order to perform a miracle, it follows that natural laws are not flexible enough for every purpose of God. He states that this is another way of saying that the original creation was imperfect. Some readers, including this one, will fail to see that this follows logically. But God declared the finished creation to be good, and the author of the book says since the creation included the existence of natural laws, the natural laws must have been good. If natural laws were good when they were made, it follows, he

says, that they must have been flexible enough for every purpose of God (page 40). Thus, if you agree with this logic, it is proved that miracles have a natural explanation, although the explanation may not be understood at present.

8. Jauncey, James H., *loc. cit.*, p. 78.

9. *Ibid.*, p. 81.

10. According to *Strong's Exhaustive Concordance of the Bible*, the word used here is the only word which is translated *iron* in all of the Old Testament except in the book of Daniel. In context the word may also mean *an implement of iron*, and it is translated *axhead* in this passage.

11. Jauncey, James H., *loc. cit.*, p. 83.

12. A Collective work, Wilson, James Maurice, one of the authors, *Evolution in the Light of Modern Knowledge* (D. Van Nostrand Co., 1925).

PROGRESSIVE CREATIONISM, THRESHOLD EVOLUTION

There was a time when the lines between evolutionists and anti-evolutionists were rather clearly drawn, but the issue is now so confused that lines are being drawn in all sorts of places. Recently a Christian man of science spoke on the subject of evolution to a group of students at a Christian college, and according to the way he defined terms, any view other than *atheistic* evolution might properly be labeled *creation*. A man like this is invited to speak where the privilege would be denied a professed evolutionist, and it seems that many Christian people are not able to discern what is being done by such a speaker.

A Christian missionary wrote an article for a Christian magazine in which he presented his credentials as a conservative Christian by saying, ". . . we believe the Bible to be the very word of God in the highest possible sense."[1] He then asked, "Does God's Word teach a view of the origin of life that forces the Christian to reject all scientific evolutionary theory?" As this is worded, it seems to be a loaded question implying the expected answer, "Oh, no! God's Word would not do that!" Lest there be any doubt about the answer expected, he answers it himself. "What shall we say then? Can a Christian who accepts the plenary [total] inspiration of the Bible believe in evolution? We answer: Why not? Of course, he must be very careful to define his theory of evolution so as not to violate any clear teaching of the Word of God."

Donald Gray Barnhouse, former Editor of *Eternity* magazine, believed that man was created, but he also believed that all other

forms of life could have evolved. He said, "May we not hold that
. . . God intervened in the past, even in the midst of a long evolutionary process, and created man as an entirely new factor?"[2] Biologists in general, of course, would not consider this for a moment.
This is an unstable position. It is unreasonable to think that evolution would go just so far and no further. Some think they can
maintain this position, but students cannot be expected to stop believing in evolution at the human level if they are taught that
everything else evolved. The trend today is to indoctrinate students
with the concept that man is an animal, so why should they stop
short of man in accepting evolution if they are told they may accept
the rest?

The position most commonly taken and taught at present by men
of science who profess to be Bible-believing conservative Christians
(they do not like the word *fundamental*) goes by such names as
threshold evolution, progressive creationism, and *scientific creationism.* These are essentially the same thing.

In the book *Evolution and Christian Thought Today,* James O. Buswell III says that anti-evolutionists may be divided into three main
categories. One of these categories, which does not meet his approval,
contains the "hypertraditionalists" [fundamentalists], who, he says,
are "bound to certain rigid interpretations of Scripture [and] who
are loath to accept any new facts which seem to contradict their
interpretations, since these are seen not as interpretations but as
literal teachings of Scripture itself."[3] Another category comprises a
large number of the Roman Catholics and the liberal Protestants
with their theistic evolution. The remaining, in-between category is
the one Professor Buswell espouses, and he says of it that "there are
creationists, many of whom have specialized in one field of science or
another, or else, as theologians, have either taken pains to keep
abreast in some measure with scientific advance, or else have sought
the council of those who have, who constantly allow their interpretations to be open to the acceptance of newly discovered facts, so that
the reintegration of their position has been free from the contradiction
of embracing one body of facts, whether from Scripture or from nature,
and excluding the other. These creationists have been given different labels of varying degrees of consistency. Carnell has called
the position 'threshold evolution'; Ramm [and Mixter follows Ramm
in this], 'progressive creationism'; others 'micro-evolution' and even
'theistic evolution.' " He goes on to say that it is not strictly an

evolutionary position at all, and he suggests the name "scientific creationism."

As Professor Buswell says, threshold evolution and progressive creationism seem to be just two labels for the same thing, and this is what we wish to discuss in this section. It may seem strange that he includes micro-evolution here. This is a term used by the evolutionists for observable changes. It is an assumption on the part of evolutionists that observable changes in organisms represent phenomena of a sort which can lead to real evolution. Some anti-evolutionists fall into a trap when they say, "We believe in micro-evolution." It is not wise to make such a statement for several reasons. For one thing, because of definitions such as that just quoted from Professor Buswell, a person who says he accepts micro-evolution may be interpreted as saying that he accepts threshold evolution or progressive creationism. On the other hand, for an anti-evolutionist to say he accepts any kind of evolution is helping the evolutionary forces in their drive to break down objection to the term *evolution* itself. The thing to do is to object to the use of the term *evolution* in connection with any real phenomenon and to insist on using a different term.

At first it may seem surprising that Professor Buswell also says that some even equate progressive creationism with "theistic evolution." Those who espouse progressive creationism usually are quite insistent that they are not theistic evolutionists. But since some do equate these two concepts, more confusion is thus added to the already great confusion in terminology.

Some consider progressive creationism to be a form of theistic evolution or a modified theistic evolution. For example, in a book called *A Christian Approach to Philosophy*, by Warren C. Young, the author lists Dr. Mixter with the creationists and also takes him as an example of an exponent of "a modified form of theistic evolution."[4] The book has a foreword by Kenneth S. Kantzer, then of Wheaton College.

Those who espouse threshold evolution or progressive creationism distinguish it from theistic evolution as follows. Theistic evolution refers to total evolution, divinely directed. Progressive creationism holds that there were a number of acts of divine creation. After each creative act there was a certain amount of diversification, but there was a limit as to how far such change could go. Because of this limitation it was necessary for the Lord to perform repeated acts of creation to lift the diversified creatures over figurative thresholds so that they could continue to diversify further.

Important questions are: How far apart were the thresholds? In other words, is the diversification which is alleged to have occurred between creative acts of sufficient magnitude to represent real evolution? Also, is there any evidence as to where espousal of this view leads?

The late Edward John Carnell of Fuller Theological Seminary is given credit as the originator of the term "Threshold evolution." He was a theologian and not a scientist. The following comments of his are pertinent to the present consideration of the problem. "Orthodoxy does not deny that nature is progressively changing, and what is this but evolution?"[5] "Nor is orthodoxy particularly disturbed by the evolution of plants and animals."[6] "While orthodoxy does not think that the evidence for human evolution is compelling, the evidence *is* sufficient to give pause. The verdict of paleontology cannot be dismissed by pious ridicule."[7] ". . . since orthodoxy has given up the literal-day theory out of respect for geology, it would certainly forfeit no principle if it gave up the immediate-creation theory out of respect for paleontology."[8] "Scripture only requires us to say that the physical antecedent of man was not denoted *man* until God performed the miraculous act of divine inbreathing. Thus, if science traces man's biological ancestry to dust, Scripture traces his spiritual ancestry to God."[9]

Dr. Carnell proposes a difficulty to which he offers no solution. He states that the paleontologists deny that man came from a single genetic line. He notes that the Apostle Paul affirms what the paleontologists deny and that Paul does so in such a manner that if we do not accept what Paul says we deny that Paul wrote with divine authority. He then says that orthodoxy can do little more to get out of this difficulty than to propose a pre-Adamic race of beings structurally similar to *Homo sapiens* but with inferior endowments. He admits that this postulate has little merit and apparently he does not accept it himself.

Bernard Ramm is a philosopher and not a scientist. However, his view must be considered here because of the great influence of his book, *The Christian View of Science and Scripture,* published in 1955. The publishers expressed the opinion that this book "marks a historical point of no return where evangelical Christian scholars will no longer in ignorance deprecate the findings of science, but will understand them with the advantage of their Christian perspectives. . . ."[10]

As to his theological position, Ramm says, "The author of this book believes in the divine origin of the Bible, and therefore in its divine inspiration; and he emphatically rejects any partial theory of inspiration or liberal or neo-orthodox view of the Bible."[11] He claims that he is not an evolutionist, not even a theistic evolutionist. He says, "The writer is not a theistic evolutionist."[12] Concerning the position he takes in this regard he says, "In summary, we accept progressive creationism, which teaches that over the millions of years of geologic history God has been fiately creating higher and higher forms of life."[13] He begins his book with a few quotations, two of which are from famous evolutionists, Goethe and Huxley.[14]

The discerning reader will notice that for one who does not espouse theistic evolution, Dr. Ramm seems to go rather far out of his way to present it favorably to his readers. Part of his logic, rather strangely, is that theistic evolution cannot be incompatible with Christian faith because the Roman Catholics accept it. He says, "We find a group of theistic evolutionists among the Roman Catholics. None can doubt the orthodox rigidity and dogmatism of Roman Catholic theology. If theistic evolution is so incompatible with Christian faith, we have the strange situation that the most dogmatic version of Christian faith is the most tolerant Church in all Christendom toward theistic evolution."[15]

In presenting the Roman Catholic position, Ramm has a hypothetical typical Catholic biologist say, "The problem of direct creation or mediate creation through evolution is immaterial to me. Neither could happen without God. Therefore, because we have established on other grounds that no motion can happen without God, it is immaterial whether life was suddenly created or slowly evolved. In either case it is God who does it and therefore evolution is neither here nor there as far as Catholic faith is concerned."[16] This is exactly what is being told to readers by the authors of many books and articles on evolution, including some college textbooks in biological science.

With the Roman Catholic view Ramm also presents the view of an "idealist philosopher," who believes that all reality is spirit or mind and that material substance does not exist (the "Christian Science" point of view). He also presents the view of a hypothetical typical fundamentalist, and of these three views he has adverse criticism only for the fundamentalist point of view.

Ramm even brings the Jews and the liberals into his argument to prove that fundamentalists are wrong in opposing the theory of evolution. He says, "It must be kept in mind that orthodox Catholic theologians with just as high a view of inspiration as evangelical Protestants, and with just as much at stake in theology, also believe in theistic evolution, not to mention the orthodox Jewish believers. Religious modernists and neo-orthodox thinkers almost to a man have accepted theistic evolution and see no incompatibility in accepting evolution with their theistic metaphysics. These various interpretations indicate that the dilemma of fiat creationism versus atheistic evolution, into which the Fundamentalist tries to force the issue, is not possible."[17]

Professor Ramm repeats this theme a number of times. In another place he says, "We have seen that evolution in a theistic form has been accepted by Catholics and Protestants alike, which means it cannot have all the evils associated with it as it is supposed to have."[18] He even goes so far as to say, "There is without question an antichristian version of the theory of evolution,"[19] implying that there are Christian versions.

To clinch his point, Ramm cites evangelical Christians. He says, "Finally, just to mention them . . . there are evangelical Christians who have espoused theistic evolution, and see no incompatibility between this acceptance and their Christian faith. Asa Gray, James McCosh, James Orr, and A. H. Strong were all evangelical believers who accepted theistic evolution."[20] He also says, "It is not true that all evangelicals believe that evolution is contrary to the Faith. Most Fundamentalists and evangelicals are opposed to evolution to be sure, but we have given evidence to show that men whose orthodoxy is unimpeachable have accepted some form of theistic evolution or at least were tolerant toward evolution theistically conceived."[21] And again he appeals to his argument that evolution cannot be so bad because it is accepted by Roman Catholics.

Asa Gray, the great American botanist, is first on Ramm's list, and the only scientist. Gray was a disciple of Darwin. In our previous discussion of the views of Professor Gray it was shown that Ramm's contention concerning him is not tenable.

James McCosh, who comes next on Ramm's list, became president of Princeton University. Evolutionists are pleased to quote him as saying that if Christians insist that the theory of evolution is inconsistent with Christian faith, the result will be that people will be driven from accepting the Christian religion. The conclusion is that therefore evolution should be accepted as consistent with Christian faith, so as not to lose these people who otherwise would be driven away.

No doubt there have been some evangelical Christians who were so impressed with the claims of the scientists that they thought it was necessary to capitulate to a certain extent. It also should be noted that some of them did not have the advantage of the perspective which more time has given us to see on the one hand that the evidences for evolution are not so impressive as they have been claimed to be, and on the other hand that compromising with evolutionists leads to liberalism and modernism.

Ramm is altogether wrong when he says concerning the effect of evolutionary thought on the Christian church: "To this point we have shown that evolution with all necessary qualifications has been adopted into both Catholic and Protestant evangelical theology and has not meant the disruption of either. To charge that evolution is anti-christian, and that theistic evolution is not a respectable position, is very difficult to make good in view of the evidence we have given."[22]

Ramm follows this with a philosophical discussion which is concerned with the matter of when evolution is in essence anti-Christian and when it is not. He says that, if men use evolution to discredit Christianity, then evangelicals must oppose it. On the other hand, he says, if evolution is viewed as a part of the divine creation, it is harmless. He concludes (italics his): "The decision as to which classification fits evolution is to be made by *competent Christian scholarship*. We have noted that already orthodox thinkers (Protestant and Catholic) have affirmed that evolution, properly defined, can be assimilated into Christianity. *This is strong evidence that evolution is not metaphysically incompatible with Christianity.* The final answer, however, must come from one with responsible leadership. It must come from the best of evangelical scholarship which is *fair, competent,* and *learned.* It must come from our better thinkers in biology, geology, and theology, and not from more vocal and less able men. It must not come by the cheap anti-evolutionary tract nor from pulpiteering, but from that evangelical scholarship which is loyal to the best of academic scholarship and to the sound teachings of Holy Scripture."[23]

Ramm proposes progressive creationism as the answer, and he says that this view goes back to Augustine. Henry Fairfield Osborn of the American Museum of Natural History, and others, have said that Augustine taught theistic evolution, but Ramm declares that what he proposes is not theistic evolution. Of this view Ramm says, "It is our hope that a theory like progressive creationism will form the basis of a new biological synthesis which will be to biology [what] relativity was to physical [science]."[24]

This, of course, is wishful thinking. The scientific approach, to which the biologists are committed, endeavors to explain *everything*, and leaves nothing to God. Evolutionary theories of the past which implied a directive force are now mentioned in books of evolution only because of their historic interest, and generally they are mentioned with contempt. It is the considered judgment of this writer that Ramm's appeal will have no effect upon the non-Christian biologists, and his influence will be most effective among those who are in transition between a conservative and a liberal position. Moreover, it may help to start such a transition in some who are conservative.

Now let us consider the views of some Christian men of science who espouse progressive creationism. As already mentioned, Professor Knobloch of the American Scientific Affiliation believes the created "kinds" of Genesis may be representatives of "phyla," the largest categories of the animal kingdom. (He feels that the chief difficulty here is that it requires some faith to accept even this much creation.) The more usual position of the progressive creationists is that the created kinds most commonly correspond to the original representatives of a type of group known technically as an "order." The carnivorous animals, for example, constitute an order. So do the odd-toed hoofed animals, the even-toed hoofed animals, the bats, the rodents, the primates, etc. What animals constitute an order may change at any time, as it has done in the past. It has been suggested that the aquatic carnivores should be placed in an order separate from the terrestrial carnivores.

An order is a rather inclusive group. Postulating that a created "kind" was a representative of an order and that all other animals of the order descended from one original pair seems to allow for quite a lot of real evolution. For example, it could be alleged that a skunk and a polar bear had the same ancestry, or even a skunk and a walrus. This could be defended as quite Scriptural on the basis that these animals belong to the same order and hence to the same "kind."

Apologists for progressive creationism sometimes deny that such an inclusive category is meant in relation to a created kind, and in support of this contention they claim that references to "kinds" apply to different types of bears, thrushes, and the like.[25] To clarify this the following quotations are pertinent.

James O. Buswell III, writing in the book *Evolution and Christian Thought Today,* says, "I propose, then, that . . . perhaps the *order* is as near to being what Genesis 1 means by the term "kind" as any single taxonomic category can be."[26] (He says that in some cases it could be a phylum and in some a genus.) In a footnote on the same page he says, "Mixter arrived at a similar conclusion, suggesting that the order is at present a reasonable approximation of 'kind.' "

Dr. Mixter explains his reason for equating the "kinds" with orders as follows: "Where shall we draw the boundaries of the groups descending from created animals? Draw [them] where the paleontologists [men who study fossils] indicate there are gaps [that is, discontinuities in the fossil record] — between the orders in practically all cases. . . ."[27] He further says, "An honest creationist will ask the paleontologist what he knows of the time of origin of animals, and draw conclusions from the data."[28]

In accordance with this, Professor Buswell points out in the footnote just mentioned that Dr. Mixter is not being inconsistent when he changes his mind about the "kinds" as George Gaylord Simpson, Harvard's eminent paleontologist and evolutionist, changes his opinion about the gaps. In this connection it is interesting to note that in 1931 Dr. Simpson described a fossil which he thought was a treeshrew, and seeing in it features which he considered to be significantly like a lemur he followed a suggestion which another zoologist had made in 1922, namely that the treeshrews are more closely related to the primates than to the animals known as insectivores. In fact, Dr. Simpson placed these animals in the order Primates. This has been generally accepted, and at present most of the men who are specialists in the study of the Primates as well as most physical anthropologists accept the treeshrews as primates. But according to J. A. Jane and others of the Department of Anatomy at the University of Illinois it has recently been shown that the fossil which Dr. Simpson studied was not a treeshrew and it was not a primate.[29]

Dr. Mixter quotes Floyd E. Hamilton, formerly Professor of Bible at Union Christian College, Korea, as follows: "Ordinary variation and mutation within the genus, or perhaps in some cases within the family, starting from a fixed point as a center and spreading in all directions, varying as it goes, would account for all these intergradients as well as the theory of evolution."[30] To this quotation Dr. Mixter adds, "My suggestion is to carry the logic one step further and say 'within the order.' "[31] In the same paragraph he also says, "It is probable that all the species within a genus and perhaps the genera within a family, and perhaps even all the families of an order may have arisen by subdivision of an original ancestral species."

Where progressive creationism leads is illustrated by the fact that it was in a discussion of one of Dr. Mixter's papers that Professor Cassel made the frequently-quoted statement, "Thus, in fifteen years we have seen develop within the American Scientific Affiliation a spectrum of belief in evolution that would have shocked all of us at the inception of our organization."[32] In the same paper Dr. Cassel interprets what Dr. Mixter says thus: "I, an evangelical Christian, can accept the basic concepts of evolution. Although not exclusively demanded by the data involved, it is certainly allowed, and in fact I can see no better or more logical way to handle the data. I believe in Creation, and simply affirm that in the light of the evidence now available, I think some evolution — that is, development of present-day forms by differentiation of previously existing forms — the most likely way God accomplished much of his creation."

One day a young man came to my office seeking help. His missionary parents were worried and did not know what to do because another son was expressing evolutionary ideas. When they tried to deal with him about this matter his reply was: Dr. Mixter believes this way so it must be all right. Progressive creationists may contend that they are creationists, but students do not always grasp such subtleties of meaning. It seems quite a coincidence that when the young man knocked on the door of my office I was engaged in writing a reply to a missionary who said I ought to apologize to Dr. Mixter because I wrote an unfavorable review of the book *Evolution and Christian Thought Today*.

NOTES

1. Wagner, C. Peter, "The Origin of Life: A Christian View," *Eternity*, 8:9:12, September, 1957, p. 13.

2. Barnhouse, Donald Grey, "Adam and Modern Science," *Eternity*, 11:5:5, May, 1960, p. 8.

3. Mixter, Russell L., Editor, *Evolution and Christian Thought Today*, Chapter by James Buswell III (Wm. B. Eerdmans Pub. Co., 1959), p. 188.

4. Young, Warren C., *A Christian Approach to Philosophy* (Van Kampen Press, 1954), p. 92.

5. Carnell, Edward John, *The Case for Orthodox Theology* (Westminster Press, 1959), p. 94.

6. *Ibid.*, p. 94.

7. *Ibid.*, p. 95.

8. *Ibid.*

9. *Ibid.*

10. Ramm, Bernard, *The Christian View of Science and Scripture* (Wm. B. Eerdmans Pub. Co., 1955), Paper jacket of book.

11. *Ibid.*, pp. 41, 42.

12. *Ibid.*, p. 293.

13. *Ibid.*, p. 256.

14. *Ibid.*, Opposite the Preface.

15. *Ibid.*, p. 282.

16. *Ibid.*, p. 254.

17. *Ibid.*, p. 265.

18. *Ibid.*, p. 301.

19. *Ibid.*, p. 262.

20. *Ibid.*, pp. 264, 265.

21. *Ibid.*, pp. 347, 348.

22. *Ibid.*, pp. 289, 290.

23. *Ibid.*, pp. 292, 293.

24. *Ibid.*, p. 272.

25. In Leviticus 11 and Deuteronomy 14, in connection with dietary laws, some birds are mentioned as not to be used for food, after their kind. The list includes the owl, and the owls constitute an order of birds. Does this have any bearing on created types reproducing after their kind, or is it a shorter way of telling the people not to eat any kind of owl? Formerly scientists put hawks and eagles in the same order with owls. Because evolutionists change their minds about what constitutes an order it does not follow that formerly bald eagles and horned owls had the same ancestry but now they do not.

26. Mixter, Russell L., *loc. cit.*, p. 183.

27. Mixter, Russell L., *Creation and Evolution*, Monograph 2, The American Scientific Affiliation, 1950, p. 17.

28. *Ibid.*, p. 18.

29. Jane. J. A., *et al.*, "Pyramidal Tract: A Comparison of Two Prosimian Primates," *Science*, 147:3654:153, January 8, 1965, pp. 154, 155.

30. Mixter, Russell L., 1950, *loc. cit.*, p. 17, Floyd E. Hamilton, *The Basis of Evolutionary Faith* (James Clarke and Co., 1931).

31. *Ibid.*, p. 19.

32. Cassel, J. Frank, "The Evolution of Evolutionary Thinking on Evolution," *Journal of the American Scientific Affiliation*, 11:4:26, December, 1959, p. 27.

THE ROMAN CATHOLIC POSITION

It may be desirable to consider the Roman Catholic position on evolution since liberal Protestants, and more recently Protestants not considered liberal, are coming ever closer to Rome in the ecumenical movement.

The Roman Catholic Church has never taken a position with regard to evolution except to declare that the soul of man did not evolve.

According to Gertrude Himmelfarb,[1] on the eve of the publication of Darwin's *Origin of Species,* Cardinal Newman urged the pope, Pius IX, not to intervene in scientific quarrels and not to make the old accepted cosmology formally binding. One can only speculate as to how much influence this had on the pope. If it had not been for the advice of the Cardinal, he might have made an outright anti-evolutionary decree. In 1864 he issued his *Syllabus of Errors,* condemning "progress, liberalism, and modern civilization." Although this was commonly understood to include evolution, no specific reference to the theory of evolution was made.

In 1950 Pope Pius XII published the encyclical *Humani Generai,* which had to do with evolution. It conceded that the evolution of the physical body is a proper subject for research. Catholic biologists today accept evolution, and a writer for a Jesuit magazine said that although the evidence for real evolution ("macro-evolution") is not very good, evolution is nevertheless preferable to special creation.[2]

It seems that Pope Pius IX had been inclined to condemn evolution, and if another cardinal instead of Cardinal Newman had advised him and had recommended that he condemn the theory of evolution, the situation might have turned out very different. The encyclical of Pope Pius XII was not particularly favorable toward evolution; if this Pope had not left a loophole for the evolution of the body, things might be very different also. Catholic biologists may believe that the popes were divinely restrained from making formal utterances condemning evolution, in accordance with the doctrine of the infallibility of the popes when speaking *ex cathedra.* But it seems that there were some very worried Catholic scholars before the pronouncements of Pope Pius XII were made known and were interpreted as permitting evolutionary views.

A recent book on evolution from the Roman Catholic standpoint may be considered authoritative. It is edited by Walter J. Ong, a Jesuit. It contains a foreword by John Wright, D.D., Bishop of Pittsburgh, and bears the "imprimatur" of Joseph E. Ritter, Archbishop of St. Louis.

In the foreword the bishop stresses the point that the Roman Catholic Church has been cautious and has not made a formal pronouncement on the subject of evolution and that the conclusions of scholars concerning evolution are tentative. He says that theologians and philosophers should make their comments "with great sobriety and humility" because "even Darwin confessed that 'the mystery of the beginnings of all things is insoluble to us.' "[3]

In the introduction Professor Ong says that one reason why theologians are deeply concerned with evolutionary processes is that the evolutionary processes help "in understanding the development theology itself undergoes as we continue our attempts further to penetrate theologically the revealed mystery of the Incarnation and Christ's continued presence in the world through His Church."[4] This seems to be about the ultimate in how far-fetched statements about Darwinian evolution can be.

Robert W. Gleason, Chairman of the Department of Theology and Religious Education at Fordham University, a Catholic university in New York City, wrote a chapter on theology and religion in this book. He says that "theologians no longer favor the effort to treat the Bible as though its apparently literal expressions were teaching facts of science."[5] He says that in the first chapter of Genesis "there are undoubtedly images, expressions, and elements of popular folklore common to other cultures besides that of the Israelites."[6] He believes that the account of the creation of man does not go back to the time of Moses, but was written later.[7] According to him, whoever wrote the account of creation shared the views of his own contemporaries, based upon personal observations and experiences, and the scientific "notions" he expressed could be in error.[8] He affirms that numerous Roman Catholic scholars today accept a form of theistic evolution, and he says, "The origin of the human body by way of evolution does not appear improbable today."[9]

As to how Adam got his body, Professor Gleason says that it could have been made directly from the dust of the ground, but he holds that this was not necessarily so. It could have been made of something else, which in turn was made from something else, and only originally came from the dust of the ground. In other words, Adam's body could have evolved from lower forms of life, and come by way of an evolutionary process from something that started originally as inorganic dust. Dr. Gleason says that "some modern theologians, approaching the text, that is, the Bible, with much more knowledge of paleontological discoveries, feel that it is also possible to interpret the text as saying that God drew the human body from an animal origin which was transformed so as to receive a human soul."[10]

The formation of Eve from a portion of the side of Adam cannot be reconciled with any theory of evolution. Professor Gleason believes this may be just figurative, and he comments, "The furthest that we can go in suggesting a solution to this problem is that Adam was at least the exemplary cause of Eve in so far as her body and her nature were fashioned after his. The exact manner in which her body was formed is uncertain from the text [that is, from the Bible], nor has tradition clarified it with any certainty."[11]

NOTES

1. Himmelfarb, Gertrude, *Darwin and the Darwinian Revolution* (Doubleday and Co., 1959), p. 375.

2. Russell, John L., "The Theory of Evolution: The Present State of the Evidence," *Month*, January, 1956, pp. 41, 45. Quoted by Gertrude Himmelfarb, *loc. cit.*, p. 376.

3. Ong, Walter J., Editor, *Darwin's Vision and Christian Perspectives* (The Macmillan Co., 1960), p. viii.

4. *Ibid.*, p. 2.

5. *Ibid.*, p. 105.

6. *Ibid.*

7. *Ibid.*, p. 106.

8. *Ibid.*

9. *Ibid.*

10. *Ibid.*, p. 108.

11. *Ibid.*, p. 112.

CHAPTER V

THE MECHANISM OF EVOLUTION

Darwin was fortunate in that the time was right when he published his *Origin of Species.* If he had published somewhat earlier, his views would not have been accepted. Another factor in his success was the impressive collection of data which he presented. However, his real contribution, and that which made evolution acceptable to the scientists, was his theory as to the way in which evolution came about. This was his natural selection theory, which Herbert Spencer called *survival of the fittest.*

Darwin's critics pointed out some weaknesses in his natural selection theory, especially the fact that it did not explain the origin of the types from which it was assumed that the fittest were selected. When Hugo de Vries proposed his mutation theory at the turn of the century, it was at first taken as a rival theory, but soon it was combined with Darwin's theory, and the two together were thought to explain the mechanism of evolution.

During the 1920's and 1930's it was realized that this combination of explanations by Darwin and de Vries was not an adequate explanation of evolution. The scientists at that time freely admitted that they did not know how evolution had come about. However, they believed that, given more time, they would find the answer. Meanwhile most of the scientists were very insistent that they were not giving up their belief in evolution, but only in the Darwinian explanation of how evolution came about. It is not surprising that the general public did not clearly understand the distinction, and when it was said that the scientists were giving up their belief in Darwinism, it was thought that they were renouncing the theory of evolution.

There were a few scientists who did say that the acceptance of evolution was losing ground, but they were a small minority. The view of the majority was that this was merely the understanding of uninformed anti-evolutionists.

A statement by Professor George H. Parker of Harvard University illustrates what was being said at that time. "At the same time that . . . biologists accept descent with modification [that is, evolution] as an actual occurrence in nature, they are most sceptical and reserved about what may be called the driving force behind descent. . . . It is this uncertainty that has been seized by a few thoughtless critics who have attempted to discredit in the eyes of the general public the well-established fact of descent with modification [evolution] by confusing it with the explanation of descent [evolution]. This confusion, commonly due to ignorance, is the source of most of the contentions now met with in evolutionary controversies. It does not characterize the clear thinker. Because biologists have not as yet discovered how evolution takes place is no reason for denying evolution itself."[1]

The views of the biologists have changed again, and natural selection and mutations are back in vogue as the explanations of evolution. Professor John Tyler Bonner, the outstanding biologist and evolutionist of Princeton University, seems to be expressing the opinion of the scientists of our day when he says, ". . . a general feeling that the mechanism of evolution is understood prevails, particularly in regard to the importance of selection and the method of formation of new species."[2] On the next page he continues, "No other hypothetical mechanisms seem to be necessary to account for the facts as we know them."

Since mutations and the principle of natural selection were both well known at the time when it was confessed that the mechanism of evolution still was not understood, the fact that they now are considered to be the basic mechanism of evolution implies that nothing better has turned up, and that in spite of much intensive research in this area, nothing better seems to be forthcoming. As an explanation of the method of evolution, natural selection and mutations are supplemented by such things as hybridization and the increase in the number of chromosomes. These, however, can only provide more combinations of hereditary material which is already present, and they do not add anything new.

The erroneous belief that the scientists were giving up evolution did not interfere with the spread of evolutionary thought as some scientists seemed to fear it might. Its effect was rather to lull the Christian public into a state of complacency. A number of students in Christian schools have expressed the view that there is no point in spending time discussing the theory of evolution, because the scientists are abandoning it. When they are asked where they got this information, they are usually vague in answering or do not know. In cases where students have an answer, it is usually traceable to statements made in the 1920's or 1930's.

Anyone who doubts that scientists accept evolution is not familiar with the current scientific literature on the subject. There are relatively few biologists who do not accept it. If there are more than a few, the others are too timid to speak up.

NOTES

1. Parker, George H., *What Evolution Is* (Harvard University Press, 1926), p. 62.
2. Bonner, John Tyler, *The Ideas of Biology* (Harper and Brothers, 1962), p. 52.

NATURAL SELECTION

Even before the basic principles of genetics were understood, it was natural for farmers to select types of animals and plants which pleased them most and to use such to propagate the next generation. By repeatedly doing this, stocks were improved in the sense that the herds and crops became more like the types which the farmers preferred. Charles Darwin proposed that a similar selection was going on in nature, and that animals and plants were being improved in the sense that those best suited to the environment were surviving and reproducing their kind at the expense of those which were not so well suited to the environment. Thus, as time went on, creatures became better and better adapted to the environment. However, Darwin went much beyond this and tried to show that this process explains how all forms of life on earth evolved from one or a few simple forms at the start.

When Darwin heard that the only mammals native to New Zealand were bats, he expressed surprise, because he thought that since there were no other mammals to disturb them or to compete with them they would have given up flight and would have become adapted to life on the ground. When he heard that a traveler in America had observed a bear swimming in a river and snapping at insects, he concluded that if this kind of food became sufficiently abundant, bears would take to the water, would develop very large mouths, and would attain a much larger size. Erik Nordenskiold in his well-known book *The History of Biology* calls this a strange conclusion and an evidence of the weakness in Darwin's speculation.[1] That this should be considered strange is rather remarkable in view of the fact that evolutionists today believe that whales and other aquatic mammals evolved from animals which walked on land.

Besides the whales, the Sirenia are the only completely aquatic mammals. They are the manatees and dugongs. A work on natural history says of them: "Shortly after the dawn of the Tertiary age, certain primitive elephants discovered a vast food supply in the rich aquatic vegetation of the tropical lakes and rivers. Life in the cool waters proved to be so pleasant and food so abundant and easily procured, that these creatures began to pass more and more of their time in the water, until at last they entirely forsook the land. Gradually colonizing the rivers, from sources to mouths, some of these earliest Sirenians at length reached the sea."[2]

Continuing, the same author says of the whales: "The Cetacea have had a very similar history since early Tertiary times, when some members of a carnivorous family . . . entered the fresh waters in pursuit of fishes, molluscs, crabs, crayfish, and other aquatic animals. They also found the water to be congenial, gradually forsook the dry land, spread from the rivers to the seas, and from Africa to all the other continents."[3] It is also interesting to note that although this author seems so certain that whales evolved from *carnivorous* ancestors, most evolutionists today seem to believe that the whales are most closely related to some of the *herbivorous* hoofed animals.

As previously mentioned, there was a time a few generations ago when it was believed by the scientists that natural selection and mutations were inadequate to explain evolution. But today textbooks are teaching the students that evolution came about mainly through natural selection and mutations. This implies that in spite of much research, nothing better has turned up and nothing better is expected. A few quotations will illustrate what the authors are saying.

Lorus and Margerie Milne of the University of New Hampshire say, ". . . that natural selection occurs and could account for a considerable part (if not all) of the evolutionary changes producing the variety of life today from the few beginnings of the past, is the considered judgment of virtually all biologists today."[4]

Julian Huxley, famous grandson of the famous Thomas Henry Huxley, says, "So far as we now know, not only is natural selection inevitable, not only is it *an* effective agency of evolution, but it is *the* only effective agency of evolution."[5]

Arthur W. Haupt, Professor of Botany at the University of California at Los Angeles, tells the students the following in his textbook. "New forms arise spontaneously by mutation; natural selection then determines whether or not they will survive. If better suited to the environment than existing forms, they tend to be preserved; if not they are eliminated. Thus the course of evolution is directed by the environment but mainly under the influence of natural selection."[6]

Professor E. O. Dodson, who has written a textbook on evolution, says in *The Encyclopedia of Biological Sciences*, "The mechanisms of evolution are now explained on the basis of mutation and selection. . . ."[7]

The late Professor Hermann J. Muller, Nobel Prize winner and one of the outstanding geneticists of our day, said, "The origin of adaptibility in organisms is the thing to be explained, not the premise to start with. The modern theory of gene mutation, coupled with Darwin's basic concept of natural selection, provides the basis for a process of evolution in which such adaptibility will come into existence by the operation of natural processes."[8]

Professor James S. Hall of Washington University tells the students this: "From myriad mutations occurring at random over the ages, there have evolved ever more varied and complex beings, including even the possessors of intelligent minds capable of attempting to comprehend the whole scheme. But how can orderly progression emerge from randomness? Some philosophically-minded students have preferred to attribute the directiveness of evolutionary change to a supernatural intelligence beyond the realm of scientific inquiry. Yet it is possible to explain the long-continued trends that we find in evolutionary history by gene mutations, recombination, and selection."[9]

The eminent geneticist Theodosius Dobzhansky of Columbia University puts it this way: "The process of mutation is the only known source of the new materials of genetic variability, and hence of evolution. . . . An apparent paradox has been disclosed. Although the living matter becomes adapted to its environment through formation of superior genetic patterns from mutational components, the process of mutations itself is not adaptive. On the contrary, the mutations which arise are, with rare exceptions, deleterious to their carriers, at least in the environments which the species normally encounters. Some of them are deleterious apparently in all environments. Therefore, the mutation process alone, not corrected and guided by natural selection, would result in degeneration and extinction rather than in improved adaptiveness."[10] He further says, "One of the basic postulates, at the present stage in the development of [a satisfactory theory of evolution] is that gene change by mutation, and gene frequency change by natural selection, are the most important common denominators in both micro- and macroevolution. Micro- and macroevolution differ simply in the number of gene changes involved."[11]

Finally, although George Gaylord Simpson, the great paleontologist and evolutionist, has some views on the mechanism of evolution which are different from the usual view, he says, "Only mutation supplies the materials for creation, but in the theories of population genetics it is selection that is truly creative, building new organisms with these materials."[12]

This is a sample of the current opinions of famous biologists and some college professors who write textbooks.[13] Among the people included in these categories there are very few dissenting voices. Although the consensus of opinion among biologists favors Darwinian natural selection again, there are problems and difficulties.

It is evident that there is much destruction of life which is not selective and which is irrelevant to superior or inferior qualities of the organisms, particularly among the very young. Some fish produce an enormous number of eggs. Sturgeons lay about seven million eggs per female, and a fish called the turbot lays over fourteen million. These are rather unusual cases, but many fish lay eggs in the thousands. Since these fish do not increase in numbers over a period of time, it is evident that all but a few of the eggs and the fish which hatch from them are destroyed before the age of reproductive maturity. If a hereditary change brought about a protective coloration or a transparent condition so that the young fish would not be so easily seen, this kind of change could have survival value, but it would not be a step in changing them into frogs or salamanders. Changes of the sort which would be significant in evolving a fish into something higher, if indeed there are changes of this sort, would have no survival value at the time when the individuals are still eggs or very young fish.

An important difficulty in the theory of natural selection is the fact that many useful characteristics would be liabilities instead of assets while still in an incompleted state of development. Intermediate stages in the evolution of a structure must have adaptive value, for otherwise the structure would never develop. It would be eliminated because individuals having these intermediate stages of a developing structure would be handicapped and they would not survive in the struggle of the survival of the fittest. Professor Garrett Hardin of the University of California at Santa Barbara quotes an engineer to the effect that the principle of natural selection "has probably precluded the development of the wheel and axle in the animal kingdom, and consequently has ruled out the possibility of flight by means of revolving propellers."[14] This is another way of saying that animals do not have wheels and propellers because such structures would be a handicap before they became perfected. This seems to imply that if evolution were true there would be no bats, for evolutionists believe that the ancestors of bats climbed in the trees. Partially evolved wings would be useless for flight and would be in the way. Natural selection would eliminate such freaks and bats never would have evolved. Since there are bats, the logical conclusion is that bats did not evolve. The same argument may be applied to many other creatures which have unusual adaptations.

It has been the custom of scientists to look upon anti-evolutionists as naive, but this matter of animals with wheels is a case in reverse. Even if natural selection did not operate against animals with partially formed wheels and propellers, there would still be many difficult problems in the development and operation of these structures in the animal kingdom. Some of the more obvious problems are the following.

If an animal had wheels, the wheels would either contain living tissue or else they would be made of non-living material like horn or oyster shell. A non-living wheel would need to be secreted by the animal (which would involve problems), and yet it would have to be free of the axle so that it could rotate freely but not come off. It would have to rotate without producing enough friction to damage the axle. An animal with wheels, and particularly one with propellers, would need a very good oil gland and an instinct to lubricate its revolving appendages properly. If the wheels contained living tissue, there would need to be a source of nourishment. Since by its nature a wheel must be a separate entity in order to revolve, there could be no blood vessels, digestive tract, or nerves connecting the animal with its wheels. Where would a wheel have a mouth? What if one wheel died? If an animal had wheels or propellers, where would be the source of power for locomotion? Would the animal be like a wheelbarrow, with wheels in front and legs behind, or would it be like a horse and cart with legs in front and wheels behind? If it had only wheels and rollerskated along, it would have difficulty in nature finding a suitable smooth habitat.

There are cases in which creatures are said to have evolved from other types although they do not seem to be better adapted to the environment than their alleged ancestors are. Even an evolutionist, M. W. de Laubenfels, then Professor of Zoology at Oregon State College, could write, ". . . worms survive well and sponges survive superlatively. Survival of the fittest does not explain the progression from microbe to man."[15]

Fish with cartilaginous skeletons, like sharks, are very well adapted to their environment. For a long time it was quite a problem to explain what advantage bony fish have over cartilaginous fish, so that bony fish evolved from cartilaginous fish. Now that it has been decided that evolution occurred the other way around and that the cartilaginous fish evolved from bony fish, the problem is just as difficult as before. There seems to be no reason why either one should have evolved from the other.

Professor J. C. Fentress of the University of Rochester observed that one species of vole (a mouse-like rodent) "froze" when it observed a moving object overhead, while another species ran for cover. The species that froze in its tracks lived in the woodland, while the species which ran for cover lived in the open field. Professor Fentress told his colleagues about his observation, but he purposely *reversed* the facts, telling them that the woodland species ran for cover and that the meadow voles froze in their tracks. The other zoologists were able to give very elaborate and satisfactory explanations why the woodland species ran and the meadow species froze, based upon conventional ideas of evolutionary theory. (This was reported in *Scientific Research,* November, 1967.)

Some animals and plants have characteristics which seem to be against the best interests of the species. Opossums are noted for "feigning death." This has long been thought of as a favorable adaptation and a means of enabling the animal to escape death from an enemy. But some authors have pointed out that the situation is really just the reverse, and that it results in the death of the animal more frequently than it leads to escape. Osmond P. Breland, Professor of Zoology at the University of Texas, says, "Whatever the reason for this performance, it appears decidedly disadvantageous to future generations of opossums. Surely any attacker, whether human or animal, would rather contend with a passive victim than with a clawing, biting, or fleeing antagonist."[16] Evolutionists say that the opossum is a very ancient species, and if the authors are correct who say that the behavior of feigning death is against the best interests of the species, natural selection should have eliminated it by this time. Meanwhile, in spite of this trait, opossums have spread their range considerably and have increased in numbers. Even if they did at some future time stop "playing possum," they still would be opossums and would not be on their way toward becoming something else.

Dr. Maurice Burton, the noted English naturalist and former Deputy Keeper of Zoology at the Natural History Museum, London, says that antelopes become terror-stricken when they get the scent of a lion they cannot see, and then become relatively calm when the lion comes into view! He says the situation is essentially the same in the case of an attack by a cheetah: "The cheetah comes into full view of a herd of antelope, sits down and surveys the scene, apparently singling out one member of the herd for attack. The antelope see the cheetah and begin to buck and bound, but without moving away. Only when the cheetah makes its sixty-mile-an-hour dash at its selected victim do any of the antelope take refuge in speed."[17]

Another example of a deleterious trait is given in *Animals of All Countries*. According to this publication, the teeth of Layard's whale become so prolonged in the male that they cross above the snout, making it very difficult for the animal to open its mouth to feed.[18]

Philip G. Fathergill of the University of Durham says of the mollusc *Gryphaea*, "As this mollusc evolved, the shell gradually became more and more coiled until finally the animal could scarcely open it, and so the animal perished."[19]

Electric eels have a remarkable adaptation which puzzled Darwin when he contemplated how it might have come about through natural selection. There is another puzzling feature about these eels besides their electricity-generating organs. John H. Heller of the New England Institute of Medical Research says it this way: "Electric eels are blind. They are not born blind; it is merely that their eyelids keep growing together until they are permanently shut — why, no one knows."[20]

Darwin himself noted the case of the loggerhead duck, or steamer duck, *Tachyeres cinereus*. When these ducks are young, they are able to fly rather well. But as they mature, the growth of the wings does not keep pace with the development of the body, and as a result the adult birds are unable to fly at all.

Burrowing animals would not be expected to develop protruding spines, for such adornments would seem to interfere with their tunneling. C. Kingsley Noble, Curator of Amphibians and Reptiles at the American Museum of Natural History, says, "Nevertheless, the rhinoceros iguana develops three horns on the snout in both sexes and manages to dig long burrows."[21]

Dr. Burton mentions some rats which invaded his garden. The young ones had very white feet and legs. This characteristic was so conspicuous that he says they appeared to be "all white feet and legs."[22] This situation is just the opposite of that in the young of many species which are protectively camouflaged. Since young rats are especially susceptible to destruction by predators, it seems that this color pattern in this kind of rat is a decided disadvantage to the species and should have been eliminated by natural selection before it became established.

D. A. Hooijer, Curator of Vertebrate Paleontology at the Museum of Natural History at Leyden, says that some species of fossil turtles apparently became extinct because they "had developed a very defective carapace [upper shell] and thus had lost their once-effective armor."[23]

The antlers of the extinct Irish elk were enormous, and it is generally assumed that it was the size of the antlers which brought about the extermination of the species. George Gaylord Simpson believes that in this case the antlers may have reached such proportions only after the age of reproductive maturity, and hence that they may not have been an important factor in the demise of these beasts as a species.

The question of why deer have antlers is an interesting one. John Paul Scott of the division of Behavior Studies of the Roscoe B. Jackson Memorial Laboratory says, "The [antlers] are of very little use against predators. When attacked, the deer usually take flight or drive at their attackers with their hoofs. Since the [antlers] may be quite heavy and impede rapid flight in bushy country, they are, if anything, a handicap to survival. Yet the male deer grow bigger and heavier antlers each year as the old ones are shed, using them only in the pushing contests which take place between the stags during the breeding season."[24] Dr. Burton believes that the antlers do not have a value even in the pushing contests mentioned by Scott. He notes that often an antlerless stag is a master stag and a successful leader of stags, and furthermore he says that an antlerless stag usually has the largest harem of females. Dr. Burton points out that if there is no survival value in the antlers, they represent a great waste, for the stag must eat a great quantity of calcium to produce the antlers. While growing, the antlers are a source of annoyance and irritability to the animal, and soon after they are fully formed they are lost. He says they do have a survival value because the deer eat them (that is why one rarely finds antlers on the ground after they are shed), and in this way the antlerless females obtain extra calcium at a time when it is needed for their developing offspring. If this is indeed the reason why deer have antlers, it would seem to tax one's faith to believe that antlers came about through Darwinian natural selection. Moreover, as Dr. Burton points out, there are species of deer in which neither males nor females have antlers, while in the reindeer and caribou both males and females have them.[25]

Even a structure so common and relatively simple as the outer ear is difficult to explain by natural selection. Some animals have quite large ears and can turn them to receive sound waves from different directions. Holding an open hand behind the ear to enlarge its area significantly aids us in hearing. However, Dr. Burton points out that birds and some other animals which have very acute hearing have no outer ears. He concludes that outer ears evolved not as aids to hearing, but as ventilators for animals with a heavy coat of fur.[26] If this is the case, it is fortunate that the ventilators developed where they did instead of on the neck, where some creatures have external gills, or some other place. It is evident that natural selection is not responsible for the fortunate position of human ears as an adaptation for wearing glasses.

Dr. Burton confesses that when evolutionists refer to adaptations, it may be largely doubletalk. He says, "As often as not, when we speak of special adaptations we mean rather that animals happen to be endowed with certain structures or certain tricks of behavior, and that they make the best use they can of those situations in which they happen to find themselves. If the structure and the situation make a nice fit we say the animal is adapted to that situation. If they do not fit, but the animal gets along the best it can, and makes a success of it, we say it is adaptable. So the root 'adapt' comes to mean almost anything we want it to do."[27]

The archer fish, *Toxotes jaculatrix,* shoots water from its mouth with great precision at insects resting on plants up to three or four feet above the water. When insects which are attacked in this manner fall into the water, the fish captures them for food. This procedure is so remarkable that when it was first reported in England in 1764 it was not accepted as true, although the man who described it was a member of the distinguished Royal Society of London. His report was followed by others, but the phenomenon was not accepted as a fact until living specimens were sent to England about forty years later and were observed in the act of shooting water at their insect prey.

The mouth of the fish is especially adapted in order that it can perform this feat, and also the eyes are modified in several ways to make it possible. The propulsive force comes from the gill covers. It is difficult to believe that all the anatomical structures and behavior patterns which are required to operate harmoniously in order to make this phenomenon possible came about through natural selection. One of the difficulties in Darwin's theory of evolution is that independent structures — such as the mouth and the eyes in this case — must be modified harmoniously in order to make the development of a new adaptation possible.

But in this case there is another factor which makes it still more difficult to explain by natural selection. This is the fact that the shooting of insects is only a "hobby" with the archer fish and not its chief means of obtaining food. According to Darwin's natural selection theory, the ability to shoot water from the mouth got started in some unknown manner, and some fish could do it better than others. Those that could do it best got more to eat than those which could not do it as well, and consequently they survived while the less proficient fish lost out in the competition for survival. But this just is not so, for even when insects are abundant and the fish are hungry, they presently tire of shooting insects and go off to obtain food in a more conventional manner.

Since these fish have such a remarkable "hobby," contrary to the principle of survival of the fittest, it follows that it is not necessary to postulate natural selection to explain how other creatures obtained some of their characteristics. Dr. K. H. Lulling, who wrote on these fish in *Scientific American,* recognizes this difficulty and says, "This raises an interesting question for evolutionary theory. Spouting, if it is so unimportant, can hardly have been a significant factor in the survival of the species or in selection and differentiation within the species."[28] He does not attempt to offer an explanation.

When Alfred Russell Wallace, Darwin's friend and the "co-discoverer" with him of the principle of natural selection, said that human intelligence could not have come about through natural selection, Darwin is said to have written a large "NO!" on the paper and underlined it three times. He wrote to Wallace, "If you had not told me you had made these remarks I should have thought they had been added by someone else. I differ greviously from you and am very sorry for it."[29] Darwin took an unscientific attitude. He did not attempt to answer Wallace's argument or to consider it. His reaction was purely emotional.

Wallace had lived for many years with uncivilized peoples in South America and in islands between Asia and Australia. He knew these people well, and he said that they were hardly inferior to Europeans in intelligence. But in their way of living they did not have a need for the intelligence they possessed. This fact is in contradiction to his and Darwin's natural selection theory, for according to their theory man's intelligence came about because those who had a higher intelligence had a correspondingly higher survival potential. But this could not be so because uncivilized people already had much more intelligence than they needed for anything they did in their culture.

The natives of an island of the New Hebrides group illustrate this in a way which is interesting because it is so unusual. Periodically they build on the side of a hill a rickety tower of poles bound together with vines.[30] The tower has platforms resembling diving boards at intervals up to eighty feet or more above the ground. Men attach to their ankles vines which are fastened at the other end to the tower, and they dive headfirst from a platform. The idea is for each man who performs to touch the ground with the top of his head without breaking his neck, and after the first rebound to land on his feet farther up the hill. To do this with a mechanism built with modern engineering skill would require a great deal of courage, but these people do it with primitive equipment. The tolerance between a successful performance and death is just the same, whether the mechanics involved is figured out by a group of engineers or a band of savages. Some men jump from a height of eighty feet or even more, and when they reach the end of their tether they are falling at a very rapid rate. As a man reaches the end of his free fall, the vines stretch and the tower sways. The ground has been dug to make it softer and to verify by the impression of the diver's head that the permance has been successul. It is considered bad form for a man to extend his arms — he has to touch the ground with his head only. To calculate so precisely how far a man will fall under such conditions seems impossible, but they do it. They may not use their brains wisely, but they have good ones.

Darwin said that natural selection could never produce anything for the sole benefit of another species.[31] With regard to this, Douglas Dewar, an anti-evolutionist, cites the example of a host-parasite relationship of two wasps named *Ibalia* and *Sirex*.[32] The *Sirex* grub burrows deep in the wood of a tree, and when it metamorphoses into the adult form, it cuts its way out with its powerful jaws. *Ibalia* parasitizes *Sirex* by laying its eggs in the hole bored by the *Sirex*. The *Ibalia* grub feeds upon the tissues of the *Sirex* grub, avoiding the vital organs and thus prolonging the life of its host and providing itself with fresh food. The mature *Ibalia*, unlike the mature *Sirex*, has weak jaws and could not bite its way out as the *Sirex* does. If other things remained the same, the *Ibalia* in the end would perish with the *Sirex*, deep within the wood of a tree. But things do not remain the same, and the parasitized *Sirex* does something which the normal *Sirex* does not do — it bores toward the surface. Thus the *Ibalia* is carried close enough to the surface so that it is able to escape. This instinctive change in the behavior of the *Sirex* is detrimental to the interest of its species and aids another species.

Different kinds of ants bring into their colonies various insects that produce a sweet exudate which is pleasing to the ants. This is a luxury item for the ants and not necessary for them. However, in some species it is a necessary part of the life cycle of the other insect to be carried to an ant colony and to develop there. In a number of these cases the ants act to their own detriment. For example, robber ants take into their nests larvae of a certain beetle and they feed the beetle ant larvae while to a certain extent neglecting the feeding of their larvae. Moreover, the larvae of the beetle eat the larvae of the ants. For some reason the ant queens become sterile in colonies harboring these beetles. Finally the ant colony degenerates and ceases to exist. The ants have established a behavior pattern which aids another species and is detrimental to their own species.

Some bean plants are said to help kill themselves because as their roots grow they exude a substance which causes the spores of a certain kind of mold to germinate, and then the mold attacks the bean plant. Research on this was done at the University of California at Berkeley, and the scientists who did the research report that the spores of this fungus approach the condition of the ideal resting spore — one which will not germinate except in the presence of its host plant and one which will germinate quickly when in the presence of this host plant.[33]

The seeds of the witchweed are said to germinate only in the presence of its host plants.[34]

There is a species of rotifer (a microscopic water creature) which attacks another kind of rotifer. But it produces a chemical which causes the eggs of the prey to develop into individuals with protective spines. These rotifers do not develop the protective spines except in the presence of the predator.

There are molds which develop traps for catching nematode worms, but they develop these traps only when stimulated to do so by a substance secreted by the worms themselves.

Darwin himself recognized difficulties because of the intricate and marvellous things which his natural selection theory would have to explain. Commenting on a communication he received about the structure of the cells in the honeycomb, Darwin wrote, "Your letter actually turned me sick with panic."[35] It had this effect upon him because he had to explain by natural selection the production of these cells in mathematical precision by neutral bees, while the reproducing bees do not make cells.

As previously mentioned, Darwin wrote to Asa Gray, "I remember well the time when the thought of the eye made me cold all over. . . ." It made him cold all over because he had committed himself to explain the evolution of life from simple forms by a process of natural selection, and he could not account for the evolution of the eye. This sentence in his letter to Gray continues, ". . . but I have got over this stage of the complaint, and now small trifling particulars of structure often make me very uncomfortable. The sight of a peacock's tail, whenever I gaze at it, makes me sick!" It made him sick because he could not explain it by his natural selection theory. But the thought of an eye no longer made him cold all over, and he wrote in his *Origin of Species*, ". . . the difficulty of believing that a perfect and complex eye could be formed by natural selection, although insuperable to our imagination, should not be considered as subversive to our theory."[36] A little further on he says, "If it could be demonstrated that any complex organ existed which could not possibly have been formed by numerous, successive, slight modifications, my theory would absolutely break down." His next sentence is: "But I can find no such case."

After reading what he said about the eye, it is understandable why he was able to say this. As he himself said, he "got over it." He did not solve the problem. He just hardened himself so that the fact that he could not solve the problem did not bother him any more.

It is very difficult, if it is possible at all, to prove that something could not happen. It has been postulated that the eye evolved from a pigment spot. Who can *prove* that it did not? In their textbook of comparative anatomy Neal and Rand say, "It is indeed difficult to imagine how the skin mucus of amphibians evolved into the milk of mammals."[37] There are very many such things which are difficult to imagine, but evolutionists glibly say they did happen. Who can *prove* they did not? Of course, if it cannot be proved that something did not happen, that does not mean that it did happen. But since their opponents cannot prove that fantastic developments in animals did not happen, evolutionists can use this as license to declare that such things did indeed really happen.

Some years ago Hollywood produced a moving picture which was the story of a man who dabbled in atomic physics and turned himself into a fly. The moving picture company offered a prize of one hundred dollars to the first person who could prove that a man could not turn himself into a fly. Is it possible to prove that a man cannot turn himself into a fly? An inquiry disclosed that a physics instructor in Indianapolis collected the award, but he did not prove that a man cannot turn himself into a fly. He was given the prize because he "gave the most plausible possibilities."[38] This is no proof at all, and far from it. A hundred dollars is nothing to a moving picture company, and it was well spent for publicity. But anyone who can *prove* that a man cannot turn himself into a fly is still eligible to collect a hundred dollars according to the terms of the agreement, for no one has proved it as yet. It would be just as hard to prove that the mucus of a salamander did not become the milk of a cow by Darwinian natural selection.

Julian Huxley volunteers a figure to illustrate the chance of a horse being produced by evolution through mutations alone, *without* natural selection. The probability would be only one chance out of a number so great that three large volumes of five hundred pages each would be required just to print the number. As a comparison, it may be mentioned that it would take less than two lines in a book to record a number larger than the estimated number of electrons in the known universe. Since Professor Huxley has shown that horses could not have come about through mutations alone without natural selection, and since there *are* horses, he concludes that this demonstrates the great importance of natural selection. This follows because he believes horses came about through the action of mutations *and* natural selection. He says that this "shows what a degree of improbability natural selection has to surmount and can circumvent."[39]

Not so very long ago an Englishman named Kettlewell gave up a medical practice of fifteen years to investigate natural selection among moths. There are in England several kinds of moths which are light in color and which sit on the trunks of trees in the daytime. Dark forms of these moths exist, and in the majority of cases the difference between the light moths and the dark moths is due to the mutation of a single gene. A hundred years ago in the days of Darwin the dark moths were a rarity, but now they are common in some areas. The reason for this is the fact that as industrialization has sprung up and increased, the smoke and fumes emitted by the factories have killed the lichens on the trees and darkened the bark so that now the light moths are very conspicuous as they sit on the trunks of the trees in the daytime, while the dark moths blend into the background and are hard to see. The situation is the reverse of what it was before the industrial revolution. In former times the light moths blended into the background and were hard to see, while the dark moths were conspicuous. Before these areas became industrialized, the birds saw the dark moths more readily and ate proportionately more of them. Therefore they remained rare. They did not become extinct because they were repeatedly renewed in the population by new mutations. Now the situation is the reverse and in industrialized areas the birds see the light moths more easily. Since proportionately more of the light moths are taken as food by the birds, the proportion of dark moths in the population has increased.

It might seem that it is hardly worth giving up a medical practice to discover this, but Dr. Kettlewell is very much pleased with his findings. They have been widely publicized in scientific and popular magazines, textbooks, and even television. Dr. Kettlewell calls this change in the ratio of dark and light moths "the most striking evolutionary change ever witnessed by man."[40] He concludes, "Had Darwin observed industrial melanism he would have seen evolution occurring not in thousands of years but in thousands of days — all within his lifetime. He would have witnessed the consummation of his life's work."[41] Thus, according to Dr. Kettlewell, if Darwin had known that birds eat more dark moths on light trees and more light moths on dark trees, he could have rested assured that it is thereby demonstrated that all forms of life on earth did indeed evolve from one or a few simple forms of life!

Another example which has been hailed by some authors as a marvellous illustration of evolution is the fact that some strains of flies have become resistant to DDT. When DDT is sprayed around and flies are killed by it, some flies survive. Many of the ones which survive do so because they have a greater natural resistance to the DDT. It is not surprising that they pass on to at least some of their offspring an inherited resistance to this insecticide. As DDT is repeatedly applied, the flies with the greatest resistance to it will be the ones most common among the survivors. Thus in such an environment there will develop a strain of flies which have a high resistance to DDT. There is no doubt that in Darwin's day some flies were more resistant than other flies, but at that time there was no DDT, and so with regard to this kind of resistance all flies were equally well adapted to their environment. However, strains of flies which have become resistant to DDT are not thereby developing into something other than flies.

Since the evolutionists make so much of examples like Kettlewell's moths and flies which have become resistant to DDT, it should be noted that they are thereby plainly advertising the poverty of evidence in their favor.

The term *natural selection* is used in two different senses. This causes confusion. Moreover, it is frequently alleged that these two ways of using the term are not really different. (1) For example, the reduction in the number of dark moths in areas not industrialized, and the reduction in number of light moths by selective feeding of birds in industrialized areas, as just explained, are instances of natural selection which cannot be denied. But the differences in the dark and light moths result from a single mutant gene, and no real evolution is involved. (2) If it could be shown — but it cannot — that moths evolved by a process of natural selection from some kind of creature which was not a moth, that would be an entirely different matter.

A recent article[42] on work with the genetic code of viruses illustrates this confusion, as the term *natural selection* is used interchangeably in these two different senses. Exchanges of amino acids in the shell of the virus represent mutations, and they occur more frequently at some places than at others. It is believed that the most frequently observed mutations may not occur more commonly than others. A more likely explanation is that they are observed more frequently because they do not harm the organism. Thus these mutations are preserved by natural selection, while other mutations are eliminated because they are deleterious. This type of natural selection is comparable to that observed by Kettlewell in his moths, where light moths predominate in some areas and dark moths in others, depending upon the shade of the treetrunks. On the other hand, the authors *assume* that the protein coat of the virus evolved through natural selection. This is an altogether different matter, and it is rather comparable to the assumption that moths evolved from something which was not a moth.

Although Darwin's natural selection theory is now back in vogue again, Ashley Montagu, the noted anthropologist and evolutionist, dared to say as recently as 1952: ". . . the development of science could well be written in terms of a history of fruitful errors. Darwin's conception of natural selection is perhaps the most outstanding example in the whole history of science of such a fruitful error."[43]

Some of the fruits of this error will be considered under the heading of *Social Darwinism.*

NOTES

1. Nordenskiold, Erik, *The History of Biology* (Tudor Publishing Co., 1935), p. 470.
2. Finn, Frank, *et al.*, *Animals of All Countries* (Hutchinson and Co.), (Not dated), Vol. 2, p. 656.
3. *Ibid.*, p. 656.
4. Milne, Lorus J. and Margery J. Milne, *The Biotic World and Man* (Prentice-Hall, 1952), p. 467.
5. Huxley, Julian, *Evolution in Action* (Harper and Bros., 1953), p. 36.

6. Haupt, Arthur W., *An Introduction to Botany*, 3d edition (McGraw-Hill, 1956), p. 258.

7. Gray, Peter, Editor, *The Encyclopedia of Biological Sciences*, Under *Evolution*, written by E. O. Dodson, 1961, p. 364.

8. Dunn, L. C., Editor, *Genetics in the Twentieth Century*, Part written by H. J. Muller (Macmillan, 1951), p. 92.

9. Hall, Thomas S. and Florence Moog, *Life Science* (John Wiley and Sons, 1955), p. 442.

10. Dobzhansky, Theodosius, "On Methods of Evolutionary Biology and Anthropology. Part I. Biology." *American Scientist*, 45:5:381, December, 1957, p. 385.

11. *Ibid.*, p. 389.

12. Simpson, George Gaylord, *Tempo and Mode in Evolution* (Columbia University Press, 1944, Third printing, 1949), p. 80.

13. The French biologists are an exception to this, and Darwinism is not popular in that country. There are cases in which French patriotism has influenced scientific research. It would be interesting to investigate how much, if at all, French patriotism has influenced the French attitude toward Darwinism.

14. Hardin, Garrett, *Nature and Man's Fate* (Rinehart, 1959), p. 74.

15. de Laubenfels, M. W., "Porifera in General Zoology," *Turtox News*, August, 1953.

16. Breland, Osmond P., *Animal Life and Lore* (Harper and Row, 1963), p. 22.

17. Burton, Maurice, "Spotted Cats," *The Illustrated London News*, 241:6436:940, December 8, 1962.

18. Finn, Frank, *loc. cit.*, pp. 693, 694.

19. Fathergill, Philip G., *Historical Aspects of Organic Evolution* (Philosophical Library, 1953), p. 274.

20. Heller, John H., *Of Mice, Men, and Molecules* (Charles Scribner's Sons, 1960), p. 113.

21. Noble, G. K., "What Produces Species?" *Natural History*, 30:1:60, January, 1930, p. 66.

22. Burton, Maurice, "Two Plagues of Grain-Eaters," *The Illustrated London News*, 241:6432:578, November 10, 1962.

23. Hooijer, Dirk Albert, "Pygmy Elephant and Giant Tortoise," *Scientific Monthly*, 72:1:3, January, 1951, p. 6.

24. Scott, John Paul, *Animal Behavior* (University of Chicago Press, 1958), p. 238.

25. Burton, Maurice, "Do Deer Chew Antlers?" *The Illustrated London News*, 238:6343:316, February 25, 1961.

26. Burton, Maurice, "Function of Pinna," *The Illustrated London News*, 230:6145:432, March 16, 1957.

27. Burton, Maurice, "A Modern Basilisk," *The Illustrated London News*, 240:6388:28, January 6, 1962.

28. Luling, K. H., "The Archer Fish," *Scientific American*, 209:1:100, July, 1963, p. 100.

29. Darwin, Francis, editor. *More Letters of Charles Darwin* (D. Appleton and Co., 1903), Vol. 2, p. 40.

30. Johnson, Irving and Electa, "South Sea's Incredible Land Divers," *The National Geographic Magazine*, January, 1955, p. 77.

31. See Julian Huxley, *loc. cit.*, p. 50.

32. Dewar, Douglas, *The Transformist Illusion* (Dehoff Publications, 1957), p. 217.

33. Schroth, Milton N. and William C. Snyder, "Effect of Host Exudates on Chlamydospore Germination of the Bean Root Fungus, *Fusarium f. phaseoli*," *Phytopathology*, 51:6:389, June, 1961, p. 392.

34. *Science News Letter*, 71:13:200, March, 1957.

35. Darwin, Francis, editor, *loc. cit.*, Vol. 1, p. 122.

36. Darwin, Charles, *The Origin of Species*, Vol. 1, chapter 6 (D. Appleton Co., printing of 1923), p. 224.

37. Neal, Herbert V. and H. W. Rand, *Comparative Anatomy* (The Blakiston Co., 1936), p. 112.

38. Private correspondence.

39. Huxley, Julian, *loc. cit.*, pp. 45, 46.

40. Kettlewell, H. B. D., "Darwin's Missing Evidence," *Scientific American*, 200:3:48, March, 1959, p. 48.

41. *Ibid.*, p. 53.

42. Fraenkel-Conrat, Heinz, "The Genetic Code of a Virus," *Scientific American*, 211:4:47, October, 1964.

43. Ashley Montagu, M. F., *Darwin Competition, and Creation* (Henry Schulman, 1952), p. 69.

SEXUAL SELECTION

Somewhat similar to Darwin's theory of natural selection is his theory of sexual selection. At present this is mainly of historic interest, for it is not widely accepted by scientists. At least it is not believed to have accomplished as much as Darwin thought it did.

The idea here is that certain traits arose and became elaborated because individuals selected mates of a type which pleased them. A trait which is considered esthetically superior in a population may become predominant in the population because individuals seek mates of this preferred type.

Certain insects, some tree hoppers for example, have bizarre, fancy structures which seem to serve no useful purpose, but it is evident that insects do not look each other over with critical esthetic appraisal.

Michael F. Guyer of the University of Wisconsin says, "While most naturalists today accept it [sexual selection] as sufficient to account for the special development of fighting organs in the males of polygamous animals, they are inclined to question its adequacy for the development of ornaments, song, and the like."[1] He quotes an undisclosed source as follows: "Undoubtedly the presumption that the females compare males and then choose only those which have the most attractive colors, the finest song, or the most agreeable odor, presents great difficulties, but it is doubtful if it is possible to replace this explanation with anything better."

In the cases of some migratory birds which have been studied it has been found that the males return first and establish their territories, and then when the females arrive they choose nesting sites or territories rather than males. A quarrel between two males with a female nearby may be interpreted by a human observer as two males fighting over a female, while in fact it may be a battle over a boundary, because the newly-arrived female has not yet learned the limits of her new home territory and has trespassed on someone else's property.

Darwin believed that the reason human beings are not covered with hair the way most mammals are is that in pre-human days the females found the males with the least hair the most attractive. Ernest Albert Hooton, the Harvard anthropologist, discussed this in several of his books. He found the problem perplexing because he believed that our hairless condition is a disadvantage on the whole instead of an advantage. His remarks are somewhat humorous, but serious. He said, "Thus Darwin, like Adam, blamed it on the woman,"[2] and commented, "Chivalry, as well as common sense, dictates a rejection of the blame-it-on-your-wife theory."[3] He concluded that none of the theories as to how we lost the hair which supposedly covered the bodies of our ancestors, "would satisfy a critical anthropoid ape."[4]

NOTES

1. Guyer, Michael F., *Animal Biology,* 4th ed. (Harper and Bros., 1948), p. 132.

2. Hooton, Ernest Albert, *Apes, Men, and Morons* (George Allen and Unwin, 1938), p. 22.

3. *Ibid.,* p. 23.

4. *Ibid.,* p. 23.

MUTATIONS

As stated before, the mechanism of evolution is thought to be based upon mutations and natural selection. Mutations are changes which are inherited, and they affect both superficial and important characteristics. Even when the effect seems superficial, however, it may be associated with detrimental physiological effects. Mutations have been studied most thoroughly in the fruit flies, *Drosophila*, where they produce such changes as abnormalities in the wings, legs, eyes, body, and bristles. In human beings mutant genes cause several kinds of colorblindness, including the common red-green color-blindness, defective enamel and other abnormalities of the teeth, hemophilia, muscular dystrophy, and other undesirable traits.

Professor Dobzhansky, one of the outstanding geneticists of our country and a strong evolutionist, admits that favorable mutations amount to less than one percent of the mutations that occur. Julian Huxley puts the figure at one tenth of one percent, for he says, "A proportion of favorable mutations of one in a thousand does not sound like much, but it is probably generous, since so many mutations are lethal, preventing the organism living at all, and the great majority of the rest throw the machinery slightly out of gear."[1]

Professor Dobzhansky says, "Most mutants which arise in any organism are more or less disadvantageous to their possessors. The classical mutants obtained in Drosophila usually show deterioration, breakdown, and disappearance of some organs."[2]

Since the great majority of mutations are injurious, it is natural to inquire why they are considered so important in evolution. The answer is that there is nothing better. There is nothing else that can furnish the basic variations required for evolutionary change. Professor Dobzhansky says in a scientific journal, "The process of mutation is the only known source of the new materials of genetic variability, and hence of evolution."[3] He repeats this in a textbook which he revised: "Since mutation is the only known method of origin of new hereditary variability, the mutation process is considered to be the prime source of the materials of evolution."[4]

Dr. L. C. Dunn, Professor of Zoology at Columbia University, says, "Such events, known as mutations, are the ultimate source of the hereditary variety characteristic of all species. It is this variety upon which natural selection and other evolutionary forces act in forming varieties, races, species, and other natural categories."[5] Similar statements may be found commonly in biological textbooks.

Professor Dobzhansky admits that "the deleterious character of most mutations seems to be a very serious difficulty."[6] Since most mutations are so deleterious and since he accepts them as the basis for evolutionary variation, he must offer an explanation. This he has done, and others have taken it up and presented it to the public and to students in their textbooks. Professor Gairdner B. Moment of Goucher College, for example, tells students in his textbook that this deleterious nature of mutations is just what is to be expected: "Generous estimates place the number of beneficial mutations at less than one percent. This, however, is exactly what is to be expected wherever animals or plants are well adapted for the life they lead. Since present-day creatures are the product of hundreds of thousands of years of adapting, it is not surprising that almost any change whatever will not adapt the animal or plant any further but do just the opposite."[7]

In other words, the bad mutations which keep appearing have appeared before and have been rejected before, while the good mutations are incorporated into the genetic constitutions of animals and plants. But creatures could not have started out with a load of bad mutations while waiting for good ones to appear and be selected. (Adam was not color blind, club-footed, hare-lipped, diabetic, etc.) Furthermore, there are many lethal mutations which kill the individual before birth. Another implication of this view of mutations is that evolution is coming to a standstill since the inferior mutations have over a long period of time been replaced by superior ones, and this situation can be changed only by a rather drastic change in the environment. However, there are some evolutionists who say that evolution is now going on faster than ever.

The case of sickle-cell anemia is used by evolutionists to illustrate how injurious mutations can become established and remain in a population. People who have a pair of genes for this trait have defective red blood cells, producing an anemia that results in death. Normal people, who do not have this kind of gene, but instead have its normal allele, are subject to malaria, while people who have one gene of each kind do not get the anemia and are immune to malaria. Thus people who carry one gene for the defect are best suited to survive in areas where malaria is prevalent. It is obvious, however, that a population of this sort will always produce both of the less well adapted types.

Granted that most mutations are harmful, another important question is: Are the *other* mutations able to produce the kinds of changes which would have to occur in order to bring about real evolution, that is, the kind of evolution which occurred if all life on earth developed from one or a few simple forms?

As previously mentioned, earlier in this century scientists rejected de Vries' mutation theory, together with Darwin's natural selection theory, as inadequate to explain the mechanism of evolution (though insisting that this should not be interpreted to mean that they were giving up their faith in evolution itself). Now that mutations and natural selection are back in vogue again, the evolutionists seem more certain than ever that mutations and natural selection are the answer to the question of how evolution came about.

John Tyler Bonner, Professor of Biology at Princeton University, says that "there is no reason to believe that these large changes [which occurred in the evolution of mammals and flowering plants from primitive aquatic forms] are not the result of the very same mechanics [which has produced dark colored moths from light colored moths in some species.]"[8] It will be remembered that a single gene mutation is sufficient to bring about the dark condition in the moths.

Professor Gairdner Moment of Goucher College tells the students who study his textbook: "Since 1900, thousands of mutations have been discovered in dozens of different kinds of animals and plants. Nevertheless, some men have objected that mutations cannot form the basis of evolution because the observed mutations are all too trivial or do not effect fundamental characteristics. Such objectors have never been able to define what they mean by fundamental characters. Yet mutations have been found in the fruit fly *Drosophila* which involve the complete absence of eyes, change in the size, shape, and veining of wings, and transformation of the proboscis into a footlike structure. *Surely these things are not trivial characters.* [Boldface type in the original.] The absence of eyes is the absence of an entire organ, while both wings and mouthparts are regarded as of fundamental importance in the classification of insects. In plants a mutation has been found which, when present in the homozygous condition, makes the formation of chlorophyl impossible. Such seedlings always die after they have used up all the stored food in the seed from which they came."[9]

Since Professor Moment is endeavoring to show that there are mutations which affect "fundamental characteristics," it is to be expected that the examples he cites are fundamental ones. First of all it will be noticed that all of the mutations he lists are undesirable, deleterious, or lethal.

The only example he gives for plants is a lethal mutation causing albinism in green plants which cannot survive without chlorophyl.

The *eyeless* gene to which Professor Moment refers reduces or brings about the absence of the compound eyes of the fruit fly. Again, the malformation or loss of an organ is a very different matter from the development of a *new* organ where none was before. Human children may be born with defects or losses due to drugs ingested by the mother. This is not the same as a mutant gene, but it illustrates that malformations and losses of parts can occur during development. This is altogether different from the production of a human child with wings.

The presence of certain ions in the water can cause fish to develop with only one eye, centrally located, but there is no comparison between this and something which would cause an earthworm to develop eyes. Moreover, if flies which have the *eyeless* gene are inbred for some time, eyes develop in spite of the presence of the mutant gene. This is not due to a reverse mutation, for when these flies are crossed with normal flies and inbred for one generation (because the gene is a recessive) the eyeless condition reappears as before.

Finally, Professor Moment mentions the replacement of mouthparts by a foot-like structure. This is a very unfortunate state of affairs for the fly, but superficially it looks impressive from an evolutionary standpoint. Professor Sewell Wright, the eminent geneticist, refutes this argument effectively in the article he wrote on *Evolution* for the *Encyclopedia Britannica*. He says, "In cases of homeosis in which a single gene may, as in the fruitfly, *Drosophila melanogaster,* replace antennae by legs, certain mouthparts by legs, balancers by wings, etc., the gene is to be looked upon not as a germinal representative of the whole complex structure but as a switch which alters conditions so as to set going a long established reaction system in a strange location."[10] In other words, he says that new structures do not come about in this way.

Another important problem, and one which is generally passed over without mention in the textbooks, is how *new* genes could come about. When a gene mutates it produces an alternative form of the structure or condition it produced before. When a gene for wing form mutates it produces another wing form, and not an eye color. When a gene for eye color mutates it produces another eye color, not a change in the form of the bristles. Thus, if we evolved from protozoa, where along the way did we get genes which produce bones, blood, and teeth, for protozoa do not have these? How could our gene complex have come about from the genes possessed by ancestral invertebrates?

There are genes which suppress the actions of other genes, and at one time these were thought to be new genes. This turned out not to be the case, and it is admitted that these genes cannot be a source of new genes.

Occasionally a part of a chromosome — a structure within the cell which contains the genes — may become duplicated. Professor H. J. Muller of Indiana University, who won the Nobel prize for his work on mutations, believes that this is a means by which new genes can be produced. He thinks that when genes are duplicated in this manner, one of the duplicates will not be needed, and can therefore become something different. He says, "And although these genes are at first, in the main at least, duplicates of others that are present, they and the others must in further evolution diverge more and more from each other through the establishment of mutations which occur independently in the two locations, so as finally to gain quite different properties."[11]

Professor Richard Goldschmidt of the University of California at Berkeley, another outstanding geneticist, commented on this explanation of the production of new genes: "I have always felt that this idea is very crude and, in addition, contrary to all we know about the action of the gene. . . ."[12] The reason he gives for rejecting this theory as contrary to what is known about the gene is that when genes mutate they merely produce an alternative effect in the same structure, and hence this is not a convincing explanation of the origin of different hereditary features. This same argument also contradicts that of Weir that "spare genes," which are not essential, mutate to something quite different and thus afford a source of new genes.[13]

Laurence H. Snyder, a famous geneticist in the field of human genetics, says, "As to the origin of genes, we know very little, although it is tempting to speculate."[14]

Although mutations generally are accepted by evolutionists as the basis for evolutionary variation — because there is nothing better — there are some who are not so certain that mutations really are the answer to this problem.

James W. Mavor, Professor Emeritus of Biology at Union College, says, "The thoughtful student will also ask whether random mutation, and isolation and natural selection . . . could have built up organisms as complicated as the higher plants and animals. At present no satisfactory direct answer can be given. That long eons of time and billions of individuals are involved is not in itself an entirely satisfactory answer."[15]

Ernest A. Hooton, Harvard's famed anthropologist, said, "Saltatory evolution by way of mutation, is a very convenient way of bridging over gaps between animal forms. . . . Now I am afraid that many anthropologists (including myself) have sinned against genetic science and are leaning upon a broken reed when we depend upon mutations."[16]

After discussing the evolution of independent parts which work together, such as the proper sort of teeth to go with a specialized digestive system, Daniel P. Quiring, Associate Professor of Biology at Western Reserve University, says, "To explain these helpful and useful changes in organ transformation, we are thrown back, as indicated, on mutations for their appearance and operation, and yet to depend upon this explanation is to make excessive demands on the mutation concept."[17]

Professor Goldschmidt, to whom reference was made previously, is the most noted opponent of the mutation theory of evolutionary variation. He maintained that there is a limit to the amount of change that can be brought about through an accumulation of mutations, and that mutations are inadequate as a means of bringing about evolution. He accepted evolution as a fact, and to explain it he suggested that there must be some sort of drastic change which can be produced. This kind of change, which is much more extensive than those produced by known mutations he designated by the term *systemic mutation.* He believed that such changes might occur during embryonic stages of development. Most individuals in which this occurred would be so abnormal that they could not survive, but he postulated that there would be occasional "lucky monsters," which would be the means of further evolution.

Goldschmidt's views about mutations have not gained acceptance to the present time. Theodosius Dobzhansky, the great geneticist of Columbia University, says that such changes as Goldschmidt's theory demands have never been found in nature. He says, "Another theorist proposes that the marvellous gifts of evolution to the living world came to birth through sudden and drastic 'systemic mutations,' which created 'hopeful monsters' that were later polished down to the final product by evolutionary selection. But these theories amount only to giving more or less fancy names to imaginary phenomena: no one has ever observed the occurrence of a 'systemic mutation,' for instance."[18]

It takes faith to believe that mutations and natural selection have brought about the world of living things. Hall and Moog of Washington University say in their textbook, "From myriad mutations occurring at random over the ages, there have evolved ever more varied and complex beings, including even the possessors of intelligent minds capable of attempting to comprehend the whole scheme. How can orderly progression emerge from randomness? Some philosophically-minded students [they do not even say religiously-minded] have preferred to attribute the directiveness of evolutionary change to a supernatural intelligence beyond the realm of scientific inquiry. Yet it is possible [they believe] to explain the long-continued trends that we find in evolutionary history by gene mutations, recombination, and selection."[19]

NOTES

1. Huxley, Julian, *Evolution in Action* (Harper and Bros., 1953), p. 45.

2. Dobzhansky, Theodosius, *Evolution, Genetics, and Man* (John Wiley and Sons, 1955), p. 105.

3. Dobzhansky, Theodosius, "On the Methods of Evolutionary Biology and Anthropology. Part I. Biology," *American Scientist*, 45:5:381, December, 1957, p. 385.

4. Sinnott, Edmund W., L. C. Dunn, and T. Dobzhansky, *Principles of Genetics*, 4th ed. (Macmillan, 1950), p. 315.

5. Dunn, L. C., *Heredity and Evolution in Human Populations* (Harvard University Press, 1959), p. 7.

6. Dobzhansky, Theodosius, *Evolution, Genetics, and Man, loc. cit.*, p. 105.

7. Moment, Gairdner B., *General Biology*, 2nd ed. (Appleton-Century-Crofts, 1950), p. 579.

8. Bonner, John Tyler, *The Ideas of Biology* (Harper and Bros., 1962), p. 48.

9. Moment, Gardner B., *loc. cit.*, p. 579.

10. Wright, Sewell, *Encyclopedia Britannica*, "Evolution," 1957.

11. Dunn, L. C., Editor, *Genetics in the Twentieth Century* (Macmillan, 1951), p. 94. This explanation was also proposed by Calvin Bridges about the same time, 1935, and was suggested by Anderson in 1920. See footnote on same page and also, Goldschmidt, Richard, *Theoretical Genetics* (University of California Press, 1955), p. 485.

12. Goldschmidt, Richard, *Theoretical Genetics* (University of California Press), 1955, pp. 485, 486.

13. *Ibid.*, p. 487. Also: Weir, J. A., "Sparing Genes for Further Evolution," *Iowa Experimental Station Journal,* Paper I-1370:313, 1953.

14. Snyder, Laurence H., *Principles of Heredity,* 4th ed. (D. C. Heath, 1951), p. 332.

15. Mavor, J. W., *General Biology* 4th ed. (Macmillan, 1952), p. 752.

16. Hooton, Ernest A., *Apes, Men, and Morons* (George Allen and Unwin, 1937), p. 118.

17. Quiring, Daniel P., *Functional Anatomy of the Vertebrates* (McGraw-Hill, 1950), p. 314.

18. Dobzhansky, Theodosius. See *Plant Life,* by Dennis Flannagan *et. al.* (Simon and Schuster, 1957), p. 131.

19. Hall, Thomas, and F. Moog, *Life Science* (John Wiley, 1955), p. 442.

HYBRIDIZATION AND POLYPLOIDY

Evolution is sometimes said to have occurred also through hybridization and polyploidy. (Polyploidy is an increase in the number of chromosomes.) In the book *Evolution and Christian Thought Today,* put out by the American Scientific Affiliation, Irving W. Knobloch says, "Many authorities [this apparently means non-Christian evolutionists] believe that interspecific hybridization [hybridization between species] has played an important role in evolution. The list of hybrids in the appendix [of the A.S.A. book], incomplete as it is, confirms their opinion."[1] Thus he says that the evolutionists are correct in believing that hybridization plays an important role in evolution.

However, it does not take a great deal of reflection to see that evolution could not get very far through hybridization. Nothing new is added, and there is merely a mixture of what is already present. For example, evolutionists believe that there was a time when there was no form of life on earth higher than fish and that all vertebrates evolved from fish. But no matter how frequently or in what combination hybridization occurred among fish, rhinoceroses and ostriches would never result. To produce these creatures something new would have to be added, something which could not be obtained through any combination of the hereditary factors found in fish.

Similarly, no real progress could be made through an increase in the number of chromosomes, for this would merely increase the quantity of hereditary factors which are already there and would add nothing new.

Through the use of polyploidy certain crosses become possible which otherwise could not be made, but this leads only to more hybridization. This technique is employed with plants, and generally is not applicable in the case of animals. Thus, if evolution proceeded in this manner, one might expect to find more species of plants than of animals, but the number of species of animals is much greater than that of plants.

The classic example of a new species produced by polyploidy is *Rapshanobrassica,* a combination of radish and cabbage. It has a root like a cabbage and a top like a radish, so it is of no value except to demonstrate that this sort of thing can happen. It is fertile with others of its kind, but not with either of the parent species. It is, however, a combination of certain properties inherent in cabbages and radishes. It is a mustard, as are cabbages and radishes. It is something new only in the sense that it has been produced by a new combination of previously existing hereditary factors. New combinations of genes and interactions of these hereditary factors in such a hybrid do not result in the sort of thing which must have happened if all the living things which we observe came from simple beginnings.

Sedges are grass-like plants that grow in moist places. Sedges of the genus *Carex* are the classic example of "evolution" through the change in number of chromosomes not in complete sets. But the various species of this genus are not on their way to becoming anything really different. They are still sedges of the same genus.

When hybridization and polyploidy are cited as methods of producing evolution, it appears to be a case of figuratively "scraping the bottom of the barrel" to find evidence which is simply not there.

NOTE

1. Mixter, Russell L., Editor, *Evolution and Christian Thought Today* (Wm. B. Eerdmans Publishing Co., 1959), p. 103.

THE EXCLUSION PRINCIPLE

According to Gause's principle, more commonly known as the exclusion principle, no difference between populations of animals or plants is really trivial if the populations are in complete competition, for by a "compound interest effect," the slight advantage which even a small difference gives to one population will eventually cause it to replace the other.

As a corollary to this, if two established populations are co-existing, they are not in complete competition with each other. An illustration of this is afforded by two species of birds, the cormorant and the shag, which nest on the same cliffs and obtain their food from the same waters. A closer study reveals that although they nest on the same cliffs, the type of nesting site is different and their food is not the same. The shag feeds on free-swimming fish, while the cormorant takes its food from among the flatfish and invertebrates which inhabit the bottom of the shallow water.

Professor Garrett Hardin of the University of California at Santa Barbara considers the exclusion principle so important that he says it plays a role in biology similar to the role which the Newtonian laws of motion play in physics.[1] He considers it central to evolutionary theory and expresses surprise that its importance has not been recognized sooner.[2]

Thus, according to the exclusion principle, if some rather small hereditary change occurs in a part of a population of animals or plants, either the two groups thus formed will have a somewhat different mode of life and will not be in complete competition, or else one will exterminate the other. If new types exterminate older types, as a series of hereditary changes occurs, a progression of types will occur, and the organisms which survive will be better adapted to their environment than the ones which were exterminated. But after such a series of changes there will remain only *one* surviving type. This does not allow for diversity. For the evolution of all forms of life found on earth from simple beginnings there would have to have been a great deal of diversity. For diversity to occur under the requirements of the exclusion principle something else is required. This something else is isolation.

If a barrier of some sort, like a mountain range, arises and separates a population into two groups, then one group may vary in one way and the other group in some other way, especially if the environment on one side of the barrier is different from the environment on the other side.

Professor Hardin admits that in most cases a physical barrier would not separate two such groups long enough to permit them to become significantly different in their habits. In other words, when they got together again, the exclusion principle would still operate, and one of them would destroy the other. Thus he believes that after being separated for some time by a barrier, variant forms of most species will still be in complete competition if the barrier is removed or becomes ineffective. Furthermore, he believes that even in many cases where the barrier separates groups for so long a time that the populations on opposite sides become different species, the "sister species" thus produced will still compete when they get together, and only one will survive.

Although one barrier could divide many kinds of organisms into separate groups at the same time, such as snakes, mice, and buttercups, and a separate barrier would obviously not be necessary for each kind of organism, still it is hard to believe that there could have been a sufficient number of barriers to bring about all the diversity we see about us.

Some authors have postulated the adequacy of short-time barriers, even such a thing as the rut of a wagon wheel, as being sufficient isolating factors for some organisms. It is also said that barriers need not be physical, and that physiological, anatomical, and behavioral differences can act as barriers to inbreeding. However, if the exclusion principle is true, these methods of genetic isolation would be ineffective, for in each case, as diversity began, one type would exterminate the other.

It is highly questionable whether real evolution — the evolution of all animals and plants and human beings from simple beginnings — could have come about through small inheritable changes. It is, however, commonly assumed by evolutionists that it did come about in this way. But now, according to the exclusion principle, this must be accompanied by a very effective isolation, an isolation so extensive that the diverging types become too distinct to compete for the same ecological niche when the barrier ceases to keep them apart.

It seems that according to the exclusion principle, evolution will not occur unless there are many isolating barriers which endure for a very long time indeed. Thus it seems that instead of being very important in explaining how evolution came about, the exclusion principle makes the theory of evolution less plausible than it seemed before the principle was suggested.

NOTES

1. Hardin, Garrett, *Nature and Man's Fate* (Rinehart and Co., 1959), p. 86.
2. *Ibid.*, p. 87.

THE SECOND LAW OF THERMODYNAMICS

According to the second law of thermodynamics, the universe is like a clock that is running down. This is so because as energy is expended, the amount of energy available for accomplishing "work" diminishes, although the total amount of energy remains the same.[1]

When a spring-type clock is wound, energy is put into the spring as it is coiled tighter and tighter. As the spring uncoils, this energy operates the clock. But less energy is available for running the clock than was put into the spring during the winding because some of the energy dissipates as heat. In any operation, some energy is lost as heat or in some other way so that it is not useful to the process. Thus the total amount of useful energy becomes less. Scientists are certain that unless there is a creative force operating in the universe, a time will come when the sun and all the stars will burn out and the universe will have "run down" completely.[2]

This "running down" of the universe poses a real problem for the atheists, for how could it have gotten "wound up" in the first place so that it can now be in the process of "running down"? This is no problem at all for Christians, for the Bible says that God created, and we are told that in the city of the New Jerusalem there will be no need for the sun or moon, for the glory of the Lord will light it. (See Revelation, chapter 21, especially verses 22 and 23.)

Gordon J. Van Wylen, Chairman of the Department of Mechanical Engineering at the University of Michigan, has written a textbook on thermodynamics. In the preface he has the customary paragraph acknowledging help from various sources, but he closes it with a statement which is very unusual for a science textbook. He says, "Also I would be remiss without acknowledging the help and grace of God, the Creator of the universe and the Author of life."[3] In his text he discusses the matter of how the universe became "wound up." The technical term employed with regard to energy relationships in this connection is *entropy*, which is said to *increase* as a mechanism is operated or runs down. He says, "The question that arises is how the universe got into the state of reduced entropy in the first place, since all natural processes known to us tend to increase entropy?" His only suggestion is creation, a phenomenon unknown to science. He concludes his discussion by saying, "The author has found that the second law [of thermodynamics] tends to increase his conviction that there is a Creator who has the answer for the future destiny of man and the universe."[4]

Another way of looking at the second law of thermodynamics is that there is a trend toward randomness in the universe. That is, the trend is toward forming less complex distributions of matter from more complex ones. A non-living structure left to itself tends to deteriorate and disintegrate. It falls apart and the pieces become scattered. A tornado can destroy a building, spreading its materials in a haphazard manner, but it will not assemble materials to form a building. The tendency toward randomness in nature is the opposite of evolution, for according to the theory of evolution, more complex forms have developed from less complex forms. Therefore it has been said that the theory of evolution is contrary to the second law of thermodynamics.

Arthur Eddington, the renowned British astronomer, has expressed the belief that this law holds the supreme position among the laws of nature. After saying that hardly any difficulty need be fatal to a theory, he adds, "But if your theory is found to be against the second law of thermodynamics I can give you no hope; there is nothing for it but to collapse in deepest humiliation."[5]

The second law of thermodynamics has not been discredited. The theory of evolution is very much in vogue today, and students and the general public are told over and over that its acceptance as a fact is practically unanimous among men of science. It follows from this that the evolutionists have been able to convince themselves that the theory of evolution is not contrary to this law. They do this by saying that there really is no contradiction because all the energy needed to bring about evolution has been supplied abundantly by an external source, namely the sun.

A human being can overcome randomness and produce a more complex configuration by doing such things as taking pigments from various sources and arranging them to represent a landscape, or even by painting a sign saying, "Keep off the Grass." To do these things requires intelligence, skill, and the expenditure of energy. It is evident that energy alone is not enough. A strong young Eskimo given a pile of random letters might not be able to arrange any of them in such a way as to communicate a message.

A bird can overcome randomness by collecting scattered materials and building a nest. This also requires an expenditure of energy, but energy alone is not enough. An ability which may be called an expression of instinct is also needed. As in the case of human beings, the energy comes from food, and it may be traced back to the sun as its origin.

An egg developing into an individual increases in complexity. This also requires an expenditure of energy, but again energy alone is not enough. An egg will not develop into a new individual unless it has a suitable genetic constitution to determine the pattern of the development.

Thus more complex arrangements of matter can be produced from simpler or from random arrangements. In each of the examples given here, the energy required can be traced to an outside source, the sun. But in each case this energy was not enough. Such things as intelligence, skill, instinct, and genetic constitution were also required.

If a watchmaker takes loose parts and puts them together to make a functional watch, he expends energy as he works. However, skill is also required. If the parts of a watch are placed in a box and shaken, more energy may be expended than is actually required to assemble the watch, but this will not put the parts together to form a watch.

As already mentioned in previous discussions, there are some men of science who profess to be Bible-believing Christians who nevertheless accept and teach a certain amount of evolution. Some of them criticize anti-evolutionists for invoking the second law of thermodynamics as an evidence against the theory of evolution. They say that there is no problem here because the sun has supplied all the energy needed. It is reasonable to ask them this question: Granted that plenty of energy is available from the sun, does this have any more bearing on the problem of evolution than the supplying of energy to a box of watch parts has to assembling a watch? One of these men was asked to comment on this watch-in-a-box analogy. His reply was that the Lord had apparently created matter with certain rules so that some combinations of atoms and groups of atoms were more likely to occur than other arrangements. This is as though the parts of the watch which belonged together had an affinity for each other, so that when they were shaken in the box and came together in the right way, they tended to stay together, while other combinations separated again.[6]

There are many kinds of groups of atoms which have an affinity for each other, and they come together and form compounds. Some can come together in one or a few definite arrangements, forming crystals. But the growth of a crystal is not comparable to the evolution of a plant or animal from some simple form of life.

Under certain conditions some organic compounds will combine to form amino acids. This is thought by the evolutionists to be a clue to the origin of life. But in animals and plants the affinities of atoms would have to be manifest in the ultimate structures of the chromosomes to be effective in evolution. This involves the problem of the origin of chromosomes, and the structure and behavior of the chromosomes of protozoa are as complex as the structure and behavior of the chromosomes in human beings.

If the affinities of atoms for each other is the answer to the problem of how to accomodate the theory of evolution to the second law of thermodynamics, it is strange that the reason given by evolutionists is that the sufficient energy from the sun is an adequate solution.

When Christians have to retreat this far in order to reconcile their theology with evolutionary biology and the theory of evolution with the second law of thermodynamics (if indeed either of these can be accomplished), they are limiting the creative work of God to the making of atoms which have affinities for each other. Some liberal, nominal Christians who are theistic evolutionists give God credit for more than that.

At a convention sponsored by the American Scientific Affiliation a Jesuit priest named Robert J. O'Connell delivered an address which was published in the *Journal of the American Scientific Affiliation* for September, 1966. The talk was about Teilhard de Chardin, the Catholic priest whose theology was so heretical that he was forbidden to teach and not allowed to publish during his lifetime. However, he has since come into high favor with an enthusiastic following.

One of the points made by the speaker seems to be that Teilhard has a message of hope for the world, namely that evolution has overcome the second law of thermodynamics. The hope for the world in this message is that the physical world is not "running down" after all, as claimed by the physicists. Since this "gospel of cosmic despair" is not true, according to Teilhard, as announced by this convention speaker, mankind need not lose interest in human betterment.

Of course this is all utterly ridiculous. Besides the audacity in announcing that the second law of thermodynamics is at fault, it should be realized that the physicists allow billions of years for the running down of the physical world while the people who are working today for the betterment of mankind are doing so without any assurance that civilization will last even one year more. That is, those who do not believe the Bible have no such assurance. Christians know that Christ will return and will reign in righteousness.

NOTES

1. In atomic reactions matter can be changed into energy and energy can be changed into matter, but in all ordinary operations the total amount of matter and energy remains the same.

2. According to the steady state theory, hydrogen atoms are constantly being created, and the universe has no beginning and no end in time. As stars burn out, according to this theory, new ones come into being from the new hydrogen atoms. For more information on the steady state theory see such books as: Hoyle, Fred, *Astronomy* (Doubleday and Co., 1962), p. 300, *et seq.* And by the same author, *Foundations of Astronomy* (Harper and Bros., 1955), p. 322 *et seq.* This theory has been discarded.

3. Van Wylen, Gordon J., *Thermodynamics* (John Wiley and Sons, 1959, Fifth printing, 1963), p. xi.

4. *Ibid.,* p. 169.

5. Eddington, Arthur S., *The Nature of the Physical World* (Macmillan, 1930), p. 74.

6. Private correspondence. Request to quote directly was not granted.

LAMARCKISM

Lamarckism is a term used to describe the passage to the next generation of traits acquired during a lifetime. For example, it has often been said that according to Lamarckian theory, the children of blacksmiths should have strong arms because blacksmiths develop powerful arms through their work. There was a time when this was rather taken for granted. Then it became controversial. More recently its acceptance was considered synonymous with ignorance. Still more recently some scientists with reputations not to be rashly jeopardized have made statements containing Lamarckian implications when seeking for an explanation of evolutionary problems. In other words, a partial return to Lamarckism appears to be another indication of the inadequacy of the orthodox explanations of the way evolution allegedly came about.

Lamarck wrote in French, and a possible misunderstanding about the translation of one word seems to have added to his troubles. There has been some disagreement about whether or not Lamarck believed that over a number of generations animals could acquire traits or parts merely because of needing them or "desiring" them. Some have ridiculed him for suggesting this, while others say he had no intention of implying this.

Some modern evolutionists, however, have not hesitated to imply the acquiring of traits due to a need. For example, G. Elliot Smith, the eminent anatomist of Oxford University, said, "In one of these groups [the tree shrews] the importance of vision became still further increased, and the result of this was to bring into existence the Order Primates."[1] This can be fitted into a Darwinian explanation, but the implication is Lamarckian. Professor Smith seems to be saying that the primates, including ourselves, came into being because tree shrews needed to see better.

Before reproductive cells were observed under the microscope and before the way they function was understood, the physical basis of heredity could not be appreciated and applied to the problems of evolution. August Weismann is the most well known of those who proclaimed late in the nineteenth century that Lamarckism is impossible because of the way the reproductive materials are passed from one generation to the next. He performed the crude but famous experiment of cutting off the tails of mice for many generations, and found that the tails of the mice of the last generation were just as long as the tails of the original parents.

The mild-mannered Charles Darwin, who had very few quarrels during his lifetime, did not hesitate to make some unkind remarks about Lamarck and about his own grandfather, both deceased, because they espoused the idea of the inheritance of acquired characteristics, which he at that time abhorred. It is therefore all the more remarkable that in later life he himself accepted ever greater amounts of Lamarckism.

With the rediscovery of Mendel's laws of inheritance and the new knowledge of the physical basis of heredity, Lamarckism seemed to be fully discredited. It was said that there was no evidence for it, and furthermore that it could not be. But there were those who would not give up. The psychologist William McDougall performed his famous experiment on the inheritance of learning in rats, but his methods were so faulty that his data are worthless. In Russia the famous Ivan Pavlov, who innocently gave the Communists the technique of brainwashing, thought he was getting smarter mice through the inheritance of acquired learning. But he changed his mind and decided that the explanation of his results was not that the mice were getting smarter but that he was becoming a better teacher of mice.

There have been a number of claims of Lamarckian inheritance in laboratory experiments, but when repeated by other investigators the results were not confirmed, or for one reason or another were not found acceptable. There are some cases where environmental factors are known to act directly upon the reproductive cells, but this is a different matter. However, when all else fails, Lamarckian inheritance can be revived to help hurdle the difficulties, in explaining evolutionary phenomena.

Considering the amount of ridicule and abuse which Lamarckism has received, a surprising amount of it may be found in biological literature. Here are a few quotations spanning a number of years to illustrate Lamarckian implications in scientific writing.

In 1930 Alexander Meek, Professor of Zoology at the University of Durham, said, "The inheritance of acquired characters as a theory fell into the background for a long period, but it is once more being advanced, for several investigators have ventured to show from experiment that acquired modifications may be inherited."[2]

In 1947 William Howells, while still at the University of Wisconsin, said, "Not long ago it was felt that Darwin had silenced Lamarck for good, but there is now less certainty."[3] (Thus when circumstances seem to demand a Lamarckian explanation it is convenient to forget that Darwin himself accepted Lamarckian explanations in his later life.)

In 1954 George C. Kent Jr., Associate Professor of Zoology at Lousiana State University, said, "The doctrine of Lamarck . . . appeared untenable with the rise of Mendelian genetics and, like many other attempts at scientific explanation, was the target of ridicule from the majority of scientists during the first half of the twentieth century. A modification of the theory is finding favor again among the zoologists, whose interpretations of the mechanisms of heredity are, like theories in other fields of scientific endeavor, undergoing a continuing, healthy evolution."[4]

It is rather commonly said by evolutionists that when our ancestors stopped using their front limbs predominantly for walking and used them more as hands to convey food to the mouth, a snout was no longer needed. For this reason the jaws became shorter. In turn shorter jaws and other related changes in the head allowed more room for brains. E. O. James of the Royal Anthropological Institute said, "Teeth were no longer used for carrying, and as a result the snout began to recede, giving an increased cranial cavity. . . ."[5] The

Lamarckian implication in this statement is evident, but he leaves no doubt about it, for on the following page he says, "Just as the mental powers of dull children are often stimulated by a course in handicraft, so the freeing of the hand . . . unquestionably reacted on the growing brain of our arboreal ancestors."

Professor Hooton of Harvard agrees, and said, "Just as increased function of a body part results in its development, so diminished use causes shrinkage. Consequently the new utilization of the liberated hands results in a recession of the jaws. The dental arches grow smaller; the projecting canine teeth are reduced to the level of their fellows. . . . To put it concisely, the brain has expanded because greater and greater demands have been made upon it, and the jaws have shrunk because the majority of their functions have been taken over by the hands and the extra-organic objects used as implements."[6] Professor Hooton admits that his statement "reeks of Lamarckianism," which he recognizes as unpopular. He seems to reject a Darwinian explanation and says that for those who reject his own Lamarckian interpretation there remains the theory of J. R. Marett, who postulates that a deficiency in the diet of certain primates caused waterlogging of body tissues and a cranial expansion. This cranial expansion was not due to an increase in the size of the brain but to "water on the brain." Nature then filled in this available space with more brains. Professor Hooton prefers a Lamarckian explanation to this and says, "I am inclined to regard unfavorably this morbid theory of human evolution. I doubt that disease has kicked an inadequate ape upstairs to humanity."

Frederick A. Lucas of the American Museum of Natural History describes alternative theories of the evolution of flight, and the descriptions sound rather Lamarckian. "According to one view, the about-to-be birds ran along the ground, or jumped into the air waving their forelimbs vigorously, until the time came when the wings were sufficiently developed to raise their owner into the air. Those who hold the other view consider that flight began by animals leaping from trees and instinctively spreading their limbs to catch at anything convenient to break their fall."[7]

George C. Kent Jr. of Lousiana State University mentions the fact that the esophagus of vampire bats is too narrow for the passage of anything but a fluid diet. He comments that it is interesting to speculate whether the small lumen of the esophagus forced the vampire to a diet of blood or whether a diet of blood for many generations resulted in the deterioration of the esophagus. He says that if the former is true, it is fortunate for these bats that they became adept at obtaining blood for their food, for otherwise they would have starved to death and become extinct.[8] Vampires have other adaptations which enable them to obtain blood for food, and it is a great oversimplification to imply that they were rather ordinary bats that took to drinking blood because their gullets became too narrow to accomodate solid nourishment.

Professor William C. Beaver of Wittenberg College tells in his textbook about an experiment in which the eggs of a single aquatic snail were divided into two groups. One group was placed in acidic water and the other in alkaline water. The snails of the former group developed thin, delicate shells, while those in the other group produced large, heavy shells. This would have presented a real problem to the taxonomist, for Professor Beaver says that the differences between these snails were so great that if the facts had not been known, it would have been thought that there was no relationship between them. He then presents this kind of environmental change as a Lamarckian basis of evolution, for he says, "Is this not suggestive of what happens in other living organisms? Many forms originally closely related develop along entirely different lines, depending upon one or more differing environmental factors. Is this not illustrative of 'descent with change?' "[9]

In attempting to explain why anthropoid apes do not have tails, Roy Chapman Andrews of the American Museum of Natural History said that "in the living anthropoids the tails disappeared far back in their evolutionary history. Just why is not clear; probably because they habitually sat on their rear ends and the tail vertebrae turned inward instead of continuing in the line of the spine."[10]

Lamarckian explanations are easy and convenient, and when it suits them to do so, some evolutionists from Darwin to the present time have not hesitated to use them. But the fact is that so far no adequate scientific evidence for this kind of inheritance has been presented.

It is rather surprising how frequently someone asks: "Is it true that women have one more rib than men?" The occasion for the question is apparent. Some anatomical part, and the Hebrew word for it is translated *rib* in the King James version of the Bible, was taken by God from the side of the first man to make the first woman. It is therefore concluded by some that men have one less rib than women.

It would be as reasonable to conclude that if a man loses an arm, his daughters and granddaughters and great-granddaughters will have one more arm than his sons and grandsons and great-grandsons. This would be Lamarckian inheritance.

However, the Bible says that when the original parents disobeyed the clear command of God, something *did* happen to them which has been passed on to all their descendants. Their nature was changed, and according to Scripture, everyone since that time has been born with a sin nature. The inheritance of a sin nature through the sinning of the man Adam is not a case of Lamarckian inheritance of an acquired characteristic, because it resulted from a direct judgment by God in accordance with a command He had made. It is due to an act of God and it is not comparable to a natural phenomenon. Since we are born with a sin nature we must be born again in order to become a part of the family of God (see the third chapter of the gospel of John). As sin came through the disobedience of one man, so the atonement for sin came through the obedience of One, the Lord Jesus Christ. He alone could atone for sin because He, being Deity, partook of human nature, yet was without sin. He alone in His incarnation in human form was not born with a sin nature. Thus salvation from the penalty of sin is afforded through His vicarious sacrifice upon the cross at Calvary. Salvation cannot be earned. It is a free gift, bestowed upon the sinner who will repent and accept Christ as his Saviour and Lord.

In the thirtieth chapter of Genesis there is recorded a procedure performed by Jacob, intended to produce speckled animals by means of maternal impressions. How prenatal impressions of the mother could affect the offspring would be as difficult to explain scientifically as Lamarckism. In trying to account for Jacob's results, it is surprising how commentators have overlooked the explanation given by the Bible in the following chapter, verses eleven and twelve. The Lord intervened in Jacob's behalf and permitted only the animals to breed which would produce the types of offspring which were to belong to Jacob. The results obtained were due to an act of God. Jacob's peeled rods had nothing to do with it.[11]

NOTES

1. Smith, G. Elliot, *The Evolution of Man* (Oxford University Press, 1924), p. 12.

2. Meek, Alexander, *The Progress of Life* (Longmans, Greene, and Co., 1930), p. 94.

3. Howells, William, *Mankind So Far* (Doubleday and Co., 1947), p. 8.

4. Kent, George C., *Comparative Anatomy of the Vertebrates* (The Blakiston Co., 1954), p. 83.

5. James, E. O., *The Beginnings of Man* (Doubleday, Doran, and Co., 1929), p. 49.

6. Hooton, E. A., *Apes, Men, and Morons* (George Allen and Unwin, 1938), p. 30.

7. Lucas, Frederic A., *Animals of the Past. American Museum of Natural History Handbook*, 7th ed., 1929, p. 68.

8. Kent, George, *loc. cit.*, p. 83.

9. Beaver, William C., *General Biology*, 5th ed. (C. V. Mosby Co., 1958), p. 683.

10. Andrews, Roy Chapman, *Meet Your Ancestors* (Viking Press, 1954), p. 15.

11. The types of sheep and goats which were to go to Jacob according to the agreement were marked with recessive traits. Thus animals of this sort would naturally recur in a mixed flock from which all that were so marked had been removed. This could have been observed at any time by anyone who tried it, but the explanation would not have been understood until modern times. But the fact that a great abundance of animals so marked occurred was due to an act of God, not to natural causes or Jacob's rods.

Chapter VI

THE EVIDENCES OF EVOLUTION

The *method* of evolution has long been a point of embarrassment to the evolutionists. Subsequent to the acceptance of Darwin's natural selection theory and De Vries' mutation theory it was admitted that these are not adequate to explain evolution. But even at that time it was emphasized that although the method of evolution was not understood, the *evidences* of evolution were so strong that evolution itself was not to be doubted.

Following is a discussion of the evidences of evolution commonly listed in the textbooks.

THE EVIDENCE FROM COMPARATIVE ANATOMY

One of the strongest evidences for evolution is said to be found in the similarities which are observed in different kinds of animals. The bones of a horse are rather strikingly different from our bones, but there is sufficient similarity so that a person who is familiar with the human skeleton can easily recognize and name the corresponding bones of the horse. The same thing may be said of other structures, such as muscles, blood vessels, and organs of the digestive tract. A fish also has these parts, but they are not as similar to ours as are the corresponding parts of a horse. This is taken as evidence that we are more closely related to horses than to fish. In other words, we are said to have had a common ancestor with horses more recently than we had with fish. Similarity of structure is interpreted to be a criterion of closeness of kinship — the greater the similarity, the closer the kinship.

Two outstanding evolutionists of a generation ago may be quoted to illustrate what evolutionists thought of this evidence at that time.

Thomas Hunt Morgan, Professor of Experimental Zoology at Columbia University, said, "If, then, it can be established beyond dispute that similarity or even identity of the same character in different species is not always to be interpreted to mean that both have arisen from a common ancestor, the whole argument from comparative anatomy seems to tumble in ruins."[1]

About ten years later Horatio Hockett Newman, Professor of Biology at the University of Chicago, made an even stronger statement. He said, "Now, a careful survey of the situation reveals the fact that the only postulate the evolutionist needs is no more or less than a logical extension of what the layman considers a truism or self-evident fact, namely, that fundamental structural resemblance signifies generic relationship; that, generally speaking, *the degree of structural resemblance runs essentially parallel with closeness of kinship.* Most biologists would say that this is not merely a postulate, but one of the best established laws of life. . . . If we cannot rely upon this postulate . . . we can make no sure progress in any attempt to establish the validity of the principle of evolution."[2]

Thus Professor Morgan said that if a case can be found in which similarity of characteristics does not relate to common ancestry, the argument for evolution from comparative anatomy appears to be of no value. Professor Newman went so far as to say that if this evidence is not reliable, it is not only the evidence from comparative anatomy which is invalid, but the theory of evolution itself.

To bring this up-to-date, Hall and Moog say in their textbook that "in general, the greater resemblance between two species, the more recent we assume the common ancestor to have been."[3]

Strausbaug and Weimer say it this way in their textbook: "The greater the similarity of structure the closer the relationship, and, wherever close relationship is found, a common ancestry is indicated."[4]

In his textbook, Ralph Buchsbaum says, "The most important kind of evidence is that based on a comparative study of the structure and development of the various groups. The use of such evidence is based on the assumption that the more closely the body plans of two phyla resemble each other, the closer their relationship and the more recent their common ancestor."[5]

Since this kind of evidence is considered so important and since professors Morgan and Newman said that exceptions would render this evidence invalid, it is of considerable interest to inquire whether any exceptional cases have been found. The answer is that they have indeed been found, and they have been found in abundance.

Concerning molluscs (sea shells), William W. Watts, Professor of

Geology at Imperial College of Science and Technology, says, "Two contemporaneous shells may appear so much alike that they have been considered to belong to the same genus or even the same species. An examination of their internal structures has often revealed such differences between the two as to compel the belief that one form was descended by modification [evolution] from an ancestor quite different from that of the other. . . ."[6]

Horace E. Wood Jr., Professor of Biology at Rutgers University, says, "One of the most striking convergences in parallel evolution is that between the woolly rhinoceros and the living white rhinoceros of Africa. The resemblance, especially in skull and teeth, is so close that it long seemed incontrovertable that they were extremely closely related. This now appears not to be the case."[7]

If Dr. Wood had taken some visitors into his laboratory before he reached this latter conclusion, he would have pointed out certain details of skull and teeth and affirmed that they afford incontrovertable evidence that these animals are extremely closely related. The average visitor would have been in no position to offer evidence to the contrary, and anyone bold enough to say, "I don't believe it," no doubt would have appeared foolish. Yet Professor Wood himself admitted later, "This now appears not to be the case."

Ruggles R. Gates, Emeritus Professor of Botany at the University of London, says, "It will be seen that parallelisms occur plentifully in whatever direction we look."[8] Continuing his discussion of these plentiful parallelisms, he says, "Their abundance also involves recognition of the fact that groups, such as mammals, which are now regarded as uniform, have had a polyphyletic origin." He is saying that although it has been assumed in the past that mammals evolved from a single ancestral type, this is not so, and mammals which are rather similar to each other are now believed to have evolved from different non-mammalian ancestries.

It is now quite common to read in the scientific literature that various taxonomic groups are believed to have had a polyphyletic origin. This means that these animals are grouped together in a classification for reasons of convenience, but in spite of their similarities they are now thought to have evolved from different ancestries.

Alfred S. Romer, the famous comparative anatomist of Harvard University, says, "The known presence of parallelisms in so many cases and its suspected presence in others suggests that it may have been an almost universal phenomenon."[9] He goes on to say, "A close student of the subject may, if pressed, be driven to the logical though absurd admission of the possibility that two animals as closely related as, for example, chimpanzee and gorilla may have evolved in parallel fashion all the way from a piscene stage!" He says that a comparative anatomist might be forced into the absurd position of having to admit that gorillas and chimpanzees could have had separate lines of ancestry all the way back to ancestral fish, and thus be more closely related to fish than to each other.

Professor Romer believes that the hoofed condition in animals originated more than once from different ancestries, and thus he does not consider it at all absurd to say that "strange as it seems, a cow is, for example, probably as closely related to a lion as to a horse."[10]

A German biologist named Ivar Broman believes that mammals and amphibians have had a separate evolutionary history all the way back to different protozoan ancestors, and he believes that he can tell that certain amphibians have evolved from different protozoa than other amphibians.[11]

Marguerite W. Jepps, formerly lecturer in Zoology at the University of Glasgow, approvingly quotes an earlier author who said that further studies might reveal such things as the possibility that the one-celled *Chlamydomonas* is more closely related to an oak tree than to the superficially rather similar one-celled *Euglena*.[12]

Since evolutionists are now freely making admissions like these, it seems that there is very little value, if any, left in the evidence for evolution from comparative anatomy.

NOTES

1. Morgan, Thomas Hunt, "The Bearing of Mendalism on the Origin of Species," *Scientific Monthly*, 16:3:237, March, 1923, p. 246.

2. Newman, Horatio Hockett, *Evolution, Genetics, and Eugenics* (University of Chicago Press, 1932), p. 53.

3. Hall, Thomas S. and Florence Moog, *Life Science* (John Wiley and Sons, 1955), p. 63.

4. Strausbaug, Perry D. and Bernal R. Weimer, *General Biology*, 2d ed. (John Wiley and Sons, 1947), p. 629.

5. Buchsbaum, Ralph, *Animals Without Backbones* (University of Chicago Press, Rev. ed., 1948), p. 335.

6. Watts, William W. (One author), *Evolution in the Light of Modern Knowledge* (D. van Nostrand Co., 1925), p. 80.

7. Jepsen, Glenn L., Editor, *Genetics, Paleontology, and Paleontology* (Princeton University Press, 1949), p. 187.

8. Gates, Ruggles R., *Human Ancestry from a Genetical Point of View* (Harvard University Press, 1948), p. 3.

9. Jepson, Glenn L., *loc. cit.*, p. 115.

10. Romer, Alfred S., *Man and the Vertebrates* (University of Chicago Press, 1941, 8th impression, 1953), p. 139.

11. See *Biological Abstracts*, 1:11035, 1927.

12. Jepps, Marguerite W., *The Protoza* (Oliver and Boyd, 1956), p. vi.

THE EVIDENCE FROM VESTIGIAL, RUDIMENTARY, AND ATAVISTIC STRUCTURES

The idea of vestigial organs as an evidence of evolution is that they are the unnecessary remnants of structures which formerly were of real value to our ancestors. As difficulties arose with this interpretation it was modified to the effect that some of these structures may still have a function but that it has been changed through evolution.

Wiedersheim, a German anatomist, compiled a list of more than one hundred eighty rudimentary structures in man, and the human body came to be thought of as a walking museum of antiquity. But as the knowledge of physiology increased, it was found that most of these organs have a useful function, and many of them are vital.

The evidence of vestigial organs is still given in the textbooks in support of the theory of evolution, but the list of such structures has dwindled to a half dozen or so. Such a list never fails to include the appendix, which seems to be the classical example of a vestigial organ in man.

The appendix and the associated cecum in man are most commonly compared with the corresponding parts of the rabbit. It is implied, and sometimes it is plainly stated, that a distant common ancestor of rabbits and men used these structures for the storage of food. Descendants of this common ancestor which became rabbits continued to use food of such a nature that this organ had survival value, and hence rabbits today have a large pocket-like structure at the junction of the small and large intestines. But descendants of this common ancestor which became men adapted themselves to a different diet and no longer had a need for this organ. Hence it has become reduced in size to a vestige, and its function has been lost.

From an evolutionary viewpoint, a rabbit is indeed a very distant relative of man. Therefore one might expect to find in animals closer to man a series of organs of this type graded in size from large to vestigial, but this is not the case. The cecum is found rather generally in mammals, but it is particularly large in marsupials, in herbivorous animals, and in some rodents. The appendix is present in the great apes, but there is a difference of opinion expressed in scientific literature as to whether any of the monkeys have one. Dr. William Straus, Jr. of the Johns Hopkins University, the famous anthropologist and specialist in the primates, says that none of the primates has an appendix except man, the four anthropoid apes, and one lemur. Some others say the same thing, but still others write of the presence of an appendix in some monkeys.[1] Weichert says that a few rodents have one.[2] Civets, which are carnivorous animals, also have an appendix. The rabbit, which is no longer classified as a rodent, has such a good one that it is customarily used by the textbook writers to compare with man's. This seems just about to complete the list of animals known to have an appendix. There is no pattern in the distribution of this organ among the different sorts of animals such as would be expected if it had once been a prominent part of the cecum and then gradually became vestigial as evolving animals became diverse. It cannot be traced down through the primates toward an ancestor we had in common with the rabbits.

The appendix is rich in lymphoid tissue and apparently helps protect the body against infection, especially in early years. In this respect it is comparable to the tonsils and adenoids, and like them, it may become so badly infected that it needs to be removed.

Professor Alfred Romer, the outstanding comparative anatomist of Harvard University, said of the appendix, "This is frequently cited as a vestigial organ supposedly proving something or other about evolution. This is not the case."[3]

Other outstanding evolutionists, including Arthur Keith and Le Gros Clark, have made statements showing that they do not consider the appendix to be vestigial. Since a number of outstanding evolutionists question the validity of calling the appendix a vestigial organ, and since the appendix is the classical example of a vestigial organ, the whole concept of vestigial structures comes under grave suspicion.

If an organ has become vestigial through an evolutionary process because it lost its value, it should, after a reasonable time, disappear entirely and not remain vestigial. Authors who view the appendix as vestigial or as harmful should be somewhat embarrassed by the fact that natural selection has not yet eliminated it entirely.

There are some organs and structures which are functional in one sex of a species and not in the other. Structures of this sort which are not functional in one sex are said to be rudimentary rather than vestigial. An example of this is the rudimentary oviducts found in the males of the leopard frog, commonly dissected by college biology students. The oviducts are the tubes through which the eggs pass after their development in the ovaries. If one attaches the same evolutionary significance to these structures which is granted to the vestigial organs characteristic to both sexes in some species, namely that they represent parts which were functional in ancestral forms, one merely arrives at the conclusion that male frogs had female frogs in their ancestry! This is not to be denied, but it certainly is not enlightening from an evolutionary standpoint.

Another possible assumption is that far distant hypothetical ancestors of frogs had functional reproductive organs of both sexes in the same individual. This implies that at some later time some of these organs became rudimentary, and the animals which survived complemented each other in such a way that all organs necessary for reproduction were retained in the two types of animals called male and female.

If one thinks of frogs as having evolved from an ancestor which had functional organs of both sexes, it is interesting to consider how far back such an ancestor might have been. It is said that a few fish have both male and female organs, but they are not in a line which is supposed to have led to amphibians. Tracing backward along the frog's supposed line of descent, none of the vertebrates would qualify. Among the pro-chordates, which supposedly help bridge the gap between the vertebrates and the invertebrates, neither the well-known Amphioxus (which has long been held by the writers of textbooks as a form close to the ancestor of the vertebrate line) nor the acorn worms (which are also generally considered close to the ancestor of the vertebrates) have both male and female reproductive organs in the same individual. Finally, the sexes are separate in the starfish, sea urchins, and most of the animals of their group. If this seems to be irrelevant, it should be pointed out that frogs as well as human beings are thought to be more closely related to these animals than to any other invertebrates. But all of this really is unnecessary, for in this attempt to trace frog ancestry back to a hypothetical hermaphroditic ancestor, we have long since passed types of animals which have no oviducts at all, even in the female, for the lampreys and hagfish have none.

From this kind of evolutionary speculation it might be concluded that rudimentary oviducts are to be found in male frogs of all species, but this is not the case. Male bullfrogs have no rudimentary oviducts, and still more surprisingly, rudimentary oviducts are found in the males of some races of leopard frogs and not in others.

Even in human beings anatomists recognize a number of rudimentary structures, including a trace of oviduct in the male. The Bible says very clearly that the human male and female were created separately. Thus in the case of human beings, similarities between male and female are clearly due to similar design by one Designer. Since it is clearly so in this case, it is reasonable to believe it is so in other cases also, and where evolutionists assume homologies to indicate closeness of evolutionary kinship, these similarities may just as well be interpreted as similarity of design by the Creator.

James W. Leach, Associate Professor of Anatomy at the Ohio State University, writes in a way which might have been considered under the heading of *fantasy* concerning the presence of rudimentary mammary glands in the human male. He says, "Their occurrence in the male is of considerable biologic interest in that it would imply a former functional significance. The inference is that in the early history of mammals the young were produced in such large numbers that the male participated in nursing them. A general biologic principle holds that the number of young produced by a species is directly proportionate to the hazards to which the young are exposed. It would follow, therefore, that with the increased protection and care afforded the young of mammals, a corresponding decrease in the number of young occurred to the point where the female alone was adequate to nourish them."[4]

It is only in the mammals that the young are nourished with milk, and in no mammal does the male participate in this. It is said that in opossums, where the young become attached for some time to the teats, that too many young may be produced to be thus accomodated, but the males are not equipped to help.

Professor Leach admits a serious difficulty to his theory, for he adds, "Further speculation fails to explain the early [early in the evolutionary history of the mammals] mechanism in the father that would have brought about his lactation to coincide with the period of its requirement."

In addition to vestigial and rudimentary structures, there are others which are called atavistic. These are not characteristic of the species but occur sporadically and are considered to represent "throw backs" to a condition found in some ancestral type.

For example, humans have no ribs in the neck, but ribs in this area occur normally in certain living and fossil reptiles. Occasionally a human being is born with a pair of ribs in the neck, and such cervical ribs are thought by evolutionists to be another indication of our reptilian ancestry.

But when cervical ribs are given as an illustration in support of evolution and of our reptilian ancestry it is not mentioned that this condition is twice as common in women as it is in men.[5] The more common a "throw back" is, the more recently this structure should be found occurring normally in the ancestor. The logical, though of course utterly absurd, conclusion from this is that women are more closely related to reptiles than men are and that men evolved from reptiles a long time before women did.

Extra ribs may also occur in the lumbar region, below the normal range of ribs. Such ribs are called "gorilla ribs" because this condition is common in gorillas. Evolutionists do not believe that we descended from gorillas, but from some ancestor which we had in common with gorillas. This occurrence of supposedly atavistic "glorilla ribs" is taken as another indication of our affinity to the apes. But it is not mentioned in this connection that "gorilla ribs" occur three times as frequently in men as they do in women.[6] The conclusion from this would be that men are more closely related to gorillas than women are, and that men evolved more recently than women from the common ancestor we shared with the gorilla.

Ribs cannot develop just anywhere, but only along the sides of the backbone. Thus extra ribs are restricted to only two locations — above and below the normal range. Thus when extra ribs occur, it is coincidental that they correspond in location to cervical ribs of reptiles and lumbar ribs of gorillas.

Occasionally ribs are forked. This condition is not considered atavistic, for there are no possible ancestral types of animals which had forked ribs.

Another anomaly in human beings is the occurrence of mammary glands in abnormal positions. They may occur near the arm pits, as they normally do in some bats. This is not taken as evidence of our affinity to bats, for this would be absurd from an evolutionary standpoint. Mammary glands may also occur in the inguinal region, as they normally do in some whales. This is not taken as a clue to our relationship with the cetacians, for this also would be absurd. In fact, mammary glands have developed at very many places on the body, including the back and the arms and the legs. There are no mammals which have mammary glands in such locations. Therefore such abnormalities are disregarded as evidence of evolution.

If such abnormalities indicate anything about our ancestral history, the more common anomalies, such as harelip and cleft palate should have some evolutionary significance. However, they are disregarded because it would be absurd to attach any evolutionary significance to them.

Anyone could make a fortune at the horse races if permitted to do what the evolutionists do with atavistic structures — choose the horses he wishes and reject the others on the basis of the outcome of the race after the race is over. In the case of the evolutionists, moreover, the choice is made not only after the alleged event and in accordance with its believed outcome, but it is used as an evidence that the event really occurred.

NOTES

1. Whether or not some monkeys have an appendix is a matter of interpretation as to whether or not a portion of the cecum should be considered as representing an appendix.

2. Weichert, Charles K., *Anatomy of the Chordates*, 2d ed. (McGraw-Hill, 1958), p. 176.

3. Romer, Alfred S., *The Vertebrate Body* (W. B. Saunders, 1949), p. 363.

4. Leach, James W., *Functional Anatomy* (McGraw-Hill, 1961), p. 15.

5. Durham, R. H., *Encyclopedia of Medical Syndromes*, 1960, p. 99.

6. Nordsiek, Frederick W., "How Your Bones Tell Your Age," *Science Digest*, 47:5:13, May, 1960, p. 15.

THE EVIDENCE FROM EMBRYONIC RECAPITULATION

Another evidence of evolution which is presented in textbooks is called embryonic recapitulation. This means that during embryonic development animals and human beings pass through stages which resemble aspects of their evolutionary history.

The beginning of the development of an animal or of a human being is an egg cell, and this is said to correspond to a single-celled protozoan. Protozoa are believed to be the ancestors of all higher forms of animal life as well as of human beings. The egg cell divides and becomes a little ball of cells, and this is said to represent a colonial protozoan, such as *Volvox*. In some species the little ball of cells pushes in on one side as it develops further, becoming cup-shaped. This is supposed to represent a stage in the evolution of higher forms of life when their ancestors resembled jellyfish or polyps.

In 1811, before scientists took the idea of evolution seriously, Johann Meckel expressed the view that embryonic stages of development in higher forms of life parallel the adult condition of lower forms. Around 1828 Karl von Baer argued that it is the embryonic stages of the lower forms and not their adult structures which are paralleled by the developmental stages of the higher forms. In 1864 Fritz Müller taught that the higher forms of life add stages to the embryonic stages which are passed through by the lower forms in their development. Two years later, in 1866, Darwin's staunchest supporter in Germany, Ernst Haeckel, combined some of Müller's views with the idea of Meckel and popularized this as "the fundamental biogenetic law." This view, also called the recapitulation theory, became very popular, and those who enjoyed erudite language liked to say, "Ontogeny [embryonic development] recapitulates [reviews in abbreviated form] phylogeny [evolutionary history]."

A *hypothesis* is a tentative possible explanation of a phenomenon. A *theory* is an explanation which has some supporting evidence. A *law* in science is something which is believed to have been established with certainty. But this view of embryonic development with its presumptuous designation of "the fundamental biogenetic law" is no longer held in high esteem by the men of science, even in a modified form, though it is still presented in the textbooks as an evidence of evolution.

For many years the biogenetic law was considered to be one of the most important evidences of evolution, and Charles Darwin evaluated it as "second to none in importance."[1] In retrospect it seems remarkable that a concept can be considered very important for a long time and then be rejected.

Professor Alfred F. Huettner of Queens College says concerning this theory in his textbook of embryology, "At its most dominant period its ever accumulating 'exceptions' and defects were diligently overlooked, and its positive evidence was stressed with such great emphasis that a wholesome reaction was soon to appear in a new attack on the problem of development."[2] (He is here referring to the beginning of the science of experimental embryology.)

Professor James W. Leach of Ohio State University says, "The undeniable tendency of a complex animal to pass through some developmental stages reminiscent of the adult conditions of a selected and graduated series of lower forms has long been described as 'The Biogenetic Law.' But as a 'law' inscribed by nature it is perhaps more full of 'loopholes' and 'bypasses' than any law thus far inscribed by man."[3]

As long ago as 1932 Dr. Waldo Shumway of the University of Illinois said, concerning the recapitulation theory, that a consideration of the results of experimental embryology "seems to demand that the hypothesis be abandoned. Those of us who were reared in the phylogenetic tradition may see it go with a sigh of regret. Those of us charged with the responsibility of explaining the law of evolution to our classes will miss a familiar maxim, easily learned, and a convenient skeleton on which to hang the discrete data of embryology. But there can be no excuse for continuing to impress plastic minds by means of discredited generalizations."[4] Would that the textbook writers were as honest as this as they produce their texts for beginning students in biology.

Professor Gavin de Beer, the eminent embryologist, says, "Until recently the theory of recapitulation still had its ardent supporters."[5] He comments, "It is characteristic of a slogan [Ontogeny recapitulates phylogeny] that it tends to be accepted uncritically and to die hard."

It has frequently been said that the recapitulation theory served a good purpose because it stimulated research in embryology. Professor de Beer thinks otherwise, and says that "the prestige so long enjoyed by the theory of recapitulation has had a great and, while it lasted, regrettable influence on the progress of embryology."[6]

In 1956 G. H. Waddington of the University of Edinburgh published a book on embryology in which he said, "The type of analogical thinking which leads to theories that development is based on the recapitulation of ancestral stages or the like no longer seems at all convincing or even very interesting to biologists."[7]

In 1959 Jane Oppenheimer of the Department of Biology at Bryn Mawr College expressed the opinion that the recapitulation theory has been so thoroughly discredited that some embryologists no longer think it worth their while to refute it. She said, "A number of embryologists now question whether attacks on the recapitulation theory are any longer necessary. Certainly a number of recent textbooks, while they still may describe the doctrine, refute it at the same time, and there seem to be increasingly fewer which labor it as tenable."[8]

William K. Gregory of the American Museum of Natural History said that "the evidence afforded by embryology . . . is often open to the suspicion that we may be mistakenly interpreting as a repetition of long past adult stages such arrangements or conditions as may be merely adaptations of the growing embryo to its own physiological needs."[9]

Hegner and Stiles, in their textbook of college zoology, say, "Among the important difficulties encountered in attempting to determine relationships between phyla are the modifications that have taken place in both adults and larval stages. The result is that what may appear to be an ancestral condition may be nothing more than an adaptation to the environment. On this account we can only speculate instead of arriving at definite conclusions."[10]

Thus there has been a truly remarkable change in the amount of importance ascribed to this evidence of evolution since the days of Darwin. From "second to none in importance," it has been demoted to a position of such poor standing that there might seem to be no point in considering it further. It is, however, still taught to students as one of the evidences of evolution.

As previously mentioned, the analogy between embryos and ancestors starts with the egg cell, which is supposed to represent a one-celled protozoan ancestor. Concerning this Professor de Beer points out that "the egg of the mammal and the unicellular ancestor are not really comparable, and in a remarkably thorough analysis Hertwig revealed this flaw in the logic of Haeckel's argument."[11]

The metazoa, or many-celled animals, are believed to have evolved in some way from protozoa. The parallel of this in embryonic development is the division of the egg cell into many cells. Dr. Libbie Hyman, the outstanding woman biologist of the American Museum of Natural History in New York City, considers this division of the egg cell to constitute strong evidence of the evolution of the metazoa from protozoa, and she says, "No direct proof exists of the origin of the Metazoa from the Protozoa, but such origin besides being necessitated by the principle of evolution is strongly indicated by the facts of embryonic development, in which each metazoan passes from an acellular to a cellular condition."[12] (She prefers to consider protozoa and egg cells as acellular instead of unicellular.) She considers the fact that an egg cell divides to be strong evidence that the many-celled animals evolved from protozoa. She says this in spite of the fact that there is no other way for an egg to develop into a multi-cellular creature but by dividing, and in spite of the fact that she is well aware of the discredit that has come to the recapitulation theory. At another place in the same book she says, "The law of recapitulation has been severely criticized in many quarters since its enunciation and has been rejected altogether by a number of present-day em-bryologists."[13]

The next stage in development is one that is important to con-sider because it has been used so very extensively in the textbooks. In the early embryonic development of some animals, the little ball of cells pushes in on one side as the cells divide, and thus the embryo becomes cup-shaped. This is the gastrula stage, and Haeckel said that it is a recapitulation of an early ancestral form which was something like a jellyfish or polyp. But the theory does not fit the facts very well, because it has been observed that in the group to which the jellyfish and polyps belong a gastrula like this seldom forms. The fundamental cupshaped structure of the jellyfish and polyps does not result from an invagination, as in the case of Haeckel's gastrula, but is formed when cells migrate past each other to reach their destinations.[14]

The textbooks place the Coelenterates — the group to which jelly-fish and polyps belong — close to the base of the evolutionary tree. This is the position demanded for these animals by the recapitulation theory. However, it is now believed by some that these animals are not primitive and therefore that do not occupy this position. Gavin de Beer says, "More recently Hadzi has attacked Haeckel's biogenetic law in its stronghold of the gastrula theory, for he has produced cogent arguments for the view that the original ancestral Metazoa were not in the least like gastrulae and that the Coelenterates are not primitive at all."[15]

Professor John Tyler Bonner, head of the Biology Department at Princeton University, makes a very frank admission when he says, "We may have known for almost a hundred years that Haeckel's blastaea-gastraea theory of the origin of the metazoa is probably nonsense, but it is so clear-cut, so simple, so easy to hand full-blown to the student."[16]

One of the most frequently cited examples of recapitulation has been the development of the mammalian kidney, which is said to recapitulate the kidneys of lower vertebrates. Three distinct kinds of kidneys are described in vertebrate animals. The type found in the hagfish (which is a cyclostome and not really a fish) is called a *pronephros*. The *mesonephros* is characteristic of true fish and amphibians. The reptiles, birds, and mammals have a kidney which is called a *metanephros*. Concerning this Professor Theodosius Dobzhansky of Columbia University says, "Why should pronephros and mesonephros, which are the kidneys of the lower vertebrates, be formed and then disappear in the embryos of the higher vertebrates? This would certainly be inexplicable if the higher vertebrates were not descendants of the lower. Again, an anti-evolutionist would have to blame God for having arranged things just to mislead the zoologist."[17]

Professor Dobzhansky clearly has an advantage when he writes like this, for although anti-evolutionists may be shocked at his rather blasphemous way of writing, few if any would be qualified to argue with him on scientific grounds. However, Professor Alfred S. Romer of Harvard University, the outstanding comparative anatomist, supplies the answer for the anti-evolutionists, although Professor Romer is himself a strong evolutionist. Concerning the stages in the development of the mammalian kidney he says, "It is often stated or implied that these three are distinct kidneys which have succeeded one another phylogenetically [that is, in evolution] as they do embryologically. Upon consideration, however, it will be seen that there is no strong reason to believe this. The differences are readily explainable on functional grounds; the three appear to be regionally specialized parts of the original holonephros which serve different functions."[18]

Thus Professor Romer says that the stages in the development of the mammalian kidney, contrary to what is frequently stated, do not necessarily have any evolutionary significance, and that they may readily be explained as being required by the functional requirements of the developing organism at the different stages of its growth.

Professor Romer's statement about the kidney illustrates a growing trend. As in the case of the argument for evolution from vestigial structures, where the list of such structures dwindled rapidly as it was found that the structures have useful functions and are not vestigial, just so it is being shown that structures which were thought to be recapitulations of ancestral organs may not be so at all, but are organs in a form which is required for the proper function of the embryo at that particular stage in its development.

Whenever the recapitulation theory is mentioned, one may be certain of hearing about the "gill slits." During embryonic development human beings have blood vessels lying parallel to each other in the region of the neck. The skin dips down between these blood vessels, forming grooves. These grooves do not become slits and there are no gills. The embryos of fish have blood vessels similarly arranged in this region. In the case of fish, grooves which form in this area do break through and gills form. This is accepted as strong evidence that we had ancestors that were fish. The evolutionist asks: "If we did not evolve from fish, why do we pass through a stage in our embryonic development in which the blood vessels are arranged in this way?" This is the same question which Professor Dobzhansky asked about the kidney, and the answer is no doubt similar.

Since the recapitulation theory has been abandoned by so many scientists as an evidence favoring evolution, it follows that such things as "gill slits" should now become an embarrassment to the evolutionists instead of, as formerly thought, an embarrassment to the anti-evolutionists. Since the "gill slits" were previously considered to be such a strong evidence for evolution, and since this kind of evidence (embryonic recapitulation) is now being discarded as invalid, the "gill slits" now should be an especial embarrassment to the evolutionists.

Since embryonic recapitulaton is not a valid evidence that evolution has taken place, it is evident that it cannot be employed, as had been hoped by evolutionists of earlier days, to clear up evolutionary history in cases of dispute. This, however, has not deterred some from trying. W. E. LeGros Clark of Oxford University says, "Embryonic evidence of evolutionary paths has not proved of great scientific value. Unhappily, however, it has often been drawn upon as a too rash assurance to give verisimilitude to theories of one kind or another."[19]

If turtles evolved from animals of a more "orthodox" structure, it is a mystery how they managed to get their shoulder bones inside their ribs. If they were outside the ribs, as in other animals, they would also be outside the shell. It was hoped that a study of the embryonic development of turtles would clarify this. This problem is discussed by Archie Carr, Professor of Biological Science at the University of Florida. He says, "It might accordingly have been hoped that the evolution of the relationship between the shell, ribs, and girdles during embryology would shed some light on the original history of these events, but such is not the case."[20]

One reason the recapitulation theory has been discredited is because a number of structures develop in an order which is the reverse of that which is assumed to have been the order of evolutionary development. For example, it is believed that we had ancestors which had teeth before any had tongues, while everyone knows that children develop tongues before teeth. We are thought to have had ancestors which had a circulatory system without a true heart, like earthworms and insects. The blood flowed because of the contraction of blood vessels and because of the pressure brought upon blood vessels by bodily movements. However, in the developing vertebrate the situation is the opposite, and the heart forms before the rest of the circulatory system.

Another type of difficulty is encountered in the fact that some forms which are rather similar in adulthood have strikingly different developments. According to the recapitulation theory it is the immature stages which should be more similar, followed by differentiation during development. Lobsters and freshwater crayfish are very much alike except for size, but the crayfish hatch from eggs as small crayfish, while lobsters pass through several different larval stages before assuming the adult shape.

Among the flies there are a number of cases in which rather similar adults have larval stages that are much more diverse. A certain mosquito of the genus *Culex* has a larva which resembles the larva of another genus more than it does larvae of other species of its own genus. Four species of flies of the genus *Austrosimulium* are said to be indistinguishable as adults, and distinguishable as species only by the respiratory organs of the pupal stage. Among the sawflies there is a species which has three geographical races that are indistinguishable, although their larvae are markedly different. Two species of sponges of the genus *Halichondra* are indistinguishable, but their larvae are quite different in shape and in size and in the arrangement of cilia.[21]

Still another difficulty results from the fact that some creatures have developmental stages which could not possibly represent a recapitulation of ancestral forms. Flies, moths, butterflies, and some other insects pass through a dormant pupal stage in their development, during which they take no nourishment and undergo a vast internal reorganization. This occurs between the larval worm-like stage and the adult insect. Structures of the body break down into a mass with a soupy consistency, and new structures are built. There could not be anything like this in the ancestry of these insects between the present time and the time when their ancestors were worm-like creatures corresponding to the larvae.

There is not a great deal of information about alleged recapitulation in plants. This is because there are so few cases which can be interpreted in this way. In some species of eucalyptus the juvenile foliage is different from that of the mature tree, and this has been interpreted as an ancestral type of foliage. Some acacias have pinnately compound leaves, while others have foliage which appears to be made up of simple leaves, but actually they are *phyllodes,* or flat swollen stems of leaves. Seedlings of the latter have foliage made up of various combinations of phyllodes and compound leaves. Professor Edmund Sinnott of Yale University mentions these examples and concludes, "These facts suggest that the seedling repeats or recapitulates ancestral traits, much as the animal embryo has been thought to do. There is much doubt in many cases, however, as to what the course of evolution actually has been and so much variation in early ontogeny [embryonic development] in many plants that it is impossible to establish the doctrine of recapitulation as an invariably useful guide to phylogeny [evolution]."[22]

Alleged evidences of evolution through recapitulation are not only anatomical, but also biochemical. The classic example of this is the change in excretory products which occur in development. Freshwater fish are able to excrete ammonia. Although it is toxic, they can conveniently dilute it and excrete it as rapidly as it forms. Animals which live on land cannot do this, and instead of excreting ammonia most of them excrete urea, which is not toxic. The tadpole of a frog is much like a fish, and it excretes ammonia. A mature frog is adapted to spend time on land, and it excretes urea. Thus a frog is said to show its fish ancestry through the recapitulation of its excretory substances. However, it is to be noted here, as in the case of the change in form of the kidney mentioned by Professor Romer, that the excretory material at each stage is suited to the habits of the animal at that stage. The same argument applies here as in the case of the structural changes: if a change during development is adaptive, that fact comprises as good (or better) an explanation for the phenomenon as does the alternative explanation that it is the result of a condition to the remote ancestry of the species.

The African clawed frog *Xenopus laevis* remains in the water as an adult. During its metamorphosis from tadpole to frog it begins to make the change from an ammonia-excreting animal to a urea-excreting animal. Thus, whatever triggers the change in other frogs does so in this one also. But it remains permanently in the water as an adult, and although it starts to make the transformation from ammonia-excreting to urea-excreting, it does not make the change, and it remains an ammonia excreter. However, if the adult is forced to live out of the water, it alters the chemistry of its excretory system in the direction of urea excretion. Thus, if there is any doubt in other cases whether a condition is related to the needs of the organism or to recapitulation, there can be no doubt in this case. Since it is evident in this case that it is an adaptation to the environment it follows that it may not be a recapitulation in other cases where the situation is not so obvious.

Concerning chemical changes of this kind in the developing frog, Earl Frieden, Professor of Chemistry at Florida State University, says, "Still others seem to have no discernible adaptive function — but even these may turn out to be essential adaptations when metamorphosis is better understood."[23]

In 1911 three men demonstrated the devotion scientists can have for the theory of evolution. They went on to what seemed to be almost certain death instead of turning back, in order to obtain some eggs of the emperor penguin which it was hoped would provide evidence favorable to the recapitulation theory.

William Wilson, H. R. Bowers, and Apsley Cherry-Garrard left the base camp of Captain Robert Scott's Antarctic Expedition in the middle of the Antarctic winter and made what has been called the worst journey in the world. Dr. Wilson considered the emperor penguins to be the most primitive birds, and reasoned that their eggs would afford particularly pertinent evidence of the evolution of birds from reptiles.

Apsley Cherry-Garrard wrote later, "The horror of the nineteen days it took us to travel from Cape Evans to Cape Crozier would have to be re-experienced to be appreciated, and anyone would be a fool who went again. It is not possible to describe it."[24]

Temperatures lower than seventy degrees below zero were encountered, but worst of all was the darkness, for at that time of the year the sun remained far below the horizon. Before they stopped for their first lunch, perspiration froze inside their clothing. Even on the coldest days they perspired, and the perspiration accumulated as ice. Some of it melted when they rested in the tent and saturated their garments and sleeping bags.

On the second day Cherry-Garrard got all his fingers frostbitten and developed large blisters. One day he raised his head to look around and the clothing around his neck froze so that he had to help pull the sledges with his head in this raised position for four hours.

On the fourth day they came to a region where the snow was so cold and grannular that it was like sand. They were not able to pull their two sledges together over this kind of snow and had to leave one while pulling the other. Besides the problem of locating the one left behind in the darkness each time, this relaying forced them to walk three times as far as they would have walked if they could have pulled the sledges together.

There were many unforseen difficulties which added to their agonies. Their feet lost feeling, and they did not know if they were frozen or not. Ordinarily one warms up with exercise, but they found it just the opposite. The longer they walked between their stops for camp, the colder they became. When they camped, it took them an increasingly longer time to get into their frozen sleeping bags. They had little consciousness of sleep. They knew that they did sleep for they had nightmares, and they could hear each other snore. They sometimes slept while walking, and woke up when they bumped into each other.

At times there was so much fog they could not tell which way to go.

When it was time to break camp, it was sometimes necessary to try five or six boxes of matches before finding a match which would strike to light a candle. Added to this was the difficulty of knowing when it was time to break camp.

They suffered from stomach cramps.

Cherry-Garrard had fits of teeth-chattering which he compared to lockjaw. The nerves of his teeth were killed and all his teeth cracked to pieces.

On one occasion the temperature rose to twenty-seven degrees below zero, and they were able to become thawed out and get some real sleep.

Crevasses are large gaping clefts in the ice, and some of them are thinly bridged with snow. They are bad enough in the daylight, when open ones can be seen and avoided, but they are a terror in the dark. The men were harnessed to the sledges so that when one fell into a crevasse, he would dangle at the end of his harness about fifteen feet down until the others pulled him up. On one occasion when they had hoped to take advantage of moonlight, the sky was overcast, and in the darkness they knew only that they were going downhill with the sledges nearly overtaking them. Suddenly the moon appeared in a patch of clear sky just in time to reveal a great crevasse three paces ahead of them. Except for this providential appearing of the moon they would all have gone over the edge with the sledges following, and this would have been the end.

For several days they were lost among pressure ridges, walls of ice piled fifty and sixty feet high. Trying a course to the right and then to the left, as in a labyrinth, they eventually came out and found that at last they had arrived at the site where they would make their headquarters while visiting the penguins, although they still had no assurance that the penguins would be there. Their sleeping bags were in such a state that it was almost impossible to get into them, and their clothing was so frozen that it seemed like lead. But they had arrived, and "Cherry" wrote in his diary, "It is wonderful how our cares have vanished."

For two days they labored to build a hut of rocks and ice, with canvas for a roof. With the hut completed they were ready to try to make contact with the penguins. This presented more problems because of crevasses, pressure ridges, and two cliffs between them and the nesting site of the birds. At one time they came to a place where they could go no farther, but they could at last hear the penguins. As they returned to seek another route they were encouraged by knowing that the birds were there. Even when they were this close and after all the hardship they had endured, they still had no assurance that they would be able to reach the penguins. But they found a way, and at last they were among the birds, except Cherry-Garrard, who had to stay at the top of the smaller cliff to pull the other two up again.

The emperor penguin is a large bird, standing about four feet high in spite of its short legs. These penguins lay their eggs in the middle of the cold Antarctic winter. A bird holds its egg on its feet to keep it off the ice, and protects it with a flap of skin. The parental instinct is so strong that if a bird has no egg it will brood a piece of ice shaped like an egg.

The men hurried as they collected five eggs and killed a few birds to provide fuel for their blubber stove, because there was evidence of an approaching storm. Two eggs were broken as they made a hasty retreat to their hut.

While a blizzard raged outside they prepared a hot meal. The blubber stove exploded and shot boiling oil into Wilson's eye. He was in great pain and thought he had lost his eye, but later recovered.

The following night the storm was much worse, and their tent blew away. The loss of the tent meant almost certain death. After the shock was over and they had time to think, they talked of digging holes in the ice on the return trip and covering the holes with the floor covering of the tent, which was with them in the hut, but even as they spoke of it they knew they would not be able to do this.

Because of the gale the canvas roof of the hut began to flap. For twenty-four hours they lay in the hut with the expectation of the roof going. Then it happened. In a moment the canvas was torn to tiny shreds with a terrific roar. Rocks from the walls of the hut fell upon them, and drifting snow piled in. It was Wilson's birthday.

This seemed to be the end. They had been out for four weeks under conditions which no man had ever endured for more than a few days. They had managed to keep going by burning plenty of oil and eating hot fatty food. Now they were exhausted; they had left only one can of oil; the tent was gone; and the wind was still howling a hurricane.

They could not move the rocks which had fallen from the walls, and they lay for two days fitting themselves around the rocks. The drifting snow helped keep them from freezing. The blizzard ended, but another threatened as, bitterly cold, they began the inevitable but apparently hopeless search for the tent. It seemed that the impossible had happened when Bowers found it. Apparently encrusting ice had kept it heavy and compact, and instead of blowing into the labyrinth of pressure ridges or out to sea, it had come to rest in a depression about a quarter of a mile away. They had hope again.

Bowers actually wanted to make another trip to the penguins. "Cherry" was willing. But Wilson said they must go back, which was the only sensible thing to do. The return trip had its own difficulties and miseries, but the men were so hardened that they were numb to suffering. Their load was lighter and they were on their way home. When they reached the home base, one of the worst journeys ever attempted was over, and they enjoyed food and rest in a way which can be understood only by those who have undergone great privation.

Of the three men who made this journey, only Cherry-Garrard got back to London. The other two perished some months later with Captain Scott on the return trip from the South Pole.

On his return to England, Cherry-Garrard wrote to the Natural History Museum that he would deliver the penguin eggs at a certain time. It might be expected that he would have been honored with a special welcome, but this was far from the case. Arriving at the museum he encountered a custodian who insulted him and threatened to call the police if he did not leave. When he reached the office of the head of the museum, he found this dignitary talking to another visitor. Cherry-Garrard waited but was ignored. At length the chief turned to him and said, "You needn't wait." "Cherry" answered politely, "I would like to have a receipt for the eggs, if you please." But he was ignored again, and returned to a position outside the door to wait. As time passed, various minor officials inquired his business, and to each his reply was, "I am waiting for a receipt for some penguin eggs." A receipt was finally handed to him and he left.

Later he visited the museum with Captain Scott's sister to inquire about the eggs, and they were told that no such eggs existed in the museum's collections. Action was forthcoming, however, when the captain's sister threatened to tell all of England the story of the eggs and the treatment of Cherry-Garrard unless something was done about investigating the evidence for evolution which they might reveal.

As a result Professor Cossar Ewart of Edinburgh University examined the embryos. In his official report he stated that although those who have devoted much time to the study of birds had assumed that feathers were developed by an evolutionary process from the scales of ancestral reptiles, a study of the embryonic development of feathers offered no evidence justifying this assumption. In the penguin embryos he found that feathers began to develop *before* scales started to form on the feet. If the feathers of birds evolved from the scales of reptiles, it would be expected, according to the recapitulation theory, that the penguin embryos would start to develop scales on their feet before feathers began to develop. But the actual findings were just the opposite of what the theory called for, as the penguins started developing feathers before scales.

Professor Ewart anticipated the possible question: What if reptiles start to develop scales on their bodies before they start developing them on their feet, as the penguins develop feathers on their bodies before scales on their feet? This was investigated and found not to be the case.

Professor Ewart's report closed with a statement that if the conclusions reached are correct "the worst journey in the world in the interest of science was not made in vain."[25] Thus Professor Ewart, an evolutionist, said that, if the anti-evolutionary conclusions drawn from his examination of the eggs is correct, the heroic effort of these men was not in vain. But the valor which they displayed and the agonies which they suffered were not appreciated at that time, nor have they been at any time since. To date, the worst journey in the world in the interest of science seems to have been in vain. Perhaps this telling of the story in honor of the three brave men will accomplish something and their valor will not go unrecognized.

NOTES

1. See Edward O. Dodson, *A Textbook of Evolution* (W. B. Saunders Co., 1952), p. 56.

2. Huettner, Alfred F., *Comparative Embryology of the Vertebrates*, Rev. ed. (Macmillan, 1949), p. 5.

3. Leach, James W., *Functional Anatomy — Mammalian and Comparative* (McGraw-Hill, 1961), p. 44.

4. Shumway, Waldo, "The Recapitulation Theory," *The Quarterly Review of Biology*, 7:1:93, March, 1932, p. 98.

5. de Beer, Gavin, *Embryos and Ancestors*, rev. ed. (Oxford University Press, 1940, Printing of 1954), p. 6.

6. *Ibid.*, p. 10.

7. Waddington, G. H., *Principles of Embryology* (George Allen and Unwin, 1956), p. 10.

8. Opperheimer, Jane, Opinion expressed in a review of *Embryos and Ancestors* by Gavin de Beer, *Science*, 129:3340:35, January 2, 1959.

9. Gregory, William D., *Our Face from Fish to Man* (G. P. Putnam's Sons, 1929), pp. 185, 186.

10. Hegner, Robert W. and Karl A. Stiles, *College Zoology*, 6th ed. (Macmillan, 1951), p. 790.

11. de Beer, Gavin, *loc. cit.*, p. 7.

12. Hyman, Libbie Henrietta, *The Invertebrates, Protozoa through Ctenophora* (McGraw-Hill, 1940), p. 248.

13. *Ibid.*, p. 273.

14. *Ibid.*, p. 252.

15. de Beer, Gavin, *loc. cit.*, p. 10.

16. Bonner, John Tyler, In a review of *Implications of Evolution* by G. A. Kerkut, *American Scientist*, 49:2:240, June, 1961.

17. Dobzhansky, Theodosius, *Evolution, Genetics, and Man* (John Wiley and Sons, 1955), p. 238.

18. Romer, Alfred S., *The Vertebrate Body* (W. E. Saunders Co., 1949), p. 382.

19. Clark, W. E. LeGros, *Early Forerunners of Man* (William Wood and Co., 1934), p. 3.

20. Carr, Archie, *Handbook of Turtles* (Cornell University Press, 1952), p. 3.

21. de Beer, Gavin, *loc. cit.*, pp. 37, 38.

22. Sinnott, Edmund W., *Plant Morphogenesis* (McGraw-Hill, 1960), p. 209.

23. Frieden, Earl, "The Chemistry of Amphibian Metamorphosis," *Scientific American*, 209:5:110, November, 1963, p. 110.

24. Cherry-Garrard, Apsley, *The Worst Journey in the World* (Dial Press, 1930), p. 236.

25. *Ibid.*, not paged, but would be between pages 300 and 301.

THE EVIDENCE FROM TAXONOMY, OR CLASSIFICATION

Carl Linnaeus was a very remarkable man. He had a passion for plants in a day when it was very difficult to make a living as a botanist. Even his name was botanical, for his father took the family name from a fine linden tree which grew on their property. His greatest achievement was the founding of our modern system of taxonomy, or classification of animals and plants.

Linnaeus did not believe in evolution, and for some time he thought that what he designated as *species* corresponded to the *kinds* of the Genesis account of creation. He performed many experiments in hybridization and in growing plants under strikingly different environmental conditions. This work impressed him with the stability of plant types, but he changed his mind about his earlier belief that his species represented the kinds spoken of in Genesis. However, a century later, when the theory of evolution became an issue, anti-evolutionists cited the great Linnaeus as their authority that the species represented the kinds. This was unfortunate, for to this very day the anti-anti-evolutionists make a big issue over their contention that those who do not believe in evolution have no alternative but to believe that every species was created in the beginning just as it is now. This charge is found over and over, *ad nauseum*, in college textbooks and books for the general public.

Heutschel and Cook, in their textbook *Biology for Medical Students* say: "To explain the presence of so many different kinds of plants and animals, two theories have been propounded. The traditional idea was that of Special Creation, in which all organisms as we know them today were invented and made in the beginning of time with the same structure as we now find them. Such is the primitive human conception of the origin of species, as exemplified in the first chapter of Genesis, and similar ideas were also current in the cosmologies of most religions of the world. The facts of biology, however, do not allow us to accept this view. The modern view is that of Organic Evolution."[1]

Hegner and Stiles, in their *College Zoology*, say, "The doctrine of special creation, that is that each species of animal was specially created, is sufficiently refuted to the satisfaction of most biologists by the facts of organic evolution."[2]

Hunter and Hunter say in their *College Zoology*, "Either the present day forms began as such and have continued to exist in their original form, or life may have started in one common form from which all the others may have developed. All the available evidence indicates that livings things started in simple form and that from this simple beginning the great diversity of present day plants and animals has developed."[3]

Professor Weatherwax in his college textbook of botany, *Plant Biology*, says: "According to the various theories of special creation, every species of plant or animal was specially created long ago, when life was first placed on earth, and each species has continued unchanged to the present time. . . . Scientists in general recognize the principle of evolution, and its influence has carried over into the field of social problems and has had a profound influence on all thought. Most religionists now realize that they really have in their field no need of solving problems of this kind and no efficient way of attempting solutions."[4]

Professor Northern says in his textbook *Introductory Plant Science*: "For many years the diversity and adaptiveness of living things was explained as an act of creation — special creation by God, who made each species to fit a prepared place in nature. This doctrine of special creation was formulated long ago when knowledge of living organisms was decidedly limited. For many centuries this idea seemed the most reasonable explanation possible. At present the concept of special creation has been replaced by the theory that present-day organisms have come from unlike progenitors which usually were less complex."[5]

Strausbaug and Weimer say in their *General Biology:* "Most of us are familiar with the account of creation in Genesis, how all species of plants and animals were created in the beginning, with the forms they now have. This explanation, called special creation, served as a satisfactory explanation until about 1880. Even today it satisfies those who have never troubled themselves to study the question objectively and scientifically."[6]

Such illustrations could be extended almost indefinitely, but as one more example, Gairdner Moment writes in his textbook, *General Biology:* "One of the oldest ideas and, until recently, the most widely accepted, is the theory of special creation. Certainly very few, perhaps no, biologists now believe that each species was separately created and has existed since the beginning of the world."[7]

Taking care not to use strong language lightly, it may be said that the often-repeated statements about special creation comprise a dishonest approach to the problem. They are dishonest because they are written by men who are sufficiently grounded in biological science to know that no one can properly define the term *species,* while at the same time they say that people who believe in special creation can distinguish species and hold that every species was created separately. Since the experts cannot rigorously define *species,* and since they frequently disagree among themselves and change their minds as to what is a species, it is absurd as well as dishonest to imply that men who are not scientists can do this. Of course these writers would readily admit that they do not expect anti-evolutionists to be experts in taxonomy, although they imply this. What they seem to be trying to do, without thinking through the implications of what they say, is to make the creationists appear very stupid.

Textbook writers charge that those who accept special creation believe that every species was created separately. To be consistent, these men must admit the absurdity that the number of creations in the beginning varies from year to year. When taxonomists decide that what has been considered ten species is really only one, it follows that what was ten creations before they changed their minds, is now only one creation. Thus the number of kinds of animals and plants created during the days of creation keeps changing. It is now different from what it was a few years ago, and in a few years from now it will be different again. This is ridiculous.

The freshwater clam *Anadonta* was formerly believed to exist in 251 species, but these have now been reduced to a single species.[8]

In 1931 Swarth studied the ground finches of the Galapagos Islands and classified them into five genera and 317 species and subspecies, but confessed that it would be as logical to put them all into a single species.[9]

These are rather extreme examples, but it is the sort of thing that is going on all the time. Some taxonomists, the "lumpers," are condensing a number of species into one, while other taxonomists, the "splitters," take single species and say that they are really several species.

In 1876 Jordan's list of fishes of North America contained 670 species. During the next ten years 125 new species were discovered. If the number of new species is added to the number previously known, the total is 795 species. However, this is not correct, for the number of species recognized at that time was 599. Thus, in spite of the fact that 125 newly discovered species were added, the total number is *less* than it was before by 71. The reason for this is that while 125 new species were added, 196 of the other species were dropped from the list because it was decided that they really were not species at all.[10]

It is well known that birds have been studied from a taxonomic standpoint more thoroughly than any other class of animals. Professor Ruggles Gates of Rutgers University says that the number of species of birds has been reduced, through changes of opinion as to what is a species, from 27,000 to about 8,500.[11]

Charles Darwin was well aware of the differences of opinion on the part of taxonomists in defining species, and he considered it to be an important piece of evidence in favor of his theory. He was interested in showing that species can change, and he extrapolated this kind of change to cover the whole scale of life from microscopic organisms to men.

The great Linnaeus never came to America, and when "poison ivy" was sent to him by a collector, he immediately recognized that it was not an ivy at all. He distinguished two species, *Rhus radicans* (climbing) and *Rhus toxicodendron* (poison tree). Since that time several taxonomists, notably one named Greene, split the poison ivies into more than thirty species. It is now generally held that all of them really amount to less than half a dozen species, including the poison oak of the west coast.

It is now commonly believed that the two species recognized by Linnaeus represent a single species, which climbs when it has something to climb upon and when it does not have something to climb upon it grows as a shrub. An examination of a number of books dealing with plants of eastern North America revealed that only two of the authors recognize these as separate species. Some who consider it a single species call it *Rhus toxicodendron* and say that it grows as a shrub or climber. Others call it *Rhus radicans.* One author took the name *Rhus toxicodendron* and applied it to a different form, which grows along the Atlantic coast from New Jersey southward. This is called the eastern poison oak and it does not climb. A number of other authors accept this. Thus there is quite a bit of confusion in the technical nomenclature of something so well known as the poison ivies.

Species may be determined by quite trifling differences. Two kinds of guinea pigs which differed by only two mutant genes, and which therefore could occur repeatedly in the same litter, were formerly accepted as distinct species.[12] There is at least one case in which a single mutant gene made a new species, in the opinion of a taxonomist. In 1922 a biologist named Weed described certain frogs in Minnesota and Wisconsin as a new species, which he called *Rana kandivehi.* In 1955 another biologist by the name of Volpe showed that this was merely a mutant form of the common leopard frog, *Rana pipiens,* differing from the common frog by a single mutant gene.[13] Such mistakes are understandable, but they should cause honest writers to be more careful in what they say about special creationists.

An abstract of a paper by E. Heitz tells that "crosses of plant species show many specific and generic characters [that is, characters which have been used to distinguish different species and different genera] are Mendelian differences [that is, differences due merely to one or a few mutant genes]." The abstract goes on to make the amazing claim that "Mendelizing characters are often not only specific but generic, or even family or ordinal. Numerous cases are cited in flowering plants. . . . In the liverwort *Marchantia,* mutations of every grade, species, genus, family, can occur."[14]

There can even be cases in which environmental factors deceive the taxonomist. The bear-gum tree of northern Florida, identified as a species and named *Nyssa ursina* by a taxonimist named Small, is apparently the same species as the swamp tuplee, *Nyssa biflora.* The difference between the two is that the former grows where fires are repeatedly set to burn off dry grass, and it is therefore stunted, while the other grows where fire is not thus employed.[15]

Biologists cannot even agree completely about the number of species of human beings. It is generally accepted that all living people belong to the same species, *Homo sapiens,* but this belief is not unanimous. Among those who would take exception to this view are Professors Henry Fairfield Osborn and Ruggles Gates, who would divide the living peoples of the earth into a number of species.[16] At the other extreme, Professor Franz Weidenreich lumps fossil hominids into the same species with us.[17]

Taxonomy is an inexact science. Professor Hooton of Harvard said, "I am convinced that a zoological classificationist may be as dissolute and irresponsible as a lightning-rod salesman."[18]

In more erudite language, Professor Ernst Mayr of the University of California says, "Systematics is in a more difficult position than other sciences . . . we have an almost unlimited diversity of opinion in answer to such questions as: What is a species? How do species originate? Are systematic categories natural? [By this he means, do they show evolutionary relationships, or are they just arbitrary arrangements?] And so forth. There is no uniform point of view among taxonomists; in fact, in regard to many of these questions there may not even be a majority opinion."[19]

Dr. James Fisher of the Zoological Society of London says concerning this, "When a collection turns up from some part of the world that has not been very well worked, the taxonomist has to be a historian, an evolutionist, a geographer, an anatomist, a bibliographer, and often a mathematician before he can be justified in assigning his specimens to their proper species, or if necessary to a new species. Even then, if he has all these qualities he may have to rely on an intuitive flair for diagnosis."[20]

Dr. Fisher also says, "Two animals belong to the same species if such is the opinion of a competent taxonomist."[21] This has been said by a number of biologists, and it is a paraphrase of the words of Charles Darwin. Professor Weidenreich, the famous anthropologist of the University of Chicago, commented on taxonomy and on Darwin's remark as follows: "Unfortunately, there is no objective gauge which can be used for measurement of the grade of morphological deviations and for the determination of the limits between individual, specific, and generic variants. Such a distinction is left entirely to the 'opinions of naturalists having sound judgment and wide experiences,' as Charles Darwin put it."[22]

There is a popular misconception that if animals or plants can be crossed and produce fertile offspring they belong to the same species; otherwise not. This is no longer recognized as an adequate criterion in taxonomy by most scientists. Dr. Fisher, for example, says, "Two animals do not necessarily belong to the same species if they interbreed in the wild. There are many examples of distinct species which have increased their range . . . so as to overlap. In this region of overlap they may interbreed, producing a mixed or hybrid population. Nevertheless this does not mean that they are the same species."[23]

Professor Michael F. Guyer of the University of Wisconsin says, "Ordinarily individuals of the same species are entirely fertile when inbred, and individuals of different species cannot or will not reproduce with each other, but there are so many exceptions to this rule that it cannot be used as a satisfactory distinction. . . . Many hybrids have been obtained, especially among fishes, by crossing species of even different genera, while on the other hand often closely related species of the same genus will not crossbreed."[24]

Professor Horatio Hackett Newman of the University of Chicago affirmed the same thing: "Hundreds of species have been successfully crossed, and the hybrids are fertile. . . . Not only are species of the same genus commonly interfertile, but not infrequently species of different genera are completely interfertile."[25]

In classifying animals and plants, certain characteristics must be compared. Just what these characteristics should be is sometimes arbitrary, and this leads to disagreements among systematists. One taxonomist may attach great significance to a characteristic which another ignores. Professor Hooton of Harvard mentions something which is humorous because it obviously has no significance, but it illustrates what can happen when arbitrary morphological characteristics are chosen to classify animals or plants. He says that a certain projection on the upper bone of the forelimb is characteristic of lower animals. A Professor Terry reported that this characteristic is found not uncommonly among Harvard graduate students, while it was exceedingly rare among criminals and prostitutes which he examined.[26]

In classifying plants, Linnaeus put emphasis upon the structure of the reproductive parts as basic. Thus even in non-technical classification the "box elder" (*Acer negundo*) is called an ash-leafed maple and not a maple-fruited ash. Ferns do not have flowers or fruits, and they were said to be more closely related to other non-flowering plants than to the flowering plants. Well-preserved impressions of fossil ferns looked so much like living ferns that many of them were classified as belonging to the same genera as living ferns.[27] However, to the great surprise of the botanists, fossils were found which showed that these plants produced seeds. Thus it was found that plants which had been placed in the same genera as living ferns were not even ferns at all. They were then called *seed-ferns*. Because of this the *living* ferns are now grouped with the flowering plants instead of with the non-flowering plants to which they had formerly been thought to be allied.[28]

Animals and plants are classified according to their supposed evolutionary relationships, and then the classification is used as an evidence of evolution. Thus the argument becomes circular.

A few typical quotations will illustrate how evolutionists ascribe to taxonomy an evidence for evolution.

Arthur W. Haupt, Professor of Botany at the University of California at Los Angeles, says, "The mere fact, then, that plants can be classified on the basis of structural similarity and that the plant kingdom can be represented in the form of a tree, signifies that evolution has taken place. In fact, it has no other rational explanation."[29]

Michael F. Guyer of the University of Wisconsin says, "The very attempt, indeed, to arrange the innumerable kinds of animals and plants into intelligent systems inevitably leads to a theory of descent with modifications, or, in other words to the *theory of organic evolution*."[30]

Claud A. Villee, Professor of Zoology at Harvard University, says it this way, "The fact that the characteristics of living things are such that they can be fitted into a heirarchial scheme of categories — species, genera, orders, classes, and phyla — can best be interpreted as indicating evolutionary relationship."[31] He adds that "present-day taxonomists are concerned with describing species primarily as a means of discovering evolutionary relationships."

But if all animals and plants came about through an evolutionary process, then the gradations between types were at one time continuous, and present-day evidences of this would also favor evolution. So, if living things can be classified into discreet groups, that favors an evolutionary explanation; but if they cannot be so classified, that also favors an evolutionary explanation! The evolutionist can't lose.

On the page following the last quotation, Professor Villee says, "If every animal and plant that ever lived were still living today, it would be a difficult matter to divide the living world into neat taxonomic categories, for there would be a continuous series grading from the lowest to the highest."

To illustrate the interdependence of taxonomy and evolution, a few examples widely separated in time and representing widely divergent forms of life may be given.

In 1889 Samuel Hubbard Scudder of Cambridge said, "Our classifications are only expressions of confessedly imperfect attempts to represent the natural affinities [evolutionary relationships] of animals, and natural affinity is but another term for blood relationship, more or less remote. It is therefore impossible in these days to consider classification without assuming as a postulate that it is a present expression of a past history [evolution]. . . ."[32]

In 1914 Samuel W. Williston, Professor of Paleontology at the University of Chicago, said, "There is very much doubt, very much uncertainty, among paleontologists about the classification of reptiles. No two writers agree on the number of orders, or the rank of many forms. Some recognize twenty or more orders, others but eight or nine. . . . The many strange and unclassifyable types which have come to light in North America, South Africa, and Europe have thrown doubt upon all previous classificatory schemes, have weakened our faith in all attempts to trace out the genealogies [evolutionary lines] or the reptilian orders; and classification is merely genealogy [evolution]. . . . With every problem solved a dozen more intrude themselves upon us. Hence classification merely represents the present condition of our knowledge, our present opinions as to the genealogies [evolutionary sequence]"[33]

In 1942 Paul Weatherwax, Professor of Botany at Indiana University, said, "Botanists still disagree widely on the proper grouping of many plants, but this is because they do not agree in their theories as to the origin of the differences which separate the groups."[34]

There are a number of cases in which forms that are identical in appearance, and which formerly would have been considered to be one species, are now listed as distinct species. This is illustrated by two species of the fungus gnat, *Sciara ocellaris* and *Sciara reynoldsi,* which the experts cannot distinguish. In spite of their identical form, they cannot be crossed, their chromosome configuration is different, and the manner of chromosome elimination (a peculiar characteristic of the Sciaras) is different.

Professor Ernst Mayr says that there are two species of brown creepers (birds) in Europe which differ in that one has a long, nearly straight claw on the hind toe, while the other has a short, curved claw. They occur together but are said never to interbreed. (According to the exclusion principle, they must not compete for the same ecological niche.) He also mentions two species of flycatchers which differ in that one has a longer tail than the other, but the difference is so slight that the species cannot be told apart unless the birds are caught and their tails measured.[35] (This is another case which should be investigated by those who stress the importance of the exclusion principle.)

Ralph Buchsbaum of the University of Chicago tells about two species of termites which are distinguished statistically by a number of measurements. "There are two species of termites which are distinguished most easily by identifying the other animals that live associated with them. Except for the difference in the 'guests' which they harbor, the termites can be distinguished only on the basis of average differences in certain body measurements made on a large number of individuals. A single termite, found away from the nest, cannot be assigned definitely to either species."[36] There must be other differences, for surely the animal "guests" do not employ statistical methods in deciding with which species to live. A difference could be physiological, as the production of different odors, not detected by human beings. On such a basis there could be many more species of various creatures which do not harbor "guests" and whose measurements do not vary in the manner of these termites, or have not been investigated, but which have different odors or some other subtle difference not distinguishable to us.

Libbie Hyman of the American Museum of Natural History says that certain protozoa which inhabit milkweeds and certain other plants and are transmitted from plant to plant by sucking insects are placed in the genus *Hepetomonas* or *Phytomonas*, and would be placed in the genus *Leptomonas* were it not for their mode of transmissal from plant to plant.[37]

There are cases where the experts say that species can be distinguished only on the basis of detailed internal anatomy. Dr. Carl Heinrich of the Smithsonian Institution of Washington says of moths of the family Phyctidae, "Anyone wishing to identify phyctids must resign himself to a tedium of dissection and slide making."[38] According to Professor Robert W. Pennach of the University of Colorado, there are some annelid worms in which "identification depends on internal details of the reproductive system, and though careful dissections are often adequate, it is frequently necessary to make stained serial sections of the segments containing the reproductive structures. Usually cross sections are sufficient, but some workers advocate longitudinal sections in addition."[39]

There are forms which differ considerably at different times of the year. The water fleas, *Daphnia*, are the classical example of this. There are species in which individuals exist in a single morphological form from October until March, but the rest of the year their offspring look like a multitude of different species.[40]

Another phenomenon which may cause trouble for the taxonomist is alternation of generations. In a number of kinds of animals each generation is very different from the one which preceeded it, but like the one before that. Every other generation is the same, but the ones between are different. The classical example of this is found in the jellyfish, but it is found also in insects and some other creatures. E. P. Felt, State Entomologist of New York, said, "One of the most striking and well established is the well-known alternation of generations in gall wasps, a divergence so marked that alternate generations up to within a few years were regarded as belonging to different genera."[41]

There are species which are distinguished physiologically. This is frequently the case in bacteria, where distinct morphological characteristics may be hard to find. Two species of the single-celled green alga *Chlorella* are identified by measuring their average rates of respiration.[42]

As previously mentioned, the anti-anti-evolutionists continually charge that anti-evolutionists must say that no new species have been formed since the time of creation. This is utterly ridiculous, for some taxonomists take trifling differences as a basis for naming new species, and they are constantly changing their minds and differing among each other as to whether a certain group of individuals represents a single species or a number of species. On the other hand, there remains the question: In spite of the fact that the term *species* cannot be defined accurately, have plants or animals been produced which may reasonably be said to be genuinely new species? The answer is probably yes. But in every case nothing mysterious is involved, the means by which the new type came about is understood, and if it has any bearing upon evolution the burden of proof is with the evolutionists.

The classical example of a new species produced by man is *Raphanobrassica,* a plant obtained by a Russian named Karpechenko by crossing cabbage and radish. This has already been discussed, and the cross was accomplished through increasing the number of chromosomes. The plant is fertile but will not cross with either of the parent plants. It is not on the way toward developing into anything of evolutionary significance.

Another example which is frequently cited to illustrate a new species is the marsh grass *Spartina townsendi,* which first appeared around the harbor of Southampton in England, somewhat over a century ago. The situation is the same as in the cabbage-radish cross, except that it occurred naturally instead of in the laboratory. It is intermediate in a number of characteristics between two other species of marsh grass which grow in that area, *Spartina stricta* and *Spartina alterniflora.* The former has 56 chromosomes and the latter has 70. The new type has 126 chromosomes, the sum of the other two. (A hybrid produced without a doubling of the chromosomes would have a number equal to the sum of half the number of chromosomes present in the parent types, or in this case 63. Such a hybrid would not be fertile.[43]) The hybrid in this case is more vigorous than either parent (a characteristic often noted in hybrids) and it is a better soil binder. It has been used on the dikes of the Netherlands and other parts of the world where a good soil binder is needed.

A third example which is frequently cited as the development of a new species is the case of the European rabbits that were liberated on an island of the Madeiras in the fifteenth century. During the intervening centuries the rabbits have become smaller, more timid, darker in color, and are said to be nocturnal. Furthermore they will not interbreed with the European rabbits. These changes are readily explainable through factors understood in modern genetics, together with natural selection, such as was observed in Kettlewell's moths. Natural selection is a fact; the trouble comes when one tries to apply it as a factor in real evolution. After the natural selection of types in a particular environment, moths are still moths and rabbits are still rabbits. Very wide ranges in size and color have been produced in different strains of rabbits in the laboratory, and these changes are hereditary. Behavior traits may also be greatly modified. An interesting illustration of this is the diving pigs of Florida. In *Hutchinson's Animals of All Countries,* Finn and Hinton say, "Domesticated pigs quickly revert to a half-wild condition and develop habits suited to a fresh environment. The diving pigs found in certain islands off the coast of Florida are an example. Their principle food is the refuse fish cast away by fishermen, and to obtain these they have developed the habit of diving under water and walking on the bottom at a depth of five feet below the surface."[44]

Mutations and artificial and natural selection, together with hybridization and chromosomal changes can produce new forms of animals and plants which may be designated as new species, or even new genera, by the taxonomists, but it remains to be shown that any known phenomenon or series of phenomena could produce the kinds of changes which had to be produced if, as the great majority of biologists profess to believe, life on earth evolved from simple beginnings. This is quite a different problem.

NOTES

1. Heutschell, C. and W. R. I. Cook, *Zoology for Medical Students* (Longmans, Green, and Co., 1947), p. 684.

2. Hegner, Robert W. and Karl A. Stiles, *College Zoology*, 6th ed. (Macmillan, 1959), p. 790.

3. Hunter, George W. and F. R. Hunter, *College Zoology* (W. B. Saunders Co., 1949), p. 687.

4. Weatherwax, Paul, *Plant Biology* (W. B. Saunders Co., 1942), p. 356.

5. Northen, Henry F., *Introductory Plant Science*, 2d ed. (Ronald Press Co., 1958), p. 432.

6. Strausbaug, Perry D. and Bernal R. Weimer, *General Biology*, 2d ed. (John Wiley and Sons, 1947), p. 622.

7. Moment, Gardiner, *General Biology* (Appleton-Century-Crofts, 1950), p. 563.

8. Mayr, Ernst, *Systematics and the Origin of Species* (Columbia University press, 1942), p. 28.

9. Huxley, Julian, *The Living Thoughts of Darwin* (Longmans, Green, and Co., 1939), p. 25.

10. Guyer, Michael F., *Animal Biology*, 4th ed. (Harper and Bros., 1948), p. 562.

11. Gates, Ruggles R., *Human Ancestry* (Harvard Univerity Press, 1948), p. 389.

12. *Ibid.*, p. 402.

13. McKinnell, Robert C., *American Naturalist*, 94:875:187, March-April, 1960, p. 187.

14. *Biological Abstracts*, 21:7945, 1947.

15. Wagner, Kenneth A., "Fire Species," *Carolina Tips*, Carolina Biological Supply Co., 26:8:31, October, 1963.

16. Gates, Ruggles, *Human Ancestry*, Harvard University Press, 1948, pp. 10, 406.

17. Weidenreich, Franz, *Apes, Giants, and Men* (University of Chicago Press, 1945), p. 3.

18. Hooton, Ernest A., *Apes, Men, and Morons* (George Allen and Unwin, 1938), p. 115.

19. Mayr, Ernst, *loc. cit.*, p. 4.

20. Fisher, James, *Watching Birds* (Pelican Books, 1940), pp. 37, 38.

21. *Ibid.*, p. 39.

22. Weidenreich, Franz, *Apes, Giants, and Men* (University of Chicago Press, 1946) p. 2.

23. Fisher, James, *loc. cit.*, p. 39.

24. Guyer, Michael F., *loc. cit.*, p. 563.

25. Newman, H. H., *Evolution Yesterday and Today* (Williams and Wilkins, 1932), p. 18.

26. Hooton, Ernest A., *loc. cit.*, p. 116.

27. For example, see Seward, A. C., *Plant Life through the Ages* (Macmillan, 1931), p. 147.

28. Formerly the ferns and horsetails were grouped together as *Pteridophytes*, while the various flowering plants were grouped together as *Spermatophytes*. Now the horsetails are by themselves as *Sphenopsida*, while the ferns and flowering plants are grouped together as *Pteropsida*.

29. Haupt, Arthur, *An Introduction to Botany* (McGraw-Hill, 1956), p. 242.

30. Guyer, Michael F., *loc. cit.*, p. 561.

31. Villee, Claude A., *Biology*, 4th ed. (W.B. Saunders Co., 1962), p. 543.

32. Scudder, S. H., *The Butterflies of the Eastern United States and Canada*, Privately Published, 1889, Vol. 1, p. 236.

33. Williston, S.W., *Water Reptiles of the Past and Present* (University of Chicago Press, 1914), p. 13.

34. Weatherwax, Paul, *loc. cit.*, p. 240.

35. Mayr, Ernst, *loc cit.*, pp. 272, 273.

36. Buchsbaum, Ralph, *Animals Without Backbones* (University of Chicago Press, Rev. ed., 1948), p. 34.

37. Hyman, Libbie, *The Invertebrates* (McGraw-Hill, 1940), Vol. 1, p. 110.

38. Heinrich, Carl, "American Moths of the Subfamily Phyctinae," *Smithsonsian Bulletin* #207, 1956, p. vi.

39. Pennack, Robert W., *Freshwater Invertebrates of the United States* (Ronald Press Co., 1953), p. 287.

40. *Ibid.*, p. 363.

41. Felt, E.P., "Origin and Evolution of Insects," *Scientific Monthly*, 16:8:588, June, 1923.

42. Buchsbaum, Ralph, *loc. cit.*, p. 34.

43. The chromosome number is 63, which is an odd number, and the chromosomes could not arrange into pairs. Furthermore, and the reason for this, is that the chromosomes are different and so could not pair in meiosis anyway. Some animals may normally have an odd number because there is no mate in certain species for the X chromosome.

44. *Hutchinson's Animals of All Countries*, Finn, Frank, *et al.* (Hutchinson and Noble, not dated), Vol. 2, p. 592.

THE EVIDENCE FROM GENETICS

Genetics is the study of the inheritance of traits by offspring from their parents. Charles Darwin realized that a great weakness in his theory was his lack of a theory of how characteristics pass from one generation to the next. Actually he came close to discovering the fundamental laws of inheritance, but he failed to do so. Finally, against the advice of his friends, he published his pangenesis theory, which, as one evolutionist has put it, is now graciously forgotten.

It was the lack of a realistic theory of inheritance which caused Darwin to repudiate, to a certain extent, his own natural selection theory, although this was his real contribution to evolutionary theory and that which made evolution acceptable to the men of science.

Credit for discovering the basic laws of inheritance is given to Gregor Mendel. There is no evidence that Darwin knew about Mendel, though Mendel certainly knew about Darwin. It is remarkable indeed that Mendel had no correspondence with Darwin, for he corresponded with Nägeli, the German botanist, who also was working on the problem of inheritance. Nägeli only discouraged Mendel and discounted the significance of his work, apparently failing to read Mendel's letters at all carefully.

Gregor Mendel and his discovery of the laws of heredity were forgotten for nearly two generations. Then three men independently achieved what Mendel had previously accomplished. The reason which was formerly given for the neglect of Gregor Mendel by the men of science was that his results were published in an obscure scientific journal and did not come to the attention of the men of science of that day. It is now admitted that this is not true, and besides, Mendel sent reprints to various scientists. Therefore a different reason had to be given as to why his work was neglected. The reason now advanced is that the biologists of that time were occupied with other matters and also because Mendel presented his results in a mathematical framework. Though the math was very simple indeed, it is said that his contemporary biologists were not accustomed to regard biological phenomena from that point of view.

R. E. D. Clark, who is not an evolutionist, has stated the opinion that the real reason why Mendel's work was not received was because it seemed to contradict Darwin's evolutionary theory.[1] Darwin believed evolution came about through continual small differences between individuals, the best of which were preserved by the process of natural selection. According to the results obtained by Mendel, inherited characteristics are stable, and moreover they can skip generations. When a characteristic skips one or more generations and then reappears, it is just the same as it was before.

By the time Mendel's laws were rediscovered, Johannsen had shown that there is a definite limit to selection. Weismann had made an impression with his germ plasm theory, which denied the possibility of the inheritance of acquired characteristics. Thus the work of Mendel, which formerly seemed to contradict the theory of Darwin, now was in accord with accepted facts. Furthermore Hugo de-Vries explained the origin of genetic differences as being through mutations. So genetics was soon looked upon as a new tool for establishing the doctrine of evolution and to explain its mechanism. But in this the evolutionists were again frustrated, and a generation later it was admitted that the mechanism of evolution still was not understood.

Now the science of genetics has progressed to the point where the molecular structure of the genetic material is being studied and there is talk of "cracking the genetic code" and of changing hereditary traits through "genetic surgery."

It is admitted that evolution must be in accord with the principles of genetics, but in spite of the great amount of work done in this area and the tremendous advance in knowledge in this field, the genetic basis of evolution is still the same as it was generations ago — mutations, hybridization, polyploidy, and such, with the greatest dependence upon mutations and natural selection. These have already been discussed and found wanting.

NOTE

1. Clark, Robert E.D., *Darwin: Before and After* (The Paternoster Press, 1958), p. 126.

THE EVIDENCE FROM ECOLOGY

Ecology as a formal discipline is one of the newest branches of science. It is a study of the relationships between living things and their environment, which includes other living things.

A college textbook published in 1965 includes ecology among the evidences of evolution.[1] It lists three kinds of evidences within the field of ecology: the progression from stereotyped to learned behavior, the development of complex interactions within a species, and the development of complex relationships between different species.

In the alleged progression from stereotyped to learned behavior, evolution is assumed on morphological grounds. It is obvious that an animal with a more complex nervous system can manifest a greater degree of learning than one with a nervous system of lesser capacity. That a dog has a greater ability to learn than a frog is only reasonable when one compares the nervous systems of these two animals. Thus this "evidence" does not seem to add anything of significance to the evidence for evolution already assumed on other grounds.

Differences in intelligence among animals generally have been held to be a matter of degree rather than of kind, and this is in accord with evolutionary theory. But M. E. Bitterman, Professor of Psychology at Bryn Mawr, has obtained results in his research which indicate that this traditional view is not correct, and that animals with a more complex nervous system have an intelligence which differs from that of simpler forms in kind, and not merely in degree.[2]

Charles Darwin was greatly perplexed as to how to explain social organization, such as the organization of an anthill or beehive. The individuals which could be affected by factors that could bring about evolution through natural selection are neuters and do not reproduce. The ones which reproduce lead sheltered lives. In the end Darwin "explained" it much as he did the evolution of the eye — merely by deciding that it should not bother him any longer. He concluded that colonies *must* respond to natural selection as individuals do. When he accepted this as a fact, he found that it was not only no longer a problem but that it increased his faith in what natural selection could accomplish! Now, instead of being a difficulty in the acceptance of the theory of evolution, complex interractions within a species are given as another evidence *for* evolution!

The third point is that evolution is evident in developing complex relationships between different species. This may be positive (mutualism) or negative (parasitism). In both kinds of cases the relationships may be so complex that an evolutionary explanation is difficult to imagine. Henry N. Andrews, a paleobotanist at the Missouri Botanical Garden, has said, "Some of these flower-insect 'cooperatives' are, however, so incredibly complex in the way in which the everyday lives of the plants and insects have been integrated as to be more than baffling to the student of evolution."[3] Again, it will be noted that what one evolutionist calls more than baffling from the standpoint of an evolutionary explanation, another evolutionist presents as an evidence *for* evolution.

NOTES

1. Cockrum, E. Landell and William J. McCauley, *Zoology* (W. B. Saunders Co., 1965), p. 621.
2. Bitterman, M. E., "The Evolution of Intelligence," *Scientific American*, 212:1:92, January, 1965.
3. Anderews, Henry N., *Ancient Plants* (Comstock Pub. Co., 1947), p. 141.

THE EVIDENCE FROM SEROLOGICAL TESTS

In 1904 George H. F. Nuttall of the University of Cambridge published the results of a very extensive amount of research into the reactions of blood sera sensitized against the sera of various animals.[1]

The serum of the blood is used because it is so convenient, but other parts of the body may be used instead. The method also has been employed with plants. The greater the reaction between the serum and the antiserum, the closer is the assumed relationship between the species concerned.[2]

Nuttall's results have been hailed as a very important evidence of evolution, and extravagant statements have been made in praise of their accuracy. Moreover it has been said to be capable of establishing evolutionary relationships where other methods fail.

In 1920 Professor Horatio Hockett Newman of the University of Chicago wrote, "The blood tests have brought very strong confirmation to the theory of evolution and from an entirely unexpected quarter; they come as near to giving a definite demonstration of the theory of evolution as we are likely to find, until experimental zoology and botany shall have been improved and perfected far beyond their present state."[3]

In 1928 Arthur Keith, the great English anatomist, said, "Early in the present century Professor G. H. F. Nuttall, of the University of Cambridge, discovered a trustworthy and exact method of determining the affinity of one species of animal to another by comparing the reactions of their blood."[4]

In 1931 Ernest Albert Hooton, Harvard's renowned anthropologist, said, "If there were no evidence of human evolution other than those proved by zoological classification [taxonomy] and by blood tests, these alone would be sufficient to convince every impartial thinker that man and the anthropoid apes have evolved from some common ape-like ancestor."[5]

In 1945 Kenoyer and Goddard wrote in their college textbook, "Nuttall developed a delicate test whereby the degree of relationship, as represented by blood similarities, may be determined."[6]

In 1952 Lorus and Margery Milne told students in their textbook that "the test is very helpful . . . in trying to learn the affinities of plants or animals which have so many differences from others in structure that their position in the classificatory scheme is not clear."[7]

In 1956 Gordon Alexander included the following in his textbook of Biology: "In recent years the most striking line of physiological evidence for organic evolution has been that provided by serology. . . . The serological method, carefully applied, has been used with success in the study of relationships among many organisms other than vertebrates — including even plants."[8]

This selection of endorsements shows how highly the serological tests in general, and Nuttall's work in particular, have been rated by textbook writers and by eminent men in the field of biological science. Nuttall's book is difficult to procure, and very few people would take the trouble to check his results and compare them with the flattering remarks presented in the textbooks.

Nuttall apologizes for some of his negative results by saying that they "are due to some common cause, which I am not at present able fully to explain."[9] Certain other reactions which he considers to be unusual he believes may have been due to the manner of death of the animal involved. Other kinds of errors are also mentioned.

Nuttall says that the anti-human sera used were more powerful than the anti-monkey sera, and he believes that this explains the fact that according to his tables placental mammals of all sorts (except two, in which there were no reactions at all) appear to be more closely related to human beings than to monkeys. Even the three families of monkeys tested are, according to his tables, more closely related to human beings than to other monkeys of their own families.[10] Since this is so obviously absurd, he looks for an explanation of the error. But what about cases where the evolutionists are using this technique to find out which animals are more closely related when they have no preconceived idea and neither of the alternative answers would be considered absurd? It seems that answers in such cases are worthless.

Since men and monkeys are supposed to be more closely related to each other than to any of the nonprimates, comparisons of various kinds of animals with men and with monkeys should agree (those closest to men should also be closest to monkeys), but they do not agree. An examination of Nuttall's results leads to the conclusion that human beings are most closely related to the hoofed animals, then to the carnivorous animals, followed by the rodents, insectivores (moles and the like), and bats. In the case of the monkeys the numbers are smaller, but the insectivores rank first, followed by the carnivores, and then the hoofed animals.

An examination of Nuttall's tables reveals the interesting feature that pigs, among the hoofed animals, and hyenas, among the carnivores, are more closely related to all sorts of animals than other animals are. For example, pigs are more closely related to cats than dogs are to cats, and also pigs are more closely related to dogs than cats are to dogs, although dogs and cats belong to the same order of animals while pigs belong to a different order. Hyenas appear to be more closely related to cats than cats are to themselves.

Nuttall's tests indicate that kingfishers and petrels (birds) are more closely related to dogs than to chickens, and that pheasants are closer to human beings than to ostriches. Among four pheasants of the same species tested, it was found that one was related to man but not to dogs, one to dogs and not to man, while the other two were related to neither. Fifteen men reacted to anti-hyena syrum and eleven did not; twenty-two reacted to anti-pig serum and six did not; four reacted to anti-dog serum and three did not.

Nuttall made a series of tests with five horses. The results of such a series of tests should be uniform, for when testing to find out if horses are related to some other kind of animal, it should make no difference what individual horse is used to furnish the serum. If it does make a difference, there is no way by which the tester can know which horse will give the correct reaction and which will not, and so the test is invalid. One of these horses showed a relationship to each of the following: man, cat, hyena, dog, seal, pig, llama, Mexican-deer, reindeer, antelope, sheep, ox (sic), and horse. One of the horses showed relationship only to sheep and other horses. One showed relationship only to man and other horses. Another showed relationship only to antelopes, and not even to other horses. The last did not show any relationship to any of the animals and not even to other horses.

Levine and Moody[11] made parallel tests with eight different kinds of rodents, to ascertain their degree of relationship to the muskrat. The only difference between the two sets of tests was that the anti-muskrat serum was produced in two different rabbits. As in the case of Nuttall's horses (in which the original *sera* were taken from different horses), this case (where the *antisera* came from different rabbits) should make no difference. If it does make a difference, the test is no good, for the tester cannot look at rabbits and tell which will produce the right kind of antiserum and which will not. Levine and Moody used more refined methods than Nuttall had employed, and they were able to present their results on a percentage basis, where 100% in this case means that the animal reacted just the way a muskrat would in the test. In other words, a result of 100% means that the animal tested is so much like a muskrat that it could be a muskrat, so far as the test is concerned.

In one series, three rodents which were not muskrats tested 100%, one tested 75%, three tested 10%, and one tested 0%, or negative. In the other series, which should have given the same result, one rodent tested 13% and the others were all 0% or negative.

It has been objected that for the sake of evolutionary perspective, rabbits should not have been used to form the antibodies, but since rabbits have been declared not to be rodents, this criticism is invalidated. Moody performed an experiment to test the relationship of rabbits to rodents, using chickens to produce the antibodies, and concluded that rabbits are more closely related to cows than to rodents (rats, mice, squirrels, muskrats).[12]

Professor William C. Boyd of Boston University recognizes such variations as a problem and says, "Another difficulty is due to the individual variation in antibodies produced by different animals of the same species. Apparently, not only do different species recognize different parts of antigens as the most significant, but different individuals may vary in this respect, so that antibodies of different specificity are obtained in different animals."[13]

In using the serological tests to discover evolutionary relationships, it is highly desirable to have a reliable measure of degree of relationship. Professor Boyd says that this is still lacking, and writing in 1956, half a century after the publication of Nuttall's work, he still feels that Nuttal's methods are preferable to later refinements. "Another problem in applying serological methods to taxonomy is that we have no certain way of expressing quantitatively the degree of relationship shown by a serological test. The method of Nuttall, though open to objections, is still in many ways better than some alternative procedures."[14]

Landsteiner and Scheer did some research involving different organs of the same species, and if interpreted in the same way as the other tests, it would seem that the trachea (wind pipe) is more closely related to the thymus gland than to the kidney, and the kidney is more closely related to the trachea than to the thymus![15]

It was found that different parts of the same organ may react differently, and even different parts of the same cell.

What if tissues other than blood are used for the tests, and the results are inconsistent? Professor Boyd recognizes this problem and says, "An interesting question which has never been thoroughly discussed now arises. Which proteins of the living organism are to be considered most indicative of its zoological relationship to other plants or animals? . . . to these questions the serologist is unable to give a definite answer, and can only reply that in the long run the decision must rest with the taxonomist. . . . An interesting point of logic comes up as we attempt to decide which antigens are most significant by comparing our conclusions about relationships with those based upon morphological comparisons, for in such a case our argument may become circular. For, clearly, if we define, the most valid serological conclusions as those which parallel most nearly those of structural lines, then serology has no independent contribution to make to taxonomy."[16]

In evolutionary studies, the serological tests should have their greatest value in solving problems of relationships where other clues fail. One such case is the ancestry of the whales. All evolutionists admit belief that the whales evolved from ancestors that walked on land, but just what these ancestors were like and what group of living animals is most closely related to whales is admittedly not clear. The hoofed animals and the carnivorous animals are the leading contestants for the honor of having the closest affinity to the whales. It is commonly asserted that the serological tests favor the hoofed animals. For example, Leslie A. Kenoyer, Head of the Department of Biology at Western Michigan College, says, "The precipitin test has been used to help assign doubtful organisms to groups and to learn something of their relationships; for example, such a test has shown that . . . whales are related most closely to the even-toed hoofed animals. . . ."[17]

A perusal of Nuttall's tables reveals that pigs react to practically any antiserum, or in other words, pigs appear to be closely related to just about everything. The Mexican-deer also shows a high degree of relationship to other animals. Data bearing on the problem of the affinities of whales are to be found at three places in Nuttall's book. The even-toed hoofed animals certainly come out ahead, but the pigs and Mexican deer are important in making this possible. Among the carnivorous animals, the hyena is the one studied by Nuttall that seems to be related to most other animals, but of the six carnivores tested to show their relationships with whales, the hyena was not included. This kind of research strongly weights the evidence in favor of the even-toed ungulates, but to see this it is necessary to procure a copy of Nuttall's book and to examine it rather carefully. It is very doubtful that textbook writers have done this. One writer makes a statement about a conclusion like this, which may or may not be justified by the facts, and other writers parrot what he says. Certainly students and the general public cannot be expected to check data like these.

Concerning plants, I. B. Balfour, Professor of Botany at the University of Edinburgh, says in the article on Angiosperms in the *Encyclopaedia Britannica*, "A phylogenetic evolutionary system based on the reaction of serum of members of various families has also been developed. It seems difficult, however, to give protein characters any higher taxonomic value than other characters, since it has been shown that the same reactive substance may occur in very distantly related families."

Since the difficulties in getting reliable information about the relationships of animals and plants from serological testing arise from characteristics intrinsic to the tissues themselves, no refinements in experimental techniques can increase the accuracy of the tests.

Among the new developments is a method of studying the composition of proteins which is called twodimensional starch-gel electrophoresis. Although the technique is quite different, it bears a relationship to the serological tests. It is now hailed as a "new and precise method" of obtaining evidence of evolutionary relationships, just as the serological tests were when they were new. A popular magazine tells the public that "the new evidence not only cements the kinship beyond all doubt but also suggests that man and ape are much closer together on the family tree than originally believed."[18]

In the same article a chemist at California Tech is quoted as remarking that "it appears that the gorilla is just an abnormal man, or man is an abnormal gorilla." Another interesting sentence in the article tells that physical anthropologists are impressed with this research and are "happy because it reinforces their own conclusions reached through imaginative deductions from woefully inadequate fossil evidence."

And so the cycle is starting over again.

NOTES

1. Nuttall, George H. F., *Blood Immunity and Blood Relationships* (Cambridge University Press, 1904).

2. Briefly the procedure and its interpretation are as follows. Suppose one wished to test by this method the statement of Professor Romer, previously mentioned, that perhaps horses and cows are more closely related to lions than to each other. Some blood would be obtained from a horse and the serum of this blood would be injected into a rabbit. The rabbit would build antibodies against this horse serum. After the elapse of a suitable amount of time for this to occur, blood would be taken from the rabbit and its serum obtained. Since this serum would contain antibodies built up by the rabbit as a natural reaction to the horse serum, it would be called anti-horse serum. If this anti-horse serum is mixed with horse serum in a test tube a reaction should occur, producing a dense clouding of the liquid and resulting in a precipitate as it settled out. If some of the anti-horse serum is introduced into two test tubes containing respectively cow serum and lion serum, the tube in which the greater reaction, if any, occurs is believed to show that the animal whose serum is in that test tube is more closely related to the horse than is the other animal.

3. Newman, Horatio Hockett, *Evolution, Genetics, and Eugenics* (University of Chicago Press, 1920), p. 104.

4. Keith, Arthur, *Concerning Man's Origin* (C. P. Putnam's Sons, 1928), p. 24.

5. Hooton, Ernest Albert, *Up from the Ape* (Macmillan, 1931), p. 45.

6. Kenoyer, Leslie A. and Henry N. Goddard, *General Biology* (Harper and Bros, 1945), p. 483.

7. Milne, Lorus J. and Margery J. Milne, *The Biotic World and Man*, 2d ed. (Prentice Hall, 1958), p. 429. In the third edition, 1965, the word "very" was dropped and there were a few minor changes in wording: ". . . the tests are helpful in trying to learn the affinities of plants or animals that differ so greatly from all others known that their position in the classificatory scheme is not clear," p. 558.

8. Alexander, Gordon, *General Biology* (Thomas Y. Crowell, 1956) p. 815.

9. Nuttall, George H. F., *loc. cit.,* p. 166.

10. In his large table, which covers forty-two pages for the placental animals, he designates four degrees of positive reaction: 1. Faint clouding. 2. Medium clouding. 3. Marked clouding. 4. Great reaction. These indicate an increasing closeness of relationship. If one assigns the value of O to tests which proved negative, and the values 1 to 4 to each of the others, as indicated above, and then divides the total by the number of tests, a convenient index is obtained. This seems to be a good approximation of the alleged relationship when the number of cases in each category is approximately the same.

11. Levine, H. P. and P. A. Moody, "Serological Investigation of Rodent Relationships," *Physiological Zoology,* 12:4:400, October, 1939.

12. Moody, Paul Amos, *Introduction to Evolution,* 2d ed. (Harper and Bros, 1962), pp. 117-119.

13. Boyd, William C., *Fundamentals of Immunology,* 3d ed. (Interscience Publishers, 1956), p. 147.

14. *Ibid.,* p. 147.

15. See Karl Landsteiner, *The Specificity of Serological Reactions* (Harvard University Press, 1947), p. 80.

16. Boyd, William C., *loc. cit.,* pp. 103, 104.

17. Kenoyer, Leslie A., *General Biology,* 3d ed. (Harper and Bros, 1953), p. 516.

18. *Newsweek,* March 2, 1964, p. 52.

THE EVIDENCE FROM ANIMAL DISTRIBUTION

The distribution of different kinds of animals over the earth is sometimes given as an evidence of evolution. It is said that if they had been created instead of having evolved, they would occur not only where they are found, but also at other places where they can survive comfortably. Rabbits have done very well in Australia after being introduced there. So the argument seems to be that if they had been created they would have been put there in the first place. This is really no argument except to those who are prepared to put themselves in the place of God and to say what God would or would not do.

J. W. Mavor, Professor Emeritus of Biology at Union College, mentions this case of the rabbits and also English sparrows, starlings, and certain insects. He points out that an animal's range seldom includes all suitable territory and may not even include the most favorable habitats. He concludes, "These facts are best explained by assuming that each species arose at a certain point on the earth's surface, called a center of dispersal, and has spread out to occupy the area it now inhabits."[1]

But Bible-believing people do not hold, as a number of evolutionists seem to think they do, that animals are found where they are because they were created there. All the terrestrial animals which were not taken into Noah's Ark were destroyed in the great deluge, and the descendants of the survivors got where they are now by dispersal from a central point. Thus creationists and evolutionists both look upon the present distribution of animals as the result of distribution from a point of dispersal. The difference is that the evolutionist may have a number of points of dispersal if he chooses, and he believes he has a great deal more time at his disposal.

Professor Paul Amos Moody, for example, in his textbook of evolution, shows great ignorance of Scripture when he belittles the position of Bible-believers in regard to the distribution of animals. He says, "We may note in passing, however, that for some people the answer is simple and clear. It is possible to be satisfied with the explanation that these continents have their present inhabitants because the latter were created in place, so to speak. Lions were created in Africa, not in South America; jaguars were created in South America, not in Africa, and so on. For people contented with this explanation the final answer has been given and there is nothing left to explain. Such an 'explanation' removes the whole matter from the field of scientific inquiry."[2]

Besides disregarding the action of the flood since the time of creation, he puts the importance of scientific inquiry above the question of truth. An honest evolutionist should consider the possibility of creation and not dismiss it on the grounds that it removes the matter from the field of scientific inquiry.

It is not easy to say how fast animals would disperse from a central point. Some creatures disperse explosively in a new environment, as did the Japanese beetles in the eastern United States some time ago. The first nest built by starlings introduced into the United States was observed in New York city in 1890. About fifty years later they had reached the west coast.

There is the highly publicized case of Hubert, the adventuring hippopotamus, who walked southward from his native habitat about a thousand miles in two and a half years. In one country he was protected as a ward of the state. He passed through a modern city, visiting a monastery and a temple. He was allowed to feed on cabbages and the like as he wished. He strayed just about as far south as it was possible for him to go when the inevitable happened in such a world as ours — a vandal shot him dead with a rifle. No hippopotamus has been known to exhibit such a *wanderlust* before or since. But it did happen, and so it is possible. Who knows what animals might have strayed long distances in the prehistoric past?

Those who discuss animal distribution tell us that animals are sometimes seen far out at sea on floating debris, washed from the land during a storm. Some of these may travel long distances in ocean currents and then be cast on a distant island, to start a colony there.

Former "land bridges" and chains of islands are postulated as a means available to animals in the past as they dispersed. The concept of land bridges has been overdone, even reaching such absurdities as the postulation that there were separate land bridges from continental land to separate mountain valleys in an oceanic island. Professor Simpson says, "Even in Darwin's day, the building of these imaginary land bridges was such a popular sport that he waxed sarcastic on the subject."[3]

Professor Simpson postulates what he calls "sweepstakes" to get animals to places where their presence is very difficult to explain. The chance of anyone in particular to win a sweepstake is small, but someone has to win. Animals may by chance get to unexpected places, but the principle is different from winning a sweepstake; none have to win.

Evolutionists rather glibly postulate solutions to some of the problems of animal distribution, but others are not always satisfied with the textbook solutions. Dr. Simpson wrote in 1958, ". . . the technical literature of zoogeography is considerably more extensive (and also considerably more complex) than that of, say, nuclear physics."[4]

Professor Simpson reviewed very favorably a new book on animal distribution by Philip J. Darlington, but in spite of his favorable attitude toward the book he said that the author's theory of animal distribution "is quite convincing, if one is willing to subordinate a great many details. Darlington does not ignore these details, but he has an Olympian way of brushing them aside — as is, indeed, necessary if one is to find fundamental underlying principles."[5]

Since the scientific experts have problems in trying to explain the distribution of animals on the earth, it is hardly to be expected that Bible-believers should be expected to give all the answers. But since the evolutionists put animal distribution on a natural basis, it is required that they produce the answers to all the questions involved or keep looking for them. The creationist does not have this responsibility or obligation. The flood was an act of God and miracles were associated with it. The Bible indicates that the animals were brought to Noah *supernaturally* and that he did not go out to seek them (Gen. 6:20, 7:9). Also it is implied in Genesis that the Lord *providentially* directed their distribution after the deluge. The Lord said that after the flood the animals would reproduce abundantly (Gen. 8:17).

NOTES

1. Mavor, James Watt, *General Biology,* 5th ed. (Macmillan, 1959), p. 592.

2. Moody, Paul Amos, *Introduction to Evolution,* 2d ed. (Harper and Brothers, 1962), p. 259.

3. Simpson, George Gaylord, Review of *Zoogeography* by Philip J. Darlington, *Natural History,* 67:3:116, p. 117.

4. *Ibid.,* p. 116.

5. *Ibid.,* p. 168.

EVIDENCE FROM THE FOSSIL RECORD

The other evidences of evolution are admittedly circumstantial, but it is sometimes said that the fossil record is a direct evidence of evolution. The textbooks present the fossils in a sequence which gives a rather convincing picture of an evolutionary sequence. It does not take a great deal of investigation, however, to discover that the alleged ancestries of animals and plants begin with hypotheses instead of with fossils.

Charles Darwin seems to have been the first to have considered seriously the fossils as an evidence of evolution. He recognized the incompleteness of the fossil record as an account of evolution, but he expressed faith that as time went on the gaps in the record would be filled. Time has gone on and a great deal more material has been found. Some of it has allegedly helped to fill gaps, but the gaps in the fossil record are now more evident than in Darwin's day because of the great mass of material which has been found.

Douglas Dewar, who writes against the theory of evolution, presented to the Zoological Society of London a paper which was unique in that he and his collaborator, Mr. C. A. Levett-Yates, seem to have been the only men who had up to that time "attempted to discover the extent to which animals are fossilized and the extent to which fossils that have been laid down have been subsequently destroyed." They studied the mammals, and concluded that with regard to these animals "the record is far less imperfect than evolutionists make out."[1] (That is, less imperfect from the standpoint of the animals which really lived.) The Zoological Society refused the paper on the grounds that "this kind of evidence leads to no valuable conclusion." In other words, evidence that the gaps in the fossil record are real gaps is said to lead to no valuable conclusion.

The evolutionists themselves admit the reality of the gaps and some of them are not expecting the gaps to be filled in with the further finding of fossils.

The largest gap of all is the first one, and it is the one most easily ignored. Darwin started his evolutionary scheme with one or a few simple forms of life, but where did they come from? Several evolutionists have stated that when there was no form of life on earth more advanced than the protozoa — the one-celled creatures — evolution had already proceeded at least half way from the beginning to human beings.

Although it is claimed that there is some evidence of life before that assigned to the time called the Cambrian Period, the fossil record begins there with a great abundance of fossils. This has to be explained, and a number of theories have been suggested. The two most commonly presented are: (1) the older rocks have been transformed by heat and pressure so that the fossils they contained were destroyed (but there are rocks of this alleged age which are not so transformed and which are suitable for containing fossils, but have none), (2) the creatures which lived at that time were too soft to leave fossils (but there are many fossil jellyfish, and what is softer than a jellyfish, and why would soft things get hard shells so suddenly?)

As a gap which allegedly has been filled let us consider the gap between amphibians and reptiles. G. A. Kerkut of the Department of Physiology and Biochemistry at the University of Southampton, himself an evolutionist, says: "*Seymouria* is sometimes thought of as a link between the amphibia and reptiles. Unfortunately *Seymouria* is found in the Permian whilst the first reptiles arose in the Pennsylvanian, some twenty or more million years earlier."[2] Thus gaps may be filled by fossils which the evolutionists admit came millions of years too late, by their chronology, to fill such a gap.

Roy Chapman Andrews of the American Museum of Natural History said that it is the anatomy which is important and not the time element in deciding ancestral forms.[3] According to this, someone sitting across from you in the New York subway could be a link between man and ape — it is the anatomy which should be the deciding factor and not the time when he lives.

Another matter which is easily overlooked is the fact that there is a very great difference between the amphibian egg and the reptilian egg. Amphibian eggs with very few exceptions develop in the water and have a mass of jelly around the embryo. In contrast to this, the reptile egg develops on land and besides a shell it has membranes around the embryo. The evolution of the reptile egg is a very difficult problem for the evolutionists, but this may be ignored when considering a fossil which has some amphibian and some reptilian characteristics. There is no way of knowing what kind of eggs were produced by a form which seems to bridge the gap between amphibians and reptiles.

William Howells is a famous evolutionist and Professor of Anthropology at Harvard University, and he proposes what may be called the "stairway theory" to explain the gaps in the fossil record. He likens the situation to an apartment house which becomes occupied as parts are finished. When the first floor is ready people move in, and as the second and higher floors become suited for occupancy they become inhabited. As people move to suitable living quarters they use the stairways, but they do not stay on the stairways very long. Similarly, he says, the evolution of different forms was very rapid between stable types, and hence there were relatively few intermediate forms. These are not likely to be found, and hence the gaps.

There are a few types of animals which can reproduce in an immature or larval stage. Some scientists believe that evolutionary lines could have developed from both immature and mature forms, and thus there could be a real continuity with an apparent gap. But even if this were true it could account for very few gaps.

Some alleged evolution may be merely effects due to a changing environment. Such a drastic change as fishes developing with a single medial eye is caused by the presence of a certain concentration of an ion in the water. Under experimental conditions a change in the acidity and alkalinity in the water has produced such difference in the development of snail eggs from the same parent that the individuals produced would not be considered to be related.

In recent years it has been admitted more and more by the evolutionists that forms which look very similar may have had quite different ancestries. It is evident that if this is admitted, the evidence for evolution from the fossil record becomes as circumstantial as the other evidences of evolution. Examples of this have been discussed already under the heading of evidence from comparative anatomy. Professor Romer admits that a comparative anatomist may be forced to admit that animals as similar as a gorilla and a chimpanzee could have evolved from different fish. Many groups which once were considered to be uniform are now believed to have had a polyphyletic origin, that is, evolutionists now believe that different animals of the same type descended by different lines from different animals of some other group (as various mammals from different kinds of reptiles).

It has been said many times that the paleontologists argue in a circle as they date the strata by the fossils they contain and the fossils by the strata in which they occur. Robert H. Rastall, formerly editor of the *Geological Magazine*, admits this in the article he wrote for the *Encyclopedia Britannica*, "It cannot be denied that from a strictly philosophical standpoint geologists are here arguing in a circle. The succession of organisms has been determined by a study of their remains embedded in the rocks, and the relative ages of the rocks are determined by the remains of organisms that they contain."[4]

Strata at a distance from each other without any connections are judged to be of the same age if they contain similar fossils. This is based upon certain assumptions. As Mr. Rastall says in the same article, "In the first place, fossils are regarded as time-indices, on the general ground that any particular species comes into existence, lasts for a certain length of time, and then dies out completely, never to recur. Therefore it would appear that if the same fossil is found in rocks in different places, these rocks must be of the same age." It will be remembered, however, that there are forms which are believed to have persisted unchanged from very early times until the present, and other forms which were thought to have been extinct for millions of years have turned up very much alive in our own day.

Sometimes strata are designated as of a certain age and then as fossils not seen at first are discovered in them, the designations are changed accordingly. Sometimes when certain fossils do not fit, it is said that they had been washed out of some other deposit and re-buried where found. These are convenient ways out so as to be able to hold on to the original assumptions.

Frequently in the geological record strata lie just above others which are believed to be very much older, and the assumed inter-vening strata are missing. The explanation of this is that the strata which came between the others was eroded away before the younger strata were laid down. But sometimes the younger lie on the older with no evidence of erosion having occurred to account for the in-tervening millions of years. This is a serious problem but it is dis-regarded.

Sometimes fossils are found in reverse order, with the older above the younger. This is explained as due to thrust-faulting, where older strata have slid across the top of younger. But this explanation is offered where there is no evidence of friction, although a very great amount of friction would have occurred if thick, heavy layers slid over others. Whitcomb and Morris in their book *The Genesis Flood* point out the absurdity of a theory which must assume that the famous Matterhorn of the Alps was pushed more than thirty miles over younger rocks, and another alpine mountain called the Mythen Peak must have been pushed to its present position all the way from Africa.[5]

N. A. Rupke of the State University of Gronigen presents a very interesting and instructive phenomenon which the paleontologists have refused to consider. There are cases where fossils, notably tree trunks, stand vertically through a number of layers of sedimentation and are cut off abruptly at a bedding plane, different trees at different planes, though standing close together.[6] (These are not trees killed by volcanic action and buried in layers of ash.) This situation does not fit the assumptions of uniformitarian geology.

Another very interesting recent development is the finding of fossil pollen grains in formations at the Grand Canyon where such pollen ought not to be according to orthodox paleontology. Clifford Burdick of the Creation Research Society has found fossilized pollen of conifers and of flowering plants even in rock classed as pre-Cambrian.[7] The reader who does not have some background in this area may not realize the extraordinary significance of this. It is like finding the fossilized skeletons of vertebrate animals where no life higher than protozoa or possibly some simple invertebrates is expected. When Leakey found his *Zinjanthropus* in Africa it was said that textbooks became obsolete overnight. The finding of pollen in pre-Cambrian formations certainly makes the textbooks of paleontology obsolete, but in a way the paleontologists do not like.

For over a hundred years the position taken by men of science with regard to geological phenomena is the view called *uniformitarianism*. According to this, the forces in the past which produced presently observed features were merely the same kinds of forces which are having effects at the present time, such as local floods, earthquakes, volcanism, glaciation, rain, frost, and the like. This is in opposition to *catastrophism*, according to which one or more catastrophes of a sort not now experienced had an influence in the past on shaping geological formations.

The concept of uniformitarianism was first propounded scientifically when James Hutton published his *Theory of the Earth* in 1785. He denied the belief held by the scientists of his day that there have been geological events in the past which were of a nature different from those we observe today. He stated that in explaining the origins of geological formations "no powers are to be employed that are not natural to the globe, no action to be admitted except that of which we know the principle." Little attention was taken of his view until 1802, when John Playfair published a book called *Illustrations of the Huttonian Theory*. The geologist Charles Lyell took up the idea and he is the one whose writing caused it to become the accepted theory among geologists ever since. In 1830 he published his *Principles of Geology: Being an Attempt to Explain the Former Changes of the Earth's surface by Reference to Causes Now in Action*. When Charles Darwin set out as a young man on his expedition with the *Beagle* he took along a copy of the first volume of this work of Lyell's. It changed his life and led him to the evolutionary views for which he later became famous.

The apostle Peter in his second epistle (II Peter 3:3-6) wrote about scoffers in the last days who would reject the promise of the Lord's return, presenting as evidence their observation that "since the fathers fell asleep, all things continue as they were from the beginning of creation." This is a description of uniformitarianism, and Peter mentions specifically that these people would willfully disregard the Scriptural account of the flood which destroyed the life that was upon the earth.

Whitcomb and Morris, in *The Genesis Flood*,[8] discuss fourteen geological phenomena which the uniformitarian principle is inadequate to explain. The concept of "flood geology," whereby much of the geological history of the earth is explained as being due to the flood of the time of Noah, is a matter of ridicule to the men of science, but it is the belief of this writer that Whitcomb and Morris have written a book which marks the beginning of the time when this must be considered seriously from a scientific standpoint.

After more than a hundred years of uniformitarianism, some geologists have recently begun to admit that there are geological phenomena which have not been explained by modern geology and that uniformitarianism is not the answer. Where does this leave those who during the last hundred years have taken the position that the experts know best, and if they accept uniformitarianism it must be all right?

The Science Editor of *Newsweek* reported in the issue of December 23, 1963, that geologists at a recent meeting of The American Geological Society "were advising the rehabilitation of catastrophism," but added that this would be "without recourse to a supernatural agent." Notice the lack of capital letters in referring to God. The editor comments that *catastrophism* is "a fighting word among geologists. It is a theory based on divine intervention." Why should geologists become so upset because some people believe God intervened in nature? Why are scientists so outraged because some people take an anti-evolutionary stand? Why do they not just ignore those who differ from their mechanistic views? But it is not so. To them *catastrophism* and *teleology* are fighting words. This attitude is unscientific and it seems to be part of a larger conspiracy aimed at the denial of a personal God, and particularly at discounting the atonement of Christ.

The Science Editor of *Newsweek* quotes Norman Newell, paleontologist of the American Museum of Natural History, as saying, "Geology suffers from a great lack of data, and in such a situation any attractive theory that comes along is taken as gospel. This is the case with uniformitarianism. . . . But since the end of World War II, when a new generation moved in, we have gotten more data and we have begun to realize that there were many catastrophic events in the past, some of which happened just once." This is quite an admission. Characteristically, Dr. Newell urges that a new word be found to describe this and that the word *catastrophism* be avoided, because it has connotations of supernatural acts of God.

It is to be noted that men who are opposed to giving God credit for manifestations of His work in nature are careful to avoid terms which have teleological implications, but frequently men who profess to be conservative Bible-believing Christians are very careless in the way they use terms which have mechanistic implications, particularly the word *evolution*. Some even make sport of the way the word *evolution* "used to" be considered a "bad word." But you will not find the evolutionists joking about how teleology "used to" be considered a "bad word" — it still is to them. While the evolutionists are exerting more and more pressure upon the public to accept evolution, a number of conservative Christians are playing into their hands by telling the Christian public that now it is all right to accept at least a certain amount of evolution.

NOTES

1. Dewar, Douglas, *The Transformist Illusion* (Dehoff Publications, 1957), p. 14.
2. Kerkut, G. A., *Implications of Evolution* (Pergamon Press, 1960), p. 136.
3. Andrews, Roy Chapman, *Meet Your Ancestors* (Viking Press, 1945, 5th printing, 1956), p. 57.
4. *Encyclopedia Britannica,* 1957, Vol. 10, p. 168.
5. Whitcomb, John C. Jr. and Henry M. Morris, *The Genesis Flood* (The Presbyterian and Reformed Pub. Co., 1962), p. 199.
6. Rupke, N. A., "Prolegomena to a Study of Cataclysmal Sedimentation," *1966 Annual,* The Creation Research Society, 3:1:16, May, 1966. Notice particularly the illustration on page 24.
7. Burdick, Clifford, "Microflora of the Grand Canyon," *1966 Annual,* The Creation Research Society, 3:1:38, May, 1966.
8. Whitcomb and Morris, *Loc. cit.* See *Uniformitarianism* in the index.

THE DATING OF REMAINS

The evolutionist relies on having a very great deal of time at his disposal. Several authors have made statements to the effect that given sufficient time, events which seem virtually impossible become not only probable, but are to be expected. But the biologists accepted evolution as a fact *before* they were given the great amount of time which is now allotted to them. Thus it is seen that they were not discouraged at a time when the time allowed for evolution was relatively short.

It is at present popular to point out that the Bible does not say when the world began, and that "In the beginning" (Gen. 1:1), can be as far back in time as one pleases. This allows time for the theistic evolutionist. In a letter to the editor of the *Journal of the American Scientific Affiliation*,[1] Dr. John R. Howitt of Toronto chides the editor for taking the compromising view that "God may have worked through a biological process of natural selection." Dr. Howitt replies that of course God could have worked through any process, but the question is not what God *could* have done but what He *did* do. He points out that all the members of the American Scientific Affiliation have signed a statement which affirms their acceptance of the historical record given in the Bible, and that Genesis is history, not poetry. The problem is not to try to make an interpretation which harmonizes with modern science, but to find out what the Bible really says in the original language.

Dr. Howitt then refers to an earlier communication in which he reported on the replies he had received to a question he addressed to Professors of Oriental Languages in nine leading universities — Oxford, Cambridge, London, Harvard, Yale, Columbia, Toronto, McGill, and Manitoba. Dr. Howitt asked: Do you consider that the Hebrew word *yom* (day) as used in Genesis 1 accompanied by a numeral should properly be translated as (a) a day, as commonly understood, (b) an age, (c) either a day or an age without preference? No reply was received from Oxford or Cambridge, but the professors of the other institutions replied unanimously that it should be translated as a day as commonly understood. Professor Robert H. Pfeiffer of Harvard added, "of 24 hours" to his reply.

The Journal of the American Scientific Affiliation reprinted an article from *Think* magazine which quotes an astronomer as saying, "In the beginning was the Word, it has been piously declared, and I might venture that the word was hydrogen gas."[2] Those who do not catch the significance of this bit of blasphemy should read carefully the opening verses of the Gospel of John, not overlooking verse 14. The astronomer is making a reference to the "steady state" theory of the origin of the universe. According to this theory hydrogen atoms are constantly being created, a phenomenon unexplained, and very slowly astronomical bodies come into being through the accumulation of the hydrogen atoms. Other elements form from these hydrogen atoms in the centers of great stars, due to intense heat and pressure. A local explosion, from a cosmological standpoint, may free this matter for evolutionary purposes. This theory has been abandoned.

In contrast to this is the "big bang" theory, according to which there was a great explosion of matter, the origin of which is not explained. The expanding universe has been expanding ever since, with the objects farthest out moving the fastest and being farthest out because they have been moving the fastest.

The current view of the scientists is that the earth is somewhere around six billion years old, more or less; that the beginning of the fossil record represents animals which lived around six hundred million years ago; and that man has been on the earth for perhaps a couple of million years, depending on how one defines *man*. A reading of the Biblical account of creation, unprejudiced by current concepts, gives the impression of a short interval of time — six days, to be exact. If it were not for a desire to reconcile Scripture with modern science, there would appear to be no reason to try to read a long period of time into the Genesis account.

Before discussing the radioactive methods of age determination, mention should be made of the fluorine method. It was originally proposed by James Middleton in 1844, and was revived by Adolphe Carnot in 1892. In recent times it was again revived by Kenneth Oakley in the 1920's.[3]

As remains lie buried they take up flourine from their surroundings, and thus the more flourine they contain the older they are assumed to be. One difficulty is immediately obvious, for the amount of fiourine available varies considerably in different localities, and thus the test is of greatest significance in comparing the ages of remains in the same general locality.

Shortly before the Piltdown remains were demonstrated to be a hoax, Oakley performed a fluorine test on the skull and jaw and announced that the test showed that they were of the same age. This bolstered the majority opinion among the scientists, namely that the skull and jaw belonged to the same individual. Shortly thereafter, however, it was revealed that the jaw was an unfossilized bone of a modern ape, stained to make it look old, while the skull, although a modern type, was mineralized. To explain away this embarrassing development it was said that the remains were deemed so valuable that samples of insufficient size were taken for the test. There was, however, no mention of such caution in taking samples when the first result was published.

Professor Duncan McConnell of Ohio State University says that in addition to the recognized difficulties inherent in this method of dating, there are still other difficulties which apparently have not even been taken into consideration up to the present time. He discusses these and says that straightforward chemical methods "can hardly be expected to give consistent age determinations."[4] He also says that since the fluorine-phosphorous ratio, a refinement of the fluorine method, introduces still another variable, it makes the situation worse instead of better. He further says that the x-ray diffraction method is also unreliable, and concludes that fluorine age determinations "must be regarded as fortuitous in view of present knowledge of the crystal structure of bone."

The radioactive methods of age determination are based on the fact that radioactive elements decay to form other elements, and the time required for half of the atoms present at any time to decay is assumed to be constant. One of the basic assumptions in the methods of age determination based on the decay of radioactive elements is that the rates of decay are constant. In this regard it is important to note that Robert V. Gentry says, ". . . my investigations of the uranium and thorium halos disclosed a startling circumstance: the radioactive decay rates have probably changed considerably during geologic time.[5]

Early in the present century it was observed that uranium in rocks decomposes through a series of transformations into helium and lead. It was suggested that by measuring the amount of one of these elements in a rock containing uranium its age could be ascertained. The helium was first used in these age determinations, but helium can escape from the rock since it is a very light gas and also it builds up considerable pressure. The helium method was abandoned, and measurements based on lead were used instead. This was complicated by the fact that two kinds of uranium produce different kinds of lead as end products, and thorium present in the rock produced a third. Besides this, other lead may be present which did not come from radioactive decay. Although it is now recognized that the earlier results were faulty, the scientists seemed just as certain of the value of their results before the various recent checks were incorporated into the technique as they do now. This attitude is characteristic of workers in various areas of evolutionary investigation, and it does not increase confidence.

Dr. L. T. Aldrich of the Carnegie Institution of Washington said in 1957 that the modern methods have not changed the basic assumptions on which the work is based. These include the assumption that the half life of the radioactive materials have not changed; that no radioactive elements which were originally in the specimen have been added, removed, or changed except by radioactive decay; that all of the end products of radioactive decay which are utilized in the test have remained in the specimen and none have been added; and other assumptions which are less obvious to the general reader.

William Lee Stokes of the University of Utah says that even after the incorporation of checks in the more refined methods, "geologists have been somewhat disappointed in the uranium-lead methods because of the many instances where the results are contradictory, inconsistent, or unreasonable."[6] He affirms that "the vast majority of uranium minerals are unsuitable for age determination by present [1960] methods,"[7] and he says of the stony meteorites that "for a number of reasons all attempts to date these minerals have proved unsatisfactory."[8]

Not only ordinary lead but radiogenic lead may be added to samples, as is said to be obvious in minerals of the upper Great Lakes region.[9] These minerals are said to be of the same geologic age, but they show large differences in isotopic composition. Since it is admitted that differences in age as obtained from the tests here are incorrect because of intrusive radiogenic leads, it leaves an open question as to the value of results where there are no clues to cast doubts upon the findings.

It has been pointed out by a number of authors that consistency in results does not necessarily mean accuracy in dating, though inconsistency does mean inaccuracy. Consistency in results merely means that the same methods are being applied repeatedly under the same conditions to the same kind of material. If the results are consistent for this reason, it does not necessarily follow that what they are interpreted to mean is correct.

The two forms of uranium present in rocks both decompose to lead, but they do so at different rates and the end products are different isotopes of lead. The type of uranium which is more useful in the dating tests because it is more abundant, is also more easily lost through being leached out of the rocks. Another factor which makes this uranium undesirable is the fact that one of the intermediate products of its decay is a gas, which may escape from the rocks.

The potassium-argon method is another test which has come into prominence. This is the test which was used to date the remains which L. S. B. Leakey found in East Africa and said were undoubtedly human (he has since changed his mind and now says they are not human), and which were named *Zinjanthropus boisei,* or the "Nutcracker man." The Geology Department at the University of California at Berkeley made the tests and announced that *Zinjanthropus* was one and three quarter million years old. The tests were not made on the remains but on various strata above and below the site where the pieces of skull were found. The stratum just *below* the skull tested a quarter of a million years *younger* than the layer just *above,* though the lower should be older. Furthermore, G. H. R. von Koenigswald, the eminent anthropologist who has done a great deal of anthropological work in Java, found that a layer of basalt below the strata in which *Zinjanthropus* was found tested nearly half a million years younger, though it should have been older. To make matters worse, von Koenigswald believes the test to be so inaccurate that the basalt is actually half a million years younger than the test shows. This would make it nearly a million years younger than the "Nutcracker man," though it should be older.

The potassium-argon method has the disadvantage that argon is a gas, and therefore can escape from the material. The other product of the radioactive decay is calcium, which cannot be used successfully in the test because it cannot be distinguished from non-radiogenic calcium.

The carbon-14 method of dating is the one which the public has heard about most. Since carbon must be present, true fossils, or mineralized remains, cannot be dated by this method. Since the half life of carbon-14 is only about 5700 years, so little of it is left after a presumed 40,000 years that dating beyond this limit is generally not considered practical. Devices have been investigated, however, for extending the testable time further back.

Dates obtained through carbon-14 are frequently expressed as years "B. P." or "before the present." Some scientists do not hesitate to facetiously substitute "B. C.," by which they mean "before carbon-14."

Radiation in the upper atmosphere causes some of the nitrogen atoms to become carbon-14 atoms.[10] (Ordinary carbon atoms are carbon-12.) Some of these carbon-14 atoms become incorporated in carbon dioxide molecules and are utilized by plants in their photosynthetic process. Animals and human beings consume plant food or eat meat which can be traced back to a plant source. Thus all living things have a certain amount of carbon-14 incorporated in their tissues. At the time of death the intake of carbon-14 ceases, and the only process involving this radioactive element is its decay back to nitrogen. Thus the amount of radioactive carbon in a sample is taken as indicative of its age — the less there is, the older the specimen.

This method of dating depends upon a number of assumptions. Of course there is the assumption that the half life of carbon-14 has not changed during the period which is being measured. It is assumed that cosmic radiation has remained constant at least during the last 50,000 years or so. However, there is evidence that there have been alterations due to changes in the earth's magnetic field, and also there seem to be evidences of changes in the radiation flux itself.

Starting with the industrial revolution, coal, oil, and gas have been burned in quantity, and the carbon dioxide produced in the process has been liberated into the atmosphere. This carbon dioxide is not radioactive. Although the industrial revolution is only about a century old, it has been found that the effect of this carbon dioxide must be taken into account in estimating ages by the carbon-14 method. It would be more difficult to estimate the amount of non-radioactive carbon dioxide released into the atmosphere by volcanic action during the past 50,000 years, and apparently this has not been done.

Neutrons released into the atmosphere by nuclear testing will increase the amount of carbon-14 in the atmosphere. It has been estimated that the amount of carbon-14 in the earth's atmosphere in 1970 will be three or four times the amount it was prior to 1962.

Another possibility which scientists do not take into account is that there may have been a vapor canopy around the earth prior to the time of the Genesis flood, producing a greenhouse effect with lush vegetation much farther north and south than now. This would increase the proportion of carbon dioxide in the atmosphere. There is Biblical evidence for this. On the second day of creation, the earth's waters were divided so that part of them were lifted above the atmosphere (Gen. 1:6, 7). We are told also that in the early days the Lord did not cause it to rain and plants were watered by a mist (Gen. 2:5, 6). The rainbow was given to Noah as a sign that there would never again be a universal flood, and if it had rained before the great deluge with the sun shining in a clear sky after a shower, there would have been rainbows before the time the Lord gave it to Noah for a sign.

Frederick Zenner, Professor Emeritus at the University of London, discusses another difficulty which was mentioned also at the carbon-

14 symposium held at Gronigen, Netherlands, in 1959. "Another serious difficulty is the possibility of uneven distribution of carbon-14 in living matter."[11] He goes on to say that it has been observed that certain isotopes are favored in the formation of certain chemical compounds, and for this reason it may be necessary in dating remains to compare only materials from the same kinds of organisms — oak wood with oak wood, land shells with similar land shells, etc.

Another difficulty, of course, is the possibility of the intrusion of foreign organic matter into old material. Charcoal and peat are noted for their ability to absorb foreign substances. It is impossible to remove fine roots of plants which have penetrated materials tested for carbon-14. Professor Stokes, among others, calls attention to the fact discrepancies due to the addition or subtraction of carbon are especially likely to occur in moist areas. He says, ". . . the degree of saturation by water and the history of all materials must be taken into account before final judgment is made."[12] It is evident that this is difficult, if indeed it is possible. It has been pointed out by various authors that carbon-14 dating within rather recent times seems to be much more reliable when the materials tested are from areas with dry climates, such as Palestine and Egypt.

The carbon-14 method was discovered by Willard F. Libby about 1949 as a by-product of work on cosmic radiation. For this discovery he received the Nobel Prize. Libby himself later said that he was very much surprised to find out that no material with a known date of more than about five thousand years was available as a standard. Thus, there was no way of knowing how much greater the percentage of error may become as older and still older objects are dated by this method. Ney and Winkler[13] have said that by employing the equations given by Libby, objects two thousand years old would be dated too old by two hundred forty years. They comment that this is hardly noticeable because it is scarcely outside the range of error anticipated for the method. But they say further that on this basis objects four thousand years old would be dated too old by a thousand years.[13] If this is true, one can see what would happen when objects are dated 30,000 or 40,000 years old.

The public has been led to believe that dates obtained by this method are accurate, but Professor Stokes says, "The original enthusiasm over carbon-14 dating was followed by a period of more cautious evaluation when many obviously incorrect dates came to light."[14]

Professor H. T. Waterbolk of the Biological-Archeological Institute at Gronigen, reporting on the 1959 carbon-14 symposium at Gronigen, said, "On the one hand, this is definitely a disappointing result, especially for those who had very high hopes for precision dating by carbon-14. But, on the other hand, it is good to be told exactly where we stand on these matters. . . ."[15]

Ernest Antevis, writing in the *Journal of Geology*, says of the carbon-14 method of dating, "Its apologists try a little too hard to make the geology fit the dates."[16] Although the radioactive dating methods are popularly hailed as being highly superior to any previous method of dating, he says, "An informed geological estimate is better than a carbon-14 date lacking geological support, even though the latter may appear attractive by giving an impression of definiteness."[17]

Charles B. Hunt, President of the American Geological Institute, says that radiocarbon dates "are sufficiently scattered and erratic to provide some determinations that will support almost any proposed correlation. Some of the radiocarbon dates, for example, support the old geologic estimates that the date of the last Wisconsin glaciation was of the order of twenty thousand years ago, but another and larger group indicates that the last great maximum occurred only ten thousand or so years ago. Which should be accepted?"[18]

A popular book, which was read in manuscript form by the Chairman of the Department of Physics at New York University and others, tells an interesting tale. According to it, two groups of archeologists disagreed on the meaning of an inscription on a doorway found in a Mayan city in Guatemala. One group said that the inscription dated the door at A.D. 741 and the other group said the inscription meant A.D. 481. Dr. Libby tested a piece of wood from the door and reported the carbon-14 test read A.D. 451, plus or minus a few years. Perhaps this should have settled the matter, but some of the archaeologists were not convinced. Another piece of wood was tested in the laboratory of the University of Pennsylvania, and thirty-three tests produced the date of A.D. 759, plus or minus a few years.[19]

The editor of *Antiquity* magazine said, "It is very important to realize that doubts about archaeological acceptability of radiocarbon dates is not obscuratism nor another chapter in the battle of science and the arts. . . . We are at a moment when some of us at least are uncertain how to answer the question: when is a carbon-14 reading an archaeological fact?"[20] It is to be remembered that dates within the range of archaeological findings are considered recent.

Professor Hunt says, "In order that a technique or discipline may be useful in scientific work, its limits must be known and understood, but the limits of usefulness of the radiocarbon age determinations are not yet known or understood. No one seriously proposes that all the determined dates are without error, but we do not know how many of them are in error — 25 percent? 50 percent? 75 percent? And we do not know which dates are in error, by what amounts, or why."[21]

This sampling of statements gives a very different picture from what the public gets in popular magazines, such as the following statement from an article on the potassium-argon method: ". . . no ordinary mechanical clock — not even the finest Swiss watch — can match our laboratory instruments for precision."[22]

It may be objected that even allowing for the errors and difficulties in the radioactive methods of dating, the times suggested are so much greater than those allowed by the Biblical account that it is irrelevant to cite instances of difficulties. The radioactive methods of dating are relatively new. As time has gone on, in spite of improvements in techniques, unforseen difficulties have arisen. Other evidences supporting evolution have been highly regarded in the beginning — embryonic recapitulation, vestigial organs, the serological tests — only to be shown later not to be the strong evidence they had been supposed to be. The future may further discredit the radioactive methods also. We believe the Bible to be the inspired account given by the Lord who made all things and who knew whereof He spoke when the record was given.

Also there are evidences that the world is younger than the scientists would have us believe. Some of these are presented by Whitcomb and Morris in their book *The Genesis Flood*.[23]

At the rate at which meteoric dust is falling and settling on the earth, a layer of this dust fifty-four feet deep should have been built up since the time it is estimated by the scientists on other grounds that the earth had a solid crust. Mixing with the surface materials cannot account for the absence of this dust. Meteoric dust is very rich in nickel, and to account for the nickel of meteoric dust mixing with the earth's surface (assuming no nickel present originally) would require a mixing to a depth of more than three miles.

Tektites or "glassy meteorites" are controversial objects. Some believe they are of terrestrial origin, but the majority opinion seems to be that they did not originate on the earth. Dated by the potassium-argon method they have been ascribed to ages varying from one to ten million years. It is interesting to note that some of them are found in geological strata that are estimated to be older than the tektites themselves. Each major occurrence of tektites is believed to represent a single shower. Those in Czechoslovakia are weathering out of Miocene strata, estimated to be from twelve to twenty-five million years old, and those in Texas are weathering out of Eocene strata, estimated to be from thirty-five to sixty million years old.

The origin of comets is unknown. Their material is constantly being dissipated, and a number of them have disintegrated within the period of human observation. The famous astronomer Fred Hoyle estimates that all of them will have disintegrated within a period of a million years. Since they disintegrate so rapidly, from the standpoint of commonly accepted cosmological time, it is quite a problem to account for their recent origin. There are several theories, but they are based upon imagination and are not substantiated by observations.

As previously mentioned, one of the end products of the decay of uranium and thorium is helium. Whitcomb and Morris point out that the amount of radiogenic helium in the atmosphere indicates a young earth. A calculation based on figures published in a scientific journal and the assumptions which go with the uranium method, indicates that the radiogenic helium from eroding primary rocks would have required about twenty-five million years instead of two billion. Evolutionists could never accept a figure like this, and even this figure is high as it does not take into account the loss of helium from rocks which have not been eroded.

In 1856 a man of the Plymouth Brethren group named Philip Gosse published a work called *Omphalos*. In it he postulated an earth of apparent age older than the actual age. His view was not well received at the time, but has been revived in recent times. Scientists who have no interest in the Bible would not consider Gosse's view, but Christians ought to give it some thought. It is evident from Scripture that Eve was formed as an adult, and Adam also was formed fully developed. When only a few hours old they had the appearance of maturity. We are not given as much detail about the rest of creation, but it is reasonable with this precedent to assume that the first animals also were created as young adults. The same thing may apply to plants. We may wonder — if a tree in the Garden of Eden had been cut down, would it have shown rings of growth? Probably so. Might not this extend to the mineral creation? Would uranium ores have shown radiogenic end products at that time? We can only speculate, but the evolutionists do a very great deal more speculating than Christians do.

NOTES

1. Howitt, John R., Letter to the Editor, *Journal of the American Scientifis Affiliation*, 15:2:66, June, 1963. See also *ibid.*, 5:1:14, March, 1953.

2. Pearson, Roy, "The Give and Take between Science and Religion," *Journal of the American Scientific Affiliation*, 15:1:4, March, 1963, p. 4.

3. Hutchinson, C. Evelyn, "Marginalia," *American Scientist*, 42:1:300, April, 1954.

4. McDonnell, Duncan, "Dating of Fossil Bones by the Fluorine Method," *Science*, 136:3512:241, April 20, 1962, p. 244.

5. Gentry, Robert V., "Cosmology and Earth's Invisible Realm," *Medical Opinion and Review*, 3:10:64, Oct., 1957.

6. Stokes, William Lee, *Essentials of Earth History* (Prentice-Hall, 1960), p. 22.

7. *Ibid.*, p. 23.

8. *Ibid.*, p. 28.

9. Farquahr, R. N. and R. D. Russell, "Anomalous Leads from the Upper Great Lakes Region of Ontario," *Transactions of the American Geophysical Union*, 38:4:552, August, 1957.

10. This is how carbon-14 is formed in nature. As cosmic rays enter the earth's atmosphere they break up various atoms which make up part of the air. Among the products of this disintegration are neutrons. When a neutron strikes a nitrogen atom it may become incorporated in the nucleus of the nitrogen atom, and when it does it causes the nucleus to emit a proton. The number of electrons which an atom has outside the nucleus is the same as the number of protons within the nucleus. Thus when the nitrogen atom loses a proton it also loses an electron. A normal nitrogen atom has seven protons in the nucleus, and seven electrons outside the nucleus. The number of protons in the nucleus of an atom determines a specific chemical element, and hence when a nitrogen atom loses a proton as it takes on a neutron, it is no longer nitrogen. The element which has six protons in its nucleus is carbon. Therefore, when nitrogen loses a proton it becomes a form of carbon. The mass number of an element is the sum of the protons and neutrons in its nucleus. Nitrogen has seven protons and seven neutrons, making a total of fourteen. Thus normal nitrogen is nitrogen-14. Carbon has six protons and six neutrons in its nucleus with a total of twelve, and so ordinary carbon is carbon-12. When a nitrogen atom gains a neutron and loses a proton it has six protons and eight neutrons. The mass number is the sum of six and eight, or fourteen, but it is now an atom of carbon, and so it is now carbon-14. Atoms of a certain element which have the same number of protons but a different number of neutrons exhibit the same chemical behavior but have different physical

properties. They are called isotopes of that element. Carbon-14 is an isotope of ordinary carbon-12. Carbon-14 is not stable, and eventually one of its neutrons decays into a proton and an electron. The proton is retained in the nucleus and the electron is emitted. The nucleus now has seven protons and seven neutrons, with a total of fourteen. An electron is soon captured in an orbit outside the nucleus to balance the new proton in the nucleus. It is now no longer an atom of carbon-14 but is again nitrogen-14, the ordinary nitrogen of the air.

11. Zenner, Frederick, Dating the Past, 4th ed., rev. (Meuthen and Co., 1958), p. 346.

12. Stokes, William Lee, loc. cit., p. 26.

13. Ney, E. P. and J. R. Winkler, Nature, 178:1226, 1956, p. 1227.

14. Stokes, William Lee, loc. cit., p. 26.

15. Waterbolk, H. T., The 1959 carbon-14 Symposium at Gronigen, p. 15.

16. Antevis, Ernest, "Geological Tests of the Varve Radiocarbon Chronologies," Journal of Geology, 65:2:129, March, 1957, p. 146.

17. Ibid., p. 130.

18. Hunt, Charles B., "Radiocarbon Dating in the Light of Statigraphy and Weathering Processes," Scientific Monthly, 81:5:240, November, 1955, p. 240.

19. Poole, Lynn and Gary Poole, Carbon-14 (McGraw-Hill, 1961), pp. 96, 97.

20. Editor, Antiquity, 34:133:4, March, 1960, p. 239.

21. Hunt, Charles B., loc. cit., p. 240.

22. Curtiss, Carniss H., "A Clock for the Ages: Potassium-Argon," The National Geographic Magazine, 120:4:590, October, 1961, p. 591.

23. Whitcomb, John C. Jr. and Henry M. Morris, The Genesis Flood (The Presbyterian and Reformed Pub. Co., 1962), p. 379 et seq.

CHAPTER VII

THE EVOLUTION OF LIFE

In practically any book which deals with evolution, the author states that evolution is a fact and is not to be doubted. If this were really so, there would be no need for so many authors to keep repeating it over and over. Chemists and physicists do not keep repeating that there really are molecules and atoms. They do not need to do so and if someone did not believe in molecules these scientists would not care at all. But it is very different with the biologists. They are in general greatly concerned with the acceptance of evolution by the public.

A recent book dealing with evolution is remarkable in that the author does not attempt to present evidence for evolution, assuming that the readers already accept it. This may start a trend among the authors of textbooks, but it is safe to predict that evolutionists will not soon relax the missionary zeal they manifest for their cult.

Although biologists present evolution as a fact categorically, they are not so sure when it comes to details. A person may choose any group of animals or plants, large or small, or pick one at random. He may then go to a library and with some patience he will be able to find a qualified author who says that the evolutionary origin of that form is not known. He can, of course, also find statements by authors who speculate on the ancestry of the group and some authors who present its alleged ancestry as a fact. Some authors discuss the evolutionary views of other authors and tell how, in their opinions, the other authors are wrong.

To illustrate, we will present a sampling of statements by qualified evolutionists in regard to groups both large and small, inclusive and specific. Most of the statements given here have been published since 1950; a few are from the late 1940's. Each statement is by a different author. We will give examples among the animal groups only, though it is just as easy or perhaps easier to do the same for plants.

Life. "We do not know how life began."[1]

Animal kingdom. "The first and most important steps of animal evolution remain even more obscure than those of plant evolution."[2]

Protozoa, the one-celled animals. "It is not known just what were the ancestors of Protozoa."[3]

Sarcodina, the amoeboid types of protozoa. "It has become commonplace to speak of evolution from amoeba to man, as if amoeba were a natural and simple beginning of the process. On the contrary, if, as must necessarily be true short of miracles, life arose as a living molecule or progene, the progression from this stage to that of the amoeba is at least as great as from amoeba to man. . . . The change from progene to protozoa was probably the most complex that has occurred in evolution, and it may very well have taken as long as the change from protozoan to man."[4]

Ciliata, the protozoa with cilia, like Paramecium. "How the ciliates arose is unknown. . . ."[5]

Flagellata, the protozoa with flagella, like Euglena. "The group seems to stand at the threshold of differentiation, and its place in the evolutionary story is blurred and uncertain."[6]

Sporozoa, non-motile protozoa, like the malaria organism, *Plasmodium.* "The origin of the Sporozoa, however, is obscure. . . ."[7]

Metazoa, or many-celled animals. "The ancestry of the metazoa is a baffling mystery."[8]

Mesozoa, microscopic parasitic animals which are solid and have no digestive cavity. "Since the discovery of the mesozoans by Krohn in 1839, almost every zoologist who has studied this group has interpreted differently their life cycle and relationship to other animals."[9]

The jellyfish group. "We can, of course, only speculate regarding their origin and differentiation."[10]

The ctenophores, which are something like jellyfish. "Nothing definite is known about the ancestry of the ctenophores."[11]

The flatworms. "Not much definite information is available in regard to the evolutionary origin of the Platyhelminthes."[12]

Tapeworms. "We do not know what its ancestors were like nor how the tapeworms adopted this parasitic way of life."[13]

Turbellarians, or free-living flatworms. "Fossil records of the transitions are lacking, and controversy thrives best when hypotheses cannot be tested."[14]

The unsegmented round worms. "From a phylogenetic [evolutionary] point of view, the relationships of this phylum to other major groups are not exactly clear because they have little in common structurally with other forms of animals."[15]

The arthropods, which include lobsters, crabs, and insects. "The evolutionary origin of the arthropods is hidden in remote Pre-Cambrian times. . . ."[16]

The crustaceans, which include crabs and lobsters. "The phylogenetic origin of Crustacea is lost in Precambrian antiquity."[17]

Spiders. ". . . we have no evidence to show that spiders have been derived from any other living or extinct group of arachnids."[18]

Mites and ticks. "The phylogeny of the Acarina is obscure. . . ."[19]

The horseshoe crabs. "The question of their phylogenetic origin and relationship still remains unsolved and confusing."[20]

The tardigrades, minute creatures called water bears. "The affinities of this group are unknown. . . ."[21]

The pauropods, very small creatures with many legs; their maximum length is about .06 inch. "The phylogeny of the pauropods is a controversial question."[22]

Insects. "There is, however, no fossil evidence bearing on the question of insect origin; the oldest known insects show no transition to other arthropods."[23]

The yellow fever mosquito, Aedes egypti. "That mosquitoes have retained generic characters since Oligocene times would seem to make any attempt to trace the history of our species [*Aedes egypti*] with the data available purely a matter of conjecture.[24]

Bugs. ". . . the phylogenetic scheme for the Hemiptera is still not entirely satisfactory."[25]

The ant-bee-wasp group. ". . . the paleontological record, going back to the Upper Jurassic, exhibits no evidence of kinship with other fossil insects."[26]

Fleas. "The origin of fleas, too, remains obscure."[27]

Butterflies and moths. ". . . it is obvious that their distinctive evolution must have been going on for a very long time and that the record is incomplete."[28]

The Geometridae, a family of moths. ". . . the paleontological evidence is not of much assistance in trying to reconstruct the past history of this family. . . ."[29]

The Phyctidae, another family of moths. "When I began this study I had hoped to write a monographic treatise and explore the phylogeny [evolutionary history] of the family, but now I find that

I know so much less than I thought I did and that the accumulated knowledge of others is so meager that any attempt along these lines would be a vain and futile performance. I don't know what a primitive phyctid was like. We don't know which forms evolved from which, or how. We weren't there. We may surmise; but the guess of one ignoramus is as good as that of another, and there is nothing to be gained by either."[30] (This statement is in a paper which was written at the completion of a twenty-five year study of this family of moths.)

The Strepsiptera, very small insects whose larvae are parasitic inside other insects. ". . . the controversy with respect to the phylogenetic position of the order still continues."[31]

The molluscs, including snails, clams, and squids. 'A great deal of discussion has been devoted to the origin of the Mollusca. . . . It is sufficient to say here that at present this question is unsettled. . . ."[32]

The Scaphopoda, or tusk shells. "The fossil record of the *Scaphoda* [or *Scaphopoda*] is still in dispute."[33]

The gastropods. They are the snails, slugs, limpets, etc. "However, one can consider the different groups [he mentioned several, including the gastropods], and hypothesize as to the nature of the ancestral type."[34]

The Planorbidae, a large family of snails. "The ancestry of the Planorbidae, as of other members of the pulmonate mollusks, is shrouded in mystery."[35]

The rotifers, the microscopic "wheel" animals. ". . . their affinities are doubtful."[36]

The brachiopods. They look something like little clams, but their anatomy is very different. "The origin and classification of these animals in the evolutionary scheme are obscure."[37]

The arrow worms (Chaetognatha). "The body plan is so different from that of any other groups that it is difficult to say what relationships they have to other invertebrates."[38]

The echinoderms, starfish, sea urchins, etc. "The fossil record of the echinoderms is one of the best. . . . But the record does not throw light upon the origin of the phylum, nor upon its possible relations to other phyla."[39]

The sea cucumbers. "The position of the holothurids in the family tree of echinoderms is uncertain."[40]

Chordates, or creatures which have, at least in embryonic life, a notochord. "Scientists have been perplexed about the origin of the chordates and have been unable to determine which lower forms gave rise to this last and perhaps most specialized group."[41]

The prochordates. These are the chordates which are not vertebrates. ". . . they stand between the animals without backbones and those with them. But instead of solving the problem of how some backboneless creatures through the eons acquired backbones, the prochordates have simply created new problems of their own. Instead of being a key, they turned out to be a headache. In other words, careful study of these animals has failed to reveal the course of evolution."[42]

The acorn worms. They used to be considered prochordates, but now some biologists are not sure. ". . . of doubtful systematic position."[43]

The vertebrates. "As our present information stands, however, the gap remains unbridged and the best place to start the evolution of the vertebrates is in the imagination."[44]

The group to which the lampreys and hagfish belong (Agnatha). (They are not really fish.) "The fossil history of the Chordata begins with the Agnatha — there are no indications of what came before."[45]

Fish. 'The geological record has so far provided no evidence as to the origin of fishes. . . ."[46]

The Chondrostei, which includes the sturgeons and paddlefish. "Although anatomically intermediate between sharks and teleoists, the phylogenetic position of the modern 'ganoids,' especially the Chondrostei with their relatively large cartilaginous skeletons, is not at all certain."[47]

The lungfish. "The lungfish presumably arose from a common ancestral stock of the Crossopterygii that led to the coelocanths, although this hypothesis does not meet with uniform acceptance by fish paleontologists."[48]

The teleosts, or ordinary bony fish. "The obvious way to determine the relationships of modern forms is to trace their genealogies back through the fossil record. But for modern teleostian groups the crucial fossil evidence is almost always lacking, at least as yet. The only alternative is to construct hypothetical genealogies."[49]

The amphibia (frogs, toads, salamanders.) "The recent discovery . . . of amphibia in the Upper Devonian of Greenland . . . raised my hopes that at last we should . . . confirm or refute the views which I had expressed on the relationships of these animals, and of the amphibia generally, to the osteolepid fish. In many ways my expectations were confirmed, but the knowledge we now have of these animals . . . raises as many new problems as it solves."[50]

The Gymnophiona, legless amphibians. "We still lack details regarding their ancestry. . . ."[51]

The reptiles. "There is no direct proof from the fossil record, but we can readily hypothesize the conditions under which it [the origin of the reptiles] came about."[52]

Snakes. "The place where snakes originated is unknown. . . . Their family tree is still adorned with questionmarks rather than branches."[53]

Birds. ". . . nearly a century after the publication of [Darwin's *Origin of Species*], there are still monumental problems that remain to be settled about the succession of life. This is especially true of the birds."[54]

Mammals. "The first successful true mammals . . . were small insectivore types whose relationship to these reptiles is not at all clear."[55]

The monotremes, or egg-laying mammals. "Their geologic history is completely unknown."[56]

The marsupials, or pouched mammals. "Their origin is extremely ancient and its sources are not known. . . ."[57]

The numbat, or banded anteater. "No bigger than a large brown rat, this banded ant-eater . . . has an origin which, in its exact details, is shrouded in mystery."[58]

The Eutheria, or placental mammals. "From some unknown, primitive, tree-living, insect-eating, and pouched animals there soon arose the earliest placental mammals."[59]

The rodents. ". . . the question of their origin must be left open."[60]

The lagomorphs (rabbits and hares). (They formerly were considered to be rodents, but now are thought to be not even related to the rodents.) "The origin of these animals is uncertain."[61]

The elephants. "The two survivors of the great Order Proboscidia are *Elephas maximus* of Asia and *Laxodonta africana* of Africa. The origins of both are obscure. . . ."[62]

The sea cows. "Their origin is still a mystery to men of science. . . ."[63]

The Aardvark. "Their prehistoric record is, however, fragmentary and offers little evidence as to their immediate ancestors."[64]

The Pinnipedia (seals, sea lions, walruses). ". . . the progenitors of the pinnipeds are completely unknown. . . ."[65]

The cetaceans, the whales and porpoises. "Agorophilus exhibits slightly more primitive features but does not furnish any clue to the affinities of whales with any known terrestrial mammalian order."[66]

The Mystacoceti, or baleen whales. "The origin of the Mystacoceti is uncertain."[67]

The Artiodactyla, or even-toed hoofed animals. ". . . their origin is uncertain."[68]

The hippopotamus. ". . . their pedigree is uncertain."[69]

The Perissodactyla, or odd-toed hoofed animals. "The Perissodactyla as an order probably originated in the northern hemisphere . . . from some as yet undiscovered relatives of the Eocene condylarths or protoungulates."[70]

Horses. "The real origin of horses is unknown."[71]

The Primates. This includes lemurs, monkeys, apes, and man. "When and where the first Primates made their appearance is also conjectural. . . . It is clear then that the earliest Primates are not yet known. . . ."[72]

The tarsier. "The evolutionary origin of these tarsiers is still in some doubt."[73]

Monkeys of the Western Hemisphere. "The phylogenetic history of the New World monkeys or platyrrhines is quite unknown."[74]

Monkeys of the Eastern Hemisphere. "As to the Old World monkeys, even less is known of their past. But they too must go back to unknown Eocene ancestors. . . ."[75]

The gibbon. "Its origin has not yet been traced."[76]

Man. ". . . there is still no general agreement as to where true *Homo sapiens,* the men of our own species, developed. Each authority has his own theory for which he will fight like a mother for her child."[77]

Neanderthal man. "Their true place in the evolution of man has never been established."[78]

Cro-Magnon man. "Cro-Magnon man is a modern man in every sense of the word, but where he came from or how he came about we have not the slightest idea."[79]

The Negritos. "It was thought at one time that they represent an earlier stage in the evolution of man, but there is no fossil evidence that man went through a pygmy stage. . . ."[80]

And finally, in conclusion, *EVERYTHING!* "We do not actually know the phylogenetic history of any group of plants and animals, since it lies in the undecipherable past."[81]

NOTES

1. Morgan, Ann H., Professor of Zoology, Mount Holyoke College, *Relationships of Animals to Man* (McGraw-Hill, 1955), p. 777.

2. Weiss, Paul B., Professor of Biology, Boston University, *The Science of Biology* (McGraw-Hill, 1963), p. 732.

3. Hickman, Cleveland P., Professor of Zoology, De Pauw University, *Integrated Principles of Zoology*, 3rd ed. (C. V. Mosby Co., 1966), p. 111.

4. Simpson, George Gaylord, Professor of Vertebrate Paleontology, Harvard University, *The Meaning of Evolution* (Yale University Press, fourth printing, 1950), pp. 15, 16.

5. Alexander, Gordon, Professor of Biology, University of Colorado, *General Biology* (Thomas Y. Crowell Co., 1956), p. 541.

6. Pauli, Wolfgang F., Bradford Junior College, in *The World of Life*, edited by Bentley Glass (Houghton Mifflin Co., 1949), p. 175.

7. Pennak, Robert W., Professor of Biology, University of Colorado, *Freshwater Invertebrates of the United States* (Ronald Press, 1953), p. 36.

8. Lwoff, Andre, editor, Head of the Department of Microbial Physiology, Pasteur Institute, *Biochemistry and Physiology of Protozoa* (Academic Press, 1951), p. 35.

9. McConnaughey, Bernard, *et al.*, Professor of Biology, University of Oregon, "Strange Life of the Dicyemid Mesozoans," *Scientific Monthly*, 79:277, 1954, p. 277.

10. Hegner, Robert W., Late Professor of Protozoology, School of Hygiene and Public Health, the Johns Hopkins University, *College Zoology*, 6th ed. (Macmillan, 1951), p. 164.

11. Kerkut, G. A., Department of Physiology and Biochemistry, University of Southampton, *Implications of Evolution* (Pergamon Press, 1960), p. 84.

12. Marsland, Douglas, New York University, *Principles of Biology*, 3d ed. (Henry Holt, 1957), p. 560.

13. Burton, Maurice, Deputy Keeper of Zoology, Natural History Museum, London, *Curiosities of Animal Life* (Sterling Pub. Co., 1959), p. 14.

14. Telfer, William H., *et al.*, University of Pennsylvania, *The Biology of Organisms* (John Wiley and Sons, 1965), p. 98.

15. Silvernale, Max N., Biology Department, Santa Monica City College, *Zoology* (Macmillan, 1965), p. 108.

16. Snodgrass, R. E. Collaborator of the Smithsonian Institution and the U.S. Department of Agriculture, "Crustacean Metamorphosis," *Smithsonian Miscellaneous Collections*, 131:10:6, 1956, p. 6.

17. Wilmoth, James H., State University of New York, *Biology of Invertebrata* (Prentice-Hall, 1967), p. 331.

18. Gretsch, Willis J., Associate Curator, Department of Insects and Spiders, The American Museum of Natural History, *American Spiders* (D. Van Nostrand Co., 1949), p. 99.

19. Baker, Edward D. *et al.*, U.S. Department of Agriculture and Department of Zoology, Duke University, *An Introduction to Acarology* (Macmillan, 1952), p. 34.

20. Petrunkevitch, Alexander, Emeritus Professor of Zoology, Yale University, *Encyclopedia Britannica*, 2:201, 1954.

21. Ross, Herbert H., Professor of Entomology, University of Illinois, *A Textbook of Entomology* (John Wiley and Sons, 1948, second printing, 1949), p. 47.

22. Fox, Richard M. *et al.*, Professor of Zoology, University of Pittsburgh, *Introduction to Comparative Entomology* (Reinhold, 1964), p. 331.

23. Carpenter, Frank M., U.S. Department of Agriculture, "Fossil Insects," *The Yearbook of Agriculture*, 1952, p. 18.

24. Christophers, S. Richard, Member of the Malaria Commission of the Royal Society, *Aedes egypti, the Yellow Fever Mosquito* (Cambridge University Press, 1960), p. 44.

25. Usinger, Robert L., University of California at Berkeley, (Ernest B. Babcock, ed.), *A Century of Progress in the Natural Sciences* (California Academy of Sciences, 1955), p. 536.

26. Whiting, P. W., University of Pennsylvania, "Some Experiments with Melittobia and Other Wasps," *Journal of Heredity*, 38:11, 1947.

27. Hollang, George P. Head, Systematic Entomology, Systematic Entomological Unit, Ottawa, (Ernest B. Babcock, ed.), *A Century of Progress in the Natural Sciences* (California Academy of Sciences, 1955), p. 588.

28. Klots, Alexander B., College of the City of New York, *The World of Butterflies and Moths* (McGraw-Hill, 1958), p. 15.

29. Rindge, Frederick H., University of California at Berkeley, *The Genus Drepanulatrix and Its Immediate Relations*, (Bound typed copy in the library of the University of California, 1949.)

30. Heinrich, Carl, The Smithsonian Institution of Washington, "American Moths of the Subfamily Phycitinae," *Smithsonian Bulletin No. 207*, 1956, p. viii.

31. Bohart, R. M., University of California at Davis, (Ernest B. Babcock, ed.), *A Century of Progress in the Natural Sciences* (California Academy of Sciences, 1955), p. 567.

32. Robson, Guy Colwin, Assistant Keeper, Zoology, British Museum, *Encyclopedia Britannica*, 15:677, 1957.

33. Pratt, Henry S., Former Professor of Biology, Haverford College, *A Manual of the Common Invertebrate Animals*, The Blakiston Co., 1951), p. 568.

34. Pimentel, Richard A., California State Polytechnical College, Department of Biological Sciences, *Natural History* (Reinhold, 1963), p. 217.

35. Baker, Frank C., Curator, Museum of Natural History, University of Illinois, *The Molluscian Family Planorbidae* (The University of Illinois Press, 1945), p. 37.

36. Bullough, William S., Professor of Zoology, University of London, *Practical Invertebrate Anatomy* (Macmillan, 1958), p. 148.

37. Etkin, William, Assistant Professor of Biology, College of the City of New York, *College Biology* (Thomas Y. Crowell, 1950), p. 659.

38. Buchsbaum, Ralph, Department of Zoology, University of Chicago, *Animals Without Backbones,* 2d ed., revised (The University of Chicago Press, 1950), p. 180.

39. Dodson, Edward O., Assistant Professor of Zoology, University of Notre Dame, *A Textbook of Evolution* (W. B. Saunders Co., 1952), p. 181.

40. Moore, Raymond C. *et al.,* Professor of Geology, University of Kansas, *Invertebrate Fossils* (McGraw-Hill, 1952), p. 658.

41. Elliott, Alfred M., University of Michigan, *Zoology,* 3rd ed. (Appleton-Century-Crofts, 1963), p. 348.

42. Coates, Christopher W. *et al.,* Curator, Aquarium of the New York Zoological Society, (Frederick Drimmer, editor), *The Animal Kingdom,* Vol. 3, p. 1402.

43. Guyer, Michael F., University of Wisconsin, *Animal Biology,* 4th ed. (Harper and Bros., 1948), p. 75.

44. Smith, Homer W., New York University, etc., *From Fish to Philosopher* (Little, Brown and Co., 1953), p. 26.

45. Moore, John A., Professor of Zoology, Barnard College and Columbia University, *Principles of Zoology* (Oxford University Press, 1957), p. 375.

46. Norman, J. R., Assistant Keeper, Department of Zoology, British Museum, *A History of Fishes,* Rev. ed. (Hill and Wang, 1963), p. 296.

47. Rand, Herbert W., Associate Professor of Zoology, Emeritus, Harvard University, *The Chordates* (The Blakiston Co., 1950), p. 436.

48. Lagler, Karl E., *et al.,* Professor of Fisheries and Zoology, University of Michigan, *Ichthyology* (John Wiley, 1962), p. 27.

49. Gosline, William A., Professor of Zoology, University of Hawaii, "Mode of Life, Functional Morphology, and the Classification of Modern Teleostian Fishes," *Systematic Zoology* 8:3, Sept. 1959, p. 160.

50. Watson, D. M. S., Professor of Zoology and Comparative Anatomy, University College, London, *Paleontology and Modern Biology* (Yale University Press, 1951), p. 91.

51. Gans, Carl, Associate Professor of Biology, University of Buffalo, "The Legless Tetrapods," *Natural History* 71:8:27, Oct., 1962, p. 27.

52. Stirton, R. A., Professor of Paleontology, University of California, *Time, Life, and Man* (John Wiley and Sons, 1957), p. 416.

53. Pope, Clifford H., formerly Curator of the Division of Amphibians and Reptiles, Chicago Natural History Museum, *The Great Snakes* (Alfred A. Knopf, 1961), pp. 22 and 164.

54. Swinton, W. E., The British Museum, "The World's Oldest Known Bird," *The Illustrated London News,* 227:6063:36, July 2, 1955.

55. Scheele, William E., Director, Cleveland Museum of Natural History, *The First Mammals* (World Pub. Co., 1955), p. 24.

56. Dunbar, Carl C., Professor of Paleontology, Yale University, *Historical Geology* (John Wiley and Sons, 1949, printing of 1952), p. 353.

57. Ryan, Francis J., Department of Zoology, Columbia University, *Encyclopedia Britannica* 18:330, 1956.

58. Fleay, David, "The Numbat: A Passing Relic of the Earth's Early Furred Animals, *The Illustrated London News* 221:5907:32, July 5, 1952.

59. Hensill, John S., Associate Professor of Biology, San Francisco State College, *The Biology of Man* (The Blakiston Co., 1954), p. 120.

60. Haines, R. Wheeler, Royal Medical College, Baghdad, "Arboreal or Terrestrial Ancestral Ancestry of Placental Mammals?" *Quarterly Review of Biology* 33:1, March, 1958, p. 19.

61. Walker, Ernest P., *et al.*, *Mammals of the World* (The Johns Hopkins University Press, 1964), p. 647.

62. Deraniyagala, P. E. P., Director, National Museum, Ceylon, *Some Extinct Elephants, Their Relatives, and the Two Living Species* (Government Press, Ceylon, 1955), p. 11.

63. Goodwin, George C., Associate Curator, Department of Mammals, American Museum of Natural History, "Whales, Porpoises, and Sea Cows," *Audubon Nature Bulletin*, Series 19, Bulletin No. 10, June, 1949, p. 4.

64. Hall, Robert T., Director, Cranbrook Institute of Science, (E. M. Weyer, ed.), "Biology of Mammals," *The Illustrated Library of Natural Science* (Simon and Shuster, 1958), p. 1637.

65. Scheffer, Victor B., Colorado State University, *Seals, Sea Lions and Walruses* (Stanford University Press, 1958), p. 31.

66. Swinnerton, H. H., Professor of Geology, University College, Nottingham, *Outlines of Paleontology*, 3d ed. (Edward Arnold Co., 1947), p. 352.

67. Harmer, Sidney F., Director, Natural History Department, the British Museum, *Encyclopedia Britannica*, 5:169, 1954.

68. Young, J. Z., Professor of Anatomy, University College, London, *The Life of Vertebrates* (Oxford University Press, 1962), p. 694.

69. Romer, Alfred S., Professor of Zoology, Harvard University, *The Vertebrate Story* (University of Chicago Press, 1959), p. 268.

70. Gregory, William K., Professor of Vertebrate Paleontology, Columbia University, *Encyclopedia Britannica* 17:527, 1957.

71. Storer, Tracy I., Professor of Zoology, Emeritus, University of California at Davis, *General Zoology*, 3d ed. (McGraw-Hill, 1957), p. 216.

72. Hill, W. C. O., University of Edinburgh, *Primates* (Edinburgh University Press, 1953), Vol. 1, pp. 25, 26.

73. Le Gros Clark, W. E., Professor of Anatomy, Oxford University, *History of the Primates*, 5th ed. (University of Chicago Press, 1965), p. 54.

74. Straus, William L. Jr., Professor of Anthropology, The Johns Hopkins University, (A. L. Kroeber, ed.), *Anthropology Today* (University of Chicago Press, 1953, printing of 1958), p. 77.

75. Howells, William, Professor of Anthropology, Harvard University, *Mankind in the Making* (Doubleday and Co., 1959), p. 102.

76. von Koenigswald, G. H. R., Paleontologist for the Netherlands East Indies, *Meeting Prehistoric Man* (Harper and Bros., 1956), p. 199.

77. Andrews, Roy Chapman, American Museum of Natural History, *Meet Your Ancestors* (the Viking Press, 1956), p. 27.

78. Gruber, Jacob W., Department of Sociology and Anthropology, Temple University, "The Neanderthal Controversy: 19th Century Version," *Scientific Monthly* 67:6:436, Dec., 1948, p. 436.

79. Ashley Montagu, M. F., Princeton University, *Man: His First Million Years* (World Pub. Co., 1957), p. 73.

80. Villee, Claude A., Harvard University, *Biology*, 3d ed. (W. B. Saunders Co., 1957, printing of 1960), p. 568.

81. Core, Earl L., *et al.*, Chairman, Department of Biology, West Virginia University, *General Biology*, 4th ed. (John Wiley and Sons, 1961), p. 299.

THE FIRST LIFE

Charles Darwin assumed one or a few simple forms of life and started from there. However, he postulated that life might have come from non-living matter by natural means. This is now the accepted point of view of biologists in general.

There have been a number of theories as to how life could have developed from inanimate matter, and it is generally held that life began in the sea. It is sometimes stated that the chemical constituency of our blood is an evidence of our origin in the ocean, and some even think that differences between the concentrations of certain substances in our blood and in the sea indicates that the sea has become noticeably more salty (though the leaching of the land and the transport of dissolved salts to the ocean by rivers) than it was when our ancestors left it. However, in a conference of outstanding physicists, astronomers, and geologists held in 1963 at the Goddard Institute for Space Studies and Space Administration, it was said that life could not have begun in the sea.

Doctors L. V. Bekner and L. C. Marshall, both of the Southwest Center for Advanced Studies, Dallas Texas, presented a paper[1] about the development of oxygen in the earth's atmosphere. They believe that essentially all the oxygen of the atmosphere came from green plants. Practically all living things, including green plants, require oxygen in order to live. But oxygen in the atmosphere, and oxygen dissolved in the water from the atmosphere, would have acted as a poison to the precursors of life, destroying them and preventing the appearance of life. There is another dilemma. Bekner and Marshall point out that before oxygen in the form of ozone was present in sufficient quantity in the upper atmosphere to screen out lethal rays from the sun, life could not have existed on the surface of the earth. Thus life must have originated in water at a depth of thirty feet or more, for that depth of water would be necessary to screen out the destructive rays of the sun which had penetrated the oxygenless

atmosphere. They observe that therefore life could not have originated in the sea, for the various movements of the waters would have
brought the developing life up into the lethal zone where it would
have been killed. They say that therefore life must have begun at a
depth of thirty feet or more below the surface of some protected
inland waters. But the problem here really is the same, for there is
turnover in ponds and lakes also.

One hundred years to the day after the publication of Darwin's
Origin of Species, at the Centennial held at the University of Chicago
in honor of the event, a panel of experts discussed the origin of life.
Ralph W. Gerard of the University of Michigan said he expected the
production of life in the laboratory to be a fact within his lifetime.
Hermann J. Muller, the noted Nobel Prize winner of Indiana University, said he believed it had been done already: ". . . those who
define life as I do will admit that the most primitive forms of things
that deserve to be called living have already been made in the test
tube. . . ."[2]

Whether or not life already has been produced in the laboratory,
whether it is likely to be produced soon, or whether it will not be
produced in the forseeable future depends upon how the word *life*
is defined. If the synthesis of some kind of molecule which can reproduce itself is accepted as the criterion of the first production of life
by man, then life has not yet been produced in the laboratory,
though scientists are optimistic about doing it within the foreseeable
future. But if or when this is accomplished, it will be very far indeed
from the production of anything as complex as the simplest bacterium,
alga, or protozoan.

Several evolutionists have expressed the opinion that when evolution had progressed to the extent that protozoa, but nothing higher,
existed on the earth it had already gone at least half way to its
culmination in human beings.[3] From the "beginning" to one-celled life
is the most difficult step for the evolutionists to explain, and it is
usually passed over without comment.

News of the possible imminence of a scientific breakthrough in
producing life has disturbed some religious people. In the January 3,
1964 issue of *Christianity Today,*[4] it is reported that a Christian young
man said to his father, a minister, "If scientists can create life in a
test tube, who needs God?" It seems that the father was troubled by
this problem also. Actually this question is less meaningful than the
question: If scientists can create life in a test tube, who needs farm-

ers? Farmers produce living things for food, but they are not worried about being replaced by scientists producing life in the laboratory. The author of the article in the magazine quite properly points out that even if the scientists synthesize something which can be defined as living, this will not minimize the creative work of God.

If scientists produce something which can be defined as living, this does not necessarily mean that life on earth was produced by a similar method. If the scientists are successful in their endeavor, it will be through much intelligent planning and the use of elaborate equipment. It will be very different from the chance actions which they postulate started the original life on earth.

A Professor Emeritus of Old Testament at the University of Chicago, later at the Southern Methodist University in Dallas, Texas, says that the author of the magazine article failed to answer the young Christian's question. He says that for all practical purposes life *has* been produced in the laboratory "and this inescapably means that life on this planet began through operations of 'natural' forces, presumably of physics and chemistry."[5] Of course, it does not mean anything of the kind. If scientists produce something which can be called living, the most that even an unbeliever can attach to it is that life *might* have started in some such way. Even from a scientific point of view it could have started in some other way. The only reason for believing it started in some natural way is because the alternative — creation — is rejected as a possibility.

Concerning the production of life in the laboratory, the professor continues his discussion and makes the following very strange observation: "It is a demonstration which Christian people should welcome with open arms. For, taken along with the great achievement of Charles Darwin a hundred years ago, it closes the last link in the line of objective evidence for the soundness of Christian faith."

In their efforts to produce life and their research in related areas the scientists are attempting to play the role of God. The fact that most of them do not believe in divine creation and many do not even believe in the God of the Bible does not alter the fact that they are endeavoring to play the role of God.

The sin of Lucifer was that he said in his heart, "I will be like the most High" (Isa. 14:14, in the context of 14:12-17). The downfall of the human race came through yielding to the temptation that by disobeying God the first parents were led to believe that they would "be as gods" (Gen. 3:5). The New Scofield Reference Bible translates this, "be as God."

It was at one time said that scientists were usurping the province of God in synthesizing organic compounds and even in separating continents in building the Panama Canal. This was comparable to the cry of "Wolf! Wolf!" when there was no wolf on the part of the boy who tended the sheep. Thus when the wolf really came, those who heard the cry paid no attention. But the wolf was real. People may have been lulled into complacency and have not paid heed to the present warning, but now even secular writers are concerned about the role of the scientists in playing God.

NOTES

1. Brancazo, Peter J. and A. G. W. Cameron, Editors, *The Origin and Evolution of Atmospheres and Oceans* (John Wiley and Sons, 1964), "The History of Growth of Oxygen in the Earth's Atmosphere," chapter by L. V. Bekner and L. C. Marshall.

2. Tax, Sol, Editor, *Evolution After Darwin* (University of Chicago Press, 1960), Vol. 3, p. 93.

3. See Frederick Drimmer, editor, *The Animal Kingdom* (Greystone Press, 1954), article by George G. Goodwin, Vol. 2, p. 857. John Tyler Bonner says it this way (The Ideas of Biology, 1962, page 18) ". . . when we think of it from the point of view of evolution it seems easier to imagine a single cell evolving into complex animals and plants than it does to imagine a group of chemical substances evolving into a cell." See also, G. G. Simpson, *The Meaning of Evolution* (Yale University Press, 1950), pp. 15, 16.

4. Holm, John R., "If Scientists Create Life," *Christianity Today*, 8:7:3 (305), January 3, 1964.

5. Letter by William A. Irwin, *Christianity Today*, 8:10:19, February 14, 1964.

THE CREATURES OF MANY CELLS

How the one-celled protozoa came into being through an evolutionary process is a very great mystery, and probably the most difficult of all the things the evolutionists need to explain. But assuming the existence of protozoa, the next question is: How did organisms become multicellular? This raises another question: In what way was it an advantage to protozoa to become multicellular?

We can think of many advantages from our point of view, but it does not follow that any of these would be influential from the point of view of the protozoa. This is an important question, but we will ignore it and assume that there was some evolutionary incentive for unicellular creatures to become multicellular. The next question is: *How* did they do it?

Libbie Henrietta Hyman is a competent and thoroughgoing lady biologist of the American Museum of Natural History in New York City. She has written a number of books on biological subjects, and in one of them she tackles this problem.

She starts out by saying, "No direct proof exists of the origin of the Metazoa [many-celled creatures] from the Protozoa, but such origin besides being necessitated by the principle of evolution is strongly indicated by the facts of embryonic development, in which each metazoan passes from an acellular [by this she means what other people call unicellular] to a cellular [that is, multicellular] condition."[1] Because she has accepted evolution in general as a fact, she says that in this case it is so because evolution is so. As to the evidence from embryonic development, this refers to the recapitulation theory, which she says elsewhere "has been rejected altogether by a number of presentday embryologists."[2] The strong evidence is merely the fact that multicellular creatures begin their development from unicellular eggs. This is accepted as "strong evidence" that the first multicellular creatures evolved from unicellular protozoa!

Dr. Hyman points out two possible routes by which single-celled animals could have become multicellular. New cell walls could have divided one cell into several, or else cells might have stayed together as an aggregate instead of separating when cells divided to form more cells. These alternatives appear to complete the possibilities. Dr. Hyman says that both methods have been advocated by prominent zoologists, "but the former has met with little acceptance because of lack of supporting evidence." This eliminates one alternative and leaves only the possibility of protozoa having become metazoa through a proliferation of cells which remained together instead of separating.

The next question is: What form was taken by the aggregate of cells which remained together instead of separating? Dr. Hyman says there are four possible shapes for colonies of cells: (1) linear (a line of cells like a string of beads), (2) arboreal (branching like a tree), (3) plate-like (a flat raft of cells), and (4) spherical (like a ball). These seem to include all the possibilities. She then says, "The first two may be disregarded. . . ." This leaves the plate of cells and the sphere. Although some noted zoologists have favored the plate of cells as a beginning for the many-celled animals, Dr. Hyman says that this is a view "for which there is little evidence." This now leaves only the sphere.

She then points out that a sphere may be solid or hollow. Although several prominent zoologists have theorized that the metazoa evolved from a solid ball of cells, Dr. Hyman says that "the theory found no acceptance." Now there is left only the hollow ball of cells.

The idea of a hollow ball of cells which pushed in on one side to become a cup-shaped structure that led to the production of the many-celled creatures is the "blastaea-gastraea" or "blastula-gastrula" theory of Ernst Haeckel. Dr. Hyman points out that this theory has been opposed by many workers but it has won acceptance and has been presented in practically all biological textbooks for over a century.

Dr. Hyman has discarded all the other possibilities and this is the only one left, but her comment concerning it is, "But it is probably one of those simplifications that are too beautiful to be true."

Professor Kerkut of the Department of Physiology and Biochemistry at the University of Southampton quotes Radl, "Everything that has ever been cited against the theory was known when the theory was put forward; nevertheless it was widely accepted. Today some still accept it, others do not."[3]

We have eliminated one by one the theories of how the metazoa could have evolved from the protozoa like children reciting the poem about the "ten little Indians" until "now there are none." But after all this, Libbie Hyman still believes that "such origin besides being necessitated by the principle of evolution is strongly indicated by the facts of embryonic development. . . ."

NOTES

1. Hyman, Libbie Henrietta, *Invertebrates*: *Protozoa through Ctenophora* (McGraw-Hill, 1940), pp. 248 to 252.

2. *Ibid.*, p. 273.

3. Kerkut, G. A., *Implications of Evolution* (Pergamon Press, 1960), p. 66.

THE VERTEBRATES

As the name implies, the vertebrates are animals which have backbones. In an effort to solve the mystery of their evolutionary origin, just about every major group of invertebrates except the molluscs (snails, clams, squids, etc.) has been suggested as ancestral to them.

The fact that so many different kinds of animals have been considered as ancestors merely reveals the magnitude of the problem.

A couple of generations ago the favored theory was that the vertebrates, including ourselves, evolved from the annelid worms. These are the segmented worms, such as the common earthworm and the clam worm. Evidences of segmentation in the human body were considered pertinent to the theory. They included the arrangement of the spinal nerves, which emerge from the spinal cord at regular intervals, that is, between the vertebrae. Since there is no other practical place for them to emerge, it is by necessity that they present an arrangement which appears as though it might be segmental. Also the arrangement of some abdominal muscles indicates segmentation. But since the evolutionists no longer derive us from the segmented worms, these alleged indications of segmentation in the human body have lost their significance.

There were some real and formidable technical difficulties in trying to derive the vertebrates from the segmented worms. The most interesting one is the fact that to become a vertebrate, the worm would have to turn over on its back. Worms do not like to do this even for a short time, not to mention staying this way while evolving into something else. Alfred S. Romer of Harvard says, "It may be that top and bottom mean little to a worm; but the reversal of position raises as many problems as it solves. We must, for example, close the old worm mouth and drill a new one through the former roof of the head, for in both worms and backboned animals the mouth lies on the underside, beneath the brain."[1] How do the animals feed during the transitional period? Transitional animals with two mouths (or none) do not seem very practical.

Perhaps the most bizarre of the theories of vertebrate origin is the arachnid theory. This theory derives us from some member of the group to which spiders and scorpions belong. It was originated by the late Professor George Patten of Dartmouth College, and he spent much of his life defending it. In deriving the vertebrates from the arachnids the same problems are encountered which caused so much difficulty in the annelid theory — the reversal of top and bottom and the necessity of closing up the mouth and opening a new mouth.

There is an alternative theory which keeps the ancestral arachnids right side up while evolving toward the vertebrates. According to this theory, the central nerve cord of the arachnid migrated to the position of the digestive tract and then surrounded the digestive tract. This changed the solid nerve cord of the arachnids into the hollow nerve cord typical of the vertebrates. Meanwhile, an entirely new digestive tract developed. This fantastic hypothesis may sound like a facetious satire, but it is serious "science."[2]

Another problem in deriving vertebrates from arachnids is what to do with the jointed feet of the arachnids. Evolutionists derive the legs of land vertebrates from the fins of fish, and as Professor Romer says, the feet of the arachnids could not possibly have evolved into the fins of fish.

The currently accepted theory of the origin of the vertebrates is the echinoderm theory. According to this theory we evolved from an ancestor related to the starfish and sea urchins, and we are more closely related to them than to any other group of invertebrates. There are a few structural similarities which we share with these creatures.

The acorn worms are sometimes looked upon as giving supporting evidence to the echinoderm theory. The larvae of acorn worms are so similar to larval echinoderms that until they were raised in the laboratory the larval acorn worms were thought to be echinoderms. Until recently it was generally believed that the acorn worms have a short notochord, which is a skeletal element characteristic of developing vertebrates. However, the opinions about this seem to be changing, and a survey of recent textbooks will reveal that some authors believe the acorn worms have a notochord, some believe they do not, and some are uncertain as to whether they have one or not.

There are two other types of animals which have a notochord but lack the skeletal elements characteristic of vertebrates. One is represented by the famous *Amphioxus*, which for generations has been portrayed in textbooks as a type of ancestor for the vertebrates. But those who know *Amphioxus* best say this cannot be so because it is too specialized. The other type is the sea squirts, which have a notochord only in the larval stage. This larval stage has been nominated as a candidate for the connecting link between the vertebrates and the invertebrates, but this view has not gained acceptance.

NOTES

1. Romer, Alfred S., *Man and the Vertebrates*, 3d ed. (University of Chicago Press, 1941, printing of 1953), p. 14.
2. Romer, Alfred S., *The Vertebrate Body* (W. B. Saunders, 1949), pp. 27, 28.

BIRDS

The derivation of birds from reptiles seems to be one of the most thoroughly accepted sequences in evolution. Thomas Henry Huxley called birds glorified reptiles, and this witicism is still frequently encountered when the evolution of birds is discussed. It is commonly stated that if the remains of *Archeopteryx*, "the earliest known bird," had been found without feathers, it would have been reconstructed as a bipedal reptile.

In 1861 the impression of a feather was found in lithographic slate being quarried in Bavaria. Later in the same year in the same quarry a feathered creature about the size of a crow was found. This is *Archeopteryx*. It has teeth in its jaws, a long tail with feathers attached along the sides of it, and claws at the ends of all four limbs. A few years later a more complete specimen, about the size of a pigeon, was discovered.

Among living creatures birds, and only birds, have feathers. Thus a feather defines a bird. This definition is extrapolated backward into the past, and *Archeopteryx* is called a bird. Although a great many other anatomical characteristics, including such things as eyes, hooves, and excretory tubules, are believed to have evolved separately in different evolutionary lines, it seems that very few evolutionists have even considered the possibility of feathers having evolved more than once. The possibility of feathers having been created is not considered at all, and they are usually said to have evolved from the scales of reptiles.

Archaeopteryx had fully developed wings. Nothing has ever been found evolving from a reptile with partially-developed wings. Since the *Archaeopteryx* has some reptilian characteristics and some avian characteristics it is considered to be a link between the reptiles and birds. But this does not necessarily mean that it does connect the reptiles with the birds. As previously mentioned, a fossil named *Seymouria* has some amphibian-like and some reptile-like characteristics. It seems to make a good connection between the amphibians and reptiles, but G. F. Kerkut points out that it cannot be, because it lived at the wrong time.[1] If a "suitable" fossil cannot be a connecting link because it lived at the wrong time, it is obvious that a "suitable" fossil is not necessarily a connecting link if it happens to live at the "right" time.

There is a difference of opinion as to whether *Archeopteryx* could fly. Gavin de Beer, Director of the British Museum of Natural History, believes it could do little more than glide. On the basis of this opinion the *Illustrated London News* published a full-page illustration showing an artist's conception of how a fossil specimen met its death — it was blown out over a shallow sea and had no choice but the fatal plunge into the water.[2] It is postulated that it was covered by dust or fine sand conveniently blown at just the right time from the land, and thus it was preserved as a fossil.

There is a living bird, the hoactzin of South America, in which the young have claws on the wings, much like *Archeopteryx*, and can climb among the branches of bushes. They later lose these claws, and the adult birds have no sign of them. Although they have large wings, the muscles are weak, and the birds cannot do much more than glide.

There are differences of opinion among the experts as to how to interpret the two specimens of *Archeopteryx*. Some believe they represent mature and immature specimens of the same species. Others think they are different species of the same genus. Still others regard them as belonging to different genera. Finally, it has been postulated that one became the ancestor of the large flightless birds — the ostriches, emus, cassowaries — while the other became the ancestor of the flying types. With such wide differences of opinion, it is evident that all of this is merely speculation.

Hesperornis is a fossil aquatic bird which had teeth. It had strong feet, apparently for swimming and diving, and it had small wings.

There are two theories as to how the flight of birds evolved. According to one theory, as certain reptiles raced along the ground on their hind feet, the scales along the margin of their raised front legs became elongated, giving added support in the air. Eventually the scales became feathers and the forelimbs became wings. According to the other theory a rather similar thing happened, except that instead of running on the ground the reptiles climbed trees and then jumped down. The scales of the fore-limbs elongated and thus helped break their fall by offering some resistance in the air. Eventually the scales became feathers and the limbs wings.

Except for the frequently repeated statement that birds evolved from reptiles, the evolution of birds is by no means clear in the minds of evolutionists. J. Arthur Thomson of the University of Aberdeen said, "Our frankness in admitting difficulties and relative ignorance in regard to the variations and selections that led from certain dinosaurs to birds cannot be used by any fairminded inquirer as an argument against the idea of evolution. For how else could birds have arisen?"[3]

W. E. Swinton of the British Museum says, "With some imagination we can link *Archeopteryx* with the forms that came later, but it requires much speculation to see the origin of even the power of flight this first known bird displays. . . . None the less, nearly a century after the publication of that monumental work [Darwin's *Origin of Species*], there are still monumental problems that remain to be settled about the succession of life. This is especially true of the birds."[4]

NOTES

1. Kerkut, G. A., *Implications of Evolution* (Pergamon Press, 1960), p. 136.
2. *The Illustrated London News*, 227:6063:37, July 2, 1955. Also see text under picture and on opposite page.
3. Thomson, J. Arthur, *The Outline of Science* (G. P. Putnam's Sons, 1922), Vol. 2, p. 368.
4. Swinton, W. E., "The World's Oldest Known Bird," *The Illustrated London News*, 227:6063:36, July 2, 1955.

HORSES

The horse is presented by evolutionists as the classic example illustrating an evolutionary series of fossil remains, and Professor Mixter tells a Christian audience that the transitions in the fossil series from the little "dawn horse to the modern horse are so gradual that there is no problem in deriving the latter from the former."[1]

In 1838 an English brickmaker named William Colchester found a tooth in some sand, and the following year an English gentleman named William Richardson found a portion of a skull with most of the teeth. These were the first finds of the now famous "dawn horse."

Richard Owen, the renowned anatomist and biologist, at first said the tooth belonged to a kind of monkey, and when the piece of skull turned up he believed it resembled "that of the Hare or other timid Rodentia."[2] (Rabbits and hares were considered to be rodents in those days.) George Gaylord Simpson, the great American paleontologist and evolutionist, says that the teeth do resemble those of a monkey more than they do those of a horse and that with the evidence available at that time "it would have been most unscientific to jump to the conclusion that this queer little beast was a sort of horse."[3] At another place Professor Simpson says, "Owen was a brilliant anatomist and he was right in concluding that the fossil teeth were more like those of a monkey than of any other living animal."[4]

Owen named it *Hyracotherium*, which means the hyrax-like beast. The hyraxes are the conies of the Bible, which "are but feeble folk, yet make their houses in the rocks" (Prov. 30:26). Quite a long time after this, O. C. Marsh, who began his paleontological work at Yale in 1866, discovered fossil material in western North America which he called *Eohippus*, which means dawn horse. It was realized that *Eohippus* and *Hyracotherium* were similar, but it was not until 1932 that C. F. Cooper, director of the British Museum of Natural History decided that they belong to the same genus.[5] In 1947 George Gaylord Simpson confirmed this.[6] Thus by the rules of scientific nomenclature, the name *Eohippus* no longer exists as a scientific name and *Hyracotherium* takes its place. But it still properly may be used as a common, non-technical name.

According to G. A. Kerkut of the University of Southampton, the story of the evolution of the horse began in 1874, when V. C. Kowalevsky drew a simple linear series which included only three types besides the modern horse. These were all fossil animals of the Eastern Hemisphere. After the American fossils were studied, other evolutionary diagrams were drawn for the horse, which did not include any of Kowalevsky's animals in the direct lineage of the horse. It may be surmised, however, that if the American fossils never had been discovered, theoretical lineages based on the Eastern Hemispere fossils would have been considered quite all right and acceptable.

It has been pointed out by a number of evolutionists, including George Gaylord Simpson, that eohippus, or *Hyracotherium*, could just as well be considered the ancestor of some other kinds of animals instead of the ancestor of the horse. But it has been so thoroughly propagandized as the ancestor of the horse that it will continue to be just that — the ancestor of the horse.

G. A. Kerkut, in his unusual book, *Implications of Evolution*, which is a somewhat anti-evolutionary book written by an evolutionist, starts his discussion of horses by saying, "The evolution of the horse provides one of the keystones in the teaching of evolutionary doctrine, though the actual story depends to a large extent upon who is telling it and when the story is being told."[7] He admits, as other evolutionists have been forced to admit, that as more and more fossils have been discovered and have been added to the family tree of the horses, the tree has become a bush. This means that instead of having a single starting point and branching from a main trunk, like a tree, there are various starting points and no main stem.

Professor Kerkut says that in this regard the story of the evolution of the horse approaches that of the elephant, and to illustrate this he quotes from an article by Henry Fairfield Osborn: ". . . in almost no instance is any known form considered to be a descendant from any other known form; every subordinating group is assumed to have sprung, quite separately and usually without any known intermediate stage, from hypothetical common ancestors in the Early Eocene or Late Cretaceous."[8] He also admits that it is not clear that *Hyracotherium* (eohippus) was the ancestral horse.[9]

In comparing the evolution of the horse with that of the elephants it is interesting to note a statement by the director of the National Museum of Ceylon in his book on elephants. He said in 1955 concerning the living Asiatic and African elephants, "The origins of both are obscure. . . . The fossil record is yet far too fragmentary for any but the vaguest conclusions as to how evolution works, but at present the Proboscidia [elephants] throw more light upon this problem than any other mammalian order."[10] If it is true that the evolutionary story is best for the elephants but even so is far too fragmentary for any but the vaguest conclusions, this does not look very good for the story of the horse.

Professor Kerkut criticizes in several particulars the story of the evolution of the horse as given by the specialists to the public. For one thing, the more recent writers do not clearly distinguish between the parts of the skeleton which have been found and the parts which are hypothetical restorations. Also it is difficult to get information about how complete the specimens are, and how many specimens have been found of the various types represented in the evolutionary tree of the horses. It makes quite a difference whether a name on a diagram represents a whole skeleton or just a tooth. After a few other criticisms he concludes, "At present, however, it is a matter of faith that the textbook pictures are true, or even that they are the best representations of the truth that are available to us at the present time."[11]

Professor Kerkut also mentions that T. Edinger reports from a study of casts of the insides of the fossil skulls of "early horses" that their brains were quite smooth.[12] The brains of living horses are highly convoluted. Therefore, evolutionists who believe that only modern horses (including zebras, etc.) evolved from these "early horses" must logically admit that any similarity between the convolutions of the brains of horses and of other animals is coincidental or a case of "parallelism." For example, Sisson and Grossman in their book *The Anatomy of Domestic Animals,* diagram and describe the brains of the horse and cow. Of fourteen fissures named, all but two have the same name in both horse and cow and correspond in location. The other two also correspond in location but are given different names.

The non-scientific public has great faith in what a paleontologist can do with a single bone. This all started with the great Georges Cuvier, the founder of modern paleontology. He believed he could reconstruct a whole skeleton from a single bone. But as Professor Simpson says, "Unfortunately, this is not true, or at least if it is true paleontologists have not yet learned the trick. . . . Today many people know this [that paleontologists can reconstruct an entire skeleton from one bone] who know nothing else about paleontology."[13] Cuvier himself made the mistake of identifying some fossil bones and teeth as belonging to an extinct hippopotamus and an extinct rhinoceros, when it turned out that they were the bones and teeth of a reptile. He later admitted his error.[14]

There were animals called chalicotheres which were something like a horse but had large claws on their feet. Concerning them Dr. Simpson says, "Cuvier was hardly in his grave when one of the most spectacular refutations of 'Cuvier's law' of correlation of anatomical parts turned up. He had concluded that certain sorts of teeth always are correlated with the occurrence of hoofs on the feet of the same animals. But a whole group of extinct animals (that of the chalicotheres) turned out to have great claws on the feet and yet have teeth such as *must* (by law!) be associated with hoofs."[15] He concludes with the significant statement: "This baffled the paleontologists of the time and enraged some of them. It has sobered paleontologists ever since."

The hypothetical story of the evolution of the horse starts with eohippus, but where eohippus came from is another problem. Back in 1942 Professor Simpson considered this and suggested five hypotheses in the search for an answer.

His first hypothesis is that eohippus "was created by divine act." His appraisal of this suggestion is, "This was accepted by scientists a hundred years ago and is still claimed by a few theologians, but it cannot now be seriously considered by any thoughtful inquirer."[16] That takes care of the first hypothesis in the opinion of Dr. Simpson.

His second hypothesis is that "the geologic record in North America was interrupted during the time when eohippus was evolving." The Christian antievolutionist may not know just what to say to that, but there is no need. Dr. Simpson obligingly answers it himself, and says, "This is a plausible hypothesis, but, as it happens, one that can now be disproved beyond any doubt."

The third hypothesis is that "certain animals unlike eohippus but related to him suddenly gave birth to a litter of dawn horses." This may seem quite far-fetched, but Professor Simpson comments, "In the nature of things, this hypothesis cannot be ruled out categorically and some respectable scientists do support it. Nevertheless it is so improbable as to be unacceptable unless we can find no hypothesis more likely to explain the observed facts." He rejects this hypothesis, but the important thing to notice is that he would be willing to accept a hypothesis he himself considers unacceptable *if he can find no other hypothesis more likely to explain the observed facts!* He repeats this for emphasis. He really would accept it if there is nothing better. This causes one to wonder how many other hypotheses may have been accepted and presented to the public merely because nothing better occurred to the evolutionists.

The fourth hypothesis is that the fossil hunters merely have failed so far in finding the pertinent fossils which connect earlier ancestors of the horse to the little eohippus. His comment is: "Again, the hypothesis cannot be disproved — who can say what may yet be discovered? It was even a likely hypothesis before much was known about the American Paleocene, but as hundreds and thousands of Paleocene fossils are found, many of them from environments suitable for eohippus, and not a scrap of a real eohippus ancestor appears, the chance that such ancestors occurred here is being reduced to the vanishing point."

Thus he does away with four of the five hypotheses. The fifth must be right, or he is left without any. The fifth is: "The dawn horse evolved elsewhere than in North America and arrived on this continent along with other invading animals." The place where eohippus and the other animals came from is unknown, and he says that perhaps it never will be known, for it is possible that it is now sunk beneath the sea. His comment is: "This is the favored hypothesis of paleontologists. It explains all the known facts, no fact contradicts it, and it is supported by other observations and theories on all sides." He concludes, "But in any case the theory [he no longer considers it a hypothesis] is established and seems almost certainly to be true."

NOTES

1. Mixter, Russell L., "An Evaluation of the Fossil Record," *Journal of the American Scientific Affiliation*, 11:4:24, December, 1959, p. 25.

2. Simpson, George Gaylord, *Horses* (Oxford University Press, 1951), p. 86.

3. *Ibid.*, p. 86.

4. Simpson, George Gaylord, "Resurrection of the Dawn Horse," *Natural History*, 46:4:194, November, 1940, p. 195.

5. Simpson, George Gaylord, *Horses, loc. cit.*, p. 115.

6. *Ibid.*, p. 115.

7. Kerkut, G. A., *Implications of Evolution* (Pergamon Press, 1960), p. 144.

8. *Ibid.*, p. 149.

9. *Ibid.*

10. Deraniyagala, P. E. P., *Some Extinct Elephants, Their Relatives, and the Two Living Species* (Government Press, Ceylon, 1955), p. 11.

11. Kerkut, G. A., *loc. cit.*, p. 148.

12. *Ibid.*, p. 149.

13. Simpson, George Gaylord, *Life of the Past* (Yale University Press, 1953), p. 38.

14. Colbert, Edwin, H., *Dinosaurs* (E. P. Dutton and Co., 1961), pp. 60, 61.

15. Simpson, George Gaylord, *Life of the Past, loc cit.*, p. 38.

16. Simpson, George Gaylord, "The Great American Invasion," *Natural History*, 49:4:206, April, 1942.

MAN

The Bible says that God created man in His own image (Gen. 1:26, 27). Some say that since God is a spirit, this cannot refer to the physical form of man. But God is not only one, but three. The Lord Jesus Christ, when He walked the earth, was God in a physical form. The Bible says that He was from the beginning and that all things were made by Him. However, we are not told about His form before the creation of man, except for the implication in the statement that we were made in His image. He appeared on the earth as a man both before and after His virgin birth in Bethlehem. In Old Testament times certain men were privileged to see and talk with God as a man, and we understand this to be the Lord Jesus, for no man has seen

God the Father at any time (John 1:18). It is evident that God made man in the form in which He wished to reveal Himself.

In contrast to this, the evolutionists look upon man as just one of a very large number of accidents which occurred in evolutionary history, and which could not have been predicted beforehand. If evolution were to start over again, man might never occur at all.

Loren Eiseley, Professor of Anthropology at the University of Pennsylvania, says, "We can still ask this varied group of fossils, why did man have to be? No answer comes back. He did not have to be any more than a butterfly or a caterpillar. He merely emerged from that infinite void for which we have no name."[1]

Ernest Baldwin, Lecturer in Biochemistry at Cambridge University, says that if fish had not developed a tolerance to different concentrations of mineral matter in the water, "man might never have been possible; logical thought, speech, and record might never have evolved, and this book would certainly never have been written."[2]

Professor Hooton says we came into being because an ape chose to go by a difficult evolutionary route, apparently in defiance of natural selection. He said, "Here, forsooth, the ape with human destiny was at the very crossroads of evolution, and he took the difficult path which led upward toward humanity."[3]

Several evolutionists have recorded their opinion that man may be considered to be the highest form of life only because it is he who does the classifying.

It has been suggested by some who speak for Christians that it may be all right for Christians to accept the evolution of animals if man be held to be a separate creation. For example, the late Donald Gray Barnhouse, former editor of *Eternity* magazine, said that as God has promised to intervene in the future to bring about the millenium, so He might have intervened in the past to create man, while other forms of life evolved. His words are: "May we not hold that in like manner God intervened in the past, even in the midst of a long evolutionary process, and created man as an entirely new factor?"[4]

This, however, is a compromise, as well as an unstable position. Evolutionists consider man to be an animal, and children are now being taught this, starting in the lower grades. For those who accept the principle of evolution there is no logical stopping place. It is folly to expect that young people can be taught that animals evolved and that man alone is a special creation. This kind of teaching merely prepares the young people to accept all of evolution.

Dr. Barnhouse also said in the article just mentioned, ". . . men have built a model for the existence of the universe. That model, now on exhibit in all the schools of the world, is called evolution. . . . Many Christians fear that model because they think it will crush faith, not realizing that faith is absolutely indestructible when it is founded upon God in Christ." We must take exception to these words of Dr. Barnhouse and say that Christians do well indeed to fear that "model," and it would be better if some feared it more than they do. The theory of evolution has been one of the principal agents in under-mining and destroying Christian faith. There are two things which Dr. Barnhouse did not seem to realize. The doctrine of evolution can prevent people from accepting a saving faith in Christ and also it can cause some who have received this faith to become backslidden. The Empress Victoria of Germany, a daughter of Queen Victoria, is said to have become a Christian, but later she became very much de-pressed and despondent as a result of the teaching of Darwinism in Germany.

This idea that the teaching of evolution is not to be feared because our position in Christ is secure is as illogical as it would be to main-tain for the same reason that the un-Scriptural and anti-Christian teachings of the cults and the modernists are not to be feared. These things need not be feared personally by those who are secure in Christ, but they may well be feared for the influence they have over others and on the affairs of our society.

A perennial question asked by perplexed Christians is: "What about the cave men?" The Cro-Magnon people, who made the famous cave paintings, seem to have been men like ourselves, and hence present no real evolutionary problem. The Neanderthals, on the other hand, have caused the evolutionists quite a lot of confusion. Jacob W. Gru-ber of the Department of Sociology and Anthropology at Temple University, said in 1948, "As more and more information has come to light concerning Pleistocene man, the problem of the Neanderthals becomes more and more confused."[5]

The first Neanderthal skull was found in a quarry at Gibraltar, but it was completely neglected for sixteen years. Therefore most text-books say the Neanderthals were discovered in 1856 in a cave in the Neander valley in Germany.

It may seem strange to us, but the Darwinians "were actually not very happy or enthusiastic about the first Neanderthal discovery."[6] They were still hoping to find *living* links between ape and man in some unexplored area of the earth. Thomas Henry Huxley, Darwin's staunchest defender, said the Neanderthals represented only a slightly exaggerated form of living Australians. An anthropologist named Pruner-Bey said the skulls showed a resemblance to the Irish. Another view was that they were Russians.

But presently the viewpoint changed, and the Darwinians found the Neanderthals to be bestial and gorilloid. Even the mild-mannered and usually cautious Charles Darwin referred to their "enormous projecting canines."[7] This is an utterly untrue description. Professor Eiseley of the University of Pennsylvania comments, "Its capacious brain-case did not prevent it from being labeled as a brute, and its characters were so transformed that, without the slightest basis in fact, it was described as possessing huge projecting canines and an appearance in the highest degree hideous and ferocious."[8]

It was said that the Neanderthals walked with a slouch, being unable to straighten their knees, and with their heads thrust forward. These allegations are still presented in current textbooks, although the conclusion of the anthropologists who have studied the remains more recently is that they are not true. It seems to be characteristic of many authors that they copy the thoughts of other authors who wrote before them. Thus, if an idea becomes expressed widely, it is carried along by its own momentum in subsequent books even after experts have made a correction.

A survey of eighteen college textbooks published after 1956 (the hundredth anniversary of the Neanderthal discovery) shows that nine told the students that the Neanderthal people could not straighten their knees (plus four more that said they walked with a slouch but did not mention the knees specifically), and eight said the head projected forward. Two made remarks about the Neanderthals being apelike.[9]

In 1956 a symposium was held in commemoration of the one hundredth anniversary of the discovery of the Neanderthals. In preparation for this symposium William S. Straus Jr., the eminent anthropologist of the Johns Hopkins University, and A. J. E. Cave of the Department of Anatomy at St. Bartholomew's Hospital Medical College in London, were permitted to examine the remains from which M. Boule had made the original description which has been the basis of the subsequent descriptions of the Neanderthals widely circulated in textbooks ever since. Straus and Cave were, of course, familiar with the literature on the subject, and they knew that the

specimen was pathological, but they say they "were somewhat un-
prepared for the fragmentary nature of the skeleton itself and for the
consequent extent of restoration required."[10]

After a thorough examination of the skeleton they concluded, "He
cannot, in view of his manifest pathology, be used to provide us with
a reliable picture of a healthy, normal Neanderthalian. Notwithstanding, if he could be reincarnated and placed in a New York subway —
provided he were bathed, shaved, and dressed in modern clothing
— it is doubtful whether he would attract any more attention than
some of its other denizens."[11] They affirm that "there is thus no valid
reason for the assumption that the posture of Neanderthal man . . .
differed significantly from that of present-day men. . . . there is
nothing in this total morphological pattern to justify the common assumption that Neanderthal man was other than a fully erect biped
when standing and walking."[12]

Two other anthropologists, C. Arambourg and E. Pattie, independently published their views at about the same time as Straus and
Cave, and they came to essentially the same conclusions, opposing
the former view that Neanderthal man walked with knees bent and
head thrust forward.[13]

Another contributor to the symposium reported that in bones other
than the skull, differences between the Neanderthals and modern populations are "much less marked than some writers in the past have
been led to believe."[14] He concludes that the skeletons are basically
modern and that former views to the contrary are untenable.

Professor Paul Amos Moody of the University of Vermont says in
his textbook of evolution (1962), "Early restorations seem to indicate
that these people did not have a fully upright posture but later
investigations have shown this interpretation to have been incorrect,
having arisen from the fact that the first specimen restored was
pathological, the skeleton of an individual suffering from severe
rickets."[15]

The heads of the Neanderthal people were shaped somewhat
differently from ours, and this has led to much speculation about their
intelligence. It is well known that their average cranial capacity was
greater than ours, and this is more remarkable when it is realized
that their average height is said to have been less than ours (about
five feet four inches in males).

G. Elliot Smith, the famous anatomist of the University of London,
published a book in 1924 in which he expressed his opinion, based

upon a study of endocranial casts, that although the average Neanderthal brain was larger in size than ours, it was inferior in quality because important parts were not well developed. This view has been widely circulated in textbooks. Straus and Cave disagree with this and they remind their readers that Professor Smith's opinions in this area are not to be relied upon. He declared that the brain of the Piltdown man, had primitive features, but it turned out that Piltdown was a hoax and the skull was a modern type.

The well-known anthropologist M. F. Ashley Montagu says, "Owing to want of a little knowledge of elementary anatomy, some of these 'authorities' who have engaged in 'reconstruction' of Neanderthal man have represented him with a bull neck, grotesque features, and walking with a stoop, during which, it was alleged, his knees knocked together! It has also often been asserted that Neanderthal man must have been of low intelligence because he had a low forehead. All these slanders are indefensible. Neanderthal man walked as erect as any modern man, he did not have a bull neck, and he was not knock-kneed. And it has long ago been proved by many independent scientific investigators that the form of the brow or of the head has nothing whatever to do with intelligence. As a matter of fact, we have very good reason to believe that Neanderthal man was every bit as intelligent as we are today."[16]

The Neanderthal people apparently buried their dead and left food and offerings with the bodies. Much flower pollen was found recently at a Neanderthal burial site, indicating that they used flowers with burials. In a cave in Switzerland there was found what has been interpreted as an altar used by Neanderthals. From these observations it has been concluded that they had a form of religion and faith in a life after death.

After the Neanderthal remains were found, a Neanderthal skull was exhibited in London between a modern human skull and the skull of an ape. For some time Neanderthal was believed to be a link between man and ape, and some champions of this view held on to it bitterly in spite of growing opposition. The consensus of opinion came to the point of view that the Neanderthals could not be ancestral to us. Part of the reason for this belief was due to the discovery of modern type skulls older than the Neanderthals. But now the cycle has reached a full completion, for several anthropologists are at present proclaiming that we did have them for ancestors after all. Of these, Professor Ashley Montagu is the most well known.

Another popular view is that we are partially descended from Neanderthals because they hybridized with modern man before becoming extinct.

As is rather characteristic in matters pertaining to evolution, one can find just about every imaginable point of view advocated by someone. Since the experts in anthropology are so confused about the Neanderthals, and since it seems clear that the Neanderthals were human beings, the whole matter hardly seems to be an issue from the Christian standpoint, except perhaps the time factor, which is discussed elsewhere.

Professor Eiseley can be depended upon to write about everything in an interesting way. He philosophizes about the Neanderthals: "And down the untold centuries the message has come without words, 'We too were human, we too suffered, we too believed that the grave is not the end. We too, whose faces affright you now, knew human agony and human love.' It is important to consider that across fifty thousand years nothing has changed or altered in that act. It is the human gesture by which we know a man though he looks out upon us under a brow suggestive of an ape. If, in another fifty thousand years, we can still weep, we will know humanity is safe. This is all we need to ask about the onrush of the scientific age."[17]

We have no assurance that such time is at our disposal. The return of the Lord always is imminent and we are told in the Bible that the situation will not be resolved through human ingenuity but by our Lord when He returns.

The next important form to consider is the "Java ape-man," formerly called *Pithecanthropus erectus* but now *Homo erectus,* and the rather similar Peking ape-man, formerly called *Sinanthropus pekinensis* but now also named *Homo erectus.*

The romantic story of the discovery of *Pithecanthropus* has been told many times. The young Eugene Dubois gave up a medical practice and security against the advice of his friends to go on a search for the missing link. He found what he was looking for on the island of Java. He also found some rather modern skulls, a fact which he refrained from mentioning for thirty years. The reason for this seems to have been that he believed these skulls would jeopardize the importance of his "ape-man."

He brought back his *Pithecanthropus* findings to the Third International Congress of Zoology at Leiden in 1885, only to find the men of science disagreeing among themselves as to what the remains represented. The creature was generally considered to be some sort of ape. Dubois removed the fossils from access to the scientists and would not let anyone see them for twenty-eight years. Meanwhile the men of science changed their views and said *Pithecanthropus* was a man. Dubois had changed his mind also; he now said *Pithecanthropus* was an ape.

The rather similar "Peking men" are said to have built fires and made artifacts. An attempt was made to remove the fossils from the country at the time of the Japanese invasion of China, but it was delayed too long, the shipment was intercepted. Where the remains are now no one seems to know.

The present view of the evolutionists is that the Java and Peking finds not only represent men instead of apes, but that they should be elevated to the genus in which we are catalogued. Whatever they really were, giving them names of one sort or another will not change whatever nature they really had, and who really knows what that was?

A generation ago the consensus of opinion of the men of science was that these forms were not on the line of evolution leading to man. At that time Franz Weidenreich, now deceased, differed from the others in believing that they were ancestral to us. Roy Chapman Andrews had sufficient faith in the opinion of Professor Weidenreich that he seems to have accepted this view as a fact, for he said, "Personally, I feel very happy about the whole thing. It is comforting to know who was one of our remote ancestors and that we need no longer wear the bar-sinister across our escutcheons."[18] As Roy Chapman Andrews and others pick which authority they will choose to believe, the Christian also has this privilege, and will choose the Authority who claims to have made man in His own image. He will be criticized for this, though there is no evidence that Dr. Andrews was criticized for his bold commitment to a minority opinion as truth.

Recently there has been much publicity about the "South African ape-men," called the Australopithecines. The first find was made in 1925, but very little was heard about these creatures for a long time, apparently because of professional jealousies. Raymond Dart named the first one *Australopithecus africanus*, which means "southern ape of Africa." A subsequent find he named *Australopithecus prometheus*, which may be translated, "the Promethean southern ape." This name was given in honor of the mythological Prometheus, who is said to have brought fire to the inhabitants of the earth as a gift from the gods. The reason Dart gave this creature this name was because he thought there was evidence that it used fire. But even Robert Broom, another prominent anthropologist of South Africa, who defended Dart's views on the Australopithecines when other anthropologists were opposing him would not accept this. It later was shown that what Dart had interpreted as charcoal was a mineral deposit instead.

Professor Dart claimed that the Australopithecines had accumulated the bones of other animals found among theirs, but some scientists believed the bones might have been brought there by hyenas. Dart made what seemed to be a very good case against this view, but it was subsequently shown that hyenas really *do* carry bones to their lairs.

Professor Dart wrote extensively about tools used by the Australopithecines, but others have expressed the belief that the alleged tools were used *on* them instead of *by* them.

In 1959 a Christian biologist published an article in which he said that the Australopithecines were men because they used tools, and since they were men we may trace our ancestry back to them and still be soundly Biblical in our views. He made the further statement that the fossil record of *their* ancestry is inaccessible because of being under water, thereby implying that except for some water we would be able to trace *our* ancestry still further back. (He since has changed his mind about this.)

A serious problem was soon recognized by those who would have the Australopithecines as our ancestors, and that was the fact that they seemed to have lived too recently in time to have permitted an evolutionary process to change them into human beings. Roy Chapman Andrews made the statement that it is the anatomical features and not the time which is important in evolution. This kind of argument could be used to show that someone sitting across from you in the New York subway really could be a link between ape and man — it is his anatomy which counts, not the time when he lives.

It became the prevailing point of view that some of the Australopithecines represented a type rather similar to the still undiscovered ancestors of man.

It was said that some of the Australopithecines were definitely too specialized to represent a type ancestral to man, for they had a bony crest along the top of the head, like male gorillas. Some authorities now place these in the genus *Parapithecus* ("near ape") as distinct from *Australopithecus*. M. F. Ashley Montagu, for one, considers *Parapithecus* to be ancestral to *Australopithecus,* and thus, in spite of the bony crest, ancestral to a type similar to our ancestors. Thus it will be seen that there is a difference of opinion not only as to what *might* have been but also as to what *could* have been.

To further complicate the situation, the famous *Zinjanthropus,* which has a bony crest on the head, is now put in the genus *Australopithecus*. The *Zinjanthropus* skull was discovered by L. S. B. Leakey in 1959 and claimed by him to be a man. Leakey's work is largely financed by the National Geographic Society, and they published in their magazine (September, 1960) a picture of a restored *Zinjanthropus* which surely would not draw a second glance in the New York subway, provided he was wearing a cap that concealed the fact that he had no forehead.

Leakey has since changed his mind and now says that *Zinjanthropus* (*Australopithecus boisei*) is an ape and not a man after all. About the same time that Leakey was changing his mind Ashley Montagu proclaimed, "The brain size of *Zinjanthropus* is that of an ape, and the skull looks in most respects like that of an ape. But *Zinjanthropus* is a man, *not* an ape."[19]

A number of anthropologists are now stressing the idea that man must be defined on the basis of what he does instead of anatomically. It is believed that if a creature was capable of chipping stone to make something usable as a tool, then he was a man. It was on this kind of basis that Leakey declared *Zinjanthropus* to be a man, and changed his mind when he found reason to believe that the tools were made by another creature, which he has named *Homo habilis* (found April 4, 1964). But *Homo habilis* has gone the way of *Zinjanthropus,* and now both are classed as Australopithecines by some authorities.

All of this is so confused that not much that is definite can be said about it except that the evolutionists definitely believe that early man was hardly to be distinguished from some sort of ape and made crude tools which can hardly be distinguished from naturally fractured rocks.

According to the Bible the first man was created as such, talked with God, knew right from wrong, named the animals, and sinned. Early men were skillful in metalwork and the handling of musical instruments.

NOTES

1. Eiseley, Loren, "The Time of Man," *Horizon*, 4:4:4, March, 1962, p. 10.

2. Baldwin, Ernest, *An Introduction to Comparative Biochemistry* (Cambridge University Press, 1937), p. 3.

3. Hooton, Ernest Albert, *Apes, Men, and Morons* (George Allen and Unwin, 1938), p. 25.

4. Barnhouse, Donald Gray, "Adam and Modern Science," *Eternity*, May, 1960, p. 8.

5. Gruber, Jacob, W., "The Neanderthal Controversy: 19th Century Version," *Scientific Monthly*, 67:6:436, December, 1948, p. 436.

6. Eiseley, Loren, "Neanderthal Man and the Dawn of Human Paleontology," *Quarterly Review of Biology*, 32:4:323, December, 1957, p. 326.

7. *Ibid.*, p. 326.

8. *Ibid.*, p. 328.

9. Guthrie, Mary J. and John M. Anderson, *General Zoology* (John Wiley and Sons, 1957), p. 643. "The characteristics of the skulls indicate somewhat ape-like features." Elliott, Alfred M., *Zoology*, 3d ed. (Appleton-Century-Crofte, 1963), p. 407. ". . . he was probably quite gorilla-like in appearance."

10. Straus, William L. Jr., and A. J. E. Cave, "Paleontology and the Posture of Neanderthal Man," *Quarterly Review of Biology*, 32:4:348, December, 1957, pp. 351, 352.

11. *Ibid.*, p. 359.

12. *Ibid.*, p. 358.

13. *Ibid.*, p. 362.

14. Howell, F. Clark, "The Evolutionary Significance of Variation and Varieties of 'Neanderthal' Man," *Quarterly Review of Biology*, 32:4:330, pp. 334, 335.

15. Moody, Paul Amos, *Introduction to Evolution*, 2d ed. (Harper and Bros., 1962), p. 243.

16. Ashley Montagu, M. F., *Man: His First Million Years*, 2d ed. (Signet Science Library, 1962), p. 58.

17. Eiseley, Loren, 1957, *loc. cit.*, p. 328.

18. Andrews, Roy Chapman, *Meet Your Ancestors* (Viking Press, 1945, fifth printing, 1956), p. 73.

19. Ashley Montagu, M. F., *The Human Revolution* (World Pub. Co., 1965), p. 64.

CHAPTER VIII

SOME MISTAKES

Everyone makes mistakes. But God is different from us and does not make mistakes. Since we believe the Bible to be a revelation to us from God, we look with suspicion at utterences of men which clearly contradict Scripture.

Bernard Ramm is representative of a number of men who are not theologically liberal but who deride Bible-believers as "hyperorthodox," and at the same time are careful not to offend those who are theologically more liberal than they themselves profess to be. Dr. Ramm uses the instance of the Piltdown hoax to show how much more noble the scientists are than the less intelligent "hyperorthodox" Bible-believing Christians.[1] The idea is that the fundamentalists gloat over the disclosure that the Piltdown findings were a hoax and say that therefore the evolutionary approach to anthropology is not trustworthy. But Dr. Ramm knows that the Christian rejection of the evolutionary approach to anthropology is more basic than this. It was proper, of course, for the scientists to announce the discovery of the hoax, but it hardly seems necessary that we admire them so much for this that we consider it unfair to point out their lack of astuteness in failing to observe the signs of forgery in the first place.

Professor Ramm makes quite a point of the fact that the hoax was discovered by scientists and not by Bible-believing Christians. The implication here is shamefully unfair. The Piltdown remains were kept in a safe in the British Museum and no Bible-believing anti-evolutionist would have been permitted a glimpse at them. When Arthur Keith, the eminent British authority in this field, wished to examine the fossils he was permitted to see them for only twenty minutes, and was forced to work with plaster casts of the originals.[2]

L. S. B. Leakey, who is famous for his anthropological work in Africa, complains, "On several occasions in the past I tried to get permission to make a detailed study of the original Piltdown fossils, but on each occasion was only shown them for a few brief moments and not allowed to examine them properly, and was given a cast to work on."[3]

Finally, in addition to all of the various kinds of evidence which had been accumulated that the material was fraudulent, a series of tests was performed, which included seven chemical tests, before the Piltdown material was admitted to be a hoax.

An anti-evolutionist would not have had the slightest chance of being permitted to prove the remains a hoax.

From the beginning, and repeatedly, people who were not anti-evolutionists declared that the whole affair was a hoax, but their words were not heeded.

The scientists overlooked a large number of rather obvious clues, any one of which should have given them reason to consider the possibility of fraud. Although this does not necessarily mean that other finds are fraudulent, the Piltdown story does expose a great weakness in the objectivity of evolutionary scientists. It reveals that they can see a great deal of what they wish to see and can overlook a great deal of what they do not wish to see. In the Piltdown case the truth has been revealed; one cannot help wondering how much fantasy may be involved in the interpretations of other cases which cannot be checked.

NOTES

1. Ramm, Bernard, *The Christian View of Science and Scripture* (Wm. B. Eerdmans Pub. Co., 1955), p. 310 ff.

2. Weiner, S. J., *The Piltdown Hoax* (Oxford University Press, 1955), p. 121. Also: *Nature*, 92:2296:267, October 30, 1913, p. 267.

3. Leakey, L. S. B., *Adam's Ancestors*, 4th ed. (Harper and Bros., 1960), p. vi.

THE PILTDOWN HOAX

On the 18th of December, 1912, Charles Dawson, lawyer and amateur antiquarian, and Arthur Smith Woodward, Keeper of the Department of Geology and Paleontology at the British Museum, reported in the lecture room of the Geological Society the finding of human remains at Piltdown. The lecture room on this occasion was packed with interested people as it never had been before nor has been since.[1] Forty-one years later, on the 21st of November, 1953, it

was announced to the world that these findings at Piltdown constituted a hoax.

Several years before the announcement of the discovery Charles
Dawson had observed workmen repairing a road with flints. Inquiring of their source, he found that they were obtained from a small
pit not far away. The laborers at the pit told him they had seen no
fossils, and he urged them to keep a careful watch for anything that
might turn up. On a subsequent visit he was handed a piece of a
human skull.

A story developed which has been widely circulated even in
scientific works, which however cannot be traced to its source and
which seems to be contradictory to the facts. According to this story
the workmen found a skull intact and broke it to pieces, thinking it
was a "petrified coconut."

More pieces of skull were found, a portion of a jawbone with teeth,
a canine tooth, and quite an assortment of animal remains. One of
the fossils found was a leg bone of an elephant, artificially pointed
at one end. This was interpreted as the handiwork of some primitive
person, although it was later agreed that a fresh bone could not have
been cut and shaped in this way. About 1914 a French archaeologist
suggested that the bone had been gnawed by a giant beaver.[2] It now
seems that the bone must have been pointed by a steel implement
after it had been fossilized.

S. J. Weiner of Oxford University, who was most instrumental in
revealing the hoax, did not make a direct accusation as to the perpetrator, though his evidence points with strong suspicion at Charles
Dawson. Rooth Moore, a journalist who writes on scientific subjects,
and the editors of *Life* magazine, state as a matter of fact that Dawson was the guilty person.[3]

From the beginning there was a controversy as to whether the
jawbone belonged to the skull. Some scientists said that it did, while
others said that it could not because it looked too much like the jawbone of an ape. As it turned out when the hoax was discovered, the
reason the jaw looked so much like that of an ape was because it
really *was* the jaw of an ape. Meanwhile, some who contended that
the jaw and the skull belonged together said that the jaw was not
really ape-like if properly reconstructed![4]

Arthur Keith, the great anatomist and anthropologist, was one of
those who believed the jaw and skull belonged together, and he went
so far as to say of those who disagreed, "This mistake could never

have been made if those concerned had studied the comparative anatomy of anthropoid apes."[5] It turned out that he was wrong in this, but he belittled the technical knowledge of those who were right.

A decade later, in 1924, George G. MacCurdy of Yale University wrote, "It is asserted by a British group that important and hitherto overlooked features of the lower jaw are positively human, and that the teeth are not only human but fundamentally unlike those of the great apes."[6] One reason for believing that the jaw went with the skull was the fact that the tops of the teeth were worn down in a manner which seemed to be characteristic of humans and not of apes. But no one noticed that the teeth had been artificially ground down to look like human teeth. No one noticed the scratches left by the abrasive agent, which the careless perpetrator of the hoax did not polish away. No one noticed that the job of flattening the surfaces of the teeth was overdone and the surfaces were too flat to be realistic. No one noticed that the teeth were so flat on top that the edges were angular instead of rounded. No one even noticed that the job had been done so carelessly that the tops of the different teeth were flattened at different angles. Also, because of the crudeness of the operation, "the Piltdown cusps exhibit dentine quite flat and flush with surrounding enamel, a state of affairs explicable only by rapid artificial rubbing down of the surface."[7]

When Kenneth Oakley made his fluorine test he found that under the surface of a tooth it was pure white. It was later shown that the surface had been artificially colored to make the jaw look old, but the whiteness just below the surface did not cause suspicion before the hoax was exploded.

When the loose canine tooth was x-rayed it was found that it had been worn down so far that the pulp cavity was exposed, a phenomenon which does not happen as a result of natural wear, and someone had filled the pulp cavity with sand! Besides all this, it was an immature tooth which would not have had time to wear down a great deal. All of this was not only overlooked as evidence that something unnatural had happened, but it was rejected when it was pointed out. A dentist named Lyne pointed out that the canine tooth could not have been worn down naturally, but his "cogent arguments were brushed aside by Woodward."[8] Professor Woodward let himself be influenced by a Dr. Underwood who "spoke in violent disagreement with Mr. Lyne's contention of the immaturity of the canine and its paradoxical nature," and who declared that the wear of the canine was "indubitably natural." Lyne was correct and Underwood was wrong, and this should have been clear at the time to anyone who had a basic knowledge of the matter.

More skull fragments were found a few miles away in a pile of stones which a farmer had raked up to make a field more suitable for agriculture. As Weiner says, "The hoaxer was determined to have his second Piltdown man — the complete answer to silence the skeptics."[9] He made a number of blunders in arranging this second man, but the scientists did not notice. Two skull fragments were found, but they did not belong to the same skull. In fact, it now seems to be established that one of these fragments belongs to the skull found at Piltdown.[10] A single tooth was also found, and no one seemed to think it strange that a loose tooth would be raked up with stones in a field. This tooth also showed obvious signs of having been ground down artificially to make it look human.

Professor Weiner says that another find at the second site was a "rhinoceros tooth whose presence in that situation is quite impossible to accept."[11] Animal remains at Piltdown which did not belong with the rest were explained by assuming that a block of older material from a different age had fallen down from somewhere and had accidentally gotten mixed up with the others. It was too much to expect that the same kind of coincidence would happen again in a field several miles away, but no one seemed to be bothered about it at the time.

It did, however, seem to be too much of a coincidence that skull fragments and a tooth similar to those found at the first location would again be associated at the second location. Therefore some of the scientists who previously maintained that the skull and jaw found at Piltdown belonged to different individuals changed their minds and agreed that they must belong together.

The skull, which originally was considered very old indeed and which for some time was said to represent the oldest human being known to science, is now admitted to be modern. The only unusual thing about it is its thickness. Oakley and Weiner believe it to be a pathological specimen.[12] Weidenreich said that the thickness is within the range of normal modern skulls.[13]

Although the skull is admittedly modern now that the hoax has been exposed, in the early days of the discovery G. Elliot Smith, the eminent anatomist and specialist on the brain, said that the skull contained "the most primitive and ape-like brain yet discovered."[14] He particularly pointed out the "pronounced gorilla-like drooping of the temporal region," and he concluded that "this feeble development of the portion of the brain which is known to control the power of articulate speech is most significant."[15] Thus he asserted that the owner of this skull, which later was shown to be modern, was so primitive that it is questionable whether he was able to speak.

As an example of what the public hears, an article datelined September 28, 1931, and published in the *New York Times* and the *Los Angeles Times* reads in part as follows: "Drawing on a lifetime of research with fossils, Professor Osborn asserted the oldest man was not the Java man as hitherto supposed but the Piltdown man, who roamed the forests of Southern England in the dim prehistoric ages. The clues which revealed the story, he declared, [were] not the famous human fossils but the fossilized teeth of prehistoric elephants which primitive man hunted for food and ivory. Professor Osborn's belief was so clear cut and confident that it startled anthropologists of the British Association. . . . Not only did he state his conclusions as facts, but he read a table of dates, giving the approximate periods at which man's primitive ancestors lived. Thus he declared that the Piltdown man lived 1,000,000 years ago. . . . Professor Osborn has been working the last few weeks in the museum collections in Great Britain trying to prove his theory that man's geologic age could be established by the teeth of prehistoric monsters. He said today that specimens proved his theory perfectly."[16]

In 1960 L. S. B. Leakey, famous for his anthropological discoveries in Africa, published the fourth edition of his book *Adam's Ancestors*.[17] The book was originally written before the Piltdown material was exposed as a fraud, but this edition was published seven years after the hoax was disclosed. Dr. Leakey added more material to bring the book up-to-date, but left the original text unchanged. Thus we find in the same volume two different versions of the Piltdown affair. At one place he says, ". . . the jaw was that of a modern ape, while the skull was that of a modern type man. . . ."[18] At another place he says, "The famous Piltdown skull agrees with *Homo sapiens* [modern man] in this one respect [that the brow ridges are similar to ours], but differs markedly in others, and so is ruled out from the species."[19] Thus at one place he says that the skull is the type of modern man, and at another place in the same book he says that it differs so much from that of modern man that it cannot be considered to belong to the same species!

When Charles Dawson brought his pieces of skull to the British Museum, Arthur Woodward of the museum pronounced the cranial capacity to be of an amount which was suited to concepts of the supposed age and primitiveness of the specimen. Professor Elliot Smith agreed with him, but Professor Arthur Keith disagreed. Keith reconstructed the skull and estimated its size as somewhat above the cranial capacity of the modern living European. Although he later reduced his estimate somewhat, it was still above the average of the living European female (the Piltdown skull supposedly being female).

Concerning the difference of opinion between himself and Dr. Keith on the cranial capacity of this skull, Elliot Smith wrote: "I should say at the outset that any anatomist, working with the plaster casts but without reference to the actual fragments from which they were molded might solve the extraordinarily difficult problem of reconstruction of the cranium in the way Professor Keith has explained so plausibly. But the bones themselves present features which make such a solution altogether inadmissable."[20] That Professor Smith could make such a statement should seem incredible to those who think that scientists are all objective searchers for truth. G. Elliot Smith would not permit the eminent Professor Keith to study the original fossil pieces and made him work with plaster casts. In an effort to have his reconstruction accepted as superior to Keith's, he admitted that he had denied Keith use of the originals. But even at that, Keith's restoration was better than Smith's, as was later shown.

Although the outstanding scientists accepted the remains at face value, there were others who contended that the whole affair was fraudulent. Members of the Sussex Archaeological Society were skeptical from the start.[21]

A paleontologist at the Natural History Museum named A. S. Kennard believed it was a hoax and claimed he knew who did it. He died in 1948 (five years before the hoax was proved) without disclosing whom he thought was guilty.[22]

Two men named Major Marriott and Captain St. Berbe said in 1913 that "Dawson was salting the mine," but not being experts in paleontology and believing that the experts would soon find this out for themselves, they said nothing publicly.[23]

A bank clerk and amateur archaeologist named Harry Morris was a strong believer that the whole thing was a hoax perpetrated by Dawson. He was deceased when the hoax was exposed, but in his collection was found a flint from Piltdown which he had labeled:

"Stained by C. Dawson with intent to deceive." With it was a card on which he had written, "I challenge the S[outh] K[ensington] Museum [the British Museum] authorities to test the implements . . . which the imposter Dawson says were 'excavated from the pit!' "[23] He believed the canine tooth found at the pit by Pierre Teilhard de Chardin had been imported from France.[24] (Incidentally, even after the hoax had been exposed by numerous tests, Teilhard was not ready to accept it as other than genuine.)

Toward the end of 1915 Dawson became ill, and no fossils were found in 1916.

A pathetic conclusion to the whole affair is seen in Arthur Smith Woodward. After his retirement from the museum he went to live near the pit so he could continue his search for more fossils in an empty pit where there were no fossils to be found.

NOTES

1. Weiner, S. J., *The Piltdown Forgery* (Oxford University Press, 1955), p. 1.

2. Oakley, Kenneth P. and S. J. Weiner, "Piltdown Man," *American Scientist*, 43:4:573, October, 1955, p. 581.

3. Moore, Ruth, *et al.*, *Man*, Time Pub. Co., 1962, p. 133.

4. Weiner, S. J., *loc. cit.*, p. 24.

5. Keith, Arthur, "Darwin's Theory of Man's Descent as It Stands Today," *Science*, 66:1705:201, September 2, 1927, p. 204.

6. MacCurdy, George G., *Human Origins* (D. Appleton and Co., 1924), Vol. 1, p. 329.

7. Weiner, S. J., *loc. cit.*, p. 46.

8. *Ibid.*, pp. 32, 33.

9. *Ibid.*, p. 146.

10. *Ibid.*, p. 143.

11. *Ibid.*

12. Oakley, Kenneth P. and S. J. Weiner, *loc. cit.*, p. 583.

13. Andrews, Roy Chapman, *Meet Your Ancestors* (Viking Press, 1956), p. 123.

14. Appendix to article by Dawson and Woodward, *Quarterly Journal of the Geological Society of London*, Vol. 69, p. 147.

15. MacCurdy, George G., *loc. cit.*, p. 325.

16. *The Los Angeles Times*, September 29, 1931, reprinted from *The New York Times*.

17. Leakey, L. S. B., *Adam's Ancestors* (Harper and Bros., 1960).

18. *Ibid.*, p. v.

19. *Ibid.*, p. 165.

20. Smith, G. Elliot, "The Piltdown Skull and Brain Cast," *Nature*,

92:2296:267, October 30, 1913, p. 267. See also *Nature*, 92:2298:318,
November 13, 1913, p. 318.
21. Weiner, S. J., *loc cit.*, p. 142.
22. *Ibid.*, pp. 162, 168.
23. *Ibid.*, p. 156, 157.
24. *Ibid.*, p. 158.
25. *Ibid.*, p. 140.

THE NEBRASKA MAN

On March 14, 1922, Henry Fairfield Osborn, Director of the American Museum of Natural History in New York City, received a package which contained a single tooth. The same day he wrote to the sender, a consulting geologist named Harold Cook, "The instant your package arrived I sat down with the tooth, in my window, and said to myself: 'It looks one hundred percent anthropoid'. . . . it looks to me as if the first anthropoid ape of America has been found."[1] Writing to Mr. Cook again eight days later he said, "The animal is certainly a new genus of anthropoid ape. . . ."[2]

Professor Osborn named it *Hesperopithecus haroldcookii*, which means, Harold Cook's ape of the west, referring to the western hemisphere, where no apes had been found previously.

Dr. William K. Gregory and Dr. Milo Hellman, both of the American Museum of Natural History and both specialists in teeth, made a careful study of the specimen and concluded that it represented a form of life which was closer to man than to apes. Although Professor Osborn had said that it was "certainly a new genus of anthropoid ape," he changed his mind and agreed with Gregory and Hellman, saying that, "it resembles the human type more closely than it does any known anthropoid ape. . . ."[3]

As the tooth had been found in Nebraska, *Hesperopithecus* became known as the Nebraska man.

About a month after the publication of the statement by Gregory and Hellman that the tooth showed closer affinities to man than to apes, the noted anatomist G. Elliot Smith published a short article in which he said that this was the oldest of all human remains known to science and that its ancestors wandered to America from Asia or Africa. He commented that this might seem like a lot to conclude from a single tooth, but justified it by saying, "But the specimen was discovered by a geologist of wide experience, and its horizon has been satisfactorily established. Moreover the determination of its affinities and its identification as one of the higher primates closely akin to the Ape-Man of Java, *Pithecanthropus,* have been made by the most competent authorities on the specific characters of fossilized mammalian teeth . . . who not only have a wider experience of such material than any other paleontologists, but also men with exact knowledge and sound judgment. One can therefore place implicit trust in their claim that the tooth, found in the Pliocene beds of Nebraska, is really that of a primitive member of the human family."[4] He wrote essentially the same thing in a book published in 1924.[5]

A year and a half after Gregory and Hellman published the paper previously mentioned they published another in which they said they could not be sure whether the tooth was more ape-like or more human, but that now Gregory favored the view that it was more ape-like while Hellman continued to believe that it was more human.[6]

The American Museum of Natural History sent men to the field to look for more teeth and other evidence of the Nebraska man, and while this search was in progress, H. H. Wilder, Professor of Zoology at Smith College, published a book in which he said that the original owner of the tooth seems to have been halfway between the Java man, *Pithecanthropus* (now called *Homo erectus*), and the Neanderthal type of man.[7]

Meanwhile an unsympathetic property owner chased the museum men from the site of the discovery of the tooth. They crossed the fence to the property of a more understanding rancher and continued their search there. Here Mr. Albert Thompson, chief field man of the expedition, made what seemed to be a very important discovery. "In undisturbed, original deposits, associated with the wonderful array of Pliocene fossil animal life . . . he found evidence of the first culture known to have been developed by the human race, and the oldest trace of humanity, by hundreds of thousands of years! . . . Some of the bones were drilled; many are shaped and sharpened in various forms; while others must have been used for pounding. Many show evidence of artificial abrasion of different types."[8] It looked as if *Hesperopithecus* was rather handy with tools.

The men from the museum also found more of the fossil material for which they were looking, and it turned out that the tooth which had caused such a sensation was the tooth of an animal which had previously been named *Prosthennops.* This was very embarrassing, because *Prosthennops* was a peccary, which is a type of pig![9]

(And nothing more was said about the human artifacts.)

It is fortunate that someone had already given this animal a scientific name, for otherwise, by the rules of scientific nomenclature, there would be an extinct species of pig forever bearing the name: "Harold Cook's ape of the west."

NOTES

1. Osborn, Henry Fairfield, "*Hesperopithecus,* the First Anthropoid Primate Found in America," *Science,* 60:1427:463, May 5, 1922.

2. *Ibid.,* p. 464. Also, same author, same title, *American Museum Noviates,* #37, 1922, p. 2.

3. *Ibid.,* p. 464.

4. Smith, G. Elliot, "The Ape-Man of the Western World," *The Illustrated London News,* June 24, 1922, p. 944.

5. Smith, G. Elliot, *The Evolution of Man* (Oxford University Press, 1924), pp. 7 and 9.

6. *Bulletin of the American Museum of Natural History,* December 4, 1923, p. 580.

7. Wilder, H. H., *The Predigree of the Human Race* (Henry Holt and Co., 1926), pp. 156, 157.

8. Cook, Harold J., "New Trails of American Man," *Scientific American,* August, 1927, p. 114.

9. Gregory, William K., "Hesperopithecus Apparently Not an Ape nor a Man," *Science,* 66:1720:579, December 16, 1927.

Chapter IX

SOCIAL DARWINISM

The application of the principle of "survival of the fittest" to human affairs came to be known as Social Darwinism. It is generally believed that Darwin did not condone the extrapolation of his natural selection theory into social relationships, but the fact is that he himself taught that human evolution proceeded through warfare and struggle between isolated clans.[1]

Robert E. D. Clark says that "Darwin often said quite plainly that it was wrong to ameliorate the conditions of the poor, since to do so would hinder the evolutionary struggle for existence."[2]

In a letter to H. Thiel in 1869, Darwin wrote: "You will really believe how much interested I am in observing that you apply to moral and social questions analagous views to those which I have used in regard to the modification of species. It did not occur to me formerly that my views could be extended to such widely different and most important subjects."[3]

Wallbank and Taylor in their textbook *Civilization Past and Present* say that Darwin's theory of the survival of the fittest "became a vogue that swept western thought in the late nineteenth century. It also became a convenient doctrine for justifying various economic and political theories."[4]

Unscrupulous industrialists took advantage of Darwin's theory to condone their unethical practices. When they put others out of business they declared that it was just another case of survival of the fittest.

The railroad magnate James J. Hill, manipulating to get more railways under his control, said that "the fortunes of railroad companies are determined by the law of the survival of the fittest."[5]

In his autobiography, Andrew Carnegie, who made his fortune in steel, describes his conversion to evolution on reading Darwin and Spencer as follows: "I remember that light came as in a flood and

350

all was clear. Not only had I got rid of theology and the supernatural, but I had found the truth of evolution. 'All is well since all grows better,' became my motto, my true source of comfort. Man was not created with an instinct for his own degradation, but from the lower he had risen to the higher forms. Nor is there any conceivable end to his march to perfection. His face is turned to the light; he stands in the sun and looks upward."[6]

John D. Rockefeller declared to a Sunday school class: "The growth of a large business is merely a survival of the fittest. . . . This is not an evil tendency in business. It is merely the working out of a law of nature and a law of God."[7]

Robert E. D. Clark comments, "Evolution, in short, gave the doer of evil a respite from his conscience. The most unscrupulous behavior towards a competitor could now be rationalized; evil could be called good."[8]

Evolution soothed the consciences of not only the big industrialists in their dealings with competitors, it also aided those who took advantage of the poor. Efforts to improve the living and working conditions of the poor and of women and children were opposed by the ruling class on the grounds that this would be contrary to the principle of evolution, for the prosperity of the wealthy and the miserable condition of the destitute was just the working out of the survival of the fittest.

Darwinism also offered a basis for acts which have resulted in racial strife. Wallbank and Taylor say: "The pseudo-scientific application of biological theory to politics . . . constituted possibly the most perverted form of social Darwinism. . . . It led to racism and anti-semitism and was used to show that only 'superior' nationalities and races were fit to survive. Thus, among the English-speaking peoples were to be found the champions of the 'white man's burden,' an imperial mission carried out by Anglo-Saxons. . . . Similarly, the Russians preached the doctrine of Pan-Slavism and the Germans that of pan-Germanism."[9]

Darwin himself, in the sixth chapter of his *Descent of Man*, postulated that the time would come when the white peoples would have destroyed the black. He also thought that the anthropoid apes would become extinct. He believed that when these two eventualities had occurred the evidence of evolution among living creatures would not be as strong as previously.

The Darwinian theory of evolution has also been used by the

militarists to glorify war. They said that the outcome of a war is determined by the principle of the survival of the fittest.

Heinrich von Treitsche, the Prussian militarist, said, "The grandeur of war lies in the utter annihilation of puny man in the great conception of the State, and it brings out the full significance of the sacrifice of fellow countrymen for one another. In war the chaff is winnowed from the wheat."[10]

The German philosopher Friedrich Nietzsche, who held Christianity in contempt, said, "You say, 'A good cause sanctifies war,' but I say, 'A good war sanctifies every cause.'"[11] Wallbank and Taylor comment, "Likewise he ridiculed democracy and socialism for protecting the worthless and weak and hindering the strong. Social Darwinism and the antidemocratic cult of naked power, as preached by advocates like Nietzsche, were laying the foundations of fascism, which would one day plunge the world into the most terrible convulsion in its history."[12]

Friederich von Bernhardi was a German soldier who retired in 1909 and wrote an inflammatory book, *Germany and the Next War*, which extolled militarism. Of this book Ashley Montagu the anthropologist says, "'War,' declared Bernhardi, 'is a biological necessity;' it 'is as necessary as the struggle of the elements of Nature;' it 'gives a biologically just decision, since its decisions rest on the very nature of things.' 'The whole idea of arbitration represents a presumptuous encroachment on the natural laws of development,' for 'what is right is decided by the arbitration of war.' In proof thereof such notions of Darwin's as 'The Struggle for Existance,' 'Natural Selection,' and the 'Survival of the Fittest' are invoked with sententiousness quite military both in logic and in sense. According to Bernhardi, it is plainly evident to anyone who makes a study of plant and animal life that 'war is a universal law of nature.' This declaration and fortification of Germany's will to war — for it had the highest official sanction and approval — was published in 1911. Three years later the greatest holocaust the world had ever known was launched. . . ."[13]

Benito Mussolini, who brought fascism to Italy, was strengthened in his belief that violence is basic to social transformation by the philosophy of Nietzsche.[14] Robert E. D. Clark says that "Mussolini's attitude was completely dominated by evolution. In public utterances he repeatedly used the Darwinian catchwords while he mocked at perpetual peace, lest it should hinder the evolutionary process."[15]

Likewise Adolph Hitler in Germany based his fascism on evolutionary theory. This is evident from his speeches and his book *Mein Kampf*. R. E. D. Clark has pointed out that in the large number of books which have appeared describing every phase of the Hitler regime, there is hardly a mention of the evolution of Charles Darwin. He interprets this to mean that the authors refrain from mentioning evolution in this context because they fear they might be considered to be anti-evolutionary.[16]

Friederich Engels, one of the founders of Communism, wrote to Karl Marx, December 12, 1859, "Darwin, whom I am just now reading, is splendid."[17] Karl Marx wrote to Freiderich Engels, December 9, 1860, "Although it is developed in the crude English style, this is the book which contains the basis in natural history for our views."[18] Again Marx wrote to Engels, January 16, 1861, "Darwin's book is very important and serves me as a basis in natural selection for the class struggle in history . . . not only is it a death blow dealt here for the first time to 'Teleology' in the natural sciences but their rational meaning is emphatically explained."[19]

Marx wished to dedicate to Darwin his book *Das Capital*, but Darwin declined the offer.

E. Yaroslavsky, a friend of Joseph Stalin, wrote a book on the life of Stalin. This book was published in Moscow by the Communists while Stalin was in power. The author says, "At a very early age, while still a pupil in the ecclesiastical school, Comrade Stalin developed a critical mind and revolutionary sentiments. He began to read Darwin and became an atheist."[20]

Yaroslavsky quotes another boyhood friend of Stalin, who relates the following:

"I began to speak of God. Joseph heard me out, and after a moment's silence said:

" 'You know, they are fooling us, there is no God. . . .'

"I was astonished at these words. I had never heard anything like it before.

" 'How can you say such things, Soso [a name for Stalin]?' I exclaimed.

" 'I'll lend you a book to read; it will show you that the world and all living things are quite different from what you imagine, and all this talk about God is sheer nonsense,' Joseph said.

" 'What book is that?' I inquired.

" 'Darwin. You must read it,' Joseph impressed on me."[21]

But as Conway Zirkle, Professor of Botany at the University of

Pennsylvania, says, "The Marxists do not accept or reject biological theories in accordance with objective evidence, but by how well they fit Communist doctrine. Darwinism does not altogether fit."[22]

T. D. Lysenko, whose ideas supplanted the science of genetics in Russia, said in 1948, "Darwin was unable to free himself from the theoretical mistakes which he committed. These errors were discovered and pointed out by the Marxist classicists."[23]

There are a few evolutionists who have been embarrassed by the social implications of evolution and who have stressed cooperation (instead of struggle) as a factor in evolution. Kropotkin and Allee may be cited here.[24] Others have said that the theory of evolution is improperly applied when it is used to defend militarism and social abuses.

Of course the application of Darwinian survival of the fittest to human affairs by unscrupulous men has no direct bearing on the question of whether human beings and other creatures evolved from simple forms of life. But these abuses have been sanctioned and abetted with evolution as an excuse, and if evolution is not true it seems all the more tragic.

NOTES

1. There is evidence of this in various places, for example the disagreement between Darwin and Wallace on the evolution of the human brain. See also R. E. D. Clark, *Darwin: Before and After*, and Arthur Kieth, *Essays on Evolution*.

2. Clark, Robert E. D., *Darwin: Before and After* (Poternoster Press, 1958), p. 120.

3. Darwin, Francis, Editor, *The Life and Letters of Charles Darwin* (D. Appleton and Co., 1896), Vol. 2, p. 294.

4. Wallbank, T. Walter and Alastair M. Taylor, *Civilization Past and Present*, 4th ed. (Scott, Foresman and Co., 1961), Vol. 2, p. 361.

5. Hofstadter, Richard, *Social Darwinism and American Thought*, Rev. ed. (Beacon Press, 1955), pp. 31, 45.

6. *Ibid.*, p. 45.

7. *Ibid.*

8. Clark, R. E. D., *loc. cit.*, p. 106.

9. Wallbank, T. W. and A. M. Taylor, *loc. cit.*, p. 362.

10. *Ibid.*, p. 362. It is quoted from: von Trietsche, H. G., *Politics*, translated by B. Dugdale and T. de Bille (Constable and Co.), Vol. 1, pp. 66, 67.

11. *Ibid.*, p. 362.

12. *Ibid.*, p. 363.

13. Ashley Montagu, M. F., *Man in Process* (World Pub. Co., 1961), pp. 76, 77.

14. *The Encyclopedia Britannica*, Mussolini. 16:27, 1957.

15. Clark, R. E. D., *loc. cit.*, p. 115.

16. *Ibid.*, p. 117.

17. Zirkle, Conway, *Evolution, Marxian Biology, and the Social Scene* (University of Pennsylvania Press, 1959), p. 85.

18. *Ibid.*, p. 86.

19. *Ibid.*

20. Yaroslavsky, E., *Landmarks in the Life of Stalin* (Foreign Languages Publishing House, Moscow, 1940), p. 8.

21. *Ibid.*, pp. 8, 9.

22. Zirkle, Conway, *loc. cit.*, p. 24.

23. *Ibid.*, p. 24.

24. Kropotkin, Peter, *Mutual Aid* (W. Heinemann, 1902), Allee., W. C., *Cooperation Among Animals,* with Human Implications (Schulman, 1951).

CHAPTER X

THE FUTURE

Some people ask: If evolution is true, why has it stopped? The answer of the evolutionists is that it has *not* stopped.[1] They say it goes on at a rate which is too slow to be apparent to us.

In contrast to this, the Bible says that God created and then rested from the work of creation. Creation is a finished work. Furthermore, since man was created in the image of God, there is no reason to expect a further evolution of man to something higher.

Kettlewell's moths, already discussed, are considered by the evolutionists as a terrific example of evolution going on.

Another frequently-mentioned example of evolution going on is the fact that some strains of flies have become resistant to DDT. When DDT is applied, the more susceptible flies succumb to it, while some of the more resistant ones survive. Thus the ones which live to produce the next generation are the ones best able to tolerate DDT, and they tend to produce more flies of the same type. After a number of generations of this, a resistant strain of flies has been produced.

The same sort of thing happened in the California citrus groves, where the concentrations of the spray used to combat the scale insects had to be increased successively, until finally all practical concentrations were ineffective and a different kind of means of control had to be sought.

By treating certain bacteria with a germicide in doses which permit some of them to survive, strains of bacteria have developed which *require* for their survival the very thing which had been lethal to their kind some generations previously.

It is said that in the early 1920's Professor Herbert Spencer Jennings of the Johns Hopkins University "was the first actually to see and control the process of evolution among living things."[2] What he did was to select for size and other differences among the progeny of a single protozoan named *Difflugia corona*. These animals reproduce by simply dividing in half, so a colony of any size can be produced by allowing the descendants of a single individual to multiply. All of them are genetically identical, except as genetic changes occur due to mutation. As Professor Jennings selected the largest and the smallest specimens, and as he selected some other contrasting characteristics, he eventually obtained different colonies characterized by these contrasting characteristics. The range of variation in one group did not overlap the range of variation in another group.

In a book called *Creation by Evolution*, Frances Mason wrote enthusiastically about this work by Dr. Jennings, using italics: "Dr. Jennings is able to follow *evolution* not as a theory but as *a thing that is actually taking place*."[3] Discussing this research in the same book, Professor Jennings defines *creation* in such a way that he can set up a straw man to knock down and take a slap at creation at the same time. He said: "Remember that there are two opposite doctrines. One holds that the constitution of organisms is permanent; that they were created as they are and do not change. The other, the doctrine of evolution, holds that the hereditary constitution slowly changes as generations pass; that a single race differentiates in the course of time into diverse ones; that from one stock many are produced. The critical observations that have been made on these minute living organisms through the passage of generations substantiates this theory; they do change and differentiate into diverse races as generations pass. The facts observed are what the doctrine of evolution demands, not what the opposite theory demands."[4]

All of these instances are considered excellent examples of evolution going on, but they leave much to be desired for those who wish to know how a fish became an elephant or how a tree shrew became a human being. All of these are cases involving mutations and they are really not comparable to the kinds of changes which would have to take place if real evolution occurs.

A college textbook published in 1947 makes a very strange statement. The authors, both full professors, say, "For instance, we cannot expect to see a cat develop bat-like wings and fly."[5] The reason for this, they say, is that such a change would take too long for anyone to observe. But if an anti-evolutionist made a statement like this, he would be denounced as incompetent to write in this field. If a cat developed bat-like wings, no matter how long it took, that would not be evolution — it would be a miracle. Anyone who suggested that cats could ever develop wings would be told that cats are too specialized for such a thing to occur, and that no evolutionist would ever dream of such a thing happening.

Popular representations of the man of the future show him with a large head and little or no hair, a small face and lower jaw, and spindly legs. This is technically known as *foetilization*. It represents a return of the adult form to that of the foetus or a juvenile condition. The young, and particularly before birth, have large heads and small faces in proportion to the rest of the body.

In this connection it may be noted that we resemble immature apes more than we do adult apes. The pictures we see of apes that look rather cute and seem so human in some ways are young chimpanzees. It is very rarely that we see the picture of an adult male chimpanzee. The adults do not look very much like humans. The ape we see pictured most frequently as an adult is the gorilla, apparently because people like to regard his rather ferocious aspect. Some biologists believe that we evolved from a line of primates which did its evolving during the immature stages, so we are more like the young than like the adult types.

The trouble with the popular concept of the man of the future is that he has already lived in the past, and he has died out. Professor Loren Eiseley of the University of Pennsylvania says, "There's just one thing we haven't quite dared to mention. It's this, and you won't believe it. It's all happened already. Back there in the past, ten thousand years ago. The man of the future, with the big brain, the small teeth."[6] He continues, "His brain was bigger than your brain. His face was straight and small, almost a child's face. He was the end evolutionary product in a direction quite similar to the one anthropologists tell is the road down which we are traveling." He says that scientists find the remains of these people widespread in layers of the ground in which they expected to find human remains of a primitive type.

Dr. Drennan of the University of Capetown says of this type, which is known as Boskopf: "It appears ultra modern in many of its features, surpassing the European in almost every direction. That is to say, it is less simian [that is, less ape-like and hence more advanced] than any modern skull."[7]

College textbooks do not discuss this. Some anthropologists believe that the Boskopf people have some living descendants and that they are the Bushmen.

The present emphasis on the evolutionary future of man lies in a different direction. The emphasis now is on improving mankind genetically rather than on producing some advanced physical type.

Hermann J. Muller of Indiana University was a leader of those who are recommending that banks be established for the storage of the reproductive cells of outstanding people. When parents have had a few children of their own they may be encouraged to take advantage of such a bank and have a child that has one parent (deceased at least twenty years according to the present recommendation) who was an outstanding musician, mathematician, or athlete. This is possible now, and Professor Muller suggested that it is time to consider and settle ethical and emotional problems involved.

With the work now being done on the ultimate structure of the chromosomes, it is anticipated that at some time in the forseeable future a way will be found to "crack the genetic code" and to manipulate the hereditary factors. This is looked upon as human beings definitely directing their own evolution.

If and when this can be done, disadvantageous inherited characteristics may be altered for the better, but already men are planning such diabolical uses of these advanced techniques as duplicating a person an indefinite number of times and producing human robots. (What legal status would such beings have? There is no limit of vileness to which a depraved dictator would go in the use of such creatures.)

A college textbook in general biology published in 1963 ends with the sentence: "The possibility of the biological improvement of our own species through a wise application of the principles of evolution makes one hopeful of the future progress and happiness of mankind."[8]

However, on the contrary, it seems unbelievable that man, who can perform such marvellous feats as photographing from a rocket a pre-arranged portion of Mars and land spacecraft at pinpointed locations on the moon, is so amazingly stupid when it comes to preserving his hard-earned liberties. If it were not for the prophecies of the Scriptures, how would these things make sense?

The optimistic picture painted by the evolutionists is pleasant but not realistic. Actually the work of the evolutionists will be largely responsible for the perilous times which are ahead, for evolution has been a large factor in bringing about the widespread godless philosophy which is characteristic of our time and which will become worse.

The Bible says, "This know also, that in the last days perilous times shall come. For men shall be lovers of their own selves, covetous, boasters, proud, blasphemers, disobedient to parents, unthankful, unholy, without natural affection, trucebreakers, false accusers, incontinent, fierce, despisers of those that are good, traitors, heady, highminded, lovers of pleasures more than lovers of God. . ." (2 Tim. 3:1-4).

But for Christians the future is bright. They are told, "When these things begin to come to pass, then look up, and lift up your heads, for your redemption draws nigh" (Luke 21:28).

NOTES

1. Some evolutionists say that evolution has essentially stopped in some areas, with the potentiality of commencing again if and when environmental conditions change.

2. Anonymous, *The Johns Hopkins Magazine*, 9:4:5, January, 1958.

3. Mason, Francis, Editor, *Creation by Evolution* (Macmillan, 1928), p. 32.

4. *Ibid.,* p. 32.

5. Strausbaug, Perry D. and Bernal R. Weimer, *General Biology*, 2d ed, 1947), p. 626.

6. Eiseley, Loren, *The Immense Journey* (Random House, 1957), p. 228 *et seq.*

7. Quoted by Professor Eiseley, *loc. cit.*

8. Stauffer, Andrew, Editor, *General Biology* (D. Van Nostrand, 1963), p. 500.

Chapter XI

THE POSITIVE APPROACH

It has been said by Bernard Ramm and others that anti-evolutionists must have a positive approach to the problem, because attacks upon the claims of the evolutionists do not constitute an adequate answer. This raises such questions as: What is a positive approach to the problem? What kind of positive approach would impress the evolutionists? Would any approach, no matter how adequate, be seriously considered by those who have accepted an evolutionary philosophy?

We have already said that both the acceptance of evolution and the rejection of evolution involve a certain amount of faith. If it were a matter of proof, the question would have been settled and there would no longer be a need to discuss it.

One kind of positive approach might be through the verification of such things as physical evidence of a relatively young earth, human footprints associated with dinosaur tracks, ancient pictographs showing dinosaurs, pollen grains in strata below the Cambrian deposits, and proof that no friction occurred between strata where thrust faulting is supposed to have taken place. Scientists will try to disqualify all evidence of such types. For example, when "impossible" fossil remains were found associated with the Piltdown skull and jaw, the scientists had an explanation. When an impossible association of fossils was found again in a field some distance away, the fact was disregarded.

J. C. Fentress of the University of Rochester made an interesting observation about voles, which are something like mice. He found that those which live in the open fields run for cover when frightened, while those which live in the woodland "freeze," or remain motionless. He reported this to his colleagues, but he intentionally *reversed* the facts, saying that the ones in the woodland run for cover while those in the fields "freeze." Evolutionists can practically always find an evolutionary explanation for everything and "These zoologists were able to give very elaborate and satisfactory explanations for this false data by using conventional ideas about selection theory."[1]

The present prestige of evolutionary philosophy and the ingenuity of the evolutionists to find plausible "explanations" makes it difficult to use effectively a positive approach in combatting evolution.

There is a well-known statement to the effect that if a million monkeys struck the keys of a million typewriters for a million years, they might by chance type a copy of a Shakesperian play. According to one version, the monkeys might type all of Shakespeare's works. Another version postulates that they might type all of the books found in the British Museum. The point of all this is to show by analogy that if evolution is given enough time it might be able to produce through a process which involves chance all known forms of life starting from lifeless material.

If we assume some facts about the typing ability of monkeys we can treat these facts mathematically[2] and see how convincing the analogy really is. Actually monkeys would soon tire of typing and would pursue more pleasing simian sports while the typewriters stood idle through most of the million years. If we assume, therefore, for the sake of the problem that these primates work diligently and find that they still are unable to produce anything of literary merit, the analogy will be shown to have no value. Indeed, the more extreme or absurd the assumptions we make favorable to their success, the more thoroughly the analogy will be discredited if the monkeys fail.

Instead of giving them standard typewriters let us give the monkeys simplified machines with only capital letters, seven punctuation marks, and a spacing key. Let us assume that each of the million monkeys types continuously twenty-four hours a day at the speed which the world's champion human typist was able to maintain for a few minutes — about twelve and a half keys per second. The only other assumption is that the monkeys type purely by chance and are as likely to strike any key as any other key.

To make their task simple, let us not inquire how long it would be expected to take them to type a whole Shakesperian play, but just the first line of Hamlet:

BER: WHO'S THERE?

The answer is that if this experiment were repeated a number of times it would be expected to take them on the average 284,000,000,-000 years.

To type the first verse of Genesis (or anything else of comparable length) would take them much longer.

IN THE BEGINNING GOD CREATED THE HEAVEN AND THE EARTH

The length of time it would be expected to require for them to type this is quite beyond our comprehension, but an illustration will help. Think of a large mountain which is solid rock. Once a year a bird comes and rubs its beak on the mountain, wearing away an amount equivalent to the finest grain of sand (about .0025 inch in diameter). At this rate of erosion the mountain would disappear very slowly, but when completely gone the monkeys would still just be warming up.

Think of a rock not the size of a mountain, but a rock larger than the whole earth. Try to think of a rock so large that if the earth were at its center its surface would touch the nearest star. This star is so far away that light from it takes more than four years to get here, traveling 186,000 miles every second. If a bird came once every million years and removed an amount equivalent to the finest grain of sand, four such rocks would be worn away before the champion super simians would be expected to type Genesis 1:1.

Of course this is quite fantastic, but it is evident that a million monkeys would never type a Shakesperian play in a million years. Evolutionists believe they are dealing with hundreds of millions of years and that almost anything could happen in this much time. However, some mathematicians have disagreed with this, using data furnished them by the evolutionists.[3]

Some outstanding evolutionists say that it is not correct to speak of evolution by chance alone because this fails to take into account the selective action of Darwin's natural selection principle. (This has already been discussed in the section on the mechanism of evolution.) A biologist at San Francisco State College takes this up and makes another analogy for those who are bothered about the monkey-and-the-typewriter analogy. He says a monkey *could* write a book by spilling type if an intelligent agent selects suitable combinations of repeatedly spilled type.[4] But in such a case the intelligent agent must have in mind a theme for the book and reject words which are not applicable. Thus the monkey is really not the author of the book. The author is the intelligent agent, who is hampered in his work because he has to wait for the monkey to produce the words he needs.

The biologist also makes another analogy which has to do with the order of shuffled cards, but this is irrelevant, because no matter how cards are shuffled they *must* be in *some* order, but there is no reason why chance aided by natural selection has to produce *any* kind of animal or plant.

Another kind of positive approach is to show that the Bible is historically reliable where events can be checked with evidence from other sources. A handicap here is the fact that human nature is such that attacks upon the historical accuracy of the Bible are well publicized, while corrections of these accusations are not. For example, there was a time when much was made of the charge that the Biblical account of the Hittites was purely fictitious, for there never had been such a people. Now the *Encyclopedia Britannica* contains some ten pages of text about the Hittites, but the general public is not interested and for the most part is unaware of this important correction of an attack upon Scripture.

Another evidence of the authority of the Biblical account of creation is miracles. Today many people utterly refuse to consider even the possibility of miracles. But this is not surprising, because miracles did not impress even the hard-hearted people who witnessed them directly. When the Lord raised to life Lazarus of Bethany in the presence of a large crowd of people, though he had been dead four days, the chief priests tried to kill Lazarus because as a result of the miracle some people had come to believe on Jesus as the Christ (John 12:10, 11). When Peter and John instantaneously healed a man who had been born a cripple, the religious leaders said, "That indeed a notable miracle has been done by them is manifest to all them that dwell in Jerusalem, and we cannot deny it" (Acts 4:16). Nevertheless they did all they could to stop the disciples in ministering the gospel. When the Israelites left Egypt and traveled through the wilderness toward the promised land, they witnessed a truly impressive number of outstanding miracles, yet even while Moses was on the mountain talking to God in their behalf, they made a calf of gold and worshipped that!

No, it is evident that miracles will not do as a positive approach to impress those who are influenced by the evidences of the evolutionists.

Another evidence of Scriptural authority is prophecy. The sign of a prophet of God is that all of his prophecies come to pass (Deut. 18:22). All of the Biblical prophecies have come to pass — many in a most remarkable way — except those which are still to be fulfilled in the future. Some of them have been fulfilled in a way so marvellous that the critics declare they were written after the events, and so represent history instead of prophecy. (See for example Isa. 44:28 and Dan. 11:2-35.)

No critic dares to say that the prophecies of the Old Testament about Christ were written after the time of the Lord Jesus. Some people have compiled over a hundred prophecies about Christ in the Old Testament which were fulfilled. This is a truly impressive credential. To illustrate the significance of this we may make one assumption and if this assumption is accepted, the rest follows. Although the probability of some of these prophecies being fulfilled by chance seems small, we will assume that from a natural standpoint each had an equal chance of being fulfilled or not being fulfilled. On this basis, the probability of ninety-two prophecies being fulfilled in an imposter is equivalent to the chance of a blindfolded person picking one colored bean from a mass of white beans the size of the earth. For ninety-three prophecies it would be like picking one bean from a mass of beans twice the size of the earth. For ninety-four the mass would be four times the size of the earth. Etc. This evidence has been available for nearly two thousand years, but it has impressed relatively few people.

Some people are impressed with what seems to be remarkable predictions by modern spiritists and the like. But these people also make mistakes. Some of these modern prognosticators may be shrewd guessers and others may actually be under the influence of diabolical powers (compare Deut. 13:1-5). There is no comparison between the prophecies of these people and the Biblical prophets inspired by God.

But people who accept the evidences of the evolutionists will not be influenced by the evidences of fulfilled prophecy of Scripture.

We have discussed various positive approaches to the problem of evolution, but none is adequate to convince a person who is reluctant to give up his belief in evolutionary philosophy. After all of this lengthy preliminary, let us present the one and only positive approach which really is effective. This is the preaching of the gospel. When a person is converted and accepts Jesus Christ as his Savior and Lord, evolutionary problems fade away. It is not a matter of refusing to examine facts, as some charge. It is a matter of substituting one faith for another.

NOTES

1. "R. B.," "Heresy in the Halls of Biology," *Research,* 2:11:59, November, 1967, p. 60.

2. For the basic formula see: William Feller, *An Introduction to Probability Theory and Its Implications* (Wiley, 1950), Vol. 1, p. 266.

3. Moorehead, Paul S., Editor, *Mathematical Challenges to the Neo-Darwinian Interpretation of Evolution* (The Wistar Institute Press, 1967). See also "R. B.," *loc. cit.,* p. 59.

4. Tomlinson, Jack, "Poker, Chance, and Evolution," *Turtox News,* 44: 9:198, September, 1966.

ADDENDUM

One of the most basic problems for the evolutionist is time. It is evident that if evolution really did occur and that this is the way living things came about, a very great deal of time is required. Astronomer Fred Whipple has said that according to the scientists the "age" of the earth has on the average doubled every fifteen years for the past three centuries.[1] But since the first printing of *Evolution and Christian Faith* more and more evidences for a shorter age of the earth have been accumulating. Many of these are based upon uniformitarian presuppositions, which in turn are basic to evolutionary theory.

Since the half-life of carbon-14 is relatively short, it was at first assumed that carbon-14 in the atmosphere had come to equilibrium long ago. But we now know that this is not so. Considering the extent of inequilibrium, an age for the earth's atmosphere of less than 10,000 years is indicated.[2]

As previously noted, the amount of carbon-14 in different things which are contemporaneous may vary considerably. Dr. Melvin Cook states that "a living mollusc is sometimes found deficient in carbon-14 to such an extent *as to appear* to have been dead as long as 3,000 years!"[3]

Admittedly the carbon-14 method does not cover a great deal of time attributed to evolutionary progression. For a longer period of time the potassium-argon method is employed where applicable. The two should not contradict each other, but mammalian bones from Leakey's "Bed-V" in the Olduvai Gorge tested as 10,100 years old by the carbon-14 method, while similar findings in the same locality tested as nearly 2,000,000 years old by the potassium-argon method.[4]

Coal, petroleum, and natural gas are said by evolutionists to have an age around 100,000,000 years, far beyond the capability of carbon-14 dating. But Dr. Robert L. Whitelaw, Professor of Nuclear and Mechanical Engineering at Virginia Polytechnical Institute, points out that when tested by the carbon-14 method they show an age of less than 50,000 years. In fact, out of more than 15,000 carbon-14 tests published in scientific journals, only three were of materials undatable by this method, while many more should have been undatable than datable.[5]

Dr. Whitelaw believes all these dates need to be corrected and when this is done they are much less. It is interesting to note that when he applies his correction and arranges in order the dates published in the scientific journals, there is a sudden and drastic decrease in the number of living things about 5,000 years ago, followed by an increase during the succeeding years. This appears to be another evidence of the flood.

Basalts in the ocean from a rift zone of the Kilauea volcano in the Hawaiian Islands were tested by the potassium-argon method. The scientists making the test believe the material is less than 200 years old and may be much more recent. Samples from the 1400 foot level tested as zero years old, or in other words as though just extruded. But samples from the 3420 foot level tested as 12,000,000 years old and material from a depth of 4680 feet tested as 21,000,000 years old.[5]

A remarkable article in *The Journal of Geophysical Research* tells of a volcanic flow in the years of 1800 and 1801 at Kaupulehu, Hualalai, Hawaii. Although this material was solidified less than two hundred years ago, eight potassium-argon tests indicated ages ranging from 160,000,000 years to 2,960,000,000 years![6]

It has rather recently been found that long periods of time are not necessary, as formerly thought, for the production of coal and oil. For example, oil can be made from garbage in twenty minutes.[7]

As is well known, sometimes when an oil well is drilled oil comes out as a gusher under considerable pressure. Dr. Melvin Cook says that under uniformitarian presuppositions pressure like this could not be obtained and maintained over the long expanse of time demanded by evolutionary geologists. He says: "Under reasonable average permeabilities . . . and geologically slow and uniform sedimentation and compaction, no abnormal pressures could possibly be attained in the very deep oil wells. Apparently only the mechanism of sudden deep burial a few thousand years ago, not even sudden deep burial millions of years ago, can explain these results."[8] He further says, "From known leakage rates (or sand permeabilities) these excessive pressures could not be retained more than a few thousand years."[9]

Data on the strength of the earth's magnetic field have been kept intermittently since 1835, and it is found that it is decreasing rapidly. It is estimated by Dr. Thomas Barnes that in about 9,000 years from now it will have essentially vanished. Since the magnetic field deflects the "solar wind" and its lethal radiation, life on earth will by that time have become impossible. Figuring backward, with a half life of only about 1400 years, the earth would have been a "magnetic star" about 8000 B.C., or about 10,000 years ago. This is impossible, and the conclusion is that the earth is not this old.[10]

The uniformitarian scientists are obliged to explain this away in order to save evolutionary theory, so they postulate repeated reversals in the magnetic field in the past. But even the technical literature on the subject reveals that the theory is fraught with difficulties. Furthermore, this theory requires the assumption of a "dynamo" of some kind to keep the magnetic field from decaying completely during geologic time. Dynamo theories of the earth's magnetic field depend upon an assumed flow of currents in the liquid core of the earth, but mathematical analysis shows that with any plausible flow of this kind—if indeed an assumed flow does occur—cannot produce a dynamo. The earth is an electromagnet and the best explanation is that its magnetism is due to currents which are decaying and which cannot be restored.

The Institute for Creation Research has published a list of seventy-six evidences for an "age" of the earth which is less than the evolutionists can accept.[11] These "ages" are based upon uniformitarian presuppositions. The average figure is about 32,000,000 years. This, of course, is not in line with Biblical chronology, and likewise it is a figure the evolutionists can in no wise accept. On a non-uniformitarian basis many of these figures can be much less than when calculated from uniformitarian presuppositions. Also the great differences in "ages" calculated from different kinds of data indicate inconsistencies in the presuppositions.

Besides the increasing evidence of a young earth, it also is becoming more evident that even if the evolutionists had all the time they think they have, it would not be enough. In 1966 a symposium was held at the Wistar Institute in Philadelphia, where biologists and mathematicians met to discuss the "Mathematical Challenges to the Neo-Darwinian Interpretation of Evolution." The case did not look so good for evolution. One of the interesting events was a talk by a mathematician from France, who programmed a recently developed computer to simulate an evolutionary situation. When the chance for evolutionary change was requested of the machine it would just jam, indicating this was beyond the range of its capability, which in this case meant less than one chance in ten to the one-thousandth power![12]

More evidence that something is wrong with the evolutionary geologic time scale is seen in the human footprints together with dinosaur tracks near Glen Rose, Texas.[13] Some footprints are large, but many are the size of people today. At Antelope Springs, Utah, apparently fossil footprints of human beings have been found together with trilobites in Cambrian strata.[14] This goes back to the beginning of the fossil record and it looks like six days of creation rather than six hundred million years of evolution, if it can be shown that men and trilobites lived contemporaneously.

A very important case is that of the finding of conifer pollen and flower pollen in and below Cambrian deposits of the Grand Canyon.[15] According to evolutionary theory there should not have been any pollen-bearing plants for many millions of years after that time. More recently, in Venezuela and British Guiana, fossil pollen has been recovered from rocks carefully protected from contamination. Through radiometric methods the rock had been dated as pre-Cambrian and some was partially metamorphosed. The men who did the work were associated with an oil company and there is no evidence that they were creationists. Some of the pollen was from flowers of the Composite Family, which the evolutionists consider to have arisen late among the flowering plants.[16]

The origin of life is one of the great unsolved problems in evolution. The famous experiment by Stanley Miller[17] is still cited as an important break-through in the search for a plausible explanation of the origin of life. Water was boiled with gases thought to be in the atmosphere of the early earth—methane, ammonia, and hydrogen, but no oxygen—and the circulating gases passed an electric spark, representing lightning. After a week some amino acids were found to have formed. Certain chemicals have an affinity for each other and it is not difficult to synthesize amino acids. But even if the young earth had an atmosphere of these gases, and if some amino acids formed, the problem would just have begun. To combine amino acids in a meaningful manner into proteins through random selections is so utterly improbable that it seems there is no need even to consider it. Furthermore, enzymes would be required, while they themselves are complex proteins. Still furthermore, if left to themselves such synthesized compounds would come to equilibrium in solution and the reactions would break down as fast as they were built up. To progress from a complex chemical to a one-called animal or plant is so far out of reason that as far as we are aware no one has ever suggested a basis for calculating a probability. When an improbable event needs to be followed by another improbable event, the probability of both of them happening is the *product* of the probability of each. When a series of events is required, the probability against them happening soon becomes a figure beyond comprehension. And then there is the second law of thermodynamics!

Some books are available which give an idea of the improbability —which amounts to impossibility—of life beginning by natural means.[18]

The knowledge of all of us—creationists and evolutionists—is incomplete. There are evidences presented for evolution and there are evidences for creation. But it appears that the observed facts fit the creationist model better than they do the evolutionary model. Furthermore, historical perspective shows that the evolutionary model is associated with atheism, agnosticism, humanism, and religious liberalism, and also with situation ethics and a breakdown in morality. On the other hand, creationism is associated with Bible-based Christian faith, absolutes in standards of morality, and suppression of evil. Finally, and most important of all, creation is the method which the Bible presents as the way in which the world was made. According to evolutionary theory there never were two individuals who were the first pair of human beings, for the transformation from beast to man was a very gradual process. Thus there was no fall into sin as described in the Biblical account and so there is no occasion for a Redeemer. Thus Christ becomes a martyr instead of the Savior.

People who call the evolution question peripheral to Christian faith do not understand the issues.

NOTES

1. Cloud, Preston, Editor, *Adventures In Earth History* (W. H. Freeman & Co., 1970), p. 101.

2. Cook, Melvin A., "Carbon-14 and the 'Age' of the Atmosphere," *Creation Research Society Quarterly*, 7:1:53, June, 1970, p. 54.

3. *Ibid.*, p. 55.

4. Whitelaw, Robert L., "Time, Life, and History In the Light of 15,000 Radiocarbon Dates," *Creation Research Society Quarterly,* 7:1:56, June, 1970, p. 60.

5. Noble, C. S., "Deep-Ocean Basalts: Inert Gas Content and Uncertainties In Age Dating," *Science* 162:3850:265, October 11, 1968.

6. *The Journal of Geophysical Research* 73:14, July 15, 1968, Table 2, p. 4603.

7. Klein, Stanley, "Profits from Pollution," *Machine Design,* May 14, 1970, p. 40.

8. Cook, Melvin A., *Prehistory and Earth Models* (Max Parrish & Co., 1966), 260.

9. Cook, Melvin A., private correspondence.

10. Barnes, Thomas G., *Origin and Destiny of the Earth's Magnetic Field* (Published by the Institute for Creation Research, San Diego, 1973).

11. Morris, Henry M., "The Young Earth. Uniformitarian Estimates— Age of the Earth," *Institute for Creation Research Impact Series, #17,* Institute for Creation Research, 2716 Madison Ave., San Diego, Calif. 92116.

12. Moorhead, Paul S. and Martin M. Kaplan, Editors, *Mathematical Challenges to the Neo-Darwinian Interpretation of Evolution* (Wistar Institute Press, 1967), p. 74.

13. "Footsteps In Stone," a film produced by Films for Christ.

14. Meister, William J., Sr., "Discovery of Trilobite Fossils in Shod Footprint of Human in 'Trilobite Beds'—a Cambrian Formation, Antelope Springs, Utah," *Creation Research Society Quarterly* 5:3:97, December, 1968.

15. See page 286.

16. Stainforth, R. M., "Occurrence of Pollen and Spores In the Roraima Formation in Venezuela and British Guiana," *Nature* 210:5033:292, 1966, reported in the *Creation Research Society Quarterly* 11:2:122, September, 1974.

17. Miller, Stanley L., "A Production of Amino Acids Under Possible Primitive Earth Conditions," *Science* 117:3046:528, May 15, 1953.

18. Gish, Duane T., *Speculations and Experiments Related to Theories on the Origin of Life* (published by the Institute for Creation Research, San Diego, 1972).

18a. Coppedge, James F., *Evolution: Possible or Impossible?* (Zondervan, 1973).

18b. Wilder Smith, A. E., *The Creation of Life* (Harold Shaw Publishers, 1970).

INDEX OF SUBJECTS

INDEX OF PEOPLE

SCRIPTURE INDEX